DIALOGUE AMONG CIVILIZATIONS

Culture and Religion in International Relations

Series Editors:
Yosef Lapid and Friedrich Kratochwil

Dialogue among Civilizations: Some Exemplary Voices
by Fred Dallmayr (2002)

DIALOGUE AMONG CIVILIZATIONS

Some Exemplary Voices

Fred Dallmayr

First published 2002 by
PALGRAVE MACMILLAN™
175 Fifth Avenue, New York, N.Y. 10010 and
Houndmills, Basingstoke, Hampshire, England RG21 6XS.
Companies and representatives throughout the world.

PALGRAVE MACMILLAN is the global academic imprint of the Palgrave Macmillan division of St. Martin's Press, LLC and of Palgrave Macmillan Ltd. Macmillan® is a registered trademark in the United States, United Kingdom and other countries. Palgrave is a registered trademark in the European Union and other countries.

ISBN 1–40396–059–3 hardback
ISBN 1–40396–060–7 paperback

Library of Congress Cataloging-in-Publication Data
Dallmayr, Fred R. (Fred Reinhard), 1928-
Dialogue among civilizations : some exemplary voices / Fred Dallmayr.
  p. cm.
  Includes bibliographical references and index.
  ISBN 1–40396–059–3 — ISBN 1–40396–060–7 (pbk.)
  1. Comparative civilization. 2. Intercultural communication.
I. Title.

CB151.D35 2002
909 — dc21

2002068412

A catalogue record for this book is available from the British Library.

Design by Letra Libre, Inc.

First edition: November 2002
10 9 8 7 6 5 4 3 2 1

Printed in the United States of America

To the memory of
Hans-Georg Gadamer

Gemeinsam lass uns atmen den Schleier
der uns voreinander verbirgt.
(Together let us breathe the veil
that hides us from one another.)

—Paul Celan, *Fernen*

We have made you into nations and tribes,
So that you can get to know and befriend each other,
Not to be boastful of your heritage.

—Qur'an 49:13

Contents

PREFACE

This book was written for the most part before the events of September 11, 2001. In its basic intent, it was meant as a salute to the opening of the new millennium, as an offering seeking to foster, in its modest way, a hoped-for new dawn in human relations: a *Morgenröte* of more amicable and peaceful relations between the peoples and civilizations of this world—after a century of unspeakable horrors and brutality. As one may recall in this context, 2001 had been designated by the United Nations the "Year of Dialogue among Civilizations," a designation that, in large part, was responsive to a plea issued by President Mohammad Khatami of Iran a few years earlier (at a time when his country was still involved in a seemingly unbridgeable conflict with the West and modern Western civilization). As its chosen title indicates, the present book was—and still is—intended as a small contribution to the civilizational dialogue recommended by Khatami and the United Nations. As it seems to me, it surely behooves people everywhere, and especially in the West, not to reject the olive branch held out by the Iranian leader, but rather to accept his plea and transform it into a gesture of welcome and goodwill toward all people in the emerging global community.

The events of September 11 have deeply shaken this goodwill and tinged with blood the dawn or *Morgenröte* of the new millennium. The events are a cause for mourning on several levels: mourning first of all for the many victims of the terrorist attacks; but, beyond this, mourning also for the terrible inhumanity still pervading humankind, for the degree of hatred, ill will, and rage exhibited in the attacks. As a result of the September events, the significance of 2001 has been called into question: in lieu of inaugurating a civilizational dialogue, the events lend credence (at least in part) to the formula of a looming "clash of civilizations" circulated for some time by prominent experts in international politics. In the wake of the events, war has been unleashed—and, in fact, a very novel kind of war, one that does not fit into the parameters of traditional inter-state wars and, in many ways, begins to shade over into a global civil war (between the forces of "order" and "disorder"). As history teaches, civil wars tend to be more gruesome and bloodier than inter-state wars: because of the Manichean polarization of combatants and because of the lack or paucity of rules of combat. Given this scenario, far from ushering in a new era of global comity, the opening years of the new millennium threaten to match in destructiveness the horrors of the twentieth century.

It is precisely in this situation, however, that President Khatami's plea shines forth with even greater urgency. In my view, the significance of 2001 is not diminished but rather intensified by September 11 and its aftermath: the attacks and the ensuing military clashes precisely underscore the urgent need to strengthen goodwill and dialogue among peoples and civilizations around the globe, as a preventive antidote to civilizational conflict. This does not mean that military action can or should never be undertaken—provided it is done for defensive purposes and as a last resort. The problem is that military leaders almost invariably favor military force as the first and only option, while sidelining or disparaging alternative avenues. In making this choice, however, military leaders tend to jeopardize the only defensible goal of warfare: peace. In this connection, they might well remember the words of the great diplomat Talleyrand that "there are many things one can do with bayonets—except sit on them." If one wishes to promote durable peace, rather than permanent warfare, between peoples, a crucial precondition is the fostering of mutual trust and goodwill, a trust that, in turn, must be anchored in a sense of justice and non-oppression. As a friend of mine rightly noted in an essay written shortly after September 11: "As we mount an effective attack against terrorism, we must also re-orient our foreign policy toward justice. . . . The ultimate defense against attack is to turn enemies into friends" (David Cortright, "For an Effective and Just Response," *Inforum*, No. 29, Fall 2001, p. 2).

In the spirit of these lines, and in the spirit of the significance of 2001, the pages of the present book explore civilizational dialogue in different dimensions, both historically and in our own time. While the first part discusses, in a theoretical or philosophical vein, the meaning, preconditions, and implications of a genuine dialogue among civilizations, the second part shifts the focus to a more concrete or applied level by making room for a number of "exemplary voices," that is, voices that illustrate or "exemplify" the meaning and potential of civilizational dialogue in different settings. Given the vast number of possible voices, the presentation in this book is necessarily selective—but not entirely arbitrary. In view of the prominent concern about "Islamic" civilization in our time, three chapters are devoted to Islamic voices—from Ibn Rushd to Hafiz to Abdolkarim Soroush. Three additional voices are linked with the Indian subcontinent—a choice that has to do mainly with my own long-standing involvement with Indian culture and philosophy.

Apart from the array of civilizational voices presented in the book, the reader will also encounter a good number of dialogue partners or interlocutors who, like me, are domiciled mainly in the West and whose arguments have been steady companions for many years: Hans-Georg Gadamer, Martin Heidegger, Charles Taylor, Jürgen Habermas, and Hannah Arendt. A little bit more recessed as interlocutors are figures such as Martin Buber, Paul Ricoeur, Amartya Sen, and Enrique Dussel. Behind these circles of dialogue partners, there is another group of voices that, even when they are not foregrounded by name, have played an important role in guiding and nurturing my thinking. It would be impossible here to enumerate all the friends and acquaintances to whom I owe an immense debt of intellectual gratitude. Still, I would feel remiss if I did not mention at least a few names: Eliot Deutsch, Tu Weiming, Chandra Muzaffer, Hwa Yol Jung, Eva and Chris Ziarek, Joseph Buttigieg, and the late Wilhelm Halbfass. Seemingly still more recessed but actually very much in the forefront are the voices of my immediate family—Ilse, Dominique, and Philip—without whose loyal support not a line would have been written. The chapters of the book have been typed and retyped with unfailing diligence by Cheryl Reed. The book is dedicated to the memory of Hans-Georg Gadamer, who passed away on March 14, 2002, at the age of 102.

South Bend, May 2002

INTRODUCTION

The year 2001 was not just any random year on the calendar: as the beginning of a new millennium it marked a kind of threshold in the historical development of humankind. As is well known, the approach of this year was accompanied in many places by a good deal of anxiety and apprehension. For some, the shift between millennia occasioned fears of grand technological mishaps or debacles; for many others—inspired by dark scriptural passages—the shift stirred up intense millenarian and even apocalyptic expectations. As it happened, none of the anticipated debacles came true—until much later in the year when calamity struck on a major scale. The calamity occasioned not only havoc in New York and huge losses of human lives (surely horrible effects); it also dimmed the more hopeful visions of human life on this planet. For, quite apart from nervous doomsday scenarios, the approach of the new millennium had also been greeted by many people around the world as the advent of a better future—a future profiled against the dark contours of a twentieth century marked by world wars, holocausts, and grim episodes of ethnic cleansing. It was in this hopeful spirit that the General Assembly of the United Nations had designated 2001 as the "Year of Dialogue among Civilizations." It was in the same spirit that 2001 was inaugurated on the first day of January by a "World Day of Peace," at which time Pope John Paul II urged people everywhere to foster the dialogue between cultures for the sake of a "civilization of love."[1]

The present volume, in its limited way, seeks to make a contribution to this dialogue of civilizations, in the hope of strengthening thereby the prospect of a more peaceful world and more amicable relations between peoples. The effort proceeds basically on two levels or along two trajectories: one more theoretical or philosophical, the other more practical and concrete—although the demarcation between the two is far from neat. The division of the volume in two parts corresponds to these two levels. Thus, the first part discusses basically the meaning of civilizational dialogue and some of its parameters, preconditions, and implications. Here the focus is chiefly on questions like these: What is the character of dialogical interaction? Can dialogue be reduced to the transmission of information or the exchange of computer messages? What is the status of civilization? Is it an encompassing concept, or does it need to be augmented or supplemented by corollary dimensions—to lend depth and significance to dialogue? Are there boundaries to civilizations, and what is the status of such boundaries? Can dialogue proceed automatically and without conditions, or does it need to be fostered and prepared in many ways? Above all, does dialogue not require some kind of equality among partners—at least what one may call a "civic equality" or an equality of trust and respect? Furthermore, can dialogue be limited to horizontal or spatial encounters—or is there not also a temporal interaction across generations? In the latter case, what role does memory or remembrance play in civilizational dialogue? How can the memory of past experiences be linked with future hopes and aspirations? Building on these and related theoretical issues, the second part offers concrete examples of both intra- and inter-civilizational dialogues or encounters, culled from different historical periods as well as from a variety of civilizational contexts. The accent here is not so much on broad cross-cultural movements as rather on some "exemplary voices" who—located in distinct historical and cultural settings—provide guideposts for the incipient dialogue of civilizations in our time.

The chapters in this volume follow, by and large, the indicated sequence of questions and themes. Since the point of these questions and themes is fairly evident, a few introductory comments should suffice. The opening chapter addresses some of the central issues of the book, by asking: What is civilization? What, in particular, do we mean by "Western" civilization? and against this background, How is civilizational dialogue feasible and how should it properly be conducted? The emphasis on Western civilization in this context is prompted by a basic assumption pervading these pages: that genuine dialogue cannot operate on an abstractly postulated universal level or be supervised from "on high" (a "view from nowhere"), but can only function and take wings through an initial attentiveness to the historical and geographical location of participants. For the author—and most English-speaking readers—this locus will be Western civilization (for good or ill). The notion of the concrete situatedness of dialogues is prominently connected with the work of the philosopher Hans-Georg Gadamer, whose arguments accordingly are invoked as principal guideposts in the first chapter. From Gadamer's vantage, every dialogue—between readers and texts, or between people across distances—has to start from the sedimented "pre-judgments" of participants, pre-judgments that are meant to function not as prison walls but rather as launching pads for excursions into unfamiliar terrain. Proceeding from this premise, his work develops a philosophical account of dialogue or a perspective that sees human encounters as necessarily dialogical. In this respect, Gadamer's outlook resembles that of Martin Buber, the celebrated proponent of the "dialogical principle," who insisted that "all real living is meeting," a meeting happening "in-between" partners and allowing an "experiencing [of] the other side."[2]

Regarding civilizational dialogue, the first chapter argues that such encounter cannot remain entirely human-centered or *polis*-centered. Despite the importance of civility and civilized discourses in "cities" (the etymological root of "civilization"), a genuine cross-cultural meeting has to take into account the deeper dimensions and resonances of human experience; differently phrased, it has to make room for certain corollaries or supplements of civilized life—corollaries that are thematized here under the rubrics of "nature" and "the divine." In this regard, it is possible to appeal again—next to Gadamer—to the work of Buber, who considered dialogue not merely an exchange of words but "a response of one's whole being to the otherness of the other" and who even ventured the belief that "a time of genuine religious conversations is beginning," from "one open-hearted person to another open-hearted person" (or persons).[3] The question remains how the relation between civilization and its corollaries is to be conceived. Are these different dimensions separated by rigid boundaries, or are they interconnected precisely through their differentiation? Modern philosophy (in the West) has tended to insist on sharp bifurcations: between reason and non-reason, between humans and nature, and between humans and the divine. But perhaps another view is possible, which sees "difference" as harboring a linkage devoid of fusion or synthesis. In recent times, such a conception of difference has been prominently articulated by Martin Heidegger and some of his followers (especially in France) who—albeit with varying accents—have explored the possibility of a complex interlacing of elements in contrast to the twin dangers of polarizing antithesis and totalizing fusion. The same outlook can also gain aid and comfort from the work of Charles Taylor, who writes at one point that the stress on boundaries, without recognition of interconnectedness, risks "stifling the response in us to some of the deepest and most powerful aspirations that humans have conceived"— which is surely "a heavy price to pay."[4]

The issue of interconnectedness is of crucial significance for civilizational dialogue in another sense. How and in what idiom is such a dialogue to be conducted? Does such a dialogue not presuppose a universal framework, a kind of a priori cosmopolitan foundation, which can give structure and significance to dialogical exchanges? In this case, are different cultural idioms simply derivative modifications subsumable under a unified syntax—obviating the need for dialogical engagement? Or, do different idioms constitute separate, perhaps incommensurable "language games"—in a manner that would render dialogue impossible? Borrowing a phrase from Michael Oakeshott, chapter 2 examines these questions under the rubric of a "conversation of (hu)mankind." In a first step, the chapter critiques some obstacles to conversation arising from narrowly political views: especially the fascination with power politics (*Realpolitik*) and with the pursuit of "Orientalist" strategies (reducing other cultures to sameness). In a second step, the discussion turns to a prominent contemporary model of communicative dialogue: the model of "communicative rationality" articulated by Jürgen Habermas. The focus here is on Habermas's essay "The Unity of Reason in the Diversity of Its Voices," which tackles the age-old problem of the relation between unity and plurality, between the "One" and the "Many." The chapter gives credit to Habermas for avoiding the twin pitfalls of a preordained holism thwarting cultural diversity and of a radical dispersal conducive to monological ethnocentrism. In the end, however, reservations are voiced regarding a certain restrictiveness of Habermasian discourse, especially his tendency to exclude or "excommunicate" voices not congruent with Western-style rationality. Returning to Oakeshott's model of conversation, the chapter at this point pleads for greater attentiveness to vernacular idioms, practices, and beliefs—that is, for a "thick" conversation between civilizations that alone can nurture genuine trust and (something like) friendship among peoples.

As can readily be seen, civilizational dialogue—like inter-human dialogue in general—is a complex undertaking fraught with many difficulties and possible derailments. If, as the first chapter argues, dialogue necessarily starts from the pre-judgments or background assumptions of interlocutors, and if, as the second chapter insists, dialogue requires a genuine openness to unfamiliar (vernacular) idioms, then dialogical interaction can easily derail in two directions: either through a strategy of appropriation (integrating the "other" into one's framework) or else through a gesture of self-abandonment (canceling the pre-judgments stimulating dialogue). Chapter 3 discusses these difficulties of civilizational dialogue with particular reference to Europe or European (Western) culture in its relation to the non-Western global context. Here, memories of colonialism and imperialism, coupled with the traumas of conquest and genocide, have induced in many observers a weariness with Europe, a tendency to depreciate or debunk European/Western culture as a synonym for cultural arrogance and conceit. The label most frequently employed in this context is that of "Eurocentrism," denoting a policy of global domination or hegemony. In some of his writings, Jacques Derrida has castigated Europe's self-image as the promontory, headmaster, or capital of the world—while counseling an exodus from European self-absorption or narcissism. As a counterpoise, many observers—both inside and outside Europe—reaffirm or seek to rekindle Europe's cultural achievements, especially the legacy of the European Enlightenment with its stress on civic equality and human liberties—a legacy that (it is felt) might serve as a bulwark against the dangers of chauvinism and ethnic or religious fundamentalism. The task here is to steer a course between "Eurocentrism" and "Euro-denial," that is, to find the balance or "mid-point" between self and other where alone dialogue can flourish. Such a mid-point, the chapter concludes, is intimated in Gadamer's hermeneutics, especially in his comments on *The Legacy of Europe* (*Das Erbe Europas*).[5]

Delineating the structure and preconditions of civilizational dialogue is not the same as showing its actual possibility in the contemporary global context. Seeing that such dialogue presupposes or requires a certain civic equality (or equality of respect) among participants, proponents of dialogue need to face up to the enormous inequalities and disproportions existing in the world today—inequalities manifest primarily in the division between North and South, between rich and poor, between "developed" and "underdeveloped" or "developing" societies. Chapter 4 examines the contemporary global structure of inequality mainly in three fields: power, wealth, and culture (including scientific and technological knowledge). In each of these three domains the chapter follows the lead of a prominent mentor or set of mentors: in the first field the political scientist and global-policy analyst Samuel Huntington; in the second the economist and Nobel laureate Amartya Sen; and in the last field the philosophers Heidegger and Gadamer. In a string of writings, Huntington has highlighted the prevailing asymmetries of global power, asymmetries that basically pit "the West versus the Rest" (where "the West" largely coincides with the United States seen as the single superpower or else as the top rung of a global "uni-multipolar" power pyramid). In the economic domain, global inequalities in income and living standards have been described in United Nations reports as "grotesque" and as fostering a class division between North and South. One way to combat this division is Amartya Sen's "capabilities" model, which seeks to combine free-market initiatives with an emphasis on the equitable empowerment of human agents. Finally, in the field of culture and knowledge, Heidegger and Gadamer have critiqued the rise of a scientific-technological "expertocracy" as well as the streamlining (and neo-colonial) effects of a cultural "Europeanization of the earth." By way of conclusion, the chapter raises the question of the compatibility of superpower hegemony with the policy of global democratization or the global dissemination of human rights. Consideration of this question leads to a plea for greater global justice, that is, for a world order anchored in civic equality (among peoples) and public legitimacy.

In light of prevailing global inequalities, the contemporary "dialogue among civilizations" will often take the form of agonal contestation or at least of a critical engagement transgressing a facile consensualism. Such a critical engagement is likely to prevail not only in the arena of lateral-spatial encounters between civilizations, but also with reference to temporal or historical trajectories. Seen from the angle of Western civilization, the crucial historical trajectory during recent centuries has been rooted in the concept of "modernity," a concept broadly linked with the historical movement from Renaissance and Reformation to Enlightenment and industrialization (a movement representing progressive waves of "modernization"). The question raised in chapter 5 is whether global modernization today amounts in fact to the relentless "Europeanization of the earth" (which, again, would collapse dialogue into consensus) or whether there is still room for different historical narratives and, more specifically, for different modalities of being modern. In a first step, the chapter examines the meaning of "modernity" as it has been developed by a series of Western social theorists and especially in the writings of Max Weber and Habermas. Next, the focus shifts to the contested character of the notion of modernity, a contest that brings into view the prospect of possibly different modernities—a prospect that, on the philosophical level, has been discussed chiefly by Charles Taylor. As Taylor writes at one point: "Instead of speaking of modernity in the singular, we should better speak of 'alternative modernities'." Although, from a global point of view, modernity is "like a wave, flowing over and engulfing one traditional culture after another," things look different on the ground where historical change involves "a people finding resources in their traditional culture which will enable them to take on the new practices." Hence, "a Japanese modernity, an Indian modernity, and various modulations of Islamic modernity will probably enter alongside the gamut of Western societies, which are also far from being uniform."[6] Following Taylor's lead, the concluding section of the chapter explores the possibility of an Islamic modernity in our time.

If historical narratives are going to matter, then memory and historical recollection will have to play an important role in our world and in the ongoing process of globalization. In many parts of the non-Western world, recollection brings to the fore memories of individual and collective suffering, sometimes memories of genocidal or near-genocidal atrocities. Chapter 6 delves into painful episodes in Central and South America during the past fifty years—in an effort not to foster hopelessness and despair but to recover indigenous resources for combating past ills and imagining a better future. In its opening part, the chapter presents a story of immense agonies undergone in Latin America during the second part of the twentieth century: a story revolving around military dictatorships, large-scale executions, "disappearances," and death squads. Highlights of this story are the "dirty war" in Argentina, the equally "dirty" repression in Chile under General Pinochet, the "killer networks" in Colombia, and the massacres performed by death squads in El Salvador and Guatemala. From this painful narrative the chapter turns next to the issue of imaginative reconstruction as seen from the angle of contemporary philosophy. Primary emphasis here is placed on the work of Paul Ricoeur, and especially on his effort to make room for social imagination by steering a course between the conceptual poles of "ideology" and "utopia" (as these terms had been defined by Karl Mannheim). Returning from this philosophical excursion, the conclusion explores the path of liberating or emancipatory imagination as articulated by two prominent Latin American theorists and writers: Enrique Dussel and Rigoberta Menchú. As both writers insist, genuine dialogue—including dialogue among civilizations—presupposes a recollection of past sufferings and of prevailing social and economic asymmetries, as a stepping-stone to social recovery, the rectification of grievances, and progressive democratic empowerment.[7]

Having laid down some theoretical or philosophical parameters, part II of the volume proceeds to illustrate the meaning of civilizational dialogue by turning to some concrete examples or "exemplary voices" taken from different historical epochs and a variety of civilizational contexts. Considering the contemporary attention given (for the right or wrong reasons) to Muslim "fundamentalism," the first three chapters of part II deal with different episodes in the historical development of

Islamic civilization. In contemporary parlance, Muslim fundamental-ism or militancy is often defined as the instrumental use of religion for strategic-political purposes, or else as the surrender of politics to a rigidly theocratic ideology—a surrender in which reason or rational judgment becomes a main casualty. Western media frequently concen-trate on this heady constellation of elements—sometimes to the point of identifying Islamic civilization as a whole with millennarian-theo-cratic leanings. What is neglected in such accounts are the numerous counter-examples in Islamic history, and especially the fact that Islamic tradition provides ample resources for structuring the relation between faith, politics, and reason along more balanced and fruitful lines. One of these counter-examples—perhaps the most inspiring one—is the age of Muslim Andalusia or Moorish Spain.

The age was remarkable both politically and intellectually: politi-cally and socially, Moorish Spain was a high point of cross-cultural and inter-religious pluralism;[8] intellectually, the same age witnessed the flowering of Islamic philosophy, a bloom evident particularly in the work of the great Ibn Rushd (known in the West as Averroes). Chap-ter 7 explores facets of Ibn Rushd's sprawling opus, with particular at-tention to his role as intellectual and political mediator. The first part of the chapter discusses his effort to delineate the proper relation be-tween reason and faith, philosophy and religion, in a treatise popu-larly known as *Fasl al-maqal*. An important ingredient in this effort is the differentiation, or differentiated correlation, of three linguistic genres (or language games): demonstrative discourse, dialectical in-quiry, and rhetorical speech; only by properly distinguishing and re-specting these genres, Ibn Rushd argues, can a peaceful correlation be maintained. Next, the chapter turns to Ibn Rushd's political thought, as reflected chiefly in his commentary on Plato's *Republic;* here again a proper balancing of groups and perspectives—a kind of ethical plu-ralism—is extolled as the highway to a just city and as the best anti-dote to political despotism (including a clerically sanctioned theocracy). The chapter's conclusion reviews Ibn Rushd's long-range influence or "effective history" (*Wirkungsgeschichte*) by tracing his legacy from medieval European philosophy through the Renaissance and Enlightenment to more recent attempts to recuperate and revi-talize his thought for the purpose of generating a pluralist, anti-elitist, and democratic Muslim polity.

Ibn Rushd has often been portrayed as a rigid rationalist, inhos-pitable to metaphysical intuitions and to a devotional kind of mysti-cism; however, the charge is probably overdrawn. What he did object to was the indiscriminate blurring of discursive genres and, above all, the privileging of an esoteric gnosticism and "illuminationism" (often found in "Eastern" Islam), with their blatantly anti-rational and elitist tendencies. His objections would most likely have vanished in the face of a genuinely non-elitist mysticism and a love-oriented (rather than power-oriented) mystical poetry. To show this "other" side of Islam, chapter 8 turns to the great Sufi poet Hafiz of Shiraz, and more particularly to the encounter between the German poet Johann Wolfgang Goethe and his Persian counterpart, as this encounter is recorded in the former's "West-Eastern Divan." Goethe's treatment of Hafiz has sometimes been critiqued as an exercise in "Orientalism," that is, as an attempt to appropriate and domesticate the East for Western consumption; however, the accusation is far off the mark, as the chapter tries to show.[9] The first part of the chapter in fact documents Goethe's deep and sustained engagement with the world of Islam, including Persian poetry—an engagement which can be traced from his early encounter with Herder through his mature years to the time of the Napoleonic wars and beyond. As befits a meeting of poets, the central part is devoted to Goethe's cycle of poems—seen as a response to Hafiz's own *Divan*—with special attention given to the themes of love and the interlacing of sensual and super-sensual devotion, of earthly and spiritual motifs. The conclusion seeks to indicate the significance of the encounter for contemporary cross-civilizational dialogue: in the pursuit of such dialogue (it is argued) much can be learned from Goethe's view of *Übersetzung* (translation), a view that steers a course between passive copying and predatory appropriation in the direction of a dialogical "letting-be."

From these excursions into the historical past the next chapter turns to a present-day setting, with the aim of illustrating the contemporary resurgence of Islamic intellectual life. Chapter 9 resumes, under new auspices, some of the themes struck in the discussion of Ibn Rushd and Hafiz: the themes of the relation between philosophy and faith, between reason and devotional mysticism, and also of the differentiated linkage of discursive genres. The focus of the chapter is on one of the leading present-day philosophers and social theorists in Iran: Abdolkarim Soroush. Thoroughly trained in modern epistemology and philosophy of science, Soroush brings to bear on contemporary Middle Eastern discussions a healthy dose of critical rationality (indebted distantly to Ibn Rushd); the same training also renders him hospitable to some aspects of Western modernity, especially the Enlightenment legacies of free inquiry and debate. Simultaneously, his writings reveal a remarkable familiarity with Islamic theology and jurisprudence (the latter harkening back again to Ibn Rushd's role as judge). Still more significantly, his work shows the imprint of Iranian Sufi poetry: above all the poetry of Hafiz and Jalal ad-Din Rumi. In all these ways, his opus resembles a large mansion giving ample room to different perspectives and discursive genres. Intellectual openness carries over into Soroush's political thought, which espouses a pluralist type of democracy—though a democracy not governed by private profit-seeking but by a kind of ethical pluralism (sensitive to religious teachings). In the first part of the chapter, this outlook is silhouetted against the backdrop of "political" Islam, especially the long-standing fundamentalist rejection of democracy in favor of clerical rule (or a quasi-theocracy). The central portion offers an exposition and interpretation of Soroush's reconciliation of Islam and democracy under the rubric of a religiously informed civil society. By way of conclusion, this perspective is inserted into the context of contemporary politics, especially the emergence of an inter-civilizational or cosmopolitan public sphere.

The final three chapters of the volume shift the accent in the direction of South Asia—a choice having to do mainly with my long-standing involvement with that part of the world. A main issue emerging from the discussion of Ibn Rushd and Soroush is the proper relation between reason and faith or (differently put) the relation between religion and the surrounding "secular" world. Under modern conditions—the Iranian thinker suggests—religion cannot (or can no longer) be defined as the property of a restricted clerical elite, but must be seen as disseminated among the peoples of the "world" (thus functioning potentially as the "salt of the earth"). Conversely, "world" or worldliness does not need to be construed in narrowly "secularist" or laïcist terms. Chapter 10 addresses the need of "rethinking secularism" in our time—a time when, in many parts of the world, societies are divided along "religious versus secular" lines. The chapter starts from the so-called secularization thesis formulated by leading social scientists—from Auguste Comte to Weber and beyond—according to which social advancement or development amounts to a progressive rationalization and "disenchantment" of social life evident in the growing obsolescence of religious faith. As an antidote or alternative to this thesis the chapter invokes the work of the prominent Indo-Hispanic philosopher of religion Raimundo Panikkar, especially his reformulation of secularization in the sense of an attunement to the "*saeculum*" or historical temporality, that is, to the lived vernacular faith of peoples. Countering both esoteric other-worldliness and anthropocentric self-enclosure, Panikkar's thought accentuates a "cosmotheandric" worldview (balancing nature, humans, and the divine) as well as a highly nuanced kind of "sacred secularity"—an outlook that in many ways resonates with Charles Taylor's notion of a "natural theology" as articulated in his Gifford lectures (of 1999).[10]

In addition to the rethinking of secularism, preceding discussions also urgently call for renewed reflection on the dominant political paradigm or worldview of our time: that of "liberal democracy" with its complex and uneasy blending of liberalism (or liberty) and democracy. Soroush's writings bear heavily upon this topic, especially by accentuating the role of freedom in democracy—where "freedom" means not only the absence of external constraints but also the taming or overcoming of internal, self-centered compulsions or forms of bondage. Chapter 11 explores specifically the meaning (or rather, meanings) of freedom or liberty by concentrating on the varying cultural and metaphysical presuppositions undergirding the use of these terms. The exploration relies for guidance on the work of the Indian philosopher D. P. Chattopadhyaya, presently the director of the Center for the Study of Civilizations in Delhi. In his book *Knowledge, Freedom and Language,* Chattopadhyaya distinguishes mainly three meanings of freedom: freedom as self-liberation or as liberation of the self (ego) from external constraints; freedom as liberation from the self or from the bondage of selfish desires; and freedom as engaged ethical (or unselfish) praxis. As he shows, the first meaning has been heavily favored by modern Western thought from Descartes to Kant to versions of liberal democracy (based on self-interest). Freedom in this version is a goal intentionally pursued by an agent; the problem is that this pursuit inevitably encounters the counter-dialectic of the causality of nature. The second alternative was the preferred approach of classical Indian thought from the Vedas and the Upanishads to the teachings of the Buddha and his successors. In this approach, freedom was to be sought through the transcendence of subjective striving, in fact through the transcendence of the subject-object dichotomy (and similar polarities) in the direction of a holistic awareness—an experience that can only be stated in aporetic or poetic-metaphorical language. Once it is seen that the issue of freedom cannot be cognitively resolved, the way is open to a perception of freedom as engaged social praxis—an avenue preeminently exemplified by the life-work of Mahatma Gandhi.

The concluding chapter is devoted to the memory of Gandhi, whose thought and practice illustrate in an exemplary fashion the meaning of genuine freedom and of an ethically suffused democracy. As the chapter tries to show, Gandhi—in addition to his many other intellectual and political achievements—also made a stellar contribution to a rethinking of democracy, namely, by raising the question central to democratic government or popular self-rule (*swaraj*): How can people properly rule or govern themselves? Differently put: How can the "people" be both the rulers and the ruled, and perform their function legitimately without domination or oppression? In the classical tradition of political philosophy, rule was considered to be just or legitimate as long as it was exercised unselfishly and virtuously for the common benefit; in the case of democracy, this means that people have to rule themselves justly and wisely—which presupposes self-restraint and the cultivation of ethical dispositions. Chapter 12 reviews first some of Gandhi's many comments on "self-rule," from his early plea for "Indian home rule" to statements made on the eve of India's independence. This review is followed by a close interpretation of Gandhi's view of self-rule (*swaraj*), an interpretation relying on recent Gandhi scholarship as well as the longer tradition of Indian thought. What emerges here is that Gandhi steered a difficult path between a "monist" or idealist view (collapsing the multiplicity of the mundane world into spiritual reality) and a "dualist" conception (radically separating the two or submerging holism in mundane flux). The chapter concludes by underscoring the continuing relevance of Gandhian self-rule and by comparing it with more recent accounts of responsible public freedom (as articulated chiefly by Hannah Arendt and Charles Taylor).

The volume, and especially its second part, might be criticized for a certain narrowness of scope: its limitation to voices emanating chiefly from India and the Islamic world, that is, to South and West Asia. Readers may wonder about the possibility and desirability of extending the range of civilizational dialogue to other parts of the world, including Africa, East Asia, and Latin America. Concerns of this kind are well-founded and legitimate—and fully shared by the author. However, desirability does not always coincide with feasibility. In the necessarily limited space of a book, selections had to be made and accents set. After exploring the philosophical and social-theoretical parameters of civilizational dialogue, the volume in part II draws attention to some "exemplary voices"—voices that exemplify or illustrate certain modes of dialogue without in any way claiming to exhaust the scope and modalities of dialogical exchanges. For readers wishing to extend the geographical scope, the author may point to some of his own earlier writings dealing with such themes as African "identity," Latin American "liberation theology," Confucian ethics, and Buddhist "*sunyata*" (emptiness)—apart from referring to a host of cross-cultural texts.[11]

A word by way of conclusion: dialogue is not the only mode of civilizational encounter. Historically and empirically, it may appear as one of the less likely forms of civilizational engagement—which does not in any way diminish its normative primacy or preferability. Apart from ethical considerations, however, there is also a concrete pragmatic consideration in its favor: in the long run, it offers the only viable alternative to military confrontation with its ever-present danger of nuclear holocaust and global self-destruction. The difficulties of civilizational dialogue are immense and are repeatedly underscored in this volume: they are both practical-political and (if one wishes) ontological or metaphysical. The deeper complexity is nowhere more fully and more eloquently expressed than in the poetry of Friedrich Hölderlin. As we read in Hölderlin's poem "Remembrance" (*Andenken*) composed around 1803/04:

> . . . But good is it
> To have dialogue [*Gespräch*] and to talk
> About the heart's thought, and to listen much
> About the days of love,
> And about deeds that have happened.

In commenting on these lines, Heidegger observes that dialogue, for the poet, involves not only speech and counter-speech, statements and rejoinders, but also a kind of world-disclosure: namely, the opening-up of a space or shared matrix holding the speakers silently together. This aspect—the excess of disclosive language over human-centered speech—is even more clearly stated in one of Hölderlin's poetic fragments, which reads:

> Much experienced or learned have humans.
> Many divinities have been named,
> Since the time we *are* dialogue
> And can hear from each other.
> (*Viel hat erfahren der Mensch.*
> *Der Himmlischen viele genannt,*
> *Seit ein Gespräch wir sind*
> *Und hören können voneinander.*)[12]

Part I

Toward a Dialogue Among Civilizations

Chapter 1

Dialogue Among Civilizations

A Hermeneutical Perspective

When asked about his view of Western civilization, the Mahatma Gandhi famously replied: "It would be a good idea." His reply reminds us that "civilization" is not a secure possession but a fragile, ever-renewable endeavor; grammatically, it has the character more of a verb than a noun. This is particularly true of the emerging global or "world civilization"—what sometimes is called the nascent "cosmopolis." Here again, caution is imperative. Anyone today who would claim to speak "in the name of" world civilization would be suspect (with good reason) of harboring hegemonic or imperialist designs. Contrary to the pretense of a facile cosmopolitanism, civilization in our time is what grammarians call a *plurale tantum* (meaning that it exists only in the plural)—notwithstanding the undeniable tightening of the network of global interactions. Hence, if there is to be a genuine civilizational encounter, participants have to proceed modestly and soberly: by taking their departure, at least initially, from their own distinct perspective or vantage point, that is, by remembering and bringing to bear their own cultural-historical "pre-judgments"—while simultaneously guarding against any form of cultural or ethnic self-enclosure.

The complexity of global encounter is sometimes recognized even by high-level public officials. Not long ago, the United Nations General Assembly declared 2001 to be the year of "Dialogue among Civilizations."[1] While signaling a welcome initiative, the declaration immediately stirs up—for philosophically minded people—a host of thorny issues or questions. What is the meaning of "civilization" in the

United Nations announcement? Is civilization equivalent here to progress in science, technology, and industry—including digital and nuclear technology? In this case, how could there be a genuine encounter—given that some civilizations (especially in the past) have not been characterized by such "progress" and that several civilizations today are classified, by United Nations criteria, as "un-" or "underdeveloped" (hence under-civilized)? Similar problems beset the notion of "dialogue." Is dialogue equivalent to commercial transactions and information exchanges carried on via digital computers or the internet (in accordance with what some analysts call our "informatic age" or age of "informatic civilization")? But in this case, quite apart from the great disparity of technical resources, is dialogue not liable to shrivel into a standardized and commodified means of communication (largely reserved for expert elites)? In the following I want to explore the meaning of "civilizational dialogue" by relying, at least in part, on teachings of the renowned "dean" of contemporary European philosophy: Hans-Georg Gadamer. My presentation proceeds in three steps. In the first section, I try to clarify the meaning of "civilization" by highlighting some of its core ingredients and drawing attention to some of its counter-terms or border zones. In a second step, I want to illustrate and concretize that meaning by taking my bearings from my own initial vantage point (or set of hermeneutical "pre-judgments"): that of "Western" civilization. The concluding section seeks to delineate the meaning or significance of civilizational "dialogue"—especially a dialogue carried on in the context of the nascent global city or emerging cosmopolis.

Civilization and Its Corollaries

The term "civilization" is ambivalent and surrounded by dispute. From Oswald Spengler's *Decline of the West* (1918/22) to Arnold Toynbee's *Civilization on Trial* (1948) to Samuel Huntington's famous (or notorious) "Clash of Civilizations" (1993), Western intellectuals have puzzled over the meaning of the term, as well as the present and future predicaments of civilized life. In his voluminous writings, Hans-Georg Gadamer has not extensively elaborated on civilization and its continued viability (or non-viability). However, his work does provide some helpful clues. Thus, in commenting on Aristotle's practical philosophy, *Truth and Method* offers these observations:

> Human civilization differs essentially from nature in that it is not simply a place where capacities and powers work themselves out. Man be-

comes what he is through what he does and how he behaves—that is, he behaves in a certain way because of what he has become. Thus, Aristotle sees *ethos* as differing from *physis* in being a sphere in which the [physical] laws of nature do not operate, yet not a sphere of lawlessness but of human institutions and human modes of behavior which are mutable and like rules only to a limited degree.[2]

Gadamer's comments accentuate an important point: namely, the linkage between civilization and human modes of behavior and specifically human institutions, which are basically the institutions of the "city" or *polis.* This point is corroborated by etymology. Historically, civilization derives from "civil" and "civility," which, in turn, go back to the Latin *cives* (citizen), the participant in a *civitas* (Greek: *polis*). In the English language, civilization is a somewhat recent innovation, dating back not farther than the late eighteenth century. When Samuel Johnson, in 1772, composed his dictionary of the English language, his friend James Boswell urged him to insert the term "civilization." Johnson, however, refused, saying that he preferred the older and more customary "civility."[3] The story is significant not as a matter of historical curiosity, but because it sheds light again on the central meaning of civilization (at least in the Western tradition): its connection with city life and citizenship. In this way, the contours of the term become clearer (as a concept always acquires focus at its boundaries). In the case of civilization, we discover two main counter-terms or boundary dimensions: (1) nature, and (2) the divine. Both dimensions delimit and transgress the city: the first by ante-dating the city and remaining its permanent substrate, the second by "transcending" the city (seen as a worldly or "temporal" institution). Probably the expression "counter-terms" is misleading in this context, because there is not necessarily opposition or mutual negation. Perhaps it would be preferable to speak of corollaries or constitutive supplements—supplements that powerfully impinge upon, and sometimes contest, the city, just as they are in turn invaded and contested by civilizational demands.

Historically, the relation between civilization and its two corollaries or supplements has always been complex. In large measure, traditional civilizations can be differentiated by examining the degree to which the relation has been construed more in terms of conflict and antagonism or more in terms of complementarity and harmony. The conventional, but by now largely obsolete divide between "East" and "West" might conceivably be explored along these lines. In the history of Western civilization, the relation has on the whole been marked by tension or conflict (or perhaps we should say that the predominant

mood of conflict was only intermittently relieved by efforts at reconciliation). Western metaphysics and social theory are replete with cat-
egorial distinctions or dichotomies. Gadamer refers to the Greek
(Aristotelian) distinction between *physis* and *polis* (or *physis* and
nomos)—although one has to say that, at that time, the terms did not
yet carry antithetical meanings. These connotations, however, did surface subsequently and with growing rigor. Modern anthropologists and
social theorists in the West are wont to distinguish neatly between "nature" and "culture" (civilization) or "nature" and "nurture," with elabo-
rate theoretical constructs erected on the basis of this distinction.[4]
Modern political philosophy is in large measure built on the division
between a primordial "state of nature" and a contractually established
"civil (or political) state," with the former populated by pre-civil sav-
ages (variously understood) and the latter by citizens enjoying the benefits of civil law, above all individual rights and freedoms. Modern
Western political thought is inconceivable without this dividing line; a
major question has been to what extent the "natural state" (or state of
nature) can or should penetrate into the civil state, and vice versa.

In the paradigmatic treatment of Thomas Hobbes, the division between nature and city is paralleled by the distinction between two kinds
of bodies: natural bodies and the "artificial" body of the state. As the
epitome of artifact, the civil state is meant to promote the development
of the arts and sciences, especially of scientific discoveries and inven-
tions and their technical (or technological) application for the improve-
ment of human comfort. As a result of the growth of science and
technology, natural bodies (and nature at large) are placed increasingly
under the tutelage of the city or "civilized" life, with its steadily expanding need for resources and commodities. In anthropological terms, the
division between natural and civil states surfaces as the opposition between reason and passion (or unreason), with the natural state being in
the grip of pre-rational impulses and the civil state pervaded or governed
by rational design—an opposition putting Western civilization again on
the path of "progress" and "enlightenment," accompanied by the eradi-
cation of natural "prejudices" and inclinations. In his wide-ranging study
of the "civilizing process," Norbert Elias places his accent squarely on
the development of the arts and sciences, particularly on the advances in
"civil" rationality triggering a spiraling dynamic pointing toward expanding levels of societal complexity and functional differentiation. To
be sure—and as Elias would not deny—one also needs to remember the
flip-side of this process: the pervasive subjugation and domination of
pre-civil "natives" or indigenous peoples under the "advanced" auspices
of Western colonialism and imperialism.[5]

Next to the nature-civilization conundrum there is a second con-
tour or boundary dimension: that of the divine. Here again, Western
civilization shows a tendency toward tension or conflict (notwithstanding episodes of accommodation). Whatever the tendency or
preference, the boundary raises difficult issues. Clearly, civilization in
the sense of civil or city life is not necessarily hostile to religion or
faith; but the two domains also cannot simply be equated or collapsed
into each other—as happens when religion is simply reduced to a "cultural" phenomenon (for example, by cultural anthropologists). Vis-à-
vis civil life, religious faith inevitably introduces an element of "excess"
or extraordinary appeal (traditionally captured by such terms as
"grace" and "promise"). The difficulty of the relation becomes immediately clear when one turns to one of the founders of Christian
thought in the West: St. Augustine. In his magisterial *Civitas Dei* (City
of God), composed around 420 A.D., Augustine identified not only
one but two cities: the earthly or mundane city (*civitas terrena*) and
the heavenly city (*civitas Dei*). While the earthly city, in his view, is
governed by worldly needs and especially the human lust for power
and self-aggrandizement, the heavenly city is founded and maintained
by grace and the divine act of salvation.[6] Ever since the time of Augustine, this distinction of cities has overshadowed the Western-Christ-
ian perspective on civilization and civilizational progress, resurfacing
powerfully during the Reformation and, more recently, in the works of
Kierkegaard, Karl Barth, Reinhold Niebuhr, and others.

As one should note, for the bishop of Hippo the two cities were not
strictly antithetical to each other (or related in the mode of mutual
negation); however, in subsequent times the relation was often construed in the latter sense—with important consequences for civil society. Once the two cities are radically separated from each other, worldly
civil and political life is inevitably denuded of intrinsic purpose or eth-
ical-spiritual significance. Differently and more sharply put: the more
the heavenly city is elevated and "transcendentalized," the more mundane civil life is de-sacralized, de-divinized, or (in Max Weber's term)
"disenchanted." In their de-sacralized or disenchanted condition, world
and nature are placed entirely in the grip of human designs and ambitions—which, in its way, provides an enormous boost to the "advances"
of modern science and technology. In the eyes of some religious
thinkers, this de-sacralization of the world is precisely one of the central achievements of Christianity (seen as a transcendental monothe-
ism). However, from an opposite position, the same process can also be
championed by secular agnostics—for example, by radical Enlightenment thinkers bent on eradicating religion by showing it to be illusory

and irrelevant. At the very least, these contrary or contradictory views point up the difficulty of the relation between the two cities and, more broadly, between civilization and the divine.

The Story of Western Civilization: An Example

These comments lead me, or have led me already, deeply into my second topic: that of Western civilization and its historical development. Here we find ourselves instantly in a cauldron of questions. Western civilization is also sometimes described as "Christian" or "Judaeo-Christian" civilization. Although useful as shorthand formulas, these labels are also confusing and intellectually troublesome. As the previous section should have made clear, religion—Christian or otherwise—cannot simply be leveled into civilization or culture without a rest; the most one can say is that Western civilization has been touched in various ways by Christian or Judaeo-Christian teachings. Apart from merging the Augustinian "two cities," the labels also suffer from other defects: notably the defect of sidestepping the precarious situation of Judaism in most traditional Western societies. In addition to these drawbacks, the labels are also obviously too narrow in that they ignore another important historical, and properly civilizational, dimension: the formative influence of Greece and Rome. Seen from this angle, Western civilization is at least as much Graeco-Roman as its is Judaeo-Christian—the main issue being how to interpret and assess the respective significance of these divergent stands of traditions.

As one of the foremost interpreters of Western traditions of thought, Gadamer inevitably had to reflect repeatedly on this divergence of formative influences. Contrary to some (recently fashionable) tendencies to counterpose "Athens" and "Jerusalem" in mutually exclusive terms, Gadamer has always recognized their tensional, but mutually supplementary, role. Commenting on Martin Heidegger's philosophy (whom he follows on this point), he emphasized that the former's outlook had been shaped *both* by (classical and pre-Socratic) Greek thought and by Christian eschatology. "Heidegger had recognized," he writes in one context, "a strong tension between the conceptual language of the Greeks, who had developed their physical and metaphysical world-experience cosmologically, and our own modern world-experience which is essentially influenced and formed by Christianity." Ever since the advent of Christianity, Western thought has been forced to grapple with these basic problems: first, how to interpret the "fundamental 'cosmological' orientation of the Greeks," and second, how to translate Greek cosmological concepts into Christian (or Judaeo-Christian) vocabulary:

> Put concretely, the reliable presence of the universe, the guarantee of its continuance, its uncreatedness and indestructibility, which Aristotle thought he had proven through the force of conceptual argumentation, is being overshadowed by man's question about himself, about his finite existence and his future. It was the Judaeo-Christian discovery of the precedence of the future, the eschatology and its promise which opened up a new dimension to understand the world.

While the Greeks knew only "peripherally" about history, being primarily concerned with cosmology (metaphysically construed), the Judaeo-Christian emphasis on salvation history brought into view another aspect of human experience: that of "hope." As a result, the whole course of Western thought—Gadamer writes—is marked by "the tension between human experience which unfolds itself historically and is directed towards the future, and the formation of concepts which had been drawn from the cosmos."[7]

What is remarkable and noteworthy about Gadamer's account is his refusal to endorse either facile synthesis or radical opposition—and above all his willingness to think together salvation history and cosmology, or Judaeo-Christian temporality and Graeco-Roman philosophy. Returning to the character of Western civilization, and focusing on its constitutive features, one can say that—during the main course of its history—it has evolved in the interstices of the two central labels: Graeco-Roman and Judaeo-Christian (while simultaneously being exposed to "outside" influences, from Africa, the Near East, and beyond). The confluence of elements is imprinted already on the birth certificate of Western Christianity as it was implanted upon, and emerged among, the ruins of the Roman or Graeco-Roman (Hellenistic) civilization. During the early years, relations between Rome and Christianity were tense and hostile, punctuated by violent persecution. Even after the conversion of Emperor Constantine and the elevation of Christianity to state religion, conflict persisted on the intellectual level. As we know, some of the Christian church fathers (like Tertullian and Irenaeus) rejected and condemned the Graeco-Roman tradition as impious and "pagan," while others (like Ambrose and Jerome) were willing to embrace a "selective learning" from the same tradition, through a practice called *usus iustus*. During subsequent centuries, Christianity and Roman civilization—despite continuing quarrels—entered into a kind of symbiosis or uneasy alliance. The

Western church, later called "Roman Catholic Church," was structured, and continues to be structured, on the model of the Roman Empire. After the coronation of Charlemagne (800 A.D.), determined efforts were made in Western Europe to reaffirm explicitly the continuity with Roman civilization, efforts giving rise to the institutionalization of the "Holy Roman Empire" governed simultaneously by two authorities (emperor and pope) as rulers of the "two cities." In a curious historical twist, Roman or Graeco-Roman cosmology was placed here in the service of Christian eschatology.[8]

This is not the place to recount in detail the history of this uneasy alliance. Suffice it to say that, in the course of several centuries, the "heavenly city" increasingly collapsed into the "earthly city," meaning that church and papacy were steadily politicized and "secularized" (with divine grace deteriorating into a worldly-political commodity). Simultaneously, the earthly city decayed due to growing internal corruption, feudal economic stagnation, and interminable rifts between princes. The rebellion against this state of affairs was two-pronged, taking the form of the Renaissance and the Reformation. Triggered in part by the influx of Greek scholars from Byzantium, the Renaissance basically sought to rejuvenate the treasures of Graeco-Roman civilization, especially its literature and philosophy, while also trying to revitalize the political city after the model of the Roman Republic.[9] In turn, the Reformation sought to restore and purify the heavenly city, that is, the dimension of faith and grace, by stripping it of pretensions to worldly power. Although there was tension between the two revivals (note, for example, the conflict between Erasmus and Luther), there was also considerable overlap: many of the great Reformers or partisans of the Reformation were also classical humanists steeped in Greek and Latin texts (figures like Melanchthon and Reuchlin being prominent exemplars). Thus, in their combined effect, the Renaissance and Reformation testified again to the complicated, profoundly hyphenated character of Western civilization (as Gadamer has noted): its character as Graeco-Roman/Judaeo-Christian.

This complex civilizational amalgam was disturbed and radically reoriented during the ensuing centuries. Pursuing the momentum of its own "civilizing process"—a momentum fueled by Baconian science and Cartesian rationalism—Western civilization steadily expanded the domain of city life (as a civil artifact), while progressively absorbing or subjugating its corollaries or horizonal supplements. Seen from this angle, Western Enlightenment signaled the upsurge of a skeptical-humanist philosophy (typified by Voltaire and Diderot) and also the triumphant ascent of empirical science and its technical/technological implementation. It is at this point that one needs to ponder whether Western civilization is not perhaps co-constituted by a third strand or ingredient: namely, the culture of "modernity" and its social and intellectual ramifications. Clearly, Western modernity stands in a difficult relation to the two earlier formative components. While borrowing from and continuing in many ways the critical-philosophical legacy of Greece and Rome, modern science and rationality also break with that tradition in important ways, especially by disowning classical cosmology and teleology. Regarding the Judaeo-Christian legacy, Western post-Enlightenment modernity is marked by its radically secularizing and often anti-religious bent—which does not prevent it from incorporating into its arsenal a good deal of the spiritual inwardness and individualism previously nurtured by (Reformed) Christian faith. In large measure, the centrality of "human rights" in modern Western civilization is explained by the confluence of Graeco-Roman (especially Stoic) teachings, Christian spirituality, and the modern infatuation with secular individualism.[10]

The profound tension introduced by modernity into the traditional fabric of Western civilization has been clearly noted by Gadamer, especially in an essay entitled "Citizens of Two Worlds"—which refers not so much to the Augustinian "two cities" as rather to the two contrasting (though often overlapping) worlds of tradition and modernity. As Gadamer writes: "The emergence of the modern empirical sciences in the seventeenth century is the event through which the previous form of the totality of knowledge, of philosophy or *philosophia* in the broadest [cosmological] sense of the word, began to disintegrate." As a result of this event, the previous—albeit fragile—"unity of our culture" was called into question and further problematized. "If this is so," he adds,

> then the formation of European [Western] civilization by science implies not only a distinction, but brings with it a profound tension into the modern world. On the one hand, the tradition of our culture which formed us determines our self-understanding by virtue of its linguistic-conceptual structure which originated in Greek dialectics and metaphysics. On the other hand, the modern empirical sciences have transformed our world and our whole understanding of the world. The two stand side by side.[11]

As is well known, the status of Western modernity is a highly contested issue, surrounded by intense philosophical, cultural, and political debates.[12] For some, the rift between scientific modernity and

Greek teleology, on the one hand, and between "secular/agnostic" modernity and Judaeo-Christian faith, on the other hand, is so profound as to be marked by irremediable rupture (which, in turn, can be either praised or condemned). For others, contrasts or divergences are mitigated by overt or covert continuities. This is not the place to rehearse this complex debate—except to note that, as a profound student of Aristotle, Hegel, and Heidegger, Gadamer himself has always tended to balance rupture or divergence with some kind of continuity. In terms of modernity's implications for the "civilizing process," a few additional comments seem in order. Judging by strictly "civic" and humanist standards, one can hardly deny the considerable accomplishments of the modern period: its contributions to the expansion of human knowledge and to the strengthening of civil-political liberty and personal autonomy. By hindsight, of course, it is also evident that some of these gains were bought at a price—a price exacted particularly from the two corollaries or supplements of civilization. Here, one should also not forget that, since its inception, modernity has steadily been accompanied—as by a shadow—by a critique of modernity and its "civilizing" effects: a critique epitomized by such names and movements as Rousseau, Romanticism, Nietzsche, existentialism, and deconstruction. Again, I shall not pursue this issue here, except to point to a caveat voiced in Gadamer's *Truth and Method*: we should not erect the legitimate critique of (aspects of) modernity into an "antithesis to the freedom of reason."[13]

Toward a Dialogue among Civilizations

These observations lead me to my final theme: the implications of the civilizing process for our global age, and especially for the emerging "dialogue among civilizations." The preceding discussion demonstrated the immense complexity of civilization, and hence of civilizational encounter and dialogue. As a result of historical sedimentations, "civilization" is an intricate, multi-layered fabric composed of different, often tensional layers or strands; moreover, every layer in that fabric is subject to multiple interpretations or readings, and so is the inter-relation of historical strands. In addition to this multi-dimensionality, one also needs to recall the embeddedness of civil life in the web of what I call its corollaries or horizonal supplements. All these features can readily be transferred from the Western context to other major civilizations in the emerging global arena. Thus, "Islamic civilization" is clearly not a uniform or compact semantic structure; as several writers have emphasized, it is possible and necessary in the case of

Islamic societies to differentiate (at a minimum) between pre-Islamic legacies, Islamic traditions, and modern cultural layers (often shaped by Western influence).[14] Considerations of this kind militate against a bland vision of global homogeneity. Reflecting diverse historical trajectories, different civilizations manage their own complexity and multiplicity in highly distinctive ways—prompting them to resort to differentiated cosmologies, ontologies, and epistemologies. With regard to civilizational encounter this means that, to be fruitful, dialogue has to be both intra- and inter-civilizational, establishing linkages across both historical and geographical boundaries.

It is precisely against this background of multiplicity that Gadamer's hermeneutics proves most helpful: namely, by centerstaging a mode of dialogue that is open-ended and hospitable to multiple and expanding horizons. The pivotal role of dialogue (*Gespräch*) in his work is well known and requires little elaboration. Commenting on the Platonic model, *Truth and Method* stresses the point that dialogue proceeds "by way of question and answer," with an accent on the primacy of questioning: "To question means to bring [an issue] into the open. The openness of what is in question consists in the unsettled state of the answer." To be sure, questioning here is not whimsical or pointless; rather, it is guided by concern for a topic or issue (*Sache*)—a concern shared by all dialogue partners in an open-ended search for truth: "To conduct a dialogue requires first of all that the partners do not talk at cross-purposes. . . . [It] means to allow oneself to be guided by the subject matter to which the partners in the dialogue are also oriented. This demands [in turn] that one does not try to argue the other down but that one genuinely weighs the other's perspective."[15]

What is particularly important in Gadamer's view of dialogue is its radically non-instrumental sense: dialoguing here involves not only an act of questioning but also the experience of being questioned or being "called into question"—often in unsettling and disorienting ways. The openness of dialoguing means precisely the readiness of participants to allow themselves to be "addressed" and challenged by the other: particularly the stranger, the different, the exile. In Gadamer's words, hermeneutical inquiry is based "on the polarity of familiarity and strangeness (*Fremdheit*)," in that a person entering dialogue must be willing to undergo questioning, even of a radical kind. Hence, he adds, dialogical understanding as the "true locus of hermeneutics" always hovers in the "in-between": between self and other, familiarity and strangeness, presence and absence. Elaborating on this point, one might say that dialoguing happens in the "middle voice," between pure activity and passivity—which is also the terrain of what Gadamer calls "hermeneutical experience (*Erfahrung*)" seen as a venturing forward into the untamed and unfamiliar. Once the aspect of the "middle voice" is taken seriously, dialoguing ceases to be a willful exercise of construction or deconstruction. As Gadamer notes, the expression "conducting a conversation (*ein Gespräch führen*)" is actually misleading. For the more genuine the conversation is, "the less its conduct lies within the will power of either partner"; it would hence be more correct to say that we "fall into conversation" or "become embroiled in it."[16]

Observations of this kind apply not only to interpersonal relations, but also—and perhaps still more forcefully—to civilizational encounters. What was called "Orientalism" in the past was precisely the effort to dominate and "talk down" the other, in such a manner that the "Occident" was never "called into question" (or never allowed itself to be questioned).[17] To avoid this outcome, civilizational dialogue must jettison self-aggrandizing or assimilationist agendas (in the sense of the old French notion of "*mission civilisatrice*"). This means that intra-civilizational discourse should not degenerate into "culture wars," just as inter- or cross-cultural dialogue should move beyond Samuel Huntington's "clash of civilizations"; but the goal in neither case is a bland amalgamation or homogenization of differences. As in the case of interpersonal relations, civilizational dialogue has to take otherness (*Fremdheit*) seriously and hence to respect differences and distances that cannot simply be wished or talked away. What is needed here is a patient reticence, a willingness to listen to the other—often in silence. There is a famous text by Heidegger titled "A Dialogue on Language" that records a conversation between Heidegger and a Japanese (on such topics as art, translation, and other matters). The dialogue is remarkable for its porousness and multi-dimensionality. In conversing with each other, Heidegger and the Japanese try to understand and come closer to each other—but they do so in a halting and reticent way, with neither party seeking to assimilate or appropriate the other's perspective. Despite several points of congruence, the exchange is perforated with puzzlement, self-questioning, and silence (even silence about silence).[18]

Respect for diversity and distances brings back into view also the corollaries or supplements of civilization mentioned before. Seen from an existential-human perspective, these dimensions can be viewed as horizons or open frontiers (though not as terrains that can progressively be settled and appropriated). Here again, Gadamer's work is helpful by accentuating the notion of "horizon" (initially introduced by Edmund Husserl) and depicting it as a "range of vision" extending beyond "what is close at hand"—though not in a way that would nullify the familiar nor assimilate the distant.[19] On the level of civilizational discourse, horizonal openness means attentiveness to other civilizations, but also to civilization's corollaries (nature and the divine)—which speak or intervene in human discourse, but do so in recessed and "non-informatic" ways. The question is whether we allow ourselves to be addressed in this fashion. In the later writings of Heidegger, openness in this sense is implicit in his comments on the "speaking of language," where language is seen as a medium opening up a primordial space: a space for the interactive entwinement of nature's earth and sky and of human finitude and the divine (what he called the "four-fold"). A similar view of language is developed in the concluding part of *Truth and Method* where Gadamer refers to the "speculative" quality of language, that is, its character as an image or mirror of holistic world relations. Language is speculative, we read there, in that "the finite possibilities of a word are linked with the intended sense in a direction toward the infinite"; for to speak means "to correlate what is said with an infinity of the unsaid in a comprehensive nexus of meaning that alone grants understanding."[20]

In the context of Western civilization and its Judaeo-Christian dimension, Gadamer indicates, this speculative quality of language—its resonance with the infinite—has strong biblical support. In sacred scripture, human speech only mirrors a depth dimension of language harboring a divine "call" or calling; thus, *Genesis* presents God as "calling" the world into being, while the New Testament describes God as the "word" (*logos, verbum*) made incarnate in Christ.[21] Other civilizations and religious traditions have different ways to articulate the speculative dimension of language and the character of a divine (or trans-empirical) calling. In a manner paralleling the divine word, nature also speaks to or addresses human life—but again in recessed ways, requiring sober attention. To give an example: if we destroy the rainforests or puncture the ozone layer, nature speaks through global warming and other climatic changes, trying to teach us about the consequences of our actions. Here again, the ongoing process of globalization renders ecological responsibility a global imperative.

By way of conclusion, let me briefly sketch or summarize some of the basic requirements of civilizational dialogue in our time. One such requirement has to be attentiveness to "civilization" seen as a form of civic or city life. As I have indicated, city life in this sense involves a mode of civility or civic conduct, governed by civil-political laws and standards. Awareness of the drawbacks of modern civilized life does not or should not cancel the need to cultivate civil society and a responsible "public sphere"—now on a global or globalizing level. Whatever its other dimensions, the emerging global community will also be a "city"—though not on the model of the nation-state—governed by fair rules of conduct and attentive to the demands of good (responsible/accountable) government. Above all, global civil life will have to nurture the virtues of practical-political citizenship: that is, a commitment to social justice and the rule of law, and a willingness to shoulder the sobering demands of civic "prudence" (*phronesis*). In addition, however, attention needs to be accorded to civilization's corollaries or supplements, speaking to us in their distinctive registers. In sum, civilizational dialogue will have to be a multi-lingual discourse carried on in multiple tonalities, including the tonalities of politics, religion, philosophy, and ecology (and—subsidarily—economics and the internet).

In this complex amalgam, politics is in many ways architectonic (as Aristotle recognized). Only by fostering a commitment to social justice and public responsibility can globalization serve not only as the pacemaker of a mega-market and (possibly hegemonic) mega-state but as the gateway to global or inter-civilizational equity and peace. Here it is well to remember the complex conditions of peace and especially its character as a gift of justice (*opus iustitiae pax*): to have genuine peace in the city, we must also be at peace with ourselves, with nature, and with the divine (no matter how the latter is theologically formulated). Any act of exclusion or domination directed against any one of these dimensions is an act of violence undermining peace. In his *Civitas Dei*, Augustine spoke of the different modalities of "peace" obtaining in the different "cities," arguing in favor of some concordance among them.[22] Closer to our time, the Mahatma Gandhi emphasized the centrality of "*ahmisa*" (non-violence), which—in his understanding—is not merely a negative injunction, but an exhortation to "let being(s) be" or to allow the different dimensions of humanity to flourish. Drawing out the implications of this view for civilizational concord, the Gandhi scholar Bhikhu Parekh observes (correctly) that—without being incommensurable—"all cultures are partial and benefit from the insights of others," with the result that genuine global universalism "can be arrived at only by means of an uncoerced and equal intercultural [or inter-civilizational] dialogue."[23]

CHAPTER 2

CONVERSATION ACROSS BOUNDARIES

E Pluribus Unum?

A door of good wishes

—Rumi

"The view dies hard," Michael Oakeshott writes, "that Babel was the occasion of a curse being laid upon mankind from which it is the business of the philosophers to deliver us, and a disposition remains to impose a single character upon significant human speech." In recent centuries (at least in the West), the "single character" imposed on speech has tended to be that of rational-argumentative discourse, a discourse closely patterned on the model of scientific inquiry. This model has been seconded and closely accompanied by the voice of practical utility, that is, by a mode of instrumental reasoning geared toward practical efficiency and success. In lieu of these preponderant types of speech—science and technical utility—Oakeshott proposes a different, more flexible and encompassing paradigm of discursive human interaction, which he labels "conversation." In his presentation, conversation is not an argumentative discourse in which speakers raise rational claims against each other; nor is it a manipulative encounter in which participants constantly seek to trump each other. Although there may be "passages of argument" in conversation, such reasoning there is "neither sovereign nor alone" nor able to structure the entire interaction. Above all, conversational encounter is not "an enterprise designed to yield an extrinsic profit, a contest where a winner gets a prize"; rather, it is "an unrehearsed intellectual adventure." This conversational paradigm,

Oakeshott proposes, is "the appropriate image of human intercourse" because "it recognizes the qualities, the diversities, and the proper relationships of human utterances." As civilized human beings we are the inheritors of conversational speech, "begun in the primeval forests and extended and made more articulate in the course of centuries."[1]

In our age of globalization, of the relentless forging of a "global village," Oakeshott's proposal gains a new and unprecedented significance. In our global (or globalizing) context it becomes urgently important to extend his paradigm beyond the domestic arena: that is, to structure not only intra-societal interactions in non-domineering and non-manipulative ways, but to explore the prospects of a similarly non-coercive global discourse conducted across national and civilizational boundaries. In Kantian vocabulary, such an exploration clearly and unapologetically pursues a "cosmopolitan intent"; at the same time, however, this intent has to be moderated and even severely restrained in the face of the rich profusion of diverse idioms and cultural voices present in our world. Above all, global discourse cannot privilege or assign prima facie validity to a particular voice or discourse (no matter how "universally" formulated); in Oakeshott's words, it cannot accept an arbiter or even "a doorkeeper to examine credentials." This caveat applies also (and perhaps especially) to modern Western discourse, heavily shaped by scientific reasoning; although surely entitled to a hearing, it cannot act as "symposiarch."[2] Differently put: Oakeshottian "conversation of humankind" has to steer a difficult path between a hegemonically imposed universalism, governed by one idiom or voice, and an array of self-enclosed, ethnocentric particularisms where no voice would be willing or able to listen to others. In the following, I shall try to move along this path by proceeding in three steps. In a first step, I shall ponder some of the formidable obstacles facing global conversation, especially obstacles arising in the field of politics and political thought; the focus here will be chiefly on forms of political "Orientalism" and on the fascination of political theorists with power (to the detriment of justice). Next, I shall discuss a prominent model of cosmopolitan discourse, advanced by a leading neo- or post-Kantian thinker (Jürgen Habermas). Finally, I shall sketch a different kind of cosmopolitan interaction, returning at this point to Oakeshott's association of conversation with interpersonal friendship.

Orientalism and the Primacy of Power Politics

From time immemorial, philosophy has favored a spectatorial or bird's-eye view. Western philosophy, in particular, has tended to privilege universal maxims over contingent phenomena, generally valid insights over local-vernacular experiences. In large measure, this privilege was at the heart of traditional Western metaphysics, with its familiar assortment of binary oppositions (transcendent/immanent, mind/body, and the like)—oppositions that typically were tilted so as to favor one side of the paired terms. In modern times, Western metaphysics became centered around the pivot of reason or the rational subject (*cogito*), a concentration accompanied again by a number of binaries seeking to screen off reason from various extra-rational dimensions, such as emotive inclinations, external nature, and the sacred or divine.[3] In its social or societal implications, this metaphysical focus entailed a number of predictable consequences, especially the growing division of society into a rational elite of experts—who increasingly became the managers of economic, technical, and administrative affairs—and the vast masses of less educated workers and artisans attached to the idiom of ordinary common sense. On the inter-societal or inter-civilizational level, the same focus gave rise to the distinction between rationally advanced and rationally backward societies, between so-called developed and underdeveloped (or developing) countries; in large measure, this distinction coincided with that between Occident and Orient, with the former assigning to the latter its status and significance in the global context—a practice that came to be known as "Orientalism."[4]

Although endemic primarily to "Orientalist" schools in Western academia, the same practice has tended to pervade other academic fields, including the discipline of political science and political theory of philosophy. At least since the rise of modern liberalism (that is, the time of Locke and Adam Smith), it has become a staple of Western political thought to draw a sharp boundary line between Western freedom and "Oriental despotism" (with the latter phrase being applied often indiscriminately to a broad swath of regimes from the Middle East to East Asia).[5] Sheltered behind this dividing line, practitioners of political thought have tended to cultivate and rehearse the so-called canon of Western political ideas and "great books," while refusing on the whole to venture beyond these canonical confines (or else venturing forward only with the imperialist gesture characteristic of Orientalism). The same canonical and ethnocentric confinement has also marked the discipline of political science as a whole, including the subfields of comparative politics and international relations. By and large, the discipline has limited itself to mapping the basic features of the modern Western nation-state—from the "input structures" of pressure groups and political parties to the "output structures" of legislative and executive branches—and then using this model as the paradigm for political analysis in general. Thus, practitioners of comparative politics have tended to employ the core insignia of Western "developed" regimes as the standard or litmus test to evaluate the performance of non-Western "developing" regimes. In turn, international relations experts, with some exceptions, have projected onto the global arena the central trademarks of the "Westphalian system" lying at the origin of modern Europe.[6]

In the field of political science, Orientalist proclivities are reinforced and further modulated by the prevailing professional fascination with political power—a fascination tending to trump or screen out concern with justice, ethics, and legitimacy. Like the modernist privileging of reason, this professional bias is not very hospitable to Oakeshottian conversation—since, predicated on command and submission, power cannot be equally shared and hence seems to call either for a "symposiarch" or else for a wordless struggle for power. The noted inhospitality is well known to political theorists. Thus, objecting to the accent on dialogue and deliberation (in the context of "deliberative" democracy), a prominent American theorist has called for an end of deliberation on the grounds that "politics is about interests and power."[7] In using this phrase to pinpoint the core of politics, the American theorist—perhaps unwittingly—echoed the view of a renowned German political thinker of the twentieth century, Carl Schmitt, who—no doubt, in a much more forceful and polemical way—voiced his disgust over the decline of German politics (during the Weimar Republic) into endless parliamentary discussion and argumentation. Among his many other intellectual contributions, Schmitt is chiefly famous (or notorious) for his pithy definition of politics in terms of the distinction between "friend and foe (or enemy)," a definition that rules out or sidelines dialogue in favor of a stark and ineluctable antithesis. As Thomas Hobbes would have said—and as he in fact did say in a slightly modified manner—between friend and enemy dialogue or conversation necessarily comes to an end, because the dispute between citizens loyal to the sovereign and those outside the bounds of the commonwealth cannot be settled by words but only by "the sword."[8]

Since the time of Hobbes, international politics has been governed basically by the friend-enemy paradigm (moderated to some extent by treaty law and shifting balances of power). No doubt, changes are afoot in the present age. Under the aegis of globalization, the old state-centered paradigm is being challenged increasingly by forces operating both above and beneath the threshold of traditional nation-states;

among these factors, broader cultural or civilizational constellations have attracted the attention of international political analysts. In his famous essay of 1993, Samuel Huntington depicted a new scenario emerging on the global horizon: a scenario tendentially replacing the traditional antagonism of states with a broader cultural conflict or (what he called) a "clash of civilizations." As he wrote at that time: "World politics is entering a new phase, and intellectuals have not hesitated to proliferate visions of what it will be. . . . It is my hypothesis that the fundamental source of conflict in this new world will not be primarily ideological or primarily economic" but "cultural." Although traditional nation-states will remain "powerful actors" in the emerging scenario, the principal global antagonisms are bound to occur between countries and clusters of countries belonging to different civilizations; hence, "the clash of civilizations will dominate global politics." In Huntington's portrayal, the projected cultural rivalry was not entirely random or haphazard; although distinguishing between some seven or eight major civilizations, his essay singled out one major rivalry as overshadowing all others: namely, the conflict between the West as the only remaining superpower—and the representative of modern aspirations of "universalism"—and all the other countries and civilizations summarily labeled as "non-Western." Despite the shift of focus from nation-states to civilizations, Huntington's scenario thus retained a central feature of the older "Westphalian system": namely, the conception of international politics as a relentless power struggle (patterned on the friend-enemy model); moreover, by centerstaging the conflict between "the West and the Rest," it paid tribute to the legacy of political Orientalism.[9]

Habermas and Communicative Rationality

As can be seen, Oakeshottian conversation faces obstacles and roadblocks on many sides. As it happens, these obstacles have not gone unchallenged. For some time now, Orientalism has tended to be a term of rebuke in academic as well as international political discourses. In its affiliation with the Orientalist paradigm, sheer power politics likewise has been critically scrutinized and contested. In this respect, older or traditional notions of just and legitimate rule have joined hands with more recent approaches to legitimation predicated on intersubjective—possibly participatory democratic—communication. An important catalyst in launching the latter approaches has been the so-called linguistic turn characterizing philosophy in the twentieth century, a turn that shifted the focus of attention from individual "monological" designs to the arena of communicative exchanges or "language games" in which individual designs are always already embedded. In the context of (so-called) Continental theorizing, a leading spokesman of this turn has been the philosopher-sociologist Jürgen Habermas, whose work is chiefly renowned for the central role it assigns to communicative action and communicative rationality (or reason). In a series of influential writings, Habermas has highlighted communicative rationality as the crucial pillar of contemporary social and political theory, and also as the guiding principle of modern intellectual life (what he has called the "philosophical discourse of modernity") and of any viable theory of social development or modernization.[10] For present purposes, these writings will be kept in the background and presupposed as relatively well known to political theorists. The following discussion shall concentrate mainly on Habermas's recent effort to develop a global or genuinely cosmopolitan model of rational communication along cross-cultural lines—that is, a model that, while recognizing the importance of cultural and historical differences, seeks to obviate the danger of an impending "clash of civilizations."

Habermas's effort is manifest in several of his recent writings; the most forthright and lucid exposition of his views on global communication can be found in an essay (of 1987/88) entitled "The Unity of Reason in the Diversity of Its Voices" (contained in his book *Postmetaphysical Thinking*).[11] In his essay, Habermas takes his departure from traditional metaphysics and its effort to reconcile unity and plurality, the "One" and the "Many." Ever since the time of Plato, he notes, metaphysics has presented itself in its dominant forms as a "doctrine of universal unity," as a theory oriented toward "the One as the origin and ground of everything." In recent times, this metaphysical legacy has become the target of an intense controversy pitting against each other defenders of holistic unity and champions of radical diversity and fragmentation. While the former—wedded to premodern life-forms—link the loss of unity with a presumed "crisis of modernity," the latter—mainly adepts of postmodern contextualism—denounce traditional holism as potentially totalitarian and appeal to the "plurality of histories and life-forms" against a unified historical *telos,* and to the "alterity of language games and discourses" against the univocity of language and speech. In Habermas's reading, *both* sides of the controversy—those privileging unity over plurality and those prioritizing plurality over unity—are in fact "secret accomplices." In opposition to both parties, his essay proposes a "third position" or third path: namely, the secular-humanist path of those "who, in continuation of the Kantian tradition, seek to salvage a skeptical and postmetaphysical, but by no means defeatist conception of reason." This approach culminates in the thesis "that the unity of reason only remains perceptible in the plurality of its voices—as the basic possibility of a contingent-occasional, but intelligible passage from one language into another."[12]

Having specified the terms of the engagement, Habermas returns briefly to the tradition of metaphysical holism as expounded by Plato, Plotinus, and their successors. As he observes, the "*to hen panta*" of Plotinus does not mean the simple diffusion of everything in an amorphous unity but rather the proposition that "the Many [or manifold things] can be traced back to the One and can thereby be conceived as a whole, as totality." In this metaphysical construal, unitary wholeness is not merely a vague preamble or speculative premise of worldly phenomena, but rather functions as the source and explanatory foundation of all things. With this vision of ultimate unity, traditional metaphysics elevated itself above the teeming polytheism of an earlier mythological age, an age content to remain at the surface of phenomenal diversity. In Habermas's words: "Through this powerful act of abstraction, the human mind gained an extra-mundane reference point," a perspectival distance that allowed the gathering of multiple events and phenomena into "a stable whole." Aiming at the intuitive blending of the philosopher's mind with the One, the "*henosis*" of Plotinus in particular signaled a movement of "ecstatic self-transgression as well as reflexive self-reassurance," which was not devoid of "emancipatory" qualities. To be sure, holistic metaphysics was from the beginning beset with formidable problems that could not ultimately be resolved. One such problem was the conundrum of immanence and transcendence: the question how the One can be reconciled with the Many without jeopardizing its oneness. For in order to be everything, the One has to be in the Many or immanent in the world; but in order to safeguard its oneness, it has to be simultaneously "above or beyond" all innerworldly things. Another major problem concerned the relation between holism and individualism or individual particularity. For if the One was the explanatory ground of all beings, the integrity of individual uniqueness was liable to evaporate—an issue that provided powerful impulses to medieval nominalism or metaphysical anti-realism.[13]

In modern times, traditional metaphysics was radically challenged—though initially without the abandonment of holistic aspirations. In Kant's philosophy, the objective unity of a cosmic order—presupposed in traditional metaphysics—was replaced by a series of synthetic achievements traceable to the capacity of human reason. "Kant,"

Habermas observes, "connected the concept of cognition with the synthetic accomplishments of productive imagination and understanding (*Verstand*) through which the manifold sensations and representations are organized into a unity of experiences and judgments." In his *Critique of Pure Reason,* Kant—while rejecting a cosmic realism—postulated the notion of a "cosmological idea," construed as an idea of pure reason, through which it is possible to transform the totality of inner-worldly phenomena into an object of rational-scientific analysis. Proceeding in this manner, Kant's treatise "downgraded the cosmos into the object domain of nomological natural sciences." To compensate for this disillusionment Kant's second *Critique* offered the vision of another, more ambitious synthesis: the synthesis of an "intelligible world" anchored in the "noumenal" realm of moral freedom. As in the case of pure reason, practical reason here projects a "synthetic unity of all possible conditions"—but now a synthesis aiming at the unity of an "ethical-civic commonwealth" organizing the multitude of citizens under the rubric of shared, objectively valid laws. Although appreciating Kant's general strategy, Habermas finds his work not immune from traditional metaphysical quandaries. Apart from the unsolved problem of individuality, this work—he states—revives traditional dilemmas "now in a transcendentally modified form: the murky coexistence of intelligible and sensible worlds translates old problems into many new questions," such as questions about the relation "between pure and practical reason, between freedom and natural causality, between morality and legality" (and the like).[14]

To overcome these and related dilemmas was the basic aim of Hegel's philosophy with its immensely complex structure of mediations. In Habermas's presentation, Hegel renewed "for the last time the holistic impulses of metaphysics"—but now against the backdrop of Romanticism, historicism, and modern liberalism; his "philosophy of reconciliation" was deliberately designed as a response to the felt need to "overcome the diremptions of modernity out of the spirit of modernity itself." Hence, the crucial importance of history for his thought. As Habermas writes:

> This background explains, first, why Hegel conceives the One as absolute subject and thus annexes metaphysics to that notion of autonomous subjectivity from which modernity derives its consciousness of freedom and its distinctive normative content of self-awareness and self-determination; and it explains, secondly, why he invokes history as the medium of the mediation of the One and the Many, of the infinite and the finite.

In Hegel's historical mediation, the unity of reason was produced in a novel fashion, different from his predecessors: "The One and the Many no longer confront each other as related entities; rather, it is now the historically mobilized relation itself which establishes the unity of its elements." For Habermas, however, this change carried a heavy price. For by opening itself to history, philosophical thought was invaded by a "host of contingencies and uncertainties" recalcitrant to mediation; Hegelian synthesis thus exposed itself to forces "whose subversive power threatened to undermine his own construction." Awareness of this difficulty prompted the philosophical interventions of Marx and Kierkegaard, with the former placing his trust in the synthetic power of collective praxis and the latter in the redemptive quality of an existential life history. By subscribing to either a collective or private teleology, however, the work of both thinkers retained a "foundationalist residue"—a residue that has become steadily less persuasive given the relentless inroad of contingencies belying all "rash syntheses."[15]

At this point, Habermas turns to more recent philosophical developments, especially to the "paradigm shift" or sea-change mentioned above: the shift from the paradigm of consciousness to that of language and communication. As he notes, in the wake of this shift, the old dilemma of the One and the Many presents itself in a new guise: namely, as the opposition between a universal and univocal language, possibly grounded in a logical syntax, and the multiplicity of heterogeneous language games. Philosophically, this opposition surfaces as the conflict between linguistic idealists or "objectivists," on the one hand, and radical contextualists or relativists, on the other. To make some headway in this debate, Habermas focuses on some recent discussions among American philosophers on this issue, choosing as his chief exemplars Richard Rorty and Hilary Putnam. In Rorty's work he finds the articulation of a circumspect and sophisticated type of contextualism, a type that avoids the self-referential paradoxes of a radical relativism. For Rorty, it is pointless to maintain the (Platonic) distinction between true knowledge and opinion, since "true" simply denotes an opinion that we consider justified according to our own standards—standards that are embedded in our culture. In accord with this view, Rorty identifies objective knowledge with an intersubjective agreement which, in turn, is buttressed by a consensually shared language and life-form; he replaces the striving for objectivity with the striving for social solidarity in a contingent language game. As a circumspect contextualist, to be sure, Rorty does not exit his given framework in the direction of comparative evaluations—even though he has to pay for this abstinence with the price of an "admitted ethnocentrism." This same abstinence has been challenged by Hilary Putnam—not in the name of a linguistic idealism or objectivism, but in favor of the porousness and permeability for all language games, that is, their reciprocal openness to each other.[16]

For Habermas, Putnam's intervention is important, especially by lending aid and support to his own program of communicative rationality. What renders Putnam's argument particularly congenial is his acceptance of the role of critical judgment, that is, of the critical amendment or emendation of prevailing linguistic and cultural standards in the light of better insights—insights that often originate outside one's frame of reference. As he comments, the possibility of the critique and self-critique of established practices can be explained only "if we take the notion of an expansion of our interpretive horizon seriously *as an idea* and relate it to the intersubjectivity of a consensus which transgresses the distinction of 'for us' and 'for them'." Whereas in Rorty's ethnocentrism every otherness ("for them") must be integrated or assimilated into "our" framework, genuine dialogue or consensus requires a reciprocity of understanding, in the sense that it is not only up to others ("them") to understand "our" perspective, but it is equally up to "us" to grasp things from "their" perspective. Seen in this light, the so-called fusion of horizons postulated by Gadamer does not signify the assimilation of others to "us," but rather the growing "convergence of our *and* their perspectives through a process of reciprocal learning." Such learning, however, is possible only against the backdrop of certain general standards or criteria operative in all language games. In Habermas's account, these standards involve concepts like truth, rationality, and justification—concepts that, although variably interpreted and applied, "play the *same* grammatical role in *every* language community." Consistently pursued, this argument leads to the notion of a "situated reason" or rationality that gains voice in validity claims that are "both context-dependent and transcendent." Differently phrased: the validity claimed for propositions and norms "transcends spaces and times"; but in each case the claim "is raised here and now, in a specific context, and accepted or rejected with concrete implications for social interaction."[17]

The notion of a "situated reason" serves as a bulwark against radical contextualism, and also as short-hand label for the theory of communicative rationality (the topic of the essay's concluding section). In Habermas's view, contextualism is a fashionable, but unpersuasive mode of contemporary *Zeitgeist*. "Today," he writes, "everything is thrust into the whirlpool of the experience of contingency"—on the premise that "everything could also be otherwise," including "the categories of understanding, the constitution of subjectivity, and the foundation of rationality itself." To some extent, this cult of contingency reflects social experiences of our time: the situation of a radically decentered and functionally differentiated society where "*everything* seems to have been pushed into the periphery." As an antidote to this kind of decentering, Habermas vindicates a concept of reason that is no longer metaphysically imposed "from above," but rather grows out of the ordinary "lifeworld" and its matrix of intersubjective communication. Transposed into this arena, the old metaphysical dilemma of the One and the Many reappears in a chastised and more manageable form: namely, as the tension (felt in the lifeworld) between "the unconditional character of context-transcending validity claims," on the one hand, and "the facticity of context-dependent and practical/pragmatic orientations," on the other. From a slightly different angle, the contrast emerges as the tension between the pre-reflective "background intuitions" of the lifeworld and the rational validity claims of discourses. As Habermas emphasizes, a situated or communicative reason of this kind is no longer a metaphysical "absolute" but at best a "critical procedure" permeated by fallibilism; although "indeed a fragile vessel," it "does not go under in the sea of contingency—even if its fragility on high seas is its only mode of coping with contingencies." In practical-political terms, situated reason remains wedded to the idea of an "un-mutilated (*unversehrt*) intersubjectivity" among social partners, to the fallible, cooperative endeavor "to reduce, abolish or prevent the suffering of vulnerable creatures."[18]

Toward Self-Transgressive Friendship

Habermas's attempt to reconcile the One and the Many is impressive and appealing in many respects. Certainly the aim of fostering an "unmutilated intersubjectivity" deserves praise and widespread support; equally praiseworthy is the desire to reduce or prevent the "suffering of vulnerable creatures"—especially in an age of horrendous sufferings produced by recurrent holocausts and ethnic cleansings. On a more theoretical or philosophical level, one cannot fail to appreciate Habermas's sensitivity for the sea-changes of our period: the change from consciousness to language, from a monological *cogito* to intersubjective communication. Behind these changes, a deeper and still more significant transformation finds recognition in his writings: the move from metaphysics to post-metaphysics, from a speculative-metaphysical apotheosis of the "One" to the post-metaphysical dispersal or dissemination of the One in the manifold of concrete phenomena. What recognition of this change entails is that unity or synthesis can no longer be presupposed a priori or postulated "from on high," but can only emerge (if at all) from the travail of multiple and criss-crossing particular experiences "on the ground." The concrete political implications of this kind of post-metaphysics are evident: the meaning and direction of social life can no longer be univocally defined by a privileged elite or compact social class, but have to be continuously negotiated and renegotiated in the absence of (what Claude Lefort called) firm "markers of certainty."[19]

The noted sea-changes are gathered or strung together in the central and most widely discussed category of Habermas's writings: communicative action or communicative rationality—a category which seems to have a distant affinity with Oakeshottian conversation. In the essay on "The Unity of Reason," communicative reason is held up as the preferred mode of reconciling the One and the Many in our time, and also as the decisive antidote to radical contextualization. In the extensive lectures on *The Philosophical Discourse of Modernity,* the paradigm of communicative reason was singled out as the basic "solution" to the theoretical and practical quandaries of the modern age—in stark opposition to a variety of anti-modern counter-discourses proliferating during the past century. It is precisely at this point that doubts or apprehensions arise regarding the character of Habermasian communication. As one will recall, *The Philosophical Discourse* basically privileged a limited number of philosophical voices, while sidelining and even "ex-communicating" a large number of other voices. The privileged forms of discourse were those of Kant, Hegel, and various post-idealist successors; the bulk of the volume, however, was devoted to illegitimate voices or idioms not fitting into modern discourse: starting from Friedrich Nietzsche, presented as the "turn-table" away from modernity, and continuing into the two main strands of Nietzsche's descendants (Heidegger and Jacques Derrida, on the one hand, and Georges Bataille and Michel Foucault, on the other).[20] By structuring his work in this manner, Habermas drew a clear demarcation between proper and improper, between rational and non-rational (or irrational) forms of communication—with the demarcation basically coinciding with the role of rational validity claims. In so doing, he reestablished a hierarchy privileging a prior "unity of reason" (in contravention of his own post-metaphysical leanings); he also installed himself in a way as the arbiter or (what Oakeshott calls) the "symposiarch" of communicative interaction.

The limitations of Habermasian communication have been noted by many observers, including readers otherwise friendly to his critical-theoretical program. Thus, in several of her writings, Iris Marion Young has endeavored to correct or augment his model by emphasizing forms of speech sidelined or neglected by Habermasian rationality: modes of greeting or salutation, of topical allusions, and of story-telling or narration.[21] However, the limitation probably goes deeper and has paradigmatic status. By making validity claims the yardstick of proper communication, his model marginalizes or excludes modes of interaction and broad domains of human experience not subsumable under argumentative reason. In a perceptive essay titled "Habermas and the Question of Alterity," Diana Coole has highlighted the strategy of exclusion and marginalization operative in his discursive framework. As she writes, Habermas is unable to attribute "any emancipatory potential to alterity or otherness" because "his basic ideas concerning communicative reason and the emancipatory project of modernity are predicated on this exclusion." For Coole, the important point is to overcome the binary dualisms of inside and outside, reason and non-reason. For the alterity suppressed by the discursive model—and valorized by postmodern "deconstruction"—is not some "mystical or primoridal" unreason, as Habermas suggests, but rather "the fault-lines and ruptures, the differences, which structure language itself." A prominent mode of such differential language is modern art and aesthetics, culminating in a "radical aesthetic of everyday life"—a domain where Habermasian discourse remains particularly weak or inadequate. Again, it is important here not to erect aesthetics into "a *model* of an alternative, harmonious subjectivity or politics" but rather to see it as "a *mode* of subversive/creative intervention—one that operates on pre-discursive levels." In social-political terms, Coole stipulates as a minimal requirement that communicative reason and discursive democracy be supplemented by "an appreciation of the prediscursive and nondiscursive levels on which power and alterity circulate," such that postmodern strategies or "decodings" can be seen as a crucial dimension of emancipatory politics.[22]

In large measure, the notion of pre- or non-discursive levels of interaction points to the recessed background matrix of the "lifeworld" and vernacular common sense—a matrix not entirely ignored in Habermas's writings. In Coole's words, Habermas's own acknowledgement of the lifeworld dimension calls attention to the "prediscursive realm and the limits of [rational] discourse." The problem, however, is the fragile and highly elusive status of that dimension in the discursive model. In several of his writings, it is true, Habermas pays tribute to the lifeworld, ascribing to it a near-redemptive quality capable of resolving or mitigating the antagonisms of modern life. Thus, *The Philosophical Discourse* invokes the holistic resources of the lifeworld as an antidote to the divisive trajectories of modern, rationalized "value spheres." As he writes there, the rationality of communication is "interwoven with the *resources* of a particular distinctive lifeworld"; and to the extent that the latter fulfills its role properly, it functions as "an intuitive, unshakeably certain, and holistic knowledge which cannot be problematized at will." As it happens, however, this passage is followed almost instantly by a reminder of the countervailing thrust of rationalization—a thrust that explains why "the weight of general [rationalized] structures can increase during the historical process of differentiation." The concluding chapter on "The Normative Content of Modernity" speaks likewise of the growing differentiation "between steering problems and problems of mutual understanding," a gap generating the prospect of the progressive "colonization of the lifeworld by the imperatives of functional systems which externalize their costs." The companion essay on "Modernity: An Unfinished Project" recapitulates the Weberian trajectory of modernization—the growing split between competing rationality spheres—while also noting its practical or experiential consequences. In the pursuit of this trajectory, Habermas acknowledges, the distance between expert domains and vernacular knowledge is liable to increase; as a result "the lifeworld threatens to become steadily *impoverished*."[23]

Impoverishment of this kind, however, poses problems not only for modernity or modernization theory; it also raises serious difficulties for a "postmetaphysical thinking" seeking to retrieve the "unity of reason" from the diversity of vernacular idioms and understandings. If modernity is tilted in the stated manner—in the direction of universally replicable rationality structures—the desired unity seems again to be presupposed or stipulated "from on high," to the detriment of prediscursive common sense operating "on the ground." Moreover, unless vernacular lifeworld matrices are more seriously acknowledged and engaged, reciprocal communication and learning are prone to be thwarted or curtailed, due to the premature equation between self and other, ego and alter ego (and hence again the exclusion of alterity). The deficit of vernacular experience and interaction in the discourse model has been prominently highlighted by Charles Taylor in several of his writings. His *Sources of the Self* describe the deficit in terms of the neglect of the background matrix or experiential "grid" against which rationality structures are profiled in the first place. What cannot be fitted into the model, he writes, are deeper human longings or aspirations, especially "the search for moral sources *outside* the subject through languages which resonate *within* him or her"; differently put, there is "no coherent place left for an exploration of the order in which we are set as a locus of moral sources." In a still more recent text, Taylor chides the neglect of this experiential matrix as responsible for a tendential erasure of the "linguistic turn," that is, the slide of communication back into monologue. This happens when communication is reduced to an exchange of self-centered interests (or an exchange between ego and alter ego). "As one might expect," he observes pointedly,

> the hold of the monological view is a lot stronger than many critics think. They tinker with the surface rather than go to the deeper assumptions. . . . Thus, Habermas demonologizes Kant, in the sense that an acceptable norm must now really be accepted by all those affected. The aim is to do real justice to everyone, and so the goal is to bring everyone to the same point. But we still conceive of the people concerned as giving their agreement as individuals. . . . What gets blocked out are what we might call essentially together-goods, where it is crucial to their being the good they are that they be lived and enjoyed together, all the way from dance to conversation, to love, to friendship, to common self-rule, to the preaching of the Word.[24]

What these comments bring into view is a mode of communication no longer narrowly tailored to rational validity claims, but open to vernacular experiences. In a slightly sharpened formulation, one might speak here of a "thick conversation" or a "thick dialogue," that is, a communicative exchange willing to delve into the rich fabric of different lifeworlds and cultures. The appeal in such exchanges is no longer merely to the rational-cognitive capacity of participants, but rather to the full range of their situated humanity, including their hopes, aspirations, moral or spiritual convictions, as well as their agonies and frustrations. In this respect, thick dialogue remains closely attentive to the "sufferings of vulnerable creatures." Most important, dialogue here is no longer a simple ego–alter ego interaction, but rather an encounter between mutually decentered agents involved in a transformative event. Taylor appropriately makes reference to Gadamer's construction of conversation as a trans-subjective happening, "more like a game or a dance than a series of causally linked monological actions." Such a construal, he notes, involves a new, no longer self-centered (or else Eurocentric) view of humanism— a view in which humans are no longer self-enclosed or self-sufficient, but constantly on a journey toward broader horizons (possibly toward a *metanoia* or change of heart). It is in this light that one should also see his association of thick conversation with love and friendship—both of which involve a form of self-transgression, in the sense that both are predicated on self-giving rather than an attempt to appropriate or assimilate the other. Transposing the discussion into an Asian-Buddhist idiom, Taylor states that self-transgression "opens the flood-gates of *metta* (loving kindness) and *karuna* (compassion)."[25]

The lessons of these observations for global diversity are evident. Conceived in terms of self-transgressive friendship, thick conversation may well be the most urgent need in our world today. The point of such conversation is not to dominate, manipulate, or lecture others "from on high," but to take them seriously in their lifeworlds as members of the global community. Differently put: the urgent need today is not so much to rationalize or control different lifeworlds, but rather to befriend people in their lived contexts all around the world. To avoid misunderstanding: to befriend people in their lived contexts does not mean to "Romanticize" these contexts or to treat them as fixed or unchangeable. In many instances, the contexts or conditions of peoples' lives are marked by squalor, misery, hardship, and exploitation. To befriend people in these conditions is not the same as to sanction or justify these conditions, but rather means to encourage, strengthen, and support people in their deepest striving for a dignified and "good" life, for a life of genuine freedom and fulfillment.[26] To this extent, thick conversation—in the sense outlined above—fully concurs with the aim of fostering an "unmutilated intersubjectivity" and of reducing or preventing the "suffering of vulnerable creatures" (to use Habermas's phrases). To go a step further: supporting the striving for a dignified or "good" life involves indeed the acknowledgment of an unconditional standard beyond contexts—but a standard that is no longer a monologically imposed imperative of reason, but rather has the character of a communicative appeal or appellation reaching us from "alterity," from the other's concrete pains and longings. "Unconditional" here means something that cannot be conditioned, manipulated, or controlled; preeminently unconditional in this sense are friendship, the divine—and the voice of poetry.

At this point, the conclusion of this chapter can be rejoined with its beginning. In his essay on the "conversation of (hu)mankind," Michael Oakeshott links genuine conversation with the voice or idiom of poetry, because poetry or "poetic imagining" is not concerned with argumentative propositions nor with efforts logically to convince readers or listeners. In the language of poetry, he writes, words are "not signs with preordained significances" nor are they "like chessmen behaving according to known rules" or like "tools with specific aptitudes and uses"; rather, their point is to offer relief "from the uniformities and rigidities of a life narrowly concentrated upon practical endeavor." Oakeshott also associates genuine conversation with love and friendship or with the world viewed *sub specie amoris,* because—he says— friends and lovers are "not concerned with what can be made out of each other, but only with the enjoyment of one another." Perhaps one may wish to supplement Oakeshott's approach here with some of the teachings of Aristotle, who, as is well known, distinguished between three kinds of friendship: those of pleasure, utility, and goodness. It is particularly in the last type, also called "perfect friendship," that love and friendship reveal their truly self-transgressive quality, by fostering a mode of loving purely for the other's sake.[27]

In the spirit of Oakeshott, it may be fitting to conclude here by honoring an eminent "voice of poetry" in the conversation of humankind: the voice of the great Persian Sufi poet Jalal ad-Din Rumi, whose constant theme was love or friendship (between humans, and between humans and the divine):

> Come now whoever you are!
> Come without any fear of being disliked.
> Come whether you are a Muslim, a Christian or Jew.
> Come whoever you are!
> Whether you believe or do not believe in God.
> Come also if you believe in the sun as God.
> This door is not a door of fear.
> This is a door of good wishes.[28]

CHAPTER 3

THE AMBIVALENCE OF EUROPE

Western Culture and its "Other"

According to Homer, Europa was the daughter of Phoenix, who was king of Phoenicia, a country in the Middle East. Because of her great beauty, the Greek god Zeus approached Europa in the form of a "white" bull and carried her away to Crete, where she became the mother of king Minos. Couched in mythological language, the story is revealing (as only thoughtful myths can be). In his account, "good Homer" (*bonus Homerus*) tells us about the ambivalence of origins, and especially about the ambivalent origin of what later came to be known as Europe. Judged in terms of that later history, beautiful Europa was by no means native or indigenous to European culture; rather, reared in the "Oriental" customs of the Near East, she was forcefully abducted by a conquering hero and only later domesticated or "naturalized" in her new surroundings. No other continent on earth (to my knowledge) has a similarly intriguing story about its origins; nowhere else is there such an explicit reference to the interlacing of identity and difference, inside and outside, familiarity and strangeness—an interlacing constitutive of the very beginnings of the continent.

Europeans today would do well to remember Homer's story, not for the sake of absconding from their history, but of living that history more soberly and generously. The following presentation seeks to foster this generosity by placing itself explicitly (or in the main) at the border of inside and outside, home and not-home. Born and raised in Europe, I myself have spent the past half-century in North America—which itself is an ambivalent offshoot of Europe. Some of my very first publications, written after World War II, were devoted specifically to the character or meaning of Europe and her place in the world[1]—issues to which I now return under changed auspices. The interlocutors chosen in the following presentation also reflect Europe's ambivalence; most of them are inhabitants of the border zone mentioned above. This is true particularly of Jacques Derrida, the Algerian-French philosopher, and Bassam Tibi, the Syrian-German philosopher. As it happens, these and other interlocutors have all reflected upon and written about the status and significance of Europe—though from different perspectives and with different accents. One of the main issues arising in the following discussion is whether and to what extent it is still possible to assert a distinctive character or identity of Europe and European (or Western) culture. Under the combined impact of universalist aspirations and charges of Eurocentrism, some commentators have counseled a resolute exit from history, a kind of self-abnegation in favor either of global unity or radical strangeness. Cautioning against premature self-denials, other commentators have pleaded for a renewed European self-awareness, though one seasoned by moderation and openness to diversity. The central effort of the following pages is to steer a course between conceit and surrender, between historical arrogance and amnesia—a course faithful to the ambivalence of Europe.

Escape from Eurocentrism

In many parts of the world today, Europe is no longer perceived as the beautiful princess from Phoenicia. As a result of colonialism and imperialism and the devastating horrors of the last century, Europe is now widely denounced as warlike and domineering (reflecting only the worst aspects of Jove's "bullish" conquest). One of the chief indictments hurled against the continent—especially (though not exclusively) by non-Europeans—is the charge of "Eurocentrism," denoting arrogant self-glorification and hegemonic mastery of the world. In explicitly polemical terms, the charge was first articulated by Samir Amin, an Egyptian trained in Paris, who attacked the claimed historical centrality of Europe as a myth and fabrication concealing the peripheral and "tributary" status of the continent during much its history. For Amin, Eurocentrism was basically a "culturalist phenomenon," a doctrine that, though parochial and ethnocentric, parades itself as a universal model whose imitation "by all peoples is the only solution to the problems" they face.[2] In a more philosophical vein, the charge was continued and reformulated by Enrique Dussel, the renowned Latin American philosopher who—as a frequent visitor to Europe (where he received part of his education)—exemplifies the ambivalence of a "border" person. In his *The Invention of the Americas,* Dussel pilloried the barbaric cruelty displayed by the European colonizers in the "New World." As he wrote, the central point of his book was not (or not principally) to explore the "emancipatory" aspirations of Europe, but to expose "the victimizing and destructive myth of a Europeanism based on Eurocentrism and the developmentalist fallacy." Drawing on the testimony of Bartolomé de las Casas, the book depicts the cruel terrors of European conquest:

> Evils accompany war: the clamor of arms, sudden, impetuous, and furious attacks and invasions; ferocity and grave perturbations; scandals, deaths, and carnage; havoc, rape, and dispossession; the loss of parents or children; captivities and the dethronement of kings and natural lords; the devastation and desolation of cities, innumerable villages, and other sites.[3]

More recently, Dussel has further elaborated on the theme, presenting Eurocentrism now as one facet or interpretation of the emerging global or planetary system of modernity. From a strictly Eurocentric perspective, he notes, this emergence is portrayed as an entirely indigenous or "*exclusively* European" process with no indebtedness to external factors, a process that originated in the European Middle Ages and later diffused itself throughout the entire world. According to this paradigm, Europe or European culture carried within itself "exceptional *internal* characteristics" that allowed it to supersede, "through its own rationality, all other cultures." The historical way stations of this process are familiar: modern consciousness or "subjectivity" developed steadily "from the Italy of the Renaissance to the Germany of the Reformation and the Enlightenment, to the France of the French Revolution," and finally to the industrial age. Construed in these terms, modernization appears as a smoothly unfolding historical narrative, and no "break" or rupture is needed, in this scheme, in order to move from Europe's past to the emerging "planetary" sphere. As opposed to this construal, Dussel adopts a more "exogenous" or planetary standpoint, a vantage that reveals modern European ascendancy as the corollary of a hegemonically imposed trajectory, that is, as the result of the "*management* of its centrality." Seen from this angle, Europe—although part and parcel of a larger "world system"—was always bent on constituting itself as center over a growing periphery, as a "superhegemonic power" whose mantle passes "from Spain to Holland, England,

and France" (and finally to North America). A crucial stepping-stone in this development was the European conquest of the New World in early modernity. The basic lesson to be learned here is that Europe's ascendancy was "not the sole fruit of an internal superiority" over other cultures but rather the fundamental effect of "the discovery, conquest, colonization, and integration (subsumption) of Amerindia" that gave Europe the "determining comparative advantage over the Ottoman-Muslim world, India, and China."[4]

In Dussel's view, a proper assessment of Europe's status requires a shift from "inside" to "outside," from an endogenous to a planetary perspective—a shift that dramatically destabilizes or deconstructs Europe's traditional self-interpretation. A similar shift has been mandated by a number of "border" thinkers domiciled in Europe, most importantly by Jacques Derrida. In Derrida's account, Europe has always presented or paraded itself as the "heading" (*le cap*) of the world—where "heading" carries multiple connotations ranging from headmaster to promontory, cape, and capital. "Europe," he writes, "has always recognized itself as a cape or headland, *either* as the advanced extreme of a continent, . . . the point of departure for discovery, invention, and colonization" *or else* as "the very center of this tongue in the form of a cape, the Europe of the middle, coiled up, indeed compressed along a Greco-Germanic axis, at the very center of the center of the cape." As he acknowledges, the notion of a "heading" or "headland" is borrowed from Paul Valéry, who had depicted Europe as a geographical promontory, in fact as an "appendix" to the vast body of the Asian continent. Beyond this geographical meaning, however, there is a deeper spiritual, even metaphysical connotation, in the sense that Europe has traditionally also donned the mantle of a "spiritual heading," signaling at once "a project, task, or infinite (that is to say universal) idea." In doing so, Europe has mingled its self-image with that of a global advancement, with "a heading for world civilization or human culture in general." To this extent, the notion of Europe's "heading" also comprises the idea of Europe's civilizing mission, of its role as commanding ruler or "captain." In dark language resonating with that of Enrique Dussel, Derrida evokes the image of a Europe

> where precisely in the name of identity, be it cultural or not, the worst violences, those that we recognize all too well without yet having thought them through, the crimes of xenophobia, racism, anti-Semitism, religious or nationalist fanaticism, are being unleashed, mixed up with each other, but also—and there is nothing fortuitous in this—mixed in with the breath, with the respiration, with the very "spirit" of the promise.[5]

For Derrida, Europe's traditional self-image today is dated and no longer sustainable. "Old Europe," he writes, "seems to have exhausted all the possibilities of discourse and counter-discourse about its own identification." As a result, its outlook tends to be increasingly backward-looking, nostalgic, and traditionalist, a purely recollective discourse marked by a "refined taste for finality, for the end, if not for death." At this point, the title chosen by Derrida for his reflections— "The Other Heading" (*L'autre cap*)—becomes significant. Literally construed, the title suggests that it is time to depart from the traditional self-image, to change destination or "head" in another direction. Beyond its role as a spatial signpost, however, the title also points to a different conception of identity or selfhood, a different relation between self and other, a different "heading" toward the other—in fact, an acceptance of the "heading *of the other*," an encounter "before which we must respond" and that may be "the first condition of an identity or identification that is not an egocentrism destructive of oneself and the other." What comes into view here is an altogether different image of Europe, a Europe nearly beside or beyond itself. "And what if Europe were this," the text asks: "the opening onto a history for which the changing of the heading, the relation to the other heading or to the other of the heading, is experienced as always possible? An opening and a non-exclusion for which Europe would in someway be responsible?" Leaving aside the pose of a detached analyst, Derrida at this juncture issues an eloquent plea:

> It is necessary to make ourselves the guardians of an idea of Europe, of a difference of Europe, *but* of a Europe that consists precisely in not closing itself off in its own identity and in advancing itself in an exemplary way toward what it is not, toward the other heading or the heading of the other, indeed . . . toward the other of the heading, which would be the beyond of this modern tradition, another border structure, another shore.[6]

Applied to the meaning and status of Europe, these passages clearly resonate with central themes of Derridean philosophy: chiefly the emphasis on the "deconstruction" of fixed conceptions or categories in favor of an opening toward unexpected possibilities or happenings. What deconstruction reveals, above all, is a profound rift or rupture inhabiting phenomena of all kinds: not only the difference of some phenomena from others, but a more radical difference of everything from itself. As "The Other Heading" indicates, the notion of "self-difference"—usually taken as a divergence from others—should also be taken in the sense of a "difference from or with itself," a difference irreducible to pure inwardness or a selfhood "at home with itself." This conception has unsettling consequences for the notion of "culture," including the distinctiveness of European culture. "What is proper to a culture," Derrida writes, "is not to be identical to itself"—which does not mean a complete lack of characteristics, but an inability fully "to identify itself, to be able to say 'me' or 'we'." Culture, from this angle, can exist and be thought of "only in the non-identity to itself or, if you prefer, only in the difference from or with itself." More sharply phrased: "There is no self-relation, no relation to oneself . . . without culture, but a culture of oneself *as* a culture *of* the other." With specific reference to Europe, this self-difference of culture—its otherness from itself—entails that Europe must forever abandon its pretense to be the advanced "heading" or promontory of the world. It must renounce the lure of being "the capital of a centralizing authority," an authority that, by means of "trans-European" (neo-colonial) mechanisms, would try to "control and standardize" the rest of the globe. Relinquishing this pretense implies a move or exodus beyond and "perhaps outside" traditional Europe—not in order to look for something empirically "outside Europe," but in order to keep open in advance "a border to the future, to the to-come (*à-venir*) of the event, to that which comes (*vient*)—which comes perhaps and perhaps comes from a completely other shore."[7]

To be sure, the move beyond or outside traditional Europe can occur in different forms and along very different trajectories. One such trajectory—not favored by Derrida—jettisons Europe and cultural distinctness per se in favor of universalism or universal sameness. As he notes, exodus sometimes justifies itself "in the name of a privilege in responsibility" and "in the memory of the universal"—in fact, in the name of post- or trans-national and even "transcendental or ontological" ideas. The problem with this move is that it remains still a "heading," though now a "heading for the universal essence of humanity." In the confines of Continental Europe, France has often presented itself as such an international avant-garde, as the symbol of a democratic culture "responsible for the universe," a culture founded on the "idea of human rights" and the "idea of international law." The same trajectory can (and has) also been followed by other societies aspiring to universal significance. What happens in these cases is that a particular context is erected into a universal standard—on the pretext of leaving all particularity behind. Sometimes, the trajectory is also emulated by high-minded philosophical discourses or approaches, especially approaches indebted to a certain kind of Enlightenment legacy. As Derrida writes—with a glance across the Rhine at German neo-Kantianism and the Frankfurt School: "Under the pretext of pleading for transparency, . . . for the univocity of democratic discussion, for 'communicative action' in public space, such a discourse tends to impose a [universal] model of language supposedly favorable to such communication." Without mentioning names, the passage clearly aims at Jürgen Habermas's language philosophy, especially at his theory of "communicative action" grounded in a model of "universal pragmatics" far removed from distinct vernacular (or cultural) practices. To some extent, the passage might also gain support from some of Habermas's more recent political-philosophical reflections, especially his comments on the emerging "post-national" constellation of global politics.[8]

A Distinct European Culture?

With regard to European culture, Habermas's position is ambivalent. As Derrida charges (with a good measure of plausibility), his work has always presented itself as "universalist" in structure and spirit, as being oriented toward univocal-universal principles superseding or leaving behind the dense multiplicity and multivocity of cultural idioms. At the same time, however, and perhaps in the same gesture, his writings have also championed as preeminent the values of Western modernity, values deeply rooted in European culture or the distinctness of European history. To this extent, his work has indeed portrayed Europe (or the West) as the promontory or "heading" of humankind, as the vanguard or avant-garde that—far from being ready to retreat—cannot help but advance itself steadily forward. As he observed in a well-known essay titled "Modernity: An Unfinished Project," contemporary European (or Western) intellectual life is marked by a deep divide or dilemma, provoked by the question of historical direction or "heading": "should we continue to hold fast to the intentions of the Enlightenment, however fractured they may be, or should we rather relinquish the entire project of modernity?" For Habermas, the latter option implied the abandonment of the entire process of "rationalization" characterizing Western modernity, a process manifest especially in the growing autonomy and refinement of the three "value spheres" of science, morality, and art. Although admitting certain limitations and perhaps one-sided construals of the modern project, his essay resolutely defended the first alternative: the continued pursuit of the European *telos* or finality: "In my view, instead of forsaking modernity and its project, we should rather learn from the aberrations that have accompanied this project and from the mistakes of rashly proposed remedies."[9]

In Habermas's account, the chief opponents or critics of the modern project were various groups of conservatives—labeled "young conservatives," "old conservatives," and "neo-conservatives" respectively—whose programs (despite differences in detail) constituted basically an "Enlightenment rearguard" in contrast to the modernizing vanguard.[10] Today, we probably need to modify and augment this account by adding a number of even more virulent dissenters from the project: ranging from neo-fascists to radical reactionaries and religious fundamentalists. Faced with challenges and attacks of this kind, exodus or self-denial may not be a sufficient response. Pressured by adversaries from within and without, Europeans as well as friends of Europe may wish to adopt a more affirmative stance—a posture that, without perhaps "essentializing" distinctness, is mindful of the many merits and accomplishments accumulated on the European "cape" or promontory. And would one really wish to "deconstruct" these accomplishments in a summary fashion? After all: besides its colonizing and predatory "aberrations," does Europe or European civilization not have to its credit a remarkable array of cultural and political achievements—achievements ranging from sublime artworks to the constitutional taming of autocracy and the broad spectrum of civil liberties and human rights, including freedom of religion and civic equality? Can one really deny the forward-pointing or avant-garde character of these advances? None of these accomplishments, one needs to recall, were simply gifts of nature or fruits of innate dispositions, but hard-won acquisitions arising out of prolonged historical struggles (from religious wars to later revolutionary upheavals). In light of these struggles, is it proper to cultivate a pose of cultural-historical amnesia—as a remedy or antidote for Eurocentric arrogance?

Rejection of cultural amnesia may be a prerogative of European traditionalists, but not necessarily so. The same attitude may be shared by "new" Europeans—for example, immigrants now residing on the Continent—who may have been attracted to Europe precisely by some its historical-political accomplishments. A case in point is Bassam Tibi, who, born in Syria, immigrated to Germany (in 1962), was educated in Frankfurt (under the guidance of Max Horkheimer and Habermas), and now teaches at the University of Göttingen. Apart from numerous other writings, Tibi is the author of a book that occasioned considerable discussion and controversy after its first publication in 1998; its title (in translation): *Europe Without Identity? The Crisis of Multicultural Society*. In this book, Tibi positioned himself both for and against Europe: *against* a Europe wallowing in self-denial or self-abnegation (that is, a Europe without distinct identity); and *for* a Europe reaffirming its Enlightenment heritage (that is, a Europe seen as "cape" of a universal modern project). In his presentation, Europe and the West during recent decades have been gripped by a vogue of self-denial and virtual self-effacement—a vogue that (in Tibi's view) can be traced in large measure to postmodernism and an insipid kind of multiculturalism that refuses to take a normative stand on cultural and political issues. Under the influence of some postmodern voices, Europeans have been lured into an exodus from their native habitat, in the direction of a non-Western world presented as "radical otherness." As he points out, however, this radical otherness—on closer inspection—has often disclosed itself as just a mode of bigotry, ignorance, or fundamentalism. Countering this exodus, he states: "I resolutely reject the acceptance of premodern cultural conceptions in the name of tolerance; at the same time, I insist on the identity of Europe as the continent of modern Enlightenment—even if the latter remains, in Habermas's words, an 'unfinished project'."[11]

In defending a mode of European identity, Tibi is far removed from vindicating traditional Eurocentrism, that is, the self-image of Europe as lord and master of the globe. As he emphasizes in the preface to his book, his argument challenges two complementary extremes, those of "Euro-arrogance" and "Euro-denial": the first extreme is "Europe seen as domineering colonial master or as intolerant Christian missionary of the past"; the second is "the contemporary self-abnegation and slavish submission of Europe to foreign cultures." In opposing the first alternative (traditional Eurocentrism), Tibi embraces the project of a de-mythologization or "de-Romanticization" of Europe or the West, to the extent that the latter postures as an "ethnic-exclusivist" culture offering no room to non-Europeans. In this pose as the "omphalos" of the world, Europe has tended to give aid and comfort to strategies of the "Europeanization" or Westernization of the world—strategies exhibiting a combination of "arrogance and ignorance" in relation to non-Western civilizations. Debunking of this posture, however, does not in any way warrant an endorsement of the second extreme. The title of the book's first part succinctly pinpoints Tibi's preferred outlook: "Farewell to the old Europe, but without self-denial!" In his eloquent words, reflecting a strong commitment: "I refuse to link the project of de-Romanticising Europe—which I endorse—with the surrender of that continent's self-identity." Among many intellectuals (sometimes self-defined as postmodernists), endorsement of the former project sometimes leads to a new mythology or a counter-Romanticism: namely, the idealization of foreign cultures coupled with the "demonization" of Europe. Despite European excesses in the past, this reversal needs to be resisted: "European civilization has not only sanctioned criminal acts, but has also produced achievements from which humankind as a whole can benefit."[12]

As an alternative to both arrogance and self-denial, Tibi's book champions a reaffirmation of central values of European or Western civilization—what he terms a "guiding culture" (*Leitkultur*) capable of serving as a model or standard for contemporary European societies. Faithful to the teachings of his Frankfurt mentors, this model basically reflects the spirit of the Enlightenment and cultural modernity: "secular democracy, human rights, primacy of reason over any religion, separation of religion and politics, and tolerance" within the confines of "clearly specified rules of the game." For Tibi, such a guiding standard is necessary as an antidote both to antimodern fundamentalism and to the leveling relativism of most multiculturalists. On a still more basic level, such a standard is required to insure the peaceful coexistence of people from different cultural backgrounds residing together in Europe today. As he writes, in language reminiscent of Habermas (and John Rawls), such coexistence "demands the rational management of differences and the existence of a consensus regarding a shared catalogue of norms and values." Within the confines of European societies, rational control of differences is provided (or should be provided) by the consensual "guiding culture" shaped by European cultural modernity—a model that, in extra-European relations, needs to be supplemented by an "international transcultural morality." At this point, a distinction between "inside" and "outside" values, between European and international standards comes into view—although the difference is not further developed in detail. What seems clear is that the "guiding culture" affirmed in the text is strongly shaped by the European Enlightenment, more particularly by a certain (liberal) version of Enlightenment placing the accent on secularism and individual autonomy. Here is how a key passage reformulates this culture:

> Primacy of reason over religious revelation, that is, over the belief in absolute religious truths; *individual* human rights (and thus *not* group rights); secular democracy based on the separation of religion and politics; a *generally accepted* pluralism coupled with a reciprocal secular tolerance. The prevalence of these values alone defines a civil society.[13]

While appreciating the importance of the preceding values or norms, one may yet note a certain narrowness in Tibi's conception of cultural modernity, that is, the tendency to privilege exclusively one model over other, competing interpretations of Western modernity. For instance, one may think of versions of this modernity in which the distinction between reason and faith, between politics and religion, is construed in less rigid, mutually exclusive ways, and also versions that more generously extend the notion of human rights (in some instances) to groups or collectivities. Concrete examples or approximations of these versions can be found in the history of England, Germany, and even North America (though perhaps not France).[14] To be sure, Tibi's formulation of modernity has a distinct, and by no means negligeable political aim: that of shielding Europe against the inroad of ethnic nationalism and religious (especially Islamic) fanaticism. However, by drawing the boundaries of his model somewhat tightly, he risks jeopardizing another valuable objective of his book: that of promoting genuine cultural dialogue both within Europe (between Europeans and immigrants) and between Europe and the rest of the world. The latter goal is a prominent, perhaps even the dominant, theme of his text. As he affirms, partly in response to the "clash of civilizations" formula: "By contrast to a continuation of the tradition of mutual hostilities, cross-cultural dialogue can serve as a dialogue of peace by helping to inaugurate a new era of the resolution of conflicts." To be sure, such dialogue cannot always proceed smoothly or harmoniously and may (or is likely to) involve "agonal" contestations. Still, to proceed as a dialogue (and not merely its semblance), participants need to show at least an initial openness or sensitivity for opposing views (which they may not end up sharing). Viewed against this background, Tibi's repeated and summary dismissal of multiculturalism—denounced as "multi-culti-ideology"—may not be entirely helpful to his purposes.[15]

The dismissal is also confusing in light of Tibi's endorsement of "cultural pluralism," predicated on the acknowledged coexistence of diverse cultural orientations in modern society. In his own words: Europe—without self-effacement—can and should "make room for cultural diversity, for an actual and concrete cultural pluralism." The dismissal is further puzzling given Tibi's favorable comments on Johann Gottfried Herder—whose outlook was hardly entirely congruent with his liberal-individualistic construal of cultural modernity.[16] The mention of Herder brings to mind another prominent interpreter of modern European or Western culture: Charles Taylor—who, as an Oxford-trained Canadian, eminently qualifies as a thinker "inside/outside" Europe. In several of his writings, Taylor has highlighted the importance of Herder for the development of the modern European conception of "identity" or selfhood, a conception carrying the dual connotations of individual autonomy and cultural distinctiveness. "I should note here," he states at one point, "that Herder applied his conception of 'originality' at two levels, not only to the individual person among other persons, but also to the culture-bearing people among other peoples." A decisive aspect here is the interconnection of levels, the fact that individual humans develop and learn about their identity in interaction with members of a language community or several language communities. As Taylor formulates this insight (dear to Herder and later hermeneutics): "The crucial feature of human life is its fundamentally *dialogical* character. We became full human agents, capable of understanding ourselves, and hence of defining our identity, through our acquisition of rich human languages of expression"— where the latter include, in addition to spoken and written language, also "the 'languages' of art, of gesture, of love, and the like."[17]

The insight has a bearing on Europe's cultural modernity and self-image. Under the influence of Herder, Hegel, and many other thinkers, modern Europe has generated a broad and highly nuanced panoply of self-images or self-interpretations—much broader than a narrow focus on liberal Enlightenment ideas might suggest. To be sure, as a respectful reader of Kant and Diderot, Herder never abandoned the modern liberal postulate of individual autonomy and civic equality; however, he proceeded to supplement and modify it through attention to deeper layers of human loyalty and affectivity. Drawing on this panoply of legacies, Taylor distinguishes between two main strands in Europe's cultural and political modernity (strands that perhaps could be multiplied): the competing perspectives of a "politics of equal dignity" and a "politics of difference." In the first perspective, modern Europe privileges a "politics of universalism" emphasizing the "equal dignity of citizens," a dignity anchored in the equal enjoyment of individual rights and entitlements. In the second perspective, political identity is construed not as identical sameness but rather as distinct uniqueness; hence, the politics of difference stresses the need to recognize "the unique identity of this individual or group, their distinctness from everyone else." In terms of public policy, the two perspectives favor competing priorities or standards: "difference-blindness" versus differential treatment. In Taylor's words: Where the politics of equal autonomy has tended to fight for "forms of nondiscrimination that were quite 'blind' to the ways in which citizens differ," the politics of difference often "redefines nondiscrimination as requiring that we make these distinctions the basis" of public policy.[18] What emerges from this account (and other accounts of a similar nature) is a modern Europe that is inherently tensional, responding to the competing demands of universality and particularity. Far from being reducible to a compact (or essential) formula, Europe is itself an emblem of openness and ongoing contestation or negotiation.

An Inside/Outside View

At this juncture, it seems proper to pause and reflect on the terrain traversed so far. In a way, after various detours, the preceding arguments have returned the discussion to the opening comments on the ambivalence of Europe. As the reader may have noticed, the preceding presentation has followed a distinct European, more specifically a Hegelian, trajectory: to an extent, the pathways of self-assertion and denial, of self-identity and cultural amnesia replicate the Hegelian categories of affirmation and negation—with no synthesis readily in sight. The trajectory may be pursued a little further. In her preface to Taylor's reflections on multiculturalism, Amy Gutmann comments thoughtfully on two different, but actually complementary modes of cross-cultural derailment: those of cultural "essentialism" and of self-erasure. A major obstacle to cultural understanding, she writes, is the belief "held in reserve by some essentialists" that they (or their cultural traditions) hold "the key to timeless moral and political truths, the truths of human nature." Judged from the height of this belief, other cultural traditions are negligeable or at best "tribal" particularities. Radically opposed to his outlook, "deconstructive" anti-essentialists erect another barrier by denying the role of cultural standards and traditions, insisting that such standards are nothing but "masks for the will to political power of dominant, hegemonic groups." For Gutmann (as for Tibi), the first view is an invitation to cultural arrogance, the second to debilitating indifference; in neither case is there a need for cross-cultural dialogue or recognition, because all issues are either settled beforehand or else elude settlement altogether. In her words:

> Whereas essentialists react to reasonable uncertainty and disagreement by invoking rather than defending timeless truths, deconstructionists react by explaining away our different viewpoints, presuming they are equally indefensible on intellectual grounds. . . . In an equal and opposite reaction, essentialists and deconstructionists express mutual disdain rather than respect for their differences.[19]

While insightful, Gutmann's comments on "deconstructionism" (like Tibi's on multiculturalism) are a bit summary and hence in need of qualification. Clearly not all deconstructionists are in favor of cultural self-erasure or the replacement of culture by power; a case in point is Derrida (whose name is most closely associated with the label). His text "The Other Heading" repeatedly strikes a note of ambivalence, pointing beyond self-identity and denial. Thus, he speaks at one point of "all the exhausted programs of Eurocentrism and anti-Eurocentrism," indicating that "we today" no longer find comfort in either of these options. At another point, the stress on innovation and cultural exodus is sharply tempered by the need for cultural memory. "Our old memory," he writes soberly, "tells us that it is *also* necessary to anticipate and to guard the heading, for under the banner . . . of the unanticipatable or absolutely new, we can fear a return of the phantom of the worst." What the present situation thus imposes on Europeans is a double responsibility, or what Derrida also calls a "double bind": namely, the dual demand to be "suspicious of *both* repetitive memory *and* the completely other of the absolutely new; of both recollective capitalization *and* the amnesiac exposure to what would no longer be identifiable at all." This double demand obliges Europeans (and their friends) to be mindful both of the accomplishments of Europe—especially the modern achievements of equal liberty, rule of law, and human rights—and the temptation of cultural self-enclosure or exclusiveness. The text speaks in this context of two tensional and even "contradictory imperatives" whose simultaneous satisfaction requires careful and vigilant negotiations: "the *duty* to respond to the call of European memory, to recall what has been promised under the name of Europe, to re-identify Europe"; but also "the *duty* of opening Europe, from the heading that is divided because it is also a shoreline: opening it onto that which is not, never was, and never will be Europe."[20]

A similar ambivalence one can also find in Dussel's writings—although his grievances regarding European arrogance and colonial subjugation are perhaps more severe. In his *The Invention of the Americas,* he acknowledges a dual obligation or a double bind: the obligation to critique an aggressive, predatory, and self-identical Europe; but, at the same time, the need to honor an "other" Europe, a Europe harboring different legacies and different future possibilities. Addressing the issue of inter-cultural dialogue, the conclusion of his study positions the possibility of such dialogue between two perils (which largely coincide with Euro-arrogance and Euro-denial). Dialogical interaction, he writes, must avoid "the facile optimism of rationalist, abstract universalism that would conflate universality with Eurocentrism and modernizing developmentalism (as the Frankfurt School is inclined to do)," without at the same time lapsing into "the irrationality, incommunicability, or incommensurability of discourses that are typical of many postmoderns." Shunning both rationalist arrogance—glorifying Europe as the universal "cape"—and radical nonidentity, a cross-cultural approach (looking at Europe from the margins) can yet rescue the "emancipative tendencies" of European modernity under the auspices of a "new transmodernity." In an appendix, Dussel further clarifies this approach by juxtaposing two "paradigms of modernity" that are also two paradigms of modern Europe. On one side, there is the "idea" of Europe that promises "rational emancipation" by opening up new possibilities for human flourishing. On the other side, there is the predatory and self-advancing Europe that treats all non-European peoples as inferior, primitive, or barbaric, often subjugating them by violent means. To salvage at least a glimmer of the former Europe, one must denounce its "mythical" supremacy. In Dussel's word:

> I propose a transmodern opposition to modernity's irrational violence, an opposition based on the *reason of the Other*. I hope to go beyond modernity by discovering as innocent the so often denied and victimized other face of modernity. . . . By denying the civilizing *myth* and the innocence of its concomitant violence, one recognizes the injustice of Europe's sacrificial practice within and outside itself. At the same time, one overcomes the limitations of emancipative [European] reason via a *liberating reason* purified of the Eurocentrism and developmentalist fallacy inhabiting hegemonic modernization.[21]

Ambivalence is also not alien to Tibi's account, despite his accent on European identity or a European "guiding culture." As he repeatedly emphasizes, his point is not to champion the rigid integration or assimilation of immigrants—especially immigrants from Muslim countries—into a compact or preordained European culture. As a Muslim *and* German citizen, Tibi insists on his right to be different or "other" (*Anderssein*) and expects to be recognized as such. Although strongly opposing the lure of ethnic or religious "ghettoization," he also favors the (non-exclusivist) cultivation of cultural values and traditions, through educational and other means. In the same direction point his comments on cultural pluralism (mentioned above) and his preference for inter-cultural dialogue (which he shares with Dussel, Taylor, and others): "If Germans [and other Europeans] really desire to live in peace with people from other cultures and civilizations, they need to search dialogically for some agreement on shared values."[22] As hinted at before, the only question one may wish to raise at this point concerns a certain narrowness of the proposed values, deriving from a restricted interpretation of Europe's modern Enlightenment legacy. While not abandoning the notion of cultural guideposts, one might perhaps adopt a more generous construal of Europe's heritage, a construal that—while resisting the "blackmail of the Enlightenment" (as Michel Foucault called it)—honors the modern Enlightenment as a part or facet of a complex historical narrative recalcitrant to univocal summary. Approached from this angle, Europe presents a diversified and ambivalent self-image (though shunning an "anything goes" relativism). As Taylor has shown in his masterful study *Sources of the Self,* modern European identity or selfhood is an outgrowth of multiple sources and strands, reaching from antiquity and the Christian Middle Ages through Renaissance and Reformation to more recent forms of "authenticity" and everydayness—with reason and faith, religion and politics embroiled in protracted negotiations. What holds these strands together is not a simple formula but an ongoing struggle for "recognition" and the meaning of a shared life, on the other side of self-enclosure and self-abandonment.[23]

To this extent, Taylor's study concurs with the outlook of Hans-Georg Gadamer, renowned both as a quintessential "European" philosopher and as one of the most prominent defenders of hermeneutical dialogue. In his numerous writings, Gadamer has continuously commemorated and re-interpreted the long history of European thought, from Plato and Aristotle to the Christian Middle Ages and the Reformation to Hegel, Schleiermacher, and Heidegger (and beyond). While paying close attention to the dense fabric of this tradition, and thus unwilling to abandon or erase it, he has also persistently emphasized the reflective and self-critical character of European thought, that is, its openness and (potential) self-transcendence toward multiple voices, including the voice of the "Other" of Europe. As he writes in his book titled *The Legacy of Europe (Das Erbe Europas)*: "To live with the Other, to live as the Other of the Other—this basic human task applies in the smallest as well as in larger contexts. Just as we, in our youth, learn to live with the Other while we are growing up and entering adult life, so also larger human groups, such as peoples and nations, undergo a similar learning experience." With particular reference to Europe, Gadamer considers it a special advantage of that continent that it always "needed to learn how to live with others, even if these others were very different." In the end, his book presents this difficult learning experience as an example from which the rest of humankind might benefit and perhaps derive lessons in our turbulent time:

So it may not be too bold to draw a final political consequence from our discussion, namely: that we may perhaps survive as humankind if—instead of simply exploiting our arsenals of power and control—we would stop and respect the Other as other, where the latter embraces nature as well as the grown cultures of peoples and nations; and if we thus could learn to experience otherness and the others as the "other" of ourselves in order to partake in one another.[24]

CHAPTER 4

GLOBALIZATION AND INEQUALITY

A Plea for Cosmopolitan Justice

Opus justitiae pax

—*Isaiah 32:17*

With 2001 having been officially designated (by the United Nations) as the year of "Dialogue among Civilizations," it appears urgent to reflect on the meaning and requisites of dialogue, especially a dialogue carried on in a global context. Dialogue here does not just mean a random exchange of information or commodities—which may leave participants neutral or disengaged. If civilization is a frame of significance allowing members to articulate their self-understanding, then civilizational dialogue must be properly "civilized" by considering participants in their intrinsic worth. Consideration of worth, however, involves a measure of equality—not perhaps a quantitative or numerical equality but a kind of qualitative equality that might be described as one of respect or of care (which is not incompatible with respect for differences). As might be expected, this invocation of equality is likely to be challenged from numerous quarters. Self-styled political "realists" are prone to denounce the invocation—and the entire idea of a dialogue among equal partners (or civilizations)—as an empty chimera or pipedream disconfirmed by the stark "reality" of power differentials both in domestic and in international politics. Curiously, this denunciation is sometimes seconded by left-leaning (especially postmodern) intellectuals who talk at length about radical asymmetry or a stark incommensurability of language games and cultures.[1]

Consciously or not, appeals to equality pay tribute to older civilizational legacies that, in turn, are inspired mainly by religious and political-philosophical teachings. In the context of the so-called Abrahamic religions, a prominent and even central theological doctrine is that of the equality of all humans in the eyes of the one transcendent God, that is, their equal status as children of the same deity. A similar conception can be found outside the Abrahamic sphere—for example in the case of Buddhism, in which all living beings are said to share in the same "Buddha-nature" (and thus to be equal in terms of "emptiness" or *sunyata*). A problem with this religious tradition is that equality often tends to be spiritualized or transcendentalized, sometimes to such an extent as to leave even egregiously oppressive inequalities in society unaffected or undisturbed.[2] This deficiency is remedied in good measure by the tradition of political philosophy, with its emphasis on a "public sphere" equally accessible to all participants. At least since the time of Aristotle, it has been a maxim of (at least Western) political thought that citizenship requires a common denominator: namely, the denominator of equal status and respect accorded to all citizens in public matters (including elections, eligibility for public office, and judicial proceedings). While circumscribed severely in ancient times during the period of the *polis,* this maxim has been embraced and steadily deepened and expanded by modern democratic theory, especially the theory of constitutional democracy with its stress on a common "rule of law" binding together all members of society in their capacity as citizens.[3]

In our age of rapid globalization, traditional religious and political-philosophical teachings face the test of entirely new and formidable challenges: the challenges posed by the emerging cosmopolis or global community. How can a measure of equality be preserved in that community given the immense diversity of cultural traditions, political practices, and levels of social-economic "development"? Or to put matters differently: how is it possible to resist or counteract oppressive inequalities in the global arena—without promoting a bland homogeneity? In the following, the accent will be placed mainly on the problem of prevailing global inequalities—but in such a way as not to lose sight of the need for diversity and human autonomy. In order to sharpen the notion of inequalities, the presentation adopts a differentiation introduced by Chandra Muzaffer to highlight the collusion and mutually reinforcing effect of numerous disparities: what he calls the "trinity of power, wealth, and knowledge."[4] Accordingly, I shall deal in sequence with the domains of political power, economic (mal-) distribution, and knowledge expertise (enlarging the latter notion to include the field of cultural self-understanding). In each of these domains, the presentation follows a prominent mentor (or set of mentors): in the first domain the political scientist Samuel Huntington; in the second the economist Amartya Sen; and in the last the philosophers Martin Heidegger and Hans-Georg Gadamer. By way of conclusion, the chapter issues a plea for cosmopolitan or global democratic justice, as a counterpoise to prevailing modes of global inequality and inequity.

Political Hegemony:
The West versus the Rest

A central form of inequality — and a perennial source of social conflicts — derives from disparities of political power. Given its prominent and undeniable role in politics of all kinds, power has always been a favorite (perhaps *the* favorite) topic of students of politics, and especially of professional political scientists and policy analysts. Among contemporary policy analysts in America one of the most distinguished is Samuel Huntington, who served for a long time as Director of the Institute for Strategic Studies at Harvard University. What makes Huntington's work particularly noteworthy in the present context is the fact that he has extended the analysis of power from domestic politics to the global or international arena, with a focus on developments since the end of the Cold War. Not long ago (in 1993), he achieved a kind of global notoriety through the publication of an essay in *Foreign Affairs* titled "The Clash of Civilizations?" Leaving aside the correctness or incorrectness of his civilizational predictions, the essay deserves to be remembered for its forthright and provocative description of power differentials operating in the international arena. Here is a remarkable passage taken from a section titled "The West versus the Rest":

> The West is now at an extraordinary peak of power in relation to other civilizations. Its superpower opponent has disappeared from the map. . . . It dominates international political and security institutions and with Japan international economic institutions. Global political and security issues are effectively settled by a directorate of the United States, Britain and France, world economic issues by a directorate of the United States, Germany and Japan, all of which maintain extraordinarily close relations with each other to the exclusion of lesser and largely non-Western countries. Decisions made at the U.N. Security Council or in the International Monetary Fund that reflect the interests of the West are presented to the world as reflecting the desires of the world community. The very phrase "the world community" has become the

euphemistic collective noun (replacing "the Free World") to give global legitimacy to actions reflecting the interests of the United States and other Western powers.[5]

The passage is memorable for a number of reasons—not the least being its revealing candor. For present purposes, it should suffice to lift up two additional aspects of Huntington's essay. One is the claim of a certain degree of objectivity, or the disclaimer of any particularly partisan or subversive intent. As he adds, in a statement both qualifying and reasserting the cited passage: "This at least is the way in which non-Westerners see the new world, and there is a significant element of truth in their view. Differences in power and struggles for military, economic and institutional power *are* thus one source of conflict between the West and other civilizations" (italics mine). The other aspect has to do with the somewhat misleading or "euphemistic" status of existing international institutions. As Huntington observes, without circumlocution: "Western domination of the U.N. Security Council and its decisions, tempered only by occasional abstention by China, produced U.N. legitimation of the West's use of force to drive Iraq out of Kuwait and its elimination of Iraq's sophisticated weapons and capacity to produce such weapons." Apart from the example of Iraq, the camouflaged role of international institutions has had particularly blatant repercussions on Islamic civilization as a whole. "After defeating the largest Arab army," he continues, "the West did not hesitate to throw its weight around in the Arab world." In effect, the West is "using international institutions, military power and economic resources to run the world in ways that will maintain Western predominance, protect Western interests and promote Western political and economic values."[6]

A few years after publication of the essay, Huntington reformulated his argument in a book—which also obtained a wide audience—titled *The Clash of Civilizations and the Remaking of World Order* (1996). In that book, Huntington toned down somewhat the emphasis on an inevitable "clash" of civilizations, in favor of the possibility of (limited) cross-cultural interactions animated by what he called "commonalities of civilization" and the potentials of "global multiculturality." At the same time, the book shifted the accent from a near-absolute supremacy of Western power in the post–Cold War world to the conception of a more limited (and possibly declining) Western preeminence or hegemony in global politics. In Huntington's words: "The West is and will remain for years to come the most powerful civilization. Yet its power relative to that of other civilizations is declining." In large measure, the decline has to do with a beginning resurgence of non-Western cultures, that is, of the "rest" vis-à-vis the West. Faced with the predominance of Western power, other societies—in Huntington's view—face a choice: some may attempt "to emulate the West" or to "band-wagon with the West"; others may try to "expand their own economic and military power" in order to resist the West. Hence, a "central axis of post–Cold War world politics" is bound to be the "interaction of Western power and culture with the power and culture of non-Western civilizations."[7]

As one should note, despite important changes of emphasis, the book did not modify or abandon Huntington's basic approach: namely, the equation of contemporary international politics with civilizational power politics. As he wrote, in a chapter devoted to the dawning "New Era in World Politics": "The central distinction is between the West as the hitherto dominant civilization and all the others which, however, have little if anything in common among them"—that is, between the West and the "rest." Although nation-states are and will remain "important actors" in world affairs, their interests, associations, and conflicts are "increasingly shaped by cultural and civilizational factors." This means that, despite the persistence of tribal and national rivalries, the conflicts that "pose the greatest dangers for stability" in the world today are those "between states or groups from different civilizations." Most important, and in line with these comments, the outstanding and most distinctive feature of Huntington's book continued to be the correlation of civilizations or cultures with power politics. In his own poignant words: "The distribution of cultures in the world reflects the distribution of power. Trade may or may not follow the flag, but culture almost always follows power."[8]

Still more recently, Huntington has further honed and refined his approach. In an essay titled "Culture, Power, and Democracy" he draws lessons from recent political developments as well as from some intellectual exchanges. Noting critical objections leveled at his accent on an impending "clash" of civilizations, he acknowledges a certain hyperbole in his earlier expressions and also the mitigating role of cultural interactions. Regarding the present or emerging international scenario, Huntington now prefers to describe it as a "uni-multipolar" system or structure—though a structure that shows signs of evolving perhaps into a multipolar arrangement at some future date. In his definition, a uni-multipolar world or system is one "in which resolution of key international issues requires action by the single superpower plus some combination of other major states and in which the single superpower is able to veto action by combinations of other states." As a global power structure, our contemporary world can be visualized as a stratified hierarchy or layered pyramid, a pyramid composed mainly of the following four layers or levels: first, and at the top, the United States as "the only superpower with unchallenged preeminence in every domain of power" and "with truly global interests extending to virtually every part of the world"; second, or at the second rung, major regional powers who are "dominant actors in important areas of the world" but with more limited interests and capabilities than the United States; third, secondary regional powers subordinated to, but often also competing with, the major regional actors; and finally, all the remaining countries that exist "in some sense apart from the power structure" and hence are basically powerless.[9]

As before, however, shifts in emphasis and formulation do not disturb the underlying assumptions of Huntington's approach. Unsurprisingly, although mitigating some of its harsher features, the essay leaves intact the basic civilizational conception of international politics. As he observes, one of the central aspects differentiating the post–Cold War scenario from the Cold War system is that now alignments and conflicts among nations are "primarily shaped by culture [or civilization], not by ideology." Recent developments in almost all parts of the world, in his view, have tended to confirm "the validity and usefulness of this cultural-civilizational approach." As in previous accounts, civilizational politics still retains all the earmarks of traditional power politics. To this extent, Huntington remains an international "realist" (though not in the sense of the older nation-state "realism"). Here is a pithy statement that articulates the core belief of political realism—and perhaps the key motto of professional political science as a whole: "While culture has particular salience for post–Cold War global politics, power is the universal and everlasting essence of all politics, and now, as in the past, power considerations shape the policies of states and relations among them."[10]

Although widely shared by his colleagues, Huntington's comments clearly invite critique. That power is the "everlasting essence" of politics is bound to be strange and disturbing news to readers familiar with the history of political philosophy—and even more disturbing news to people committed to democracy and democratic accountability. As previously indicated, Western political thought since Aristotle has emphasized the need for a certain equality—we may call it civic equality—among members of a political community. More important, following Aristotle, political philosophy has distinguished political regimes or forms of government not only in terms of their power, but in terms of their justice and legitimacy; differently phrased: political writers have drawn a demarcation between just or legitimate and unjust or illegitimate types of rule—the basic criterion being whether political rule is exercised for selfish ends of the rulers (their lust for power) or for the benefit and well-being of the population at large. In the case of democracy, this distinction means that, in order to be legitimate, democratic rule has to be responsible and continuously accountable to the "governed." Considerations of this kind have important repercussions for contemporary international politics or the global "world order." In an age of democratization, when global politics is increasingly infiltrated by democratic demands, this global "order" cannot permanently shield itself from the standard of justice and democratic legitimacy—an issue to which I shall return at the end of this chapter. As this happens, however, the pyramidal structure itself gives way not simply to multipolar power politics but to a global community honoring a degree of global civic equality.

Economic Inequality and Capabilities

Political hegemony is not the only problem besetting the global community. As mentioned before, inequality of power is in collusion with, and reinforced by, other types of inequality: above all, disparities of wealth or affluence. Here it may be useful to cite some global statistical figures. According to the Human Development Report issued by the United Nations in 1999, global inequalities in income and living standards have now reached "grotesque proportions." For example, the combined wealth of the world's three richest families (about $135 billion) is greater than the annual income of 600 million people in the economically least-developed countries. In large measure this polarization of income is due to the rapid process of economic globalization which, in the words of the report, is moving in "fast forward," leaving behind considerations of equitable distribution. While thirty years ago, the gap between the richest one-fifth of the world's population and the rest stood at 30-to–1, by 1990 it had widened to 60-to–1 and today stands at 74-to–1. United Nations figures, as presented in the same report, also show that, over a four-year period (1995–1999), the world's 200 richest people doubled their wealth to over $1 trillion, while the number of people living on less than $1 a day has remained steady at 1.3 billion.[11] Findings of this kind are supported by the World Bank (International Bank for Reconstruction and Development) in its World Development Report 2000/01. According to World Bank data, the average income in the richest twenty countries is today thirty-seven times the average in the poorest twenty—a gap that has doubled in the past forty years.[12]

The vast, even "grotesque" disparities arising from gallopping economic globalization have not escaped the attention of (critical) economists and social theorists. Thus, economists such as Andrew Hurrell and Ngaire Woods have analyzed the persistent and steadily deepening strains of "inequality" in the global arena, while others have highlighted the international class division or class structure emerging as a result of "predatory" forms of globalization.[13] One of the most eloquent critical voices has been that of Charles Derber, author of *Corporation Nation* (1998). According to Derber, economic globalization is producing, and has already produced, a new kind of hegemony fusing power and wealth, which he calls "corpocracy" and defines as "a world-wide nexus of financial markets and corporations that now dominates the world." Among the constitutive elements of "corpocracy," financial institutions are particularly prominent and important because the 100 largest banks control $21 trillion in assets (about three-fourths of the world's total wealth). This situation is compounded by the role of speculative and portfolio capital. In Derber's words: "With over $1.5 trillion racing around the planet for maximum profit each day, the financial markets are the ultimate masters of the universe, controlling not only governments but the corporations themselves."[14]

While powerful in their diagnosis of global economic disparities, critical economists often fall short in offering viable remedies. The main reason is the difficulty of reconciling free markets with (a measure of) economic and social equality. A crucial defect of traditional socialism has been its policy of transferring control of the economy from private (capitalist) hands into the hands of the state—a policy that undermined economic freedom and initiative while magnifying the power of a centralized bureaucracy. It is precisely in this respect that contemporary theorizing can benefit from the work of the economist and Nobel Laureate Amartya Sen. A central feature of Sen's voluminous writings has always been his emphasis on the economy as part of civil society (vis-à-vis the state), and more particularly on economic freedom defined not as an abstract individual license but as part of concrete and socially nurtured human "capabilities." With his accent of "capabilities," Sen has been able to infuse economics again with a sense of social responsibility, a responsibility not imposed from the top down but instilled through social interactions—interactions that also imply or require a certain form of interactive equality. As he wrote in his well-known book *Inequality Reexamined* (1992), a basic question in all social and economic theory is the question "Equality of what?" While the principle of equality advanced as an abstract postulate may have little real significance, the desire for some kind of equality—namely, equality "in some space that is seen to be particularly important"—is far from vacuous or an empty demand. Once this space is specified or delimited, the demand for equality imposes some "ranking of patterns," which, in turn, have mushrooming effects in many parts of social life.[15]

The answer provided by Sen to this crucial question is as far removed from a doctrinaire egalitarianism as it is from an equality-bashing libertarianism or market ideology. This becomes immediately evident in his discussion of poverty in different economic contexts. As he notes, poverty should not just be identified with "low utility" or else with "low income" or a deprivation of primary goods. Viewed from a "capability-based approach," poverty invokes not merely "low well-being," but rather "the inability to pursue well-being" induced in part by the lack of economic means; moreover, the adequacy of such means cannot be judged independently of the possibility a person has to convert incomes and resources into real-life courses of action. This means that, from Sen's perspective, considerations of social equity and a fair distribution of capabilities are not (or should not be placed) in opposition to the commitment to human freedom—as well as a prudent regard for economic efficiency and the role of differential economic incentives. As he writes in the conclusion of his book, the "capability approach" has something to offer both to the evaluation of concrete "well-being" and to the assessment of practical human "freedom." This is due primarily to a basic shift of focus: namely, from the traditional concentration on material means and economic "opulence" (measured in terms of income, consumption levels, and the like) to the domain of practical functionings seen as "*constitutive* elements of human well-being."[16]

A chief merit of Sen's work is the extension of his theorizing to the contemporary global arena—an arena dominated, in large measure, by liberalization and "structural readjustment" policies. In his justly celebrated *Development as Freedom* (1999), he cites with approval T. H. Huxley's statement that, "It is the customary fate of new truths to begin as heresies and to end as superstitions," adding: "Something very much like this seems to have happened about the truth of the importance of markets in economic life." This does not mean, of course, that Sen has abandoned his emphasis on the crucial role of freedom in modern social and political life. On the contrary, as he writes forcefully, his analysis of development in the world "treats the freedoms of individuals as the basic building blocks," giving special attention to "the expansion of the 'capabilities' of persons to lead the kind of lives they value—and have reason to value." Freedom and development, from this angle, are closely connected, in the sense that exercise of freedom leads to higher levels of social-economic achievement or "success," while higher levels of development tend to expand the range of practical freedom (seen as capability). In Sen's words: "Greater freedom enhances the ability of people to help themselves and also to influence the world, and these matters are central to the process of development," especially once the latter is viewed from the "agency aspect" of individuals.[17]

To be sure, in Sen's presentation, the role of market freedoms needs to be carefully calibrated against the perils of infringements of capability by market forces. Like the earlier study, *Development as Freedom* offers a reassessment and redefinition of poverty and other forms of economic hardship (such as unemployment) in terms of the curtailment of human agency. Social and economic policies aimed at remedying these ailments can be justified precisely in terms of human freedom and well-being construed as capability. For Sen, the crucial task of contemporary economics, especially on the global level, is to find a "many-sided" approach that would assess the role of markets and "freedom-inequality problems" simultaneously and even-handedly. Such an approach needs to concentrate both on curbing the "overactivity of the state" in running the economy and on removing its "underactivity" in the field of agency-enhancing social opportunities. The task of public policy, however, extends beyond the realm of remedial interventions (to overcome poverty and the like) to the very constitution of the public realm itself. For, as Sen observes, there are important goods that are "nonmarketable" in the sense that they cannot be sold to, or consumed by, one person at a time. This is the sphere of "public goods" that people "consume *together* rather than separately." While the rationale of the market is geared basically to private ends, a case can be made for the "provisioning of public goods" beyond market transactions—basic education, public health care, and environmental protection belonging to this sphere of goods.[18]

Sen's arguments need to be seen against the backdrop of the statistical figures cited above. Judged in light of these figures, it is evident that the enormous (even grotesque) disparities in wealth and income in the world today are bound to have damaging and disabling repercussions on the development of human capabilities, and hence on the effective exercise of freedom and responsible agency among the vast majority of the world's population. To the extent that the contemporary world is coalescing into a kind of global community or global civil society, the same disparities also stifle or prevent the "provisioning of public goods" such as general educational and ecological programs—goods without which the global society is unable to function or survive for any length of time. Given the obvious significance of Sen's analyses for contemporary economics and politics, it is not surprising that his work is increasingly invoked by social and political theorists (as well as critical economists) concerned with issues of social equity and democratic agency. Thus, David Crocker appeals to Sen-style capability criteria in his effort to articulate a global "developmental ethic" transcending both utilitarian selfishness and state-centered controls of human freedom. In turn, Iris Marion Young advances an ideal of "social justice" defined in terms of human "self-development and self-determination"—notions that are largely derived from, and congruent with, Amartya Sen's concept of equal capabilities (and that I shall invoke again in my conclusion).[19]

Expertocracy and "Europeanization of the Earth"

Power and wealth are only two elements in Chandra Muzaffer's "trinity" of inequality; what compounds and further aggravates their role are the prevailing global asymmetries of knowledge and cultural self-understanding. Asymmetries of knowledge here refer to the vast gap between developed and (so-called) third world countries—or between the West and the rest—in terms of scientific, technological, and industrial expertise. Indicative of this gap is the fact that today roughly four-fifth of the world's total scientific and technological "output" is generated in Western societies, with a concomitant concentration of scientists and technological experts in the same part of the world.[20] Existing knowledge inequalities are sharpened in a number of domains by political or strategic policies, such as the classification and hording of types of knowledge for "security" reasons. As one should note, gaps of knowledge or expertise are a prominent feature not only of the international arena, but also of domestic conditions in many societies (including Western societies)—an issue often thematized under the rubric of technocracy or "expertocracy." Questions of knowledge, however, are related to the role of cognitive and interpretive frameworks—frameworks rooted in a language community that, in turn, sustains and gives room to a certain from of cultural self-understanding. To this extent, modern science and technology are linked with the advances characterizing modern Western civilization or culture, a linkage that, in a global-developmental perspective, fuels charges of neo-colonialism, Eurocentrism, or Western cultural hegemony.

In recent decades, the lure of technocracy has been intensified and rendered more complex and pervasive by a major development of our time: the ongoing "information revolution" with its repercussion in the media, the internet, and other modes of telecommunications. According to the Italian political theorist Danilo Zolo, the political consequences of this revolution have been profound, in the sense that most Western societies are steadily moving in the direction of "post-representative democracies" or techno-oligarchies. Elaborating on the work of Zolo and other media analysts, Wayne Gabardi perceives in the ongoing process of "high-tech globalization" the seeds of an emerging "mediacracy" or "mediocracy," which complements and reinforces the move toward "corpocracy" and "technocracy." As he writes: "It is not an exaggeration to say that the axis of governance today is a media-information complex or 'mediocracy' (rule by means of images)." This complex, he adds, is a function of "high-tech innovations such as fiber optics, digital transmission, cable TV, video-cassettes, satellite dishes, new computer software, and the Internet, combined with neoliberal strategies of deregulation and privatization." Faced with the surplus of symbols, signs, and images produced and manipulated by the media, non-specialists or ordinary lay citizens are increasingly disempowered and thrown into a condition known as "hyperreality" or "virtual reality" with little or no connection with actual public policies. Instead of engaging or participating in public agency, they become image-consumers and pliant tools of "telegenic politicians and pundits" ruling over a "televisual" or phantom democracy.[21]

As in the case of political and economic inequalities, prevailing cultural and knowledge differentials have attracted the critical attention of social theorists and socially concerned philosophers; among the latter, it should suffice here to invoke the names of Martin Heidegger and Hans-Georg Gadamer. One of the persistent preoccupations in Gadamer's work has been the rise of "expertocracy" and its effects on social and political praxis. In his well-known book *Reason in the Age of Science,* Gadamer brings the problem of expert knowledge in close connection with the advances of modern science since the time of the Renaissance and Enlightenment, and the related tendency to devalue both philosophy and political praxis. As he writes there, humankind today seems willing to accept the fact that, with the growing mastery over nature, "the domination of human beings over other human beings is not eliminated but, contrary to all expectations, keeps steadily growing, thus threatening freedom from within [society]." Hence, the advances of modern science and technology—which, in the Enlightenment view, were destined to foster human freedom and emancipation—are uncannily producing a boomeranging effect by tightening social controls and encouraging the kind of social conformism that de Tocqueville had predicted long ago (but had ascribed to different motives). As Gadamer notes, in a nearly Tocquevillian vein, it is a result of technology that, via expertocracy, it promotes "such a manipulation of human society, of the formation of public opinion, of ordinary life-conduct and the partitioning of life between job and family, that it takes our breath away."[22]

Concerns about expertocracy are further fleshed out and intensified in his essay on "What is Praxis?" (contained in the same volume). A major emphasis of that essay is on the need to differentiate clearly between "application (*Anwendung*)" and "praxis"—where the former term refers to the simple implementation of scientific formulas or blueprints, and the second to the public exercise of human freedom. In Gadamer's account, the accent on application is a corollary of the rise of modern science and technology and their methodological aims. By removing themselves from ordinary life-experience, science and technology develop into a knowledge of experts geared toward the prediction and control of events, and hence also toward the construction, application, and manipulation of consequences. "This," he writes, "is what has ultimately brought about the civilizational pattern of modernity in which we live." The scientific ideal of construction and application has made possible "the nature of our machines, our transformation of nature, and our outreach into space." With the extension of application to social life, the model of a technocratic society or expertocracy comes into view, a model in which people have recourse to experts and look to them not only in strictly scientific matters but also in "the discharging of practical, political and economic decisions they have to make." In recent times, the contours of this model have been further sharpened by the "informatic revolution" and the steadily expanding influence of the media on opinion formation. For, as Gadamer observes, dissemination of information involves selection, and selection implies control of opinion by media experts:

> It is inevitable that the modern technology of communication leads to an ever more powerful manipulation of minds, . . . hence, possession of the news media becomes the decisive issue. . . . Seen against this background, the expansion of information does not necessarily mean a strengthening of social or public reason. Instead—and this seems to me the real problem—there is a danger of the loss of [independent] identity among people today . . . through the elevation of purely adaptive qualities to privileged status.[23]

For Gadamer, the greatest peril posed by the rule of experts, especially media experts, is the progressive atrophy of human freedom, particularly the kind of freedom exercised in public in the form of political praxis. In a manner paralleling arguments of Hannah Arendt, one of his central concerns is the revitalization of the "*vita activa*" construed as the enactment of creative freedom in a public realm. Amplifying Arendt's vistas with some Aristotelian teachings, he defines praxis as the exercise of "considered or prudential choice, right deliberation, and right coordination under some common ends"; the latter ends, moreover, involve the ordering of social life and political conduct in terms of "right and wrong," that is, under the yardstick of social and political justice. What is important in the present context is that, for Gadamer, the cultivation of human agency and public justice is an urgent concern not only in European (or Western) societies, but in the contemporary international arena marked by the relentless process of globalization. As he writes poignantly at the end of his essay: "The confined work place [*Werkstatt*] of the earth is ultimately the destiny of us all"—a realization that is slowly pervading political reasoning in many parts of the world. "I believe," he concludes hopefully, "in the rediscovery of solidarities that could animate a future society of humankind."[24]

As it happens, it is precisely in the global arena that inequalities of knowledge today are becoming increasingly pronounced; moreover, expertocracy is compounded by the near-monopoly wielded by Western (or Western-trained) elites—an aspect linking expert knowledge with the broader issue of cultural hegemony or supremacy. It is this broader cultural asymmetry that raises profound problems for cross-cultural encounters, and particularly for a "dialogue among civilizations." In this domain, some of the most incisive formulations have been advanced by Martin Heidegger (Gadamer's teacher). Among Heidegger's more disturbing insights is the claim that global encounters or dialogues today are typically not conducted between equal cultural partners, but rather on the basis of a linguistic and conceptual framework supplied entirely by Western (or European) civilization. In his famous "Dialogue on Language" (with a Japanese), he speaks of the "complete Europeanization of the earth and of humankind," and adds somberly: "The delusion is growing, so that we are no longer able to see how the Europeanization [Westernization] of the earth and humankind erodes every genuine being at the source. It seems that all sources are bound to dry up." In another essay, titled "On the Question of Being" ("Zur Seinsfrage"), Nietzsche is singled out as the philosopher who first clearly perceived the onset of the struggle for global or

planetary domination or supremacy. Given the ongoing Westernization of the globe, Heidegger was keenly aware of the enormous obstacles standing in the way of cultural encounters, and especially of a
dialogue of civilizations. In the same essay, "On the Question of
Being," he ponders soberly the difficulties faced by a genuinely global
thinking. "No prophetic gifts are required," he writes, "to realize that,
on the planetary level, encounters are looming ahead for which none
of the participants today is prepared." This holds true both for the Occident and the Orient, both for "European and East Asian language,"
and especially for the "space of their possible dialogue
[*Zwiesprache*]"—a space "neither side is able to open up unilaterally."[25]

A Plea for Cosmopolitan Justice

Having reviewed the predominant forms of global inequality, I want to
return, at the end, to Chandra Muzaffer's "triad." It is clear—and recognized by most perceptive observers (from Huntington to Gadamer
and Heidegger)—that the prevailing inequalities of power, wealth, and
knowledge coalesce today into a formidable pyramidal structure, that
is, the structure of an unprecedented global hegemony. By way of conclusion, I want to ponder briefly the political effects of this structure,
more particularly its implications for the promotion of justice in the
emerging "global city" or global civic framework. It is in this domain
that the arguments of international experts or global policy analysts
tend to be most deficient. Thus, although writing about the relations
between "culture, power, and democracy" (in the essay cited above),
Huntington fails entirely to reflect on the implications of democracy
and its expansion for global power and (what he calls) "the hegemon
problem." While worrying extensively about the prospects of "democratization" in Latin America, China, and the Muslim world, his discussion bypasses completely the required democratization of the global
structure itself, that is, the need to render global power legitimate and
hence to hold global hegemons democratically accountable.

This deficiency is shared, in large measure, by some of Huntington's
most prominent colleagues. Thus, in an essay on "Democracy's Uncertain
Triumph," Zbigniew Brzezinski draws attention to some "key factors" in
contemporary international politics, chiefly these two: "the primacy of
American global power" and "the global appeal of democracy"—but
without exploring the impact of the latter's appeal on the former primacy. In a still more forthright manner, Robert Kagan—in writing about
"American Democracy at Home and Abroad"—emphasizes the "centrality of the United States" in global politics today. As he states: "Those who

favor a policy that seeks to promote democracy around the world" need to grasp "a few central facts: The present international order was built by American strength and American principles working in tandem; to the degree that either America's power or its commitment to the universality of its principles begins to decline, so will that international order."[26]

The issue here is not the promotion of "democracy around the world" nor the value or validity of American democratic "principles," but rather the relevance of these principles for the global hegemonic structure. By democracy or democratic principles here I do not mean merely formal procedures or legal safeguards but rather the effective chance of people around the world to engage in political participation and will-formation and thus to exert their capabilities. If it is true, as many political thinkers hold, that, to gain legitimacy, public policies require the endorsement (or at least consultation) of all affected, then global policy-making needs to rely on the broadest possible participation on a global scale. The notion of democracy invoked at this point concurs in many ways with the view of Sheldon Wolin, whose writings have persistently sought to reinvigorate popular agency in the face of its growing curtailment or "domestication" by established elites. For Wolin, democracy is not just a regime of governance or power but a way of life in which ordinary people become "political beings through the self-discovery of common concerns and modes of action for realizing them." As he wrote in an essay titled "Fugitive Democracy," people through their practical engagement renew the political space "by contesting the forms of unequal power that democratic liberty and equality have made possible and that democracy can eliminate only by betraying its own values."[27]

The widening or globalization of popular participation, however, contributes not only to the legitimacy of particular policies but also to the fostering of a genuine sense of global or cosmopolitan justice. The close connection between democracy and justice has been correctly and eloquently stressed by Iris Marion Young in several of her writings. As she observes in her recent book *Inclusion and Democracy,* there are good reasons to believe that "democratic process is the best means for changing conditions of injustice and promoting justice." Although "actually existing democracies" often exhibit "a reinforcing circle between social and economic inequality and political inequality that enables the powerful to use formally democratic processes to perpetuate injustice or preserve privilege," open democratic participation provides an antidote: "One means of breaking this circle, I argue, is to widen democratic inclusion." As one should note, justice for Young is not an abstract philosophical doctrine far removed from peoples' ordinary lives or aspirations. Two central maxims of social justice stand out in her account—maxims that must be firmly concretized and contextualized to meet actual needs: "self-development and self-determination." These two standards or criteria function as correctives to "two general conditions of injustice": namely, oppression with regard to self-development, and domination with regard to self-determination. As she makes clear, "self-development" is an adaptation of Amartya Sen's conception of capabilities (discussed before) with its emphasis on chances of human well-being above and beyond levels of income or material goods. "Self-determination," on the other hand, consists in being able to participate "in determining one's course of action" and "in making the collective regulations designed to prevent domination."[28]

Significantly, *Inclusion and Democracy* extends the linkage of democracy and social justice to the global arena, to the arena of a global or cosmopolitan democracy. As Young insists, given the scope of contemporary global interactions, concerns for social justice also need to be globalized today, in the sense that the maxims of self-development and self-determination are proper aspirations of peoples around the world. "With cosmopolitans," she writes, "I argue against the widespread belief that obligations of justice extend only to co-nationals or only members of the same nation-state. Especially under contemporary conditions of global interdependence, obligations of justice extend globally." For Young, the objective is not the establishment of a global governmental structure, especially a structure dominated by a limited number of national actors or nation-states. Sensitive to the needs of local or regional self-development and self-determination— needs construed in open-ended, non-parochial ways—her approach opts more for an intensification of cross-cultural and inter-societal interaction and recognition (without dismissing the importance of ongoing reforms of existing international institutions). To this extent her perspective makes a contribution to the "dialogue among civilizations" recommended by the United Nations. Above all, her argument center-stages not so much individual or private morality as rather the need for a cosmopolitan justice anchored in an equitable global public sphere.[29]

The plea for global justice, however, would be empty without the indication of a path leading to its accomplishment or approximation. *Inclusion and Democracy* is important in this respect as well, by offering or at least sketching an avenue designed to overcome existing roadblocks to global dialogue, especially the roadblocks of injustice and inequality. For Young, the proper and, in fact, the only path is "struggle," a struggle for more inclusive democratic participation. As she writes, in a society marked by "significant injustice" and inequality, democratic politics will inevitably be "a process of struggle," that is, a process of "communicative engagement of citizens with one another." In domestic as well as in global society, the field of engagement is "not level," because some groups or sectors are usually at a disadvantage. Under these circumstances, oppressed or disadvantaged groups have "no alternative but to struggle for greater justice under conditions of inequality." A crucial point here is the manner or method of struggle. For Young, the method has to be non-violent, because the means have to be appropriate to the end: if the end is justice, the proper way is to struggle justly or ethically.[30] On this score, Young's argument coincides with the teachings and practices of Mahatma Gandhi (who is the topic of chapter 12).

CHAPTER 5

GLOBAL MODERNIZATION

Toward Different Modernities?

Our world—one says today—is rapidly shrinking, and there is evidence to support this claim. In its most obvious meaning, globalization denotes the progressive shrinkage of the world into a relatively circumscribed cosmopolis, a "global village" or a "spaceship earth." These expressions are more than metaphors. With accelerating speed, space explorations, jet travel, and the internet demonstrate the spatial contraction of the earth, the steady attenuation, perhaps even elimination of spatial distances. Yet, despite their plausibility, images of this kind miss an important point. What is usually neglected in globalization accounts is the fact that human societies and cultures live not only in space but also in time, and there is no evidence of a collapse of temporal distances. One way to put the matter is to say that, in different cultures, history has a different significance and obeys different narrative structures. In the context of Western civilization, it is customary among historians to distinguish between the periods of antiquity, the Middle Ages, and modernity; however, it would be futile to try to generalize or "globalize" this periodization. Thus, in the long unfolding of Chinese civilization one would look in vain for a period corresponding to the European Middle Ages. More pointedly still: the time period of the European Middle Ages coincides in Islamic civilization with Islam's gloriously vibrant "classical" age; and the same period witnessed in China the impressive flourishing of the Sung dynasty.[1] Thus, among the great world civilizations, history has not been, and is not presently, synchronized.

This lack of temporal equivalence has consequences especially for the notion of "modernity." By and large, this term is taken from the arsenal of

Western historiography—where it designates in the main developments triggered by Western Renaissance, Reformation, and Enlightenment. Against this background, given the absence of equivalent Middle Ages, modernity cannot possibly mean quite the same thing in non-Western societies and cultures. This difference is aggravated and compounded by another factor: namely, the steady expansion of Western civilization precisely during the modern period. In large measure, the blessings of modernity have come to non-Western societies through the vehicle of colonialism and imperialism—a vehicle replaced in our time by the West's pervasive hegemony in military, economic, and technological domains. To this extent, the term "globalization" tends to be basically synonymous today with "modernization," meaning the diffusion of Western cultural preferences around the globe.[2] In this situation, the notions of modernity and modernization clearly need to be approached cautiously and with circumspection. The following discussion seeks to heed this requirement, proceeding in three steps. The first section examines the meaning of "modernity" as it has been developed by a sequence of Western social theorists, and especially by the German philosopher-sociologist Jürgen Habermas. In the second section, the focus shifts to the question, Is the Western notion of modernity univocal and internally consistent?, leading to the corollary question, Might there be multiple varieties of modernity or different "modernities"? The concluding section seeks to exemplify the latter possibility by turning to Islamic civilization and, in particular, to arguments advanced by such leading Muslim intellectuals as Mohammed al-Jabri and Abdolkarim Soroush.

Modernity and Modernization

In the Western context, the terms "modernity" and "modernization" enjoy wide currency, sometimes being used nearly interchangeably with progress, advancement, and prosperity. Given this broad currency, the meaning of these terms is often amorphous and hard to pinpoint. Still, despite their fluctuating usage, some recurrent accents can readily be discerned; in the main, these accents have to do with advances in science, human rationality, and economic efficiency (associated with capitalism)—and a corresponding decline of tradition, habit, and the authority of religion. Thus, Sir Henry Maine spoke prominently of the transition from "status" to "contract," that is, from a stationary to a rationally constructed society, while Emile Durkheim expressed the same process in terms of a move from pre-ordained (mechanical) to deliberately chosen norms. In turn, Reinhard Bendix focuses on the dissolution of traditional life-forms in favor of "enlightened" practices, while Bruce Lawrence identifies modernity mainly with processes of "increasing bureaucratization and rationalization as well as [growing] technical capacity." Other writers add features like urbanization, industrialization, and centralization of state power. Correlating many of these aspects, Richard Falk has offered a summary description whereby modernity is

> associated with the ascendancy of reason, science, and statist forms of political organization as they emerged in Europe during the 13th to 17th centuries, culminating in the triumph of industrial capitalism in the 19th century and, finally, complemented by the October Revolution in Russia that brought state socialism into the world. . . . A strong feature of [modernity] was its basic secularism, finding meaning in the combination of materialist and scientific developments that made knowledge the equivalent of what an earlier age had regarded as salvation.[3]

These and similar formulations have no doubt intuitive plausibility; yet, the correlation and respective priorities of elements still remain obscure. As it happens, during the course of the twentieth century, major efforts have been undertaken by leading social theorists to sharpen the meaning of modernity and modernization; most prominent among them are Max Weber, Talcott Parsons, and Jürgen Habermas. In the following, my focus will be chiefly on the writings of Habermas—given the central position he occupies in contemporary discussions of the topic; for the sake of brevity (and narrative simplicity), other social theorists will be treated as seen mainly through Habermasian lenses. The issue of modernity and modernization has been a recurrent theme in the German theorist's evolving opus; however, the distinctive contours of his outlook emerged only slowly over the years. Thus, without directly addressing the issue, one of his earliest writings—titled *Toward a Rational Society*—paid tribute to an important thesis of modernization literature: that of the growing rational transparency of societies as they emerge from archaic or traditional forms of opacity. In a more explicit manner, two of his subsequent publications enlisted insights culled from theories of social development and evolution: *Legitimation Crisis* and *Communication and the Evolution of Society*. Still, both texts were mainly "receptive" in orientation, recapitulating (sometimes with new accents) mainstream arguments developed in recent sociology and social psychology. The breakthrough to a distinctive perspective occurred mainly in a text that is sometimes celebrated as Habermas's magnum opus: *The Theory of Communicative Action*—a text that was soon followed by a sequel sharply critiquing counter-positions: *The Philosophical Discourse of Modernity.* Given that the second text relies conceptually entirely on the first, my discussion here will be limited to the former.[4]

Habermas's *The Theory of Communicative Action* is a sprawling work with a somewhat rambling structure. Organized in two volumes, the text acquaints the reader with a great variety of pertinent theorists—from Weber, Durkheim, and Mead to Parsons and Adorno—while offering only intermittent or dispersed glimpses of the author's preferred position. In order to gain a better historical and narrative sequence, it is necessary to rearrange somewhat the book's composition. The chapter dealing with Max Weber's "theory of rationalization" is preceded by some backward glances at Enlightenment precursors—glances meant to profile more sharply Weber's own approach. Most prominent among these precursors was the Baron de Condorcet, who, for the first time, established a close linkage between modernity (or modernization) and social "progress." In Habermas's account, Condorcet's outlook was predicated mainly on four premises. First of all, he construed progress or perfection along the model of scientific advancement, that is, he conceived "the history of humankind on the model of the history of modern science." Second, progress for Condorcet involved the overcoming of past prejudices—a move that, "as if with one blow, devalues traditional religious, philosophical, moral, and political opinions." Third, defined as "enlightenment," this move establishes a bridge between scientific progress, on the one hand, and moral perfection and political emancipation, on the other: "In the battle against the traditional powers of church and state, enlightenment requires the courage to make use of one's own reason, that is, autonomy or maturity (*Mündigkeit*)." Finally, given the close linkage between science and moral and political advancement, Condorcet expected the universal transformation of social conditions around the globe. In Habermas's words, citing a passage of the Frenchman's text: "Condorcet has no doubt that *all* nations will one day 'attain that state of civilization which the most enlightened, the freest and least prejudiced—such as the French and the Anglo-Americans—have already reached'."[5]

In large measure, Condorcet's premises were taken over by nineteenth-century evolutionary theory—although some of them were modified in line with more empiricist or "positivist" canons of inquiry, and in line with the newer experiences of industrialization and capital accumulation. It is against this backdrop of nineteenth-century evolutionism that Max Weber's approach gains its characteristic contours.

According to Habermas, Weber both continued and significantly modified the arguments of his predecessors—mainly in three respects. Firstly, under the influence of historicism and related developments, Weber could no longer accept the exemplary status of scientific progress or the coincidence between the "natural" and the "human" (or cultural) sciences with regard to social development. This change of outlook prompted Weber to examine the process of social evolution "along the lines, not of scientific progress but of the transformation [and disenchantment] of religious worldviews." Secondly, and closely linked with this point, Weber could not endorse the idea of an automatic or linear moral progress (along the lines of "ethical naturalism"). Under the impact of neo-Kantian teachings, he insisted on a more careful segregation of empirical explanations from normative or moral standards of action. Moreover, partly in response to Nietzsche, he embraced a pronounced pluralism of "value orientations," while simultaneously casting doubt on the generally beneficial effects of science on human and social praxis. Finally, with regard to the broad sweep of evolutionary assumptions, Weber adopted a cautious middle road, navigating between the universalism of modern Enlightenment and the relativisim sponsored by historicism. In this dispute, Habermas notes, Weber assumed a cautiously univeralistic position: He did not "regard processes of rationalization as a phenomenon peculiar to the West (or Occident), although the kind of rationalization demonstrable in all world religions led at first only in Europe to a form of rationalism that exhibits both peculiar Occidental features and those general features characteristic of modernity as such."[6]

Following up on these demarcation points, the Weber chapter develops in detail his "theory of rationalization"—an account of which I can give here only the barest outline. In contrast to Condorcet, Weber anchored the notion of modernization not solely or centrally in scientific progress but in a series of multiple and parallel developments that he described as processes of "rationalization," and ultimately as forms of "Occidental rationalism." Following a schema first sketched by Talcott Parsons, Habermas divides these processes into the three domains of culture, personality, and society (with the last one functioning more or less as dependent variable). It is primarily in the field of culture that Weber introduced a differentiation of "value spheres," unknown to his predecessors, between science, ethics, and art—all of them obeying distinct modes of "cultural" rationalization. In the field of science, rationalization means progress in terms of the explanation, prediction, and possible control of empirical phenomena. In the field of ethics or morality, progress denotes the increasing formalization and rational abstractness of moral rules (as compared with the substantive quality of older worldviews). In the field of art, modernization leads to the growing "autonomy" and self-sufficiency of art and aesthetics (again through segregation from traditional worldviews). One of the most distinctive and well-known contributions of Weber's analysis resides in the field of personality structures, particularly his elaboration of a typically modern "methodical life form." It is here that one encounters the familiar model of the so-called Protestant ethic, a model characterized (among other things) by "an inner-worldly asceticism of restless vocational labor" and the "methodical rigor of a principled, self-controlled, autonomous life conduct." These modes of rationalization are complemented on the societal level by the emergence of a utility-governed, capitalist economy and the establishment of a law-bound, bureaucratically administered modern state.[7]

Based on this differentiated schema, Habermas proceeds to examine the meaning of rationality and rationalization in Weber's work. In his view, it is possible to differentiate both between "rationalization steps (or advances)" and between distinct types or concepts of rationality. In terms of historical steps, one can distinguish between the broad rationalization or disenchantment of worldviews leading to the separation of modern "values spheres," and the subsequent transposition of cultural change into societal rationalization. In terms of rationality types, the main distinction is between purposive or instrumental rationality (*Zweckrationalität*) and "value" rationality (*Wertrationalität*), a distinction also captured by the labels of "formal" and "material" rationality. For Weber, instrumental rationality meant basically the efficient employment of suitable means or instruments for the achievement of chosen ends. In this context, ends or values were not considered to be rational in themselves (but rather privately selected); yet, indirectly, values or ends could be rationally evaluated depending on the degree to which they enabled the pursuit of an autonomous and "methodical" life conduct. In Habermas's words, "even the ends themselves can be more or less rational, that is, be chosen correctly in an objective sense in light of given values, means, and circumstances." To this extent, purposive rationality (*Zweckrationalität*) includes not only the instrumental employment of means, but also the "rationality of choice" (*Wahlrationalität*) in the selection of ends. In Weber's usage, both the instrumentality of means and the rationality of choice formed the core of (what he called) "formal rationality" as contrasted to the "material" assessment of substantive preferences and worldviews. As Habermas summarizes these points:

The instrumental rationality of an action is measured by the effectively planned employment of means for given ends. In turn, rationality of choice is measured by the correct calculation of ends in the light of precisely conceived values, available means, and boundary conditions, while normative rationality is measured by the unifying, systematizing power and effectiveness of action-guiding standards and principles. Weber called actions that satisfy the conditions of means and choice rationality "purposive-rational" and those satisfying the conditions of normative rationality "value-rational."[8]

In *The Theory of Communicative Action,* the summary of Weber's rationalization theory is immediately joined with some critical observations—observations that, though faithful to some Weberian insights, channel the notions of modernity and modernization in a new, normatively more ambitious direction. In agreement with Weber, Habermas sees modernization basically as a sequence of "rationalization steps," catapulted by the disenchantment of worldviews. As he writes: "Rationalized worldviews satisfy to a [steadily] greater degree the requirements of *a modern understanding of the world,* which categorically presupposes the *disenchantment* of the world." He also follows Weber and Talcott Parsons regarding the progressive differentiation of cultural "value spheres" (and the corresponding segregation of societal structures). At this point, however, several disagreements come into view. One important issue has to do with his predecessors' focus on purposive-instrumental rationality—a focus Habermas tries to counterbalance and correct through a normatively enriched notion of rationality (especially the concept of "communicative" rationality). At the same time, and from the same angle, the distinction of value spheres is tied no longer to fortuitous preferences but rather to the stringent demands of rational "validity claims" (especially the claims of scientific "truth," ethical "rightness," and aesthetic "authenticity"). In his words: "To the degree that distinctive value spheres are profiled in their rational consistency, we become conscious of those universal validity claims against which cultural advances or 'value increases' are measured." Closely connected with this feature is perhaps the most significant Habermasian departure: his embrace of a strong sense of cultural and normative universalism. Going resolutely beyond Max Weber's ambivalence in this domain, *The Theory of Communicative Action* states:

> If we construe Occidental rationalism not from the conceptual angle of purposive rationality and mastery of the world, if instead we take as our

point of departure the rationalization of worldviews that results in a decentered understanding of the world, then we have to face the question:
whether there is not a formal stock of universal structures of consciousness manifest in the cultural value spheres that develop, according to
their own logics, under the abstract standards of truth, normative rightness, and authenticity. . . . The universalist position does not have to
deny the pluralism and incompatibility of historical versions of civilizations; however, it regards this multiplicity of life forms as limited to *cultural contents,* and it asserts that every culture—if it is at all to attain a
certain degree of "self-awareness" or "sublimation"—must share certain
formal properties of the modern understanding of the world. Thus, the
universalist position relies on certain necessary structural features of
modern life forms as such.[9]

Guided by considerations of this kind, the opening chapter of the
text develops in detail Habermas's own conception of modernity and
modernization. Following (as well as amending) central Weberian
teachings, Habermas depicts modernization basically as a process of
rationalization involving the progressive differentiation or segregation
of cultural value spheres and societal subsystems. As in Weber's case,
rationalization for him denotes chiefly a growing "disenchantment" of
worldviews—an aspect analyzed in the text through a juxtaposition of
"mythical" and "modern" modes of "world-understanding." For Habermas (and many prominent anthropologists), mythical worldviews are
characterized by a totalizing synthesis or fusion of all dimensions of
experience, a fusion devoid of reflective distantiation. "The deeper
one penetrates into the network of a mythical worldview," he writes,
"the more strongly the totalizing power of the 'savage mind' stands
out." Totalizing synthesis here means the non-differentiation of the
domains of nature and culture, subject and object, inner world and
outer world, church and state, language and reality. Most astonishing
for the modern mind, Habermas notes, is the fusion or "levelling" of
the domains of nature and culture that, in mythical thought, are "projected onto the same plane." From this amalgamation of spheres there
results, on the one hand, "a nature endowed with anthropomorphic
features and drawn into the network of social agents," and on the
other hand, "a culture that is (so-to-speak) naturalized or reified and
absorbed into the objective nexus of anonymously operating powers."
In its effects on social agency, the fusion of nature and culture basically
entails passivity and the constraining "reification of the [dominant]
worldview."[10]

In contrast to mythical fusionism, modernity or the modern
"world-understanding" is characterized by the progressive separation

or segregation of spheres—especially the spheres of nature and culture (as well as culture and religion). In terms of the text, modernization involves the growing rationalization and disenchantment (or "demythologization") of worldviews, which in turn leads to the "desocialization of nature" and the "denaturalization of society." Habermas introduces at this point the idea of different or multiple "worlds" (as opposed to the mythical-archaic *one*-world) and of different "basic attitudes" (*Grundeinstellungen*) toward these worlds. In accordance with the mentioned validity claims, he distinguishes basically between three modern (or rationalizable) worlds: the objective, social, and subjective worlds—with the "lifeworld" functioning as a recessed, supplementary backdrop. The "objective" world, in this scheme, refers to the world of facts or "existing states of affairs" that we approach in an empirical or "objectifying" attitude (subject to the standard of truth). The "social" world, on the other hand, refers to the fabric of interpersonal relations governed by legitimate norms to which we can adopt a "conformist or nonconformist" attitude. The "subjective" world, finally, has to do with the sum of inner experiences tied to an "expressive" attitude (governed by criteria of authenticity or truthfulness). In Habermas's presentation, a core feature of modernity resides precisely in the disaggregation of holistic structures and the steadily more rigorous distinction between worlds and corresponding attitudes. As he writes, with specific reference to the distinction between objective and social worlds:

> We need to proceed behind the differentiation of domains to the difference separating a basic attitude toward the objective world of what is factually the case from a basic attitude toward the social world of what can legitimately be expected, commanded, or morally required. We make the correct conceptual cuts [*Schnitte*] between causal connections of nature and normative orders of society to the extent that we become conscious of the changes in perspective and attitude that we effect when we pass from observing or manipulating to following or violating legitimate expectations.[11]

As one should note, modernization here does not only refer to the distinction between social functions or subsystems (as in Parsons's case), but to the progressive rationalization of social interactions in such a way as to render them amenable to the application of general or universally binding validity claims. For Habermas, "rationality" basically has to do with the quality of utterances and communicative exchanges and ultimately depends on the willingness of participants to raise such general claims and to have their views tested or contested by the same standards. Behind the range of rational or rationalizable worlds, one should remember, there hovers the backdrop of the life-world (*Lebenswelt*), seen as a matrix of "more or less diffuse, always unquestioned or unproblematized background convictions"; modernization on that level means the progressive rationalization of convictions such that a passively accepted or "normatively ascribed" consensus is replaced by "communicatively achieved agreement." In the course of this development, traditional cultural beliefs—which are always particular and contingent—steadily give way to formalized and universally binding rationality structures: "Cultural beliefs are not universal, but—as their name indicates—are located in the horizon of a distinctive cultural lifeworld. . . . Only the truth of propositions, the rightness of norms, and the comprehensibility of symbolic expressions constitute, by their very meaning, universal validity claims testable in discourses."[12]

Modernity in the Crossfire

As one can see from the preceding account, Habermas is a resolute defender—perhaps the most resolute and eloquent defender—of Western modernity and its universal scope. Although critical of earlier science-based conceptions, he certainly does not regard modernity as a *cul-de-sac*, but rather as a "project" in need of further development or completion.[13] In adopting this stance, his argument runs headlong into an opposing view that has gained considerable attention and prominence in the course of the twentieth century: that of the outright rejection or dismissal of modernity (sometimes styled as "antimodernism"). The literature in this regard is voluminous and impressive. From Oswald Spengler's *The Decline of the West* (1918) to René Guénon's *La crise du monde moderne* (1928), Romano Guardini's *Das Ende der Neuzeit* (1950), and Alasdair MacIntyre's *After Virtue* (1984), a lengthy and powerful indictment has been drawn up against Western modernity. Among the many charges leveled against modernity, the following are particularly prominent: the demotion of traditional religious or cosmological worldviews in favor of a calculating rationality, manifest in modern science and technology; the steady dissolution of traditional community bonds in favor of a self-centered individualism (often shading over into narcissism and solipsism); the weakening and even demolition of traditional virtues, making room instead for the celebration of arbitrary whims and emotions; and finally the abandonment of quiet contemplation in favor of a restless activism and programs of social engineering. Some writers add to this list a number of further charges: the alliance of modernity with concentrated state power and bureaucratization; its complicity with Eurocentric colonialism and imperialism; its subservience to the economic dictates of capitalism; and its contribution to the devastation of natural resources.[14]

Charges of this kind are surely serious and need to be taken as such; however, many of them are misdirected or do not fully come to grips with the Habermasian conception of modernity and modernization. With regard to the linkage of modernity with reason or rationality one might possibly adopt a more benign assessment. Remembering the Socratic motto that "the unexamined life is not worth living," one might credit modernity with cultivating a mode of rational reflexivity and with critiquing traditional life-forms that have lost any intelligible justification. This favorable assessment is buttressed by Habermas's multidimensional notion of rationality, that is, his refusal to reduce modernity to scientific progress. Surely, the charge of a wanton abandonment of "virtue" in favor of passions becomes dubious in light of his strong insistence on normative rightness claims, patterned in part on Kantian and neo-Kantian teachings. Probably the most serious shortcoming of the opponents of modernity, however, is their inability to grasp the significance of the modern differentiation of value spheres and social subsystems (as articulated by Weber and Habermas). What is involved in the disaggregation or "decentering" of traditional holistic worldviews is actually a major political development: the decentering or decentralization of totalizing power structures that, in most traditional societies, were monopolized by privileged elites (kings, emperors, aristocratic and priestly castes). Seen against this background, the hankering of anti-modernists for the "good old" (pre-modern) [days loses some of its romantic innocence and charm; while nostalgic for ancient forms of "spirituality," critics of modernity often turn a blind eye to the political abuses of traditional societies: the concentration of power in a few hands, the collusion of political and religious domination, and the exclusion of women and marginalized classes from the public sphere. Although not directly thematized in his text, modernization as decentering clearly signals for Habermas a process of democratization, that is, the emergence of a society in which no individual or group has a monopoly of power. Contradiction

To be sure, these comments do not fully exonerate modernity in the eyes of its critics; yet, there is room to examine further some of the charges. Thus, regarding the linkage between modernity and colonialism/imperialism, one may wonder whether the linkage is strictly necessary or only contingent—and in the first case, whether necessity mars only a "Eurocentric" kind of modernity (or any other kind).[15] A similar question affects the relation between modernity and capitalism, a relation anchored by Weber in the "Protestant ethic"; here again, much further examination needs to the done (and is actually being done by numerous social scientists), with no conclusive verdict so far in sight.[16] Leaving these matters aside, it may still be the case—and in fact I want to claim—that there are shortcomings besetting Habermas's own, admittedly highly nuanced conception of modernity. Perhaps the central defect or shortcoming may actually be a corollary of his major achievement: the meticulous segregation of value spheres and social subsystems in modern times under the aegis of "rationalization" or "disenchantment." As has been shown, modernization for Habermas depends basically on a deepening of divisions—or, as he says, on our ability to make the right "cuts" (*Schnitte*) between different spheres or domains. As can readily be seen, this process of disaggregation or cutting is actually just a reversal of earlier holistic or totalizing structures—and, as such, remains tied to these structures in the mode of negation or antithesis. It is precisely in this domain that recent philosophy—especially under "postmodern" or "transmodern" auspices—has introduced new departures or initiatives aiming (one might say) at a different understanding of difference. Under such labels as "*Unterschied,*" "*différance,*" and "*chiasm,*" leading Western thinkers have tried to articulate a mode of differentiation that resists the lure both of totalizing synthesis and radical segregation or mutual negation. If these initiatives are taken seriously, it clearly becomes imperative to rethink—along non-antithetical and non-synthetic lines—the relation between rationality and non-rationality, reason and faith, nature and culture, and form and content.[17]

As one should add, the noted shortcoming of Habermas's approach is aggravated by another problematic feature: his valorization of one side of modern divisions or dichotomies over its respective counterparts. Strictly construed[modernization for him means the steady ascent of reason over belief (*mythos*), of culture over nature, of form over content, and segregation over holism]To this extent, his approach entails a series of exclusions or marginalization, all attesting to the supremacy of *logos*. Seen against this background, charges of "logocentrism" leveled by recent writers against Western modernity (including Habermas's version) do not seem far off the mark. Other charges could readily and plausibly be added. Thus, given the rootedness of Habermas's three worlds in basic human attitudes (*Grundeinstellungen*), the label of "anthropocentrism" does not seem ill-fitting; likewise, the stress on progressive disenchantment supports the verdict of an immanentist "secularism" (or laïcism). In all these respects, correctives are clearly called for. In light of present-day global realities, the nature-culture liaison surely needs to be carefully rethought, in a way that would pay closer attention to ecological needs.[18] Equally important (and closely related with this point) is a broader reassessment of the status of humans in the world (or *cosmos*), a reassessment that should steer clear both of a scientific reification of the world and of its reduction to an anthropocentric construct or commodity. Along the same lines, the complex issue of the immanence-transcendence relation urgently needs reconsideration. There are plenty of signs in our time that a narrowly confined immanence cannot satisfy human longings and aspirations. What needs to be recognized is that longings for transcendence, even a transcendental holism, are vibrantly alive today in many societies on the level of the ordinary lifeworld—far removed from traditional holistic power structures.[19]

What these considerations bring into view is the need to find a path between (Habermasian) modernity and its radical opponents (or anti-modernists), a path that acknowledges the beneficial or emancipating dimensions of modernity while refusing to canonize its defects. Among contemporary Western thinkers, such a path has been most famously and eloquently charted by Charles Taylor, in a series of writings. In one of his popular and more accessible essays, *The Ethics of Authenticity*, Taylor distinguishes sharply between wholesale promoters and radical opponents of modernity, what he calls modernity's "boosters" and "knockers." As he writes: "Modernity has its boosters as well as its knockers. Nothing is agreed here and the debate continues." What is unfortunate about this debate is that it often degenerates into polemics, with the result that basic issues tend to be misconstrued or misunderstood. In forging his own path in this debate, Taylor distances himself both from straight promoters and radical enemies of modernity. At the same time, his path is not that of a half-hearted compromise favoring a "simple trade-off between the advantages and costs of, say, individualism, technology, and bureaucratic management." Rather, his aim is to renew serious reflection on the meaning of modernity and its possible future directions. In his words:

> What I am suggesting is a position distinct from both boosters and knockers of contemporary culture. Unlike the boosters, I do not believe that everything is as it should be in this culture. Here I tend to agree with the knockers. But unlike them, I think that [modern] authenticity should be taken seriously as a moral ideal. I differ also from various middle positions. . . . The picture I am offering is rather that of an ideal that

has degraded but that is very worthwhile in itself, and indeed, I would like to say, unrepudiable by moderns.[20]

The path favored by Taylor was further developed or fleshed out in one of his larger studies, *Sources of the Self,* especially its concluding section titled "The Conflicts of Modernity." In that section, Taylor also positions himself more clearly vis-à-vis Habermas's conception of modernity and modernization, carefully navigating between sympathy and critique. Contrary to the view of radical "knockers," Taylor does not fail to perceive the liberating or empowering elements in Habermas's approach. As he notes, the latter's communicative model "certainly gives us reason to be less pessimistic about democracy and self-management" than his detractors would grant. What he finds uncongenial, however, is Habermas's narrowly rationalistic "logocentrism," and especially his insistence on slicing apart domains of experience in a manner that privileges anthropocentrism over broader human aspirations (on the level of ordinary life). One serious effect of this slicing strategy is the nature-culture dichotomy where it would surely "greatly help in staving off ecological disaster if we could recover a sense of the demand that our natural surrounding and wilderness make on us." Equally or still move damaging are the effects of the strategy on broader holistic longings that—Taylor states—fall through the "grid" of Habermas's scheme. As he writes: what cannot be fitted into this grid is "the search for moral sources *outside* the subject through languages which resonate *within* him or her, the grasping of an order which is inseparably indexed to a personal vision." To be sure, the point is not to recapture holism through a nostalgic return to totalizing power structures of the past—a return that would truncate modern (and postmodern) sensibilities. In an age in which a publicly sanctioned cosmic order of meanings has become untenable, the only promising way to "explore the order in which we are set, with an aim to defining moral sources, is through the part of personal resonance."[21]

One of the most exciting and promising aspects of Taylor's approach is his nuanced critique of modernity—a critique pointing in the direction not of its denial but its differentiation, that is, the direction of different or multiple modernities. As it happens, Taylor himself has more recently taken pioneering steps in this respect: namely, in his Marianist Award Lecture (of 1996) titled *A Catholic Modernity?* As the title indicates, Taylor again does not simply dismiss modernity, but rather seeks to amend its defects. In fact, his lecture valorizes the modern gains in human freedom and emancipation precisely from a Christian faith perspective. As he writes: "Modern liberal political culture is characterized by an affirmation of universal rights—to life, freedom, citizenship, self-realization"—an affirmation that would have been inconceivable under holistic power structures of the past. In the West, these power structures were largely identified with established Christian religion—which Taylor calls "Christendom," adding that it would have been difficult if not impossible for Christendom to accept "full equality of rights for atheists, [and] for people of a quite alien religion." As it happens, in the course of the Renaissance, Reformation, and Enlightenment, the power structures of Christendom were "broken open," leading to a process of democratization in which no single doctrine can be triumphant and the public sphere remains "the locus of competing ultimate visions." Although bemoaned by nostalgic traditionalists, this process actually can be welcomed by Christians because modern freedom—prized by many different people for different reasons—also has its "Christian meaning," as it entails "the freedom to come to God on one's own or, otherwise put, moved only by the Holy Spirit." Seen from this angle, modernization signals a new potential for the "practical penetration of the gospel in human life," freed from imperial or hegemonic designs:

> This kind of freedom, so much the fruit of the gospel, we have only when nobody (that is, no particular outlook) is running the show. So a vote of thanks to Voltaire and others for (not necessarily wittingly) showing us this and for allowing us to live the gospel in a purer way, free of that continual and often bloody forcing of conscience which was the sin and blight of all those "Christian" centuries.[22]

As in his previous writings, Taylor locates the shortcoming or downside of modernity mainly in its narrowly rationalistic and "secularizing" bent. In tune with its central theme, the Marianist Lecture finds evidence for this bent in modernity's neglect of transcendence or its inability to grasp the immanence-transcendence nexus. As he writes, modernity for many people seems to accredit the view that "human life is better off without transcendental vision altogether." For people holding this view, transcendence is often identified with a confining church doctrine, perhaps an oppressive theological or theocratic structure—a construal ignoring its transgressive or transformative quality. In Taylor's words: "Acknowledging the transcendent means being called to a change of identity," that is, responding to the call for "a radical decentering of the self" in relation with the divine. Denial of transcendence, by contrast, means a confinement in mundane immanence, with its lineaments of death, decay, and violence. To be sure, for a Christian, especially a Catholic Christian, acknowledging transcendence cannot signify a hankering for a restored, hegemonic Christendom. Under modern auspices, the universalism of Christian faith, its intrinsic "holism" (the original meaning of "catholicity"), has to be understood in a new way: from the ground up, foregoing "potential echoes of triumphalism." Differently phrased: the wholeness promised by the gospel is not equivalent to unity as uniformity, but rather evocative of a transformative process: that of reconciliation in the midst of diversity. Here are some powerful lines from Taylor's text:

> [For Christians] redemption happens through incarnation, the weaving of God's life into human lives; but these human lives are different, plural, irreducible to each other. Redemption-incarnation brings reconciliation, a kind of oneness. This is the oneness of diverse beings who come to see that they cannot attain wholeness alone, that their complementarity is essential, rather than of beings who come to accept that they are ultimately identical. . . . Human diversity is part of the way in which we are made in the image of God.[23]

Toward an Islamic Modernity?

Taylor's observations clearly are not narrowly restricted to a Catholic or Christian context. In an age of global modernization, it becomes timely and urgent to ponder the possibility of other alternatives, such as the prospect of Islamic, Confucian, or Hindu modes of modernity. For present purposes, the discussion will be limited to the issue of a possible Islamic modernity (or a set of Islamic modernities).[24] As is well known, Islamic civilization has had its share of "knockers" and "boosters" of modernity—although, during recent decades, the knockers have tended to monopolize the limelight of public attention (at least in the West). What in Western literature is described as Islamic "fundamentalism" or political Islamism coincides almost completely with the position of radical knockers, a position bent on devalorizing or debunking modern Western culture as a whole (while often borrowing from modern scientific and technological advances). As one should realize, the case of Islamic anti-modernists is powerfully bolstered by the legacy of Western colonialism and imperialism, that is, by the insidious contamination of modernization with Westernization or the imposition of Western hegemonic imperatives. What in Iran is called "*gharbzadegi*" (Westoxication) captures precisely this toxic confluence of modernity and Western hegemony in its deleterious effects on traditional culture and Islamic faith.[25]

The mixture of elements explains in large measure the vehemence or stridency of the rhetoric employed by many radical Islamicists. Among Egyptian fundamentalists, no one has been more emphatic in the denunciation of modern Western culture than Sayyid Qutb (1906–1966). As Qutb wrote late in his life, curiously echoing some Western "crisis of culture" literature: "Humanity is standing today at the brink of an abyss, not because of the threat of annihilation hanging over its head . . . but because humanity is bankrupt in the realm of 'values'." The danger for him was particularly evident in the modern Western world, "for the West can no longer provide the values necessary for [the flourishing of] humanity." In Qutb's view, modern culture, especially in the West, was marked by skepticism, anomie, and ignorance of truth (*jahiliyya*), chiefly ignorance of the revealed teachings of Islam; the remedy for him—as for many Western critics of modernity—was a return to the traditional holistic worldview, particularly the acknowledgement of God's absolute supremacy and sovereignty.[26] Qutb's stance has been, and continues to be, shared by numerous intellectuals and clerics both inside and outside his native Egypt—and sometimes even by intellectuals not partial to his brand of radical fundamentalism. Thus, in Iran, the slogan of "*gharbzadegi*" has often been embraced by writers otherwise quite distant from popular fundamentalist movements. Here are some lines penned by an urbane Iranian, the theosophist Seyyed Hoseyn Nasr:

> Modern civilization as it has developed in the West since the Renaissance is an experiment that has failed—failed in such an abysmal fashion as to cast doubt upon the very possibility of any future for man to seek other ways. It would be most unscientific today to consider this civilization, with all the presumptions about the nature of man and the universe which lie at its basis, as anything other than a failed experiment.[27]

The pervasive influence of *gharbzadegi* can be gauged from the extent to which it has been able to structure—at least in part—contemporary philosophical discourse in Iran. Thus, one of the most distinguished Iranian philosophers, Reza Davari, has paid tribute to its spirit. Paralleling Nasr's indictment, some of Davari's early publications denounced modern Western culture as corrupt in its very core, claiming that, since the Renaissance, Western modernity was anchored in selfish individualism, secular humanism, and agnosticism—doctrines that are like withered branches of a dying or dead tree. As he wrote in 1983: "Modernity is a tree that was planted in the West and has spread everywhere. For many years we have been living under one of the dying and faded branches of this tree and its dried shadow, which is still hanging over our heads"—adding: "What can be done with this dried branch?" (leaving the answer to his readers). Davari's denunciation extended to modernity's social and political manifestations, especially the rise of democracy, which he found incompatible with the traditional Islamic postulate of a supreme law-giver and prophet (patterned in many ways on Plato's philosopher-being). Summarizing the ills of Western modernity, another publication of 1984 stated:

> It [modern culture] is a way of thinking and a historical practice which started in Europe more than four hundred years ago, and has since expanded more or less universally. The modern West signals the demise of the holy truth and the rise of a humanity which views itself as the sole proprietor and focus of the universe. Its accomplishment is to appropriate everything in the celestial cosmos. Even if it proceeded to prove the existence of God, it would be done not to show obedience and submission but in order to glorify itself.[28]

In Iran, *gharbzadegi* has been criticized by a number of intellectuals, especially by Hamid Enayat and Abdolkarim Soroush. For Enayat, denunciations of Western modernity by Islamic knockers were often prompted by ignorance or mere hearsay knowledge. Moreover, *gharbzadegi* in many instances served as an invitation to nativist self-enclosure or self-indulgence—a retreat unconducive to critical inquiry and debate. As it happens, such a retreat was often encouraged by "Orientalizing" intellectuals in the West. As Enayat noted (in 1980), Western praise for Eastern "spiritualism, simplicity, and unhurried pace of life" has often been eagerly embraced by people in the East— but at a price: "This perverted Eastern attraction to itself through the West's condescending love for the exotic has been deservedly censured by Frantz Fanon, whose ideas have gained popularity among Muslim intellectuals opposed to cultural imperialism." In more recent years, Enayat's comments have been seconded as well as fleshed out and philosophically deepened by Soroush. Addressing the company of radical knockers of the West, Soroush asked in 1988: "Where do you draw the boundaries of the West? Is this moral decline present wherever there is the West, or wherever there is the West is there moral decline?" What seemed particularly obnoxious to Soroush in *gharbzadegi* was its resort to hyperbole and summary condemnation—a hyperbole evident in such expressions as "essence of the West," "destiny of the

West," or "spirit of the West." Without endorsing everything contained under the broad label of Western modernity, Soroush (like Enayat) insisted on the need to exercise critical judgment—a judgment seasoned through cross-cultural interrogation. Above all, modernization—despite its publicized ills—also harbored some liberating or empowering features, evident (for example) in the differentiation of the spheres of religion, knowledge, politics, and aesthetics.[29]

In March 2000, Soroush attended a conference on "Islam and the Modern World" in Leyden, Netherlands. In an interview conducted at the time of the conference, Soroush articulated concisely his views on modernity and modernization—disclosing an outlook in many ways akin to that of Charles Taylor (now transposed into an Islamic register). Facing the topic squarely, his comments valorized an aspect of modernity most frequently attacked by anti-modernists: progressive "disenchantment" or "demystification." Far from bemoaning it, Soroush saw this feature as a sign of a "healthy epistemological skepticism," of a willingness to engage in critical inquiry that "opens the way to plurality and diversity," while also mounting a challenge to "the worldview of the past." As for Taylor, this traditional worldview for him was largely focused on constraining obligations anchored in holistic power structures (monopolized by political and clerical elites). A major innovative feature of modernity, by contrast, is its emphasis on "the language of rights"—the rights "to speak, think, learn, work, and act." In Soroush's account, this emphasis marks "the crucial difference between the traditional way of life in the past and life in the present modern age." As he adds pointedly: "The traditional notion of God was almost a tyrannical one: God for us was a supreme being who demanded our devotion and love at all costs." Tied exclusively to obligations, the image of God in the past tended to be that of an "intolerant, almost cruel" overlord. Seen against this background, the rise of modernity did not necessarily signal an abandonment of religion or scriptural faith; rather, it opened the door to a new relation to the divine, a new freedom to worship God freed from external coercion (by kings and mullahs). In Soroush's words: "Our view of God has also changed, for now we feel that it is our right to worship Him and show our love to Him freely." Understood as a God (also) of rights, God in the modern age is "closer to the individual believer" and also to an uncoerced community of believers.[30]

To round out this discussion, I would like to draw attention to another Muslim intellectual whose arguments in many ways resemble those of Soroush: the Moroccan Mohammed al-Jabri. In his recently published *Arab-Islamic Philosophy: A Contemporary Critique,* al-Jabri calls for a modernization that is mindful of indigenous cultural and religious traditions; in the context of the Maghreb, this means a call for a Muslim and, move specifically, an "Arab modernity." As he points out, there is not "*one* single absolute, universal and planetary modernity"; rather, there are "*numerous* modernities that differ from era to era and from place to place." The kind of modernity that emerged in Europe is necessarily different "from either Chinese modernity or Japanese modernity," given the non-coincidence and lack of synchronicity between cultural traditions; attempting to transfer the European model to the Maghreb would be futile, since it is "foreign to Arab culture and its history" and hence could not possibly strike roots or trigger a dialogue "likely to engender movement in its midst." To be viable, modernization, for al-Jabri, must develop a sense and a "modern vision of tradition"—which is far removed from a nostalgic traditionalism. Turning against radical knockers of modernity, he chides their hankering for self-enclosure, for a "narcissistic retirement within oneself" that "can only lead to a suicidal exile and self-marginalization." Although not unaware of certain defects marring Western rationalism and modernity— such as the bent toward ecological devastation and possible nuclear destruction—al-Jabri is unwilling to abandon reason itself (which has always been integral to Islamic civilization) nor the liberating potential of modern reason. As he writes: "Modernity is above all reason and democracy," meaning: "a rational and critical approach to all aspects of our existence." He concludes his book with these comments:

> We really ought to set the problematics as follows: how can contemporary Arab thought regain and reinvest the rational and "liberating" gains from its own tradition—in a similar perspective to that within which they were invested the first time: the struggle against feudalism, superstition, fatalism, and the will to found a city of reason and justice, to build the free, democratic, and socially responsible Arab city?[31]

CHAPTER 6

MEMORY AND SOCIAL IMAGINATION

Latin American Reflections

Milan Kundera writes somewhere: "The struggle of man against power is the struggle of memory against forgetting."[1] These are powerful words, words worth remembering in our time of rapid globalization—a time when, attracted by the lure of technocracy and technopolis, humankind seems ready to plunge into global historical amnesia. Kundera stresses memory or memory-work—not in order to foster nostalgia, but to retrieve resources of empowerment and social imagination, resources enabling humans, especially the oppressed and marginalized, to "struggle against power." Kundera's words find an echo in the work of Herbert Marcuse who, in *Eros and Civilization*, wrote that "the restoration of remembrance to its rights, as a vehicle of liberation, is one of the noblest tasks of thought." As in the case of Kundera, remembrance for Marcuse was not equivalent to nostalgic escapism; partly under the influence of Freudian teachings he argued that, through memory-work, the "forbidden images and impulses of childhood begin to tell the truth that reason denies." With specific reference to Marcel Proust he added that, in opposition to a narrow empiricism, "the orientation to the past tends toward an orientation to the future: the *recherche du temps perdu* becomes the vehicle of future liberation."[2]

In commenting on the liberating potential of remembrance, Marcuse linked memory with imagination and, in this connection, appealed explicitly and at length to Immanuel Kant's theory of imagination, especially "productive imagination." As he noted (and as most commentators would concur), Kant treats productive imagination as a constructive agency, as a kind of innovative bridge-builder between sensibility and intelligibility, or between sensual experience (the experience in the ordinary lifeworld) and rational-cognitive understanding. The role of bridge-builder, however, is complicated by the temporality of experience: in guiding thought from sensibility to intelligibility, imagination leads to an understanding not only of what "is" (factually), but of what "can be"; differently phrased, it opens the path not only to cognitive-empirical analysis, but to the imaginative retrieval of possibilities—thus to a reconciliation of past and future. In the following, I want to pursue this path of imaginative retrieval by proceeding in three steps. First, in order to reduce the hazards of philosophical abstractness, I take my departure from a concrete historical and geographical setting: Latin American experience during the second part of the twentieth century. Here, the accent is on re-telling a story of collective suffering. In a second step, I make room for some broader theoretical reflections on social imagination, taking my bearings especially from the work of Paul Ricoeur. In a third and final step, I return to the concrete setting of Latin America, invoking as my guides some leading Latin American social thinkers and writers: primarily Enrique Dussel and Rigoberta Menchú.

A Story of Collective Suffering

Memory-work in Latin America is hard and taxing—but absolutely necessary if social imagination is ever to take wings in this part of the world. As Friedrich Nietzsche observes at one point, the history of most peoples is written in blood and tears, with agonies vastly outweighing episodes of happiness or tranquillity. These comments seem nowhere more pertinent than in Latin America. Despite intermittent episodes of peace and recovery, the history of Latin America has been punctuated by immense catastrophes and unspeakable atrocities. Above all, the history of the "common" people—including native Indians, blacks, mestizos, and poor peasants—has been a long story of suffering, oppression, and even genocidal "ethnic cleansing." The opening thunderbolt of this story happened in 1492, the beginning of the European invasion and conquest of the Americas. It is estimated (quite reliably) that, in the wake of the conquest, some sixty to seventy million native Indians perished as a result of killings, starvation, or disease—certainly one of the largest cases of genocide in human history.[3] Those native inhabitants who survived were subjected to semi-slavery and harsh subsistence levels of survival, conditions that they soon shared with slaves imported from Africa. With the coming of constitutional forms of government, outright modes of enslavement were progressively abolished—only to be replaced by subtler forms of social-political and economic marginalization instigated by land-owning and military elites (often acting in alliance with the "colossus" to the north). This is not the place to rehearse in detail the story of social struggles since the days of independence. Here it must suffice to recall briefly some episodes and experiences of the past fifty years—experiences that are grim and sobering (and scarcely relieved by recent accounts of "transitions to" or "consolidations of democracy"). What I have in mind is the story of military dictatorships, large-scale executions, "disappearances," and death squads. I limit myself to a few reminders. The first thing to remember is that "disappearances" have not been the monopoly of Argentina and its so-called dirty war. Turning first to Argentina's northern neighbor, one needs to recall the period of military-presidential rulers in Brazil (1960s and 1970s) and their "dirty" belligerence against dissidents and political opponents. The Commission on Politically Disappeared Brazilians (Comissão pelos Desaparecidos Politicos Brasileiros) has published a list containing the names of at least 170 victims of political assassination and of at least 130 political "disappearances" during that period (and the list is limited only to members or friends of the Marxist left).[4] No doubt, however, that the most "dirty" belligerence was carried out subsequently in Argentina, following the ouster of Isabel Perón (1976). Much has been written about the horror of that period—but the horror still needs to be remembered. In the stirring words of Marguerite Feitlowitz:

> Brutal, sadistic and rapacious, the "Dirty War" junta, which ruled Argentina from 1976 to 1983, was intensely verbal and used language with diabolical skill to confuse, disorient, and terrorize.... From the moment of the coup, there was a constant torrent of speeches, proclamations, and interviews.... As the commanders talked, some 30,000 suspected "subversives" were kidnapped from the streets, tortured in secret concentration camps, and "disappeared." Victims died during torture, were machine-gunned at the edge of enormous pits, or were thrown, drugged, from airplanes into the sea. These individuals came to be known as "the missing," or *desaparecidos*.[5]

Regarding the "constant torrent" of words unleashed by the military junta, its cynicism defied belief. As Jo(sephine) Fischer reports, General Videla, who headed the three-man junta, assured the public in his speeches that the country would be governed "by the values and morality of Christianity, patriotism, and the family. 'The common good,' he said, 'is achieved by the resolution of conflicts and by the energetic protection of the human rights of all members of the community'." The same General Videla has also been quoted as saying in one meeting: "In order to achieve peace in Argentina, all the necessary people will die." Regarding the methods used by the junta, Fischer offers these details: most of the operations were "carried out at night after first diverting the traffic with roadblocks and cutting off the electricity supply, and were executed with the maximum display of violence to instil a terror which would paralyze public reaction and ensure the silence of neighbors and friends." A word also needs to be said about the complicity of other Latin American governments in the "dirty war." To quote Fischer again: "With the collaboration of the security forces of neighboring countries which had also fallen under authoritarian regimes—including Brazil in 1964, Bolivia in 1971, and Chile and Uruguay in 1973—the Argentine military were able to extend their operations across national frontiers, unobstructed by considerations of national sovereignty. . . . [Thus] Argentine security forces kidnapped and assassinated foreign exiles or transferred them to secret detention centers in their own countries." A particularly sad or distressing part of the "dirty war" was another kind of collusion: the widespread complicity of the Catholic Church in the activities of the junta, evident both in public pronouncements of Church leaders and in local policies of closing church doors to victims of persecution.[6]

Fortunately, the unfolding story of the "dirty war" was not entirely bleak. One of the more uplifting aspects of the *proceso* was the formation and insurgency of the mothers of the disappeared, known as Madres de Plaza de Mayo. As their courageous actions have frequently been chronicled, I shall refrain from a detailed discussion—except to extend a brief salute to these remarkable women. In the words of Marguerite Guzman Bouvard:

> Fueled by anger at the disappearance of their children and by an extraordinary courage, a group of middle-aged women belied the perception in a traditional, patriarchal society that the aged and women in general are powerless. Against the military values of hierarchy, obedience, and the unchecked use of physical force, the Mothers practiced pacifism, cooperation, and mutual love. They developed a political organization and style which contradicted that of a culture whose politics historically had been based upon ideological fragmentation and military intervention.[7]

And here are some words of Hebe de Bonafini, one of the leaders of the Mothers, criticizing President Menem for pardoning the junta (in

1990): "Our country is different from his. His is the military, money, and the United States, power, a Ferrari. Ours is the working men and women who give their lives for it, our children, the Plaza, life, the earth."[8] These are statements worth remembering—not least for showing the power of social imagination, the power to imagine a different country and a different future through the recollection of the "disappeared."

As we know, dirty belligerence extended far beyond the confines of Argentina and Brazil. In Chile, during the regime of General Pinochet (1973–1989), it is estimated that over 3,000 civilians had been killed by the military, while an equal number of disappearances have remained unresolved. A dark scenario emerges also in Colombia—with only part of the darkness being attributable to drug cartels. In a report issued in 1996, Human Rights Watch carefully examined and analyzed Colombia's so-called killer networks, focusing in this context particularly on the "military-paramilitary partnership" in that country and its close linkage with the United States.[9] With appropriate modifications, similar stories could be told about Bolivia, Peru, and Ecuador. For present purposes, however, I want to shift attention briefly to Central America. There too, the past fifty years have witnessed violence on a massive scale, executed with incredible cunning and brutality. According to the Asociaciòn Centroamericana de Familiares de Detenidos-Desaparecidos (ACAFADE), killings and disappearances have been rampant in Central America especially during the 1980s. In Honduras, the number of disappearances at the hands of the Honduran military had by 1988 reached 140, while the operation of military and paramilitary death squads was steadily on the rise. In El Salvador, nine years of civil war had by the same date left some 60,000 civilians killed and 7,000 disappeared, while in Guatemala ACAFADE was investigating the cases of over 38,000 disappeared persons.[10]

Given the staggering number of victims, a few additional comments seem appropriate on the last two countries. In the case of El Salvador, one may usefully recall a report issued by Ramsey Clark, former Attorney General under President Johnson. In Clark's words:

> On January 22, 1980, a peaceful demonstration of more than 200,000 in San Salvador was fired on by the army, killing 49 and wounding hundreds. Archbishop Oscar Romero, radicalized and, in the eyes of the populace, sainted by the violence . . . denounced the government in weekly sermons heard on radios throughout the country. He publicly declared that the "most repressive sector" of the military was in control, and he opposed even nonlethal aid from the United States to the

Salvadoran military. In his last sermon, the day before he was murdered, he said: "No soldier is obliged to obey an order contrary to the law of God. . . . Thou shalt not kill." He was assassinated on March 24, 1980, as he led prayers in the chapel of the cancer hospital where he lived. At his funeral, 75,000 mourners were dispersed with grenades and rifle fire, leaving more than 30 dead and 400 injured. . . . A week after Romero's murder, the U.S. Congress appropriated $5.7 million in additional military aid to strengthen the Salvadoran army.[11]

In his opposition to the military, Archbishop Romero gave an example of "prophetic witness" by daring to "speak truth to power"—and he was crushed as many prophetic witnesses before him. Unfortunately, his assassination did not bring to an end the ordeal of witnessing. In December of 1980, three Maryknoll nuns and a lay volunteer were raped and murdered on the road from the airport to the capital. A year later—still according to Ramsey Clark—hundreds of Salvadorans, mostly women and children, "were murdered at El Mozote by troops trained in the United States."[12]

If possible, the situation in Guatemala has been even more somber and gruesome. According to another documentary report published in 1988, some 40,000 people had disappeared in Guatemala since 1965— which equals 44 percent of the 90,000 disappeared persons in all of Latin America during that period. In addition, some 100,000 Guatemalans had been killed by military and paramilitary forces, while additional hundreds of thousands were displaced, forced into "model cities," or were surviving in the mountains.[13] Much of the violence was directed against the native Indian population: the Mayans. Theirs has been a particularly bitter history. During the three centuries that Guatemala was ruled by Spain (1520 to 1820), Mayan lands were expropriated while Mayan labor was coerced through systems of tributory or compulsory semi-slavery. During the nineteenth and twentieth centuries, the country was ruled by a series of dictators, while the nation's economy came increasingly under British and North American influence or control. As is generally acknowledged, the United Fruit Company (aided by the CIA) was directly responsible for toppling the democratically elected government of Jacobo Arbenz in 1954—an event ushering in decades of political violence ("*la violencia*") carried out with unspeakable brutality: whole villages were massacred, rivers poisoned, forests burned down. Here is one report of a village massacre:

> They left the poor mothers hanging, one with a little baby on her back. Three other children were on top of her, hanging. They strangled them;

they cut the throats of the little ones. Some of them, they grabbed by their arms and stoned them against the floor, on their little heads. My husband buried them. You can't leave them for the dogs to eat.[14]

So far, little or no effort has been made to bring the guilty to justice.

Paul Ricoeur on Social Imagination

After this plunge into memory-work—in Latin America mainly a remembrance of suffering—I want to return to the issue of social imagination, and especially the role of imagination in regenerating and re-orienting social life (in accordance with Bonafini's words: "Our country is different from his . . ."). Contemporary philosophy has devoted considerable attention to the role of imagination and the "imaginary," examining the topic from a great variety of theoretical angles.[15] One of the most helpful and insightful treatments of the topic, in my view, has been provided by Paul Ricoeur. In an essay titled "Imagination in Discourse and Action," Ricoeur highlights the linkage between imagination and semantic innovation or the "metaphorical redescription" of reality. Instead of deprecating imagination as flawed or decayed perception, he writes, the idea of "metaphorical redescription" brings into view a possible change of semantic fields: "The theory of metaphor invites us to relate the imagination to a certain type of language use, more precisely, to see in it an aspect of semantic innovation characteristic of the metaphorical uses of language." What this means is that imagination is basically the apperception, or sudden realization, of a new kind of pertinence: of a new way of seeing and articulating the world by means of a "restructuring of semantic fields." For Ricoeur, this view concurs with the teachings of the later Wittgenstein (as well as with Heidegger's *Being and Time*). More crucial still, redescription coheres with Kant's view of productive imagination, and especially with the Kantian theory of "schematism," where schematism means a way of giving images to understanding. In this productive schematization, he notes, seeing appears basically as "seeing as": "We see old age as the close of the day, time as a beggar, nature as a temple or living pillars, and so forth."[16]

In his essay, Ricoeur is intent on differentiating imagination from private whim or empty day-dreaming. Although liberating us from the bondage of external reality, imagination puts us in touch with deeper human longings and aspirations—which he calls (somewhat ambiguously) a "second-order reference." What is suspended or bracketed in imagination is only a naïve type of empiricism or objectivism, that is, an "ontic" reference to objects governed by empirical interests, especially the interest in "controlling and manipulating" the world. But this is only part of the story. "By holding in abeyance this [manipulative] interest and the sphere of meaning it governs," he observes, in a Heideggerian vein, "poetic discourse allows our deep-seated insertion in the life-world to emerge; it allows the ontological tie uniting our being to other beings and to Being to be articulated." This linkage of imagination with deep-seated aspirations is particularly important in the field of social practice or action—an arena in which "redescription" shades over into, or gives way to, projective re-orientation and transformation. Taking some cues from Kant's *Critique of Judgment,* Ricoeur at this point articulates the transition to practice as a move from "I see" or "I say" (in discourse) to the mode of "I do" or "I can" (in action), that is, from the metaphorical "seeing as" to a transformative reshaping as. In his words: "The form of the practical imaginary has its linguistic equivalent in expressions such as: I could do this or that, if I wanted. . . . It is in the realm of the [practical-social] imaginary that I try out my capacity to do something, that I take the measure of 'I can'."[17]

It is precisely in the field of social action or the "social imaginary" that Ricoeur's argument proves to be most instructive. His essay takes its bearings here from Karl Mannheim's famous *Ideology and Utopia* (first published in 1929). In that work, Mannheim had basically deprecated ideology as a from of distortion and repression, while celebrating utopia as the path to liberating innovation. Ricoeur follows Mannheim in accepting the distinction between ideology and utopia; however, he departs from Mannheim by re-interpreting the meaning of both terms and by detecting a basic tension or polarity operating within each of these concepts. Regarding ideology, he rejects Mannheim's purely pejorative (and quasi-Marxist) reduction of the term to distortion. Following Max Weber and Lévi-Strauss, Ricoeur views ideology (in one of its senses) as a primary mode of the "social imaginary," that is, as a synonym for the symbolic constitution of social ties. No society, in his account, could operate without this primary form of symbolization, without this practical mode of "seeing as" and reshaping as. In the terminology of Hans-Georg Gadamer, ideology on this level appears equivalent to the role of "pre-judgments"—which (for Gadamer) are constitutive of social experience and understanding as such. In Ricoeur's words, ideology in this sense

seems related to the need every group has to give itself an *image,* to "represent" itself, in the theoretical sense of the word, to put itself on stage, to play itself. Perhaps no social group can exist without this indirect relation to its own being through a representation of itself. . . . In truth, we cannot speak of a real activity which would be [radically] pre-ideological or non-ideological. . . . All that Marx contributes which is new and unquestionably valid stands out against this initial background of the symbolic constitution of social ties in general.[18]

Standing over against this "positive" or integrative side of ideology looms a "negative" or pejorative meaning of the term: its role as an instrument of political distortion, dissimulation, and repression. As Ricoeur notes: "The function of dissimulation clearly surpasses that of integration when ideological representations are monitored by the system of authority in a given society." The motive for this monitoring resides in the desire of public power or authority to "make itself legitimate," an ambition that usually involves the manipulative abuse of the resources of primary symbolization. Once instrumentalized by political elites, ideology turns into a dubious or unwarranted "prejudgment," that is, into a mere prejudice shielded from critical scrutiny. It was this uncritical acceptance of the *idola fori* that modern Enlightenment sought to challenge—and Marx simply followed in its footstep: "His own contribution concerns the legitimating function of ideology with respect to the relations of domination stemming from the division into classes and the class struggle." For Ricoeur, a similar tension or polarity operates inside the field of "utopia" seen as the arena of social re-orientation and projective transformation. In his account, the central idea here is that of a lack or constitutive absence: the idea "of *nowhere* implied by the word itself and by Thomas More's description." Crucial to the notion of utopia is the aspect of displacement, exodus, and re-spatialization. For it is "beginning from this strange spatial extraterritoriality—this non-place in the literal sense of the word," he writes, "that we can take a fresh look at our reality, in relation to which nothing can henceforth be taken for granted. The field of the possible now extends out beyond the real." The question for Ricoeur is whether and how imagination can play its role in this ek-static enterprise, in this "leap outside" ordinary (ontic) reality. In contrast to the primary function of ideology of providing for social integration, utopia basically is tied to the counter-function of "social subversion." In this respect, utopia joins or complements the second or "negative" meaning of ideology, namely, by unraveling distortion, dissimulation, and repression, and by suggesting "other ways" of organizing social, economic, and political relations.[19]

In projecting such "other ways," the social imaginary of utopia displays its important and constructive role in social life. However, just as in the case of ideology, Ricoeur finds in utopia also a "negative counterpart," a kind of pathological derailment: namely, the tendency toward totalization, toward eschatological, millennarian, and possibly totalitarian social schemes. Despite its uplifting and empowering features, he observes, we cannot fail to detect in utopia also "a tendency to hold reality in the throes of a dream, a fixation on perfectionist designs." Once this fixation triumphs, utopia falls pray to Manichean blueprints, to the "logic of all or nothing," coupled with the disdain for intermediary degrees or mediating judgments. A further feature of totalizing utopias is the neglect of memory-work, that is, the lofty disregard of situated experiences, including the agonies and travails of ordinary people in their historical contexts. Ricoeur's basic conclusion is the need to correlate or complement ideology and utopia, both terms taken in their "most constructive" and empowering senses. Although seemingly at odds, he notes, ideological integration and utopian subversion "dialectically imply one another." Thus, even the most "conservative" ideology bent on conformist integration is a social imaginary only by virtue of a "gap"—the lurking possibility of social reconfiguration and transformation. Conversely, although appearing utterly "ek-centric," utopia is not simply a synonym for escapism and wishful thinking. The essay invokes at this point a poem by Paul Celan entitled "A Step Outside the Human," where Celan depicts utopia in these terms: "Inside a sphere directed towards the human, but excentric." As Ricoeur comments: "We see the paradox here. It has two sides: On the one hand, there is no movement towards what is human which is not first excentric; on the other, elsewhere leads here."[20]

Liberating Imagination: Dussel and Menchú

From this excursion into contemporary philosophy—more particularly Ricoeur's account of social imagination—permit me to return to a more concretely situated mode of social imagining: an imagining nurtured by Latin American experience. One of the most innovative and "imaginative" Latin American thinkers today is the Argentine (or Argentine-Mexican) philosopher Enrique Dussel, known chiefly for his formulation of a "philosophy of liberation." In his formative philosophical experience, Dussel was strongly influenced by the teachings of Heidegger, Ricoeur, and Gadamer. With Heidegger he shares, among other things, the emphasis on concretely situated human existence, on *Dasein* as "being-in-the-world," where "world" is co-constitutive of human being. With all three thinkers he shares a commitment to hermeneutics or hermeneutical interpretation, that is, the conviction that seeing is always a "seeing as" and hence action an imagining or "shaping as" inspired by sedimented memories and pre-judgments. In pursuing his intellectual trajectory, Dussel was increasingly attracted to the writings of Emmanuel Levinas—although the latter never fully eclipsed his earlier philosophical commitments. What attracted him in Levinas's work was especially the debunking of egocentrism, that is, the insistence on non-totality in the sense of an openness to the ethical demands of the "Other"—where "Other" stands basically for the disadvantaged: "the poor, the stranger, the widow, the orphan." What emerged from this confluence of mentors was (what Michael Barber terms) an "ethical hermeneutics," that is, a hermeneutics that takes its departure from the vantage of the marginalized and oppressed (paralleling the "preferential option for the poor" favored by liberation theology).[21]

Another distinctive feature of Dussel's approach is the so-called analectical mode of reasoning and interacting, a mode that differs from Hegel's "dialectical" method by refusing to "sublate" the self/other relation in a higher synthesis (which would incorporate and "totalize" the Other and thereby negate the Other's otherness). In Dussel's own words:

> The *dia*-lectic method is the path that the totality realizes within itself. . . . What we are discussing now is a method (or the explicit domain of the conditions of possibility) which begins from the Other as free, as one beyond the system of the totality; which begins, then, from the Other's word, from the revelation of the Other, and which, trusting in the Other's word, labors, works, serves, and creates.[22]

From an analectical angle, interaction with the Other involves indeed dialogue, but one that respects fully the gap (*dia*) between self and other—with the result that the Other can be thematized only as "analogical," never simply as alter ego (or replica of the self). In Dussel's view, Western philosophy has never fully acknowledged this analogical otherness. This is particularly true of modern European thought, which has been deeply marred by "Eurocentrism"—a myopia closely linked with colonialism and imperialism. This kind of Eurocentrism goes back to 1492 and its tragic aftermath. As Dussel writes in his *The Invention of the Americas*, subtitled *Eclipse of the "Other" and the Myth of Modernity:*

> The birthdate of modernity is 1492. . . . Whereas modernity gestated in the free, creative medieval European cities, it came to birth in Europe's confrontation with the Other. By controlling, conquering, and violating

the Other, Europe defined itself as discoverer, conquistador, and colonizer of an alterity likewise constitutive of modernity. Europe never discovered (*des-cubierto*) this Other *as* Other but covered over (*encubierto*) the Other as part of the same: i.e., Europe. Modernity dawned in 1492 and with it the myth of a special kind of sacrificial violence which eventually eclipsed whatever was non-European.[23]

Although emphasizing and affirming the Other's distinctness and integrity, Dussel does not erect otherness into a shibboleth—which would open an unbridgeable gulf between peoples. Countering certain (postmodern) claims of radical separateness and incommensurability, he is intent on fostering dialogue—in an analectical-analogical manner. To avoid a vapid consensualism, however, such dialogue in his view has to embrace memory-work: above all, by recollecting the asymmetry between oppressor and oppressed. As he writes: "I want to develop a philosophy of dialogue as part of a philosophy of liberation of the oppressed, the excommunicated, the excluded, the Other. It will be necessary [hence] to analyze the historical, hermeneutical conditions of the possibility of intercultural communication." Guarding against historical amnesia, such a hermeneutics has to steer clear of a facile universalism or globalism neglectful of social-historical experiences. In this respect, Dussel sides with the Peruvian philosopher Augusto Salazar Bondy, who counsels vigilance against hegemonic or imperialist forms of synthesis and universal integration. The only way to pursue universalization, for Dussel, is to build from the ground up, by taking seriously the sufferings of the marginalized and oppressed in their concrete particularity. As he observes pointedly in an essay on inter-faith relations:

> Within the dialogues of the periphery have arisen differences among Africa, Asia, Latin America, and between center and periphery. Some bridges offering possible solutions have also arisen, first of all, for understanding the position of the Other, and then, for arriving at some method and some categories which might be capable of opening to a future *mundial* theology. This new analogical totality will be built up in the twenty-first century beginning from affirmed and developed particularisms (among these, as particulars, Europe and the United States).[24]

As one should note well, in starting from particularity Dussel does not simply deny universalizing hopes and aspirations. Contrary to the charges of some of his critics, he is not unaware of the perils of a self-centered or self-enclosed particularism, and above all, of the dangers of an untutored and aggressive "populism."[25] As an avenue to liberation, dialogue in his view has to be critical of both external and internal forms of oppression, that is, of both colonialism and domestic-indigenous modes of resentment and hostility. In Barber's words: as opposed to sheer negation or negativity, "authentic liberation springs neither from hatred nor a desire for struggle in itself, but is moved by love and by appreciation for the value of the exterior [other] culture." An illustrious exemplar of this attitude (of prophetic witness), for Dussel, was Bartholemé de las Casas, the Spanish priest who, at the time of the conquest, "underwent tutelage at the hands of the oppressed and learned to admire the beauty, culture, and goodness of the indigenous, the new, the Other." In a Levinasian sense, Las Casas discovered the "exteriority" of indigenous peoples in their positivity and "out of his love begins a critique of their unjust totalization." In his *The Invention of the Americas,* Dussel ably summarizes the preconditions of a non-imperialist, analogical dialogue of liberation. The idea of such a dialogue, he writes,

> should not (1) fall into the facile optimism of a rationalist, abstract universalism that would conflate universality with Eurocentrism and modernizing developmentalism (as the [recent] Frankfurt School is inclined to do); nor should it (2) lapse into irrationality, incommunicability, or incommensurability of discourses that are typical of many postmoderns. The philosophy of liberation affirms that rationality can establish a dialogue with the reason of the Other, as an alternative reason. Today, such rationality must deny the irrational sacrificial myth of modernity as well as affirm (subsume in a liberating project) the emancipative tendencies of the Enlightenment and modernity within a new transmodernity.[26]

By way of conclusion I want to descend still more deeply into Latin American agonies, into the liberating struggles waged in Latin America, by calling attention to, and saluting briefly, a great Guatemalan writer, exile, and Nobel laureate: Rigoberta Menchú. The life-story of Rigoberta Menchú replicates the broader history of her people, the Mayan Indians: their long-standing suffering and exploitation, but also their stubborn defiance and untamed longing for freedom. Born in 1959 into a poor peasant family, she spent her childhood helping her family with farm and plantation work. While still a teenager, she became involved in social reform and women's rights movements, and her family was soon accused of being involved in guerrilla activities. Her father Vincente was imprisoned and tortured and, on his release, joined the recently founded Committee of Peasant Union (CUC), an organization in which Rigoberta also became a member. In 1979, her brother was arrested, tortured, and killed by the army. A year later, her father was killed when security forces in the capital stormed the Spanish Embassy in which he and some other peasants had sought refuge. Shortly afterwards, her mother also died after having been arrested and raped. These grim experiences only further radicalized Rigoberta. In 1980 she figured prominently in a strike organized by CUC, and in May 1981 she was active in large-scale demonstrations in the capital. Faced with repeated threats of torture and killing, she first went into hiding and finally fled to Mexico where she soon co-founded the United Representation of Guatemalan Opposition, while also participating in the National Coordinating Committee of CUC. In 1992, precisely five hundred years after Columbus's arrival in America, she was awarded the Nobel Peace Prize for her role as "a vivid symbol of peace and reconciliation across ethnic, cultural and social dividing lines."[27]

Let me end with a few lines from Rigoberta's book *Crossing Borders* (of 1998), from a marvelous chapter on "Understanding and Accepting Diversity" that resonates with Dussel's "ethical hermeneutics" and also with his spirit of liberation:

Indigenous peoples [today] are always on the periphery. They are never the ones who make decisions. It is our responsibility to see that one day these people become the central protagonists of their own destiny and culture. The power we feel crushing us is the power to buy, to sell, and to earn: the power of intolerance, arrogance, silence, indifference and insensitivity. I believe that there are important values, and beautiful things, that can never be bought or sold. They include the memory of indigenous peoples. They include life itself. . . . It is something we cultivate. There is a time to sow, a time to grow, and a time to reap.[28]

PART II

SOME EXEMPLARY VOICES

CHAPTER 7

REASON, FAITH, AND POLITICS

A Journey to Muslim Andalusia

As many times before in human history, reason and faith are at loggerheads today. What renders our contemporary situation distinctive, however, is the intensity of the confrontation and the radicality of opposing claims. Ever since the Enlightenment, modern philosophy—trusting in "unaided" reason alone—has launched an assault on traditional dogmas and all kinds of rationally unvalidated premises and beliefs. The situation is further aggravated by the steady advances of modern science and the premium placed in our time on scientific and technological expertise—a premium that militates against any reliance on untested assumptions (thereby equating faith with ignorance). Unsurprisingly, the modern assault on faith has engendered a vigorous counter-offensive against modern rationality, an offensive operating both inside and outside of academia. In academic and literary circles, this offensive tends to take the form of a radical fideism (sometimes curiously allied with philosophical agnosticism)—a posture bent on debunking philosophical reasoning as such in favor of an untrammeled spirituality or self-styled transcendentalism. In more concrete social contexts, anti-rationalism often surfaces as a wholesale attack on modern forms of public life, an attack drawing inspiration from premodern autocratic or "theocratic" conceptions of politics. To a large extent, the revolutionary upheavals of modernity thus continue to shape contemporary thought and practice, now on a global scale: akin to post-revolutionary France, many societies around the world today are internally split—into the factions of the "Black" and the "Red," that is, the factions representing respectively traditional faith and emancipatory reason.[1]

Viewed against this background, the relation between reason and faith is not merely of detached scholarly interest, but reveals itself as part of a profound historical drama. This does not mean, of course, that there is no room for scholarly inquiry; in fact, there is today a sprawling literature on the topic.[2] What is frequently neglected, however, is the contextual character of the topic—the aspect that there is a third dimension operative in the reason-faith relation. This dimension is the domain of politics or political praxis, a domain powerfully molding the character of the relation. The constellation of factors is clearly evident in the case of Islam. As most people will agree, the conflict between reason and faith is nowhere as intense and troubling today as in the context of Islamic civilization. This clash and its repercussions provide ample grist for Western media and journalistic denunciations of "fundamentalism." What media accounts usually ignore, however, is the fact that this same Islamic civilization also provides resources for tackling the conflict and for nurturing a fruitful, though always tentative reconciliation under politically tolerant auspices. To discover these resources it is necessary to travel back in time to the great age of Islamic philosophy, particularly to the period of Moorish or Arabic Spain. The following presentation hence takes the form of a "journey to Andalusia," more specifically: a journey to that flourishing Andalusian empire that, at its height, counted among its luminaries the great philosopher Ibn Rushd, known in the West as Averroes. The discussion proceeds in three steps. The first section explores the arguments that Ibn Rushd himself advanced on the topic of the relation between reason and faith (or philosophy and religion), mainly in a text popularly known as *Fasl al-maqal* or simply *Fasl*. In a second step, attention shifts to Ibn Rushd's broader political conception in which the nexus of philosophy and religion necessarily played a major part. By way of conclusion, an effort will be made to draw out the implications of Ibn Rushd's arguments for contemporary intellectual and political tensions in the Muslim world and, beyond that, for the emergence of a multicultural global polity.

Philosophy and Faith as "Milk-Sisters"

Before proceeding further, some historical recollections seem in order. Ibn Rushd—whose full name was Abu'l Walid Muhammad ibn Ahmad ibn Muhammad ibn Rushd—is also known as the philosopher of Cordoba, which then was a center of "Western" Islam (comprising the Maghrib and Southern Spain). He was born in Cordoba in 1126 into a distinguished family of lawyers—his grandfather and father having served there as chief justices—and he himself came to occupy a high legal position in that city (following the so-called Malikite school of law). Having spent his later years at the caliph's court in Marrakesh and having died there in 1198, his body was returned home and buried again in Cordoba. Although greatly innovative and distinguished, Ibn Rushd was by no means the first serious philosopher—in the classical Greek sense of philosophy—in the broad ambit of Islamic civilization, and not even within the narrower confines of Western Islam. In the broader Islamic context, he was preceded by such illustrious "Eastern" thinkers as al-Farabi (870–950) and Ibn Sina (Avicenna, 980–1037). In the confines of the Western, Andalusian world, his philosophical inquires could build on the initiative of such thinkers as Ibn Masarra (883–931), Ibn Bajja (Avempace, 1106–1138), and Ibn Tufayl (d.1185)—although it appears difficult to establish any direct influence of their writings on the young Cordoban. As it happens, little is known about Ibn Rushd's properly philosophical training, although there is ample evidence testifying to his firm legal education and also to his thorough training in medicine and his exposure to some works of contemporary theology (*kalam*), especially works of the Ash'arite school.

Despite its increasingly prominent role, it is important to remember that philosophy—or "*falsafa*"—encountered severe suspicions and restrictions in the context of the Islamic civilization of the time. For one thing, due to its Greek origins, philosophy was often seen as a foreign import designed to undermine a basically Arabic-Islamic culture. As Oliver Leaman notes, Greek philosophy had been introduced through a wave of translations from the eighth century onward, but its "foreign nature" was "bitterly resented and disparaged by the intellectual elite of the Islamic world."[3] This intellectual elite included above all the lawyers or practitioners of jurisprudence (*fiqh*) who, insisting on the practicality of Islamic law, were averse to theoretical speculation. In this connection it is worth remembering that—in entering the Islamic world—philosophy presented itself no longer in its strictly classical mode but in a late-Hellenistic garb marked by a heavy dose of Neoplatonism and a certain penchant for speculative-mystical insight. The Islamic elite most vigorously opposed to the inroad of philosophy, however, was the group of religious clerics and theologians (*mutakallimun*) intent on preserving or safeguarding the literal integrity of sacred scriptures as well as their own doctrinal authority and preeminence, which was challenged by philosophical questioning. The power wielded by these clerics was formidable as they could brand philosophical opinions either as heresy (*bida*) or else as outright unbelief (*kufr*), the latter being punishable by death. As a result of these and other counter-offensives, the status of philosophy in the Islamic world tended to be precarious, with the relation between reason and faith often resembling a battlefield. The mutually destructive effects of this conflict were vividly highlighted by a Persian scholar, Nasir-e Khosraw, who commented around 1064:

> As the [clerics] have denounced as infidels the students of created things, the explorers of the how and why have become silent and the practitioners of science have turned mute so that ignorance has over-powered the people. . . . In this land, nobody now remains who is capa-ble of uniting the practice of true religion, which is the product of the Holy Spirit, with the knowledge of creation, which is an emblem of phi-losophy. The philosopher relegates the so-called scholars [clerics] to the rank of beasts and on account of their ignorance despises the religion of Islam, while clerics declare the philosopher to be an infidel. As a result, neither true religion nor philosophy remains any more in this land.[4]

When Nasir penned these lines, the "most stunning blow to philosophy"—as George Hourani writes—had not yet been deliv-ered. This attack was mounted not by practical-minded lawyers nor by half-educated clerics but by one of the most illustrious intellec-tuals of Islamic civilization: Abu Hamid Muhammad ibn Muham-mad al-Tusi al-Shafii al-Ghazali, known as Ghazali (1058–1111). Although himself thoroughly trained in Greek philosophy, espe-cially its Neoplatonic variety, and serving for a time as head of Bagh-dad's leading university, Ghazali in his later life turned resolutely away from philosophical reasoning in favor of a reaffirmation of re-ligious orthodoxy coupled with a strong dose of trans-rational mys-ticism. In a major treatise composed around 1095, he sought to demonstrate the inability of philosophical reasoning to ground itself rationally and hence the utter "incoherence of philosophers" and the entire enterprise of philosophy (as stated in its Arabic title *Tahafut al-falasifa*). A few years later, adopting the standpoint of Is-lamic law, Ghazali proceeded to charge Muslim philosophers with various forms of heresy and disbelief (*kufr*), leaving punishment to the appropriate authorities.

Such was then the condition of philosophy when Ibn Rushd arrived at the scene: an enterprise buffeted and beleaguered from many quar-ters, including legal pragmatism, scriptural orthodoxy, and a "decon-structive" transcendentalism. His entire life-work was devoted to the task of salvaging the integrity and legitimacy of human reason and re-flection in the face of these combined attacks. In pursuing this task, he found it important to cleanse Greek philosophy from later accretions, and especially to rescue Aristotle's work from its fusion with quasi-mystical or "illuminationist" strands (a fusion often characterizing Muslim thinkers in the East).[5] In his rebuttal of Ghazali, Ibn Rushd accordingly did not attempt so much to defend the former's Neoplatonic target as rather to vindicate a more genuine Socratic-Aristotelian mode of thought; proceeding in this manner, he was able to show the inescapability of human reasoning—the fact that, in debunking philosophy, Ghazali himself had extensively relied on philosophical argumentation, thereby disclosing the "incoherence of the [presumed] incoherence" of philosophy (the title of Ibn Rushd's rebuttal, *Tahafut al-tahafut*).[6] In close conjunction with this rejoinder, Ibn Rushd sought to counter the serious legal and political charges advanced by Ghazali and orthodox clerics: those concerning the intrinsic impiety or disbelief of philosophy. To respond to these charges was the basic aim of *Fasl al-maqal*, a relatively short treatise composed around 1180.

The book (*kitab*) *Fasl al-maqal* carried originally a somewhat cumbersome title that might be transliterated as "the book of the decision or distinction of the discourse, and a determination of what there is of a connection between religion and philosophy." According to George Hourani, the title phrase *Kitab fasl al-maqal* could be rendered as "the decisive treatise" or "the book of the decision of the discourse." However, the emphasis on "decision" can be misleading if it suggests that the relation between religion and philosophy is one of arbitrary decision or choice (unless the term is taken in the difficult German sense of *Ent-scheidung*). In his own edition of the book, Hourani uses as title "Averroes on the Harmony of Religion and Philosophy"—a phrasing that is dubious or problematical in its own way. For Ibn Rushd does not simply wish to "harmonize" religion and philosophy—if by harmony one understands a fusion or synthesis between the two (something he precisely criticizes in Eastern illuminationism). Rather, the aim of the book seems to be to assert both the compatibility *and* mutual distinctness of religion and philosophy, that is, their relatedness without synthesis or coincidence. For this reason, *Kitab fasl al-maqal* might perhaps preferably be rendered as "the book of difference"—the latter term taken in the Heideggerian and Derridean sense of difference (*différance, Unterscheidung*) involving non-antithetical distinction. This sense emerges already in the opening section of the book where Ibn Rushd underscores the differential approaches taken by humans to deal with religious and philosophical "truth." Although Islamic religion establishes a distinct standard of belief, he notes, recognition of this standard is allotted or appointed "for every Muslim by the method of assent which his temperament and nature require";

for "the natures of humans are on different levels with respect to their paths to assent." A bit later, the text speaks of "the diversity of people's natural capacities and the difference of their innate dispositions with regard to assent."[7]

In speaking of differential approaches Ibn Rushd does not merely mean that, though following different paths, humans ultimately arrive at a uniform or identical formulation of (transcendent) truth. His claim is in fact more radical: although honoring a common horizon of truth, human articulations of the latter are necessarily differentiated due both to a diversity of human aptitudes and the variety of available linguistic or discursive genres. In *Fasl*—as also in his lengthier *Tahafut al-tahafut*—Ibn Rushd distinguishes basically between three kinds of discourse or reasoning (*qiyas*), which ultimately can be traced back to Aristotelian teachings: namely, demonstrative, dialectical, and rhetorical modes of speech. While the first type (*burhan*)—which might also be called the strictly logical-deductive type—proceeds from valid premises to valid conclusions, the dialectical genre relies on probable or approximate conjectures and the rhetorical genre on everyday, common-sense assumptions. As *Fasl* states: In inquiries of any kind, it is important first to have grasped or understood "the kinds of arguments and their conditions of validity and in what respects strictly theoretical (i.e., demonstrative) reasoning differs from dialectical, rhetorical and merely fallacious reasoning." This grasp, however, is not possible unless one has previously learned "what reasoning itself is and how many kinds it has" and in which way such kinds are valid or invalid. One probably need not quibble here about *Fasl*'s equation of philosophy with "demonstrative" or apodictic truth—a claim anchored in Platonic-Aristotelian metaphysics (which today seems no longer fully persuasive). More important here is the book's endeavor to link kinds of discourse with different groups of people: namely, by declaring demonstration to be the province of philosophers, dialectical conjecture the pastime of clerics and theologians (*mutakallimun*), and rhetorical speech the habitual genre of ordinary people. Even more important, in the context of Islamic religion, is the corollary claim that revealed scripture (especially the *Qur'an*) addresses itself equally to all people according to their aptitude and degree of understanding, and that its interpretation hence should not be monopolized by one group or discursive genre.[8]

To be sure, *Fasl* does not merely present an academic typology devoid of a critical edge; its significance only emerges against its historical backdrop: the siege laid to philosophy and its frequent indictment as disbelief (*kufr*). This backdrop provides profile to the book's bold opening section: its assertion that philosophical inquiry is not only not contrary to religion and revealed scripture but is in fact recommended, perhaps even demanded by the latter. "If philosophical inquiry," *Fasl* states, "is nothing more than the study of existing beings and reflection on them as indications of their maker . . . and if religious law has encouraged and urged reflection on such beings, then it is clear that such inquiry is either obligatory or at least recommended by religion." Ibn Rushd proceeds in fact to opt for the obligatory nature of inquiry (for philosophically minded people)—which is perhaps on overstatement, but one fully intelligible given the heavy onus placed on philosophy in his time. If philosophical inquiry is recommended and perhaps even commanded by religion, however, it follows that philosophers have to obtain training in all the tools and intellectual requisites necessary for their inquiry. Just as lawyers—including Muslim lawyers—have to obtain training in legal reasoning and the handling of legal categories and syllogisms, so also philosophers have to acquire and diligently cultivate the methods and pathways of philosophical reasoning. The question then becomes, How can such training be acquired and where can the appropriate methods and pathways be found? To his question Ibn Rushd offers again a bold reply, which was bound to upset many contemporary clerics. In the absence of any predecessors, he writes, present-day philosophers would have to undertake their inquiries "from scratch"—which is a nearly impossible task for any one person or generation. Fortunately, the situation was different:

> But if someone other than ourselves has already examined that subject, it is clear that we ought to seek help towards our goal from what has been said by such a predecessor on the subject, regardless of whether this other one shares our religion or not. For when a correct operation is performed with a certain instrument, no account is taken . . . of whether the instrument belongs to one who shares our religion or to one who does not, so long as it fulfills the conditions of correctness. By "those who do not share our religion" I refer to those ancients who studied these matters before Islam [i.e., the Greeks].[9]

By appealing to resources outside Islamic culture and religion, Ibn Rushd did not at all seek to place himself—or any philosopher for that matter—beyond the pale of his/her social community or *umma*. The charge is sometimes advanced that, by distinguishing between "theory" and mere rhetoric, medieval Muslim philosophers aimed to establish an invidious and divisive hierarchy, one that allowed them to celebrate arrogantly their "esoteric" wisdom while snubbing the unwashed multitudes of believers.[10] Although perhaps applicable to some Neoplatonists and illuminationists, the charge is completely un-founded in the case of Ibn Rushd. As a good Aristotelian, Ibn Rushd was firmly committed to a shared horizon of social-political praxis, a horizon linking together people of the most diverse aptitudes. Follow-ing Aristotle's ethical teachings, he saw the chief goal of practical life in the cultivation of "virtue," above all the fostering of sound "judg-ment" and the commitment to justice—a goal that was fully supported by sacred scripture (*Qur'an*) and genuine religion in general. Given this shared framework of praxis, the role of the philosopher was not that of the iconoclast or haughty schoolmaster, but of an engaged, unpreten-tious counselor—counseling pursuit of the "good life" and avoidance of destructive-fanatical excesses. Ibn Rushd's commitment to a shared horizon of praxis is evident in *Fasl* where he writes that, with regard to practical matters, everyone agrees that "the truth about them should be disclosed to all people alike," adding that "to reach concurrence in these matters we consider it sufficient that the question at issue should have been widely discussed" and that "no report of controversy should have been handed down to us." The same commitment is also evident in his stipulation that, ideally, philosophers should have two qualities: first, natural intelligence, and second, "religious integrity and practical virtue"—with the second quality being a disposition ex-pected among all members of a community.[11]

Agreement on practical matters, of course, was not the primary concern of *Fasl;* much more central were raging disputes regarding theoretical, doctrinal, or theological issues. On a rudimentary level, orthodox literalists routinely objected to the philosophers' penchant for a flexible, metaphorical interpretation of scripture. However, the situation was more complex as all Muslims—including most clerics and theologians—were agreed on the need of a differentiated reading: some passages were held to be accessible to a literal approach while others required a metaphorical exegesis. Differently phrased: some passages readily disclosed their manifest or apparent meaning (*zahir*) while others demanded exploration of a deeper, recessed or hidden meaning (*batin*). Faithful to his practical Aristotelian leanings, Ibn Rushd was by no means eager to disturb the public consensus (*ijma*) to the extent that it was firmly established in such scriptural matters. The problem arose in the absence of such consensus, that is, in all those— quite extensive—areas of scripture where neither Muslims at large nor the scholarly community offered any clear guidance. It was in this do-main that Ibn Rushd sought to vindicate the legitimacy and impor-tance of philosophical exegesis. As he wrote, consensus in such scriptural matters can "never be reached with certainty, as it can be in practical matters"; for, to do so, one would have to specify a given historical period, have knowledge of all the scholars existing in that period, and finally establish that all these scholars were firmly agreed regarding the precise dividing line "between apparent and inner or recessed meaning of scripture." Such a task, however, generally exceeds human capabilities. Hence, although concurrence in practical matters may be possible, "in matters of doctrine [or doctrinal interpretation] the case is different."[12]

For Ibn Rushd, the task of a metaphorical or non-literal reading of scripture—in non-consensual areas—should be consigned to philosophers, mainly because they are trained in clear reasoning and (still more important) because their inquiries are ultimately directed toward "truth" (the same horizon of truth disclosed in revealed scripture). In the words of *Fasl:* If lawyers are routinely entitled to offer interpretations in cases of religious law (*shari'ah*), "with how much more propriety is this done by the guardians of philosophical (demonstrative) reasoning." By contrast, *Fasl* throws doubt on the ability of clerics and would-be theologians (*mutakallimun*) to perform deeper exegesis (*batin*): by being harnessed to merely probable conjectures, such clerics were liable to move back and forth randomly between recessed and apparent, common-sense meaning, thereby ending up in a confused mélange of philosophy and religion jeopardizing the integrity of both. To some extent, this procedure was also manifest in some Eastern Muslim thinkers who were prone to mix philosophical reasoning with intuitive-esoteric speculation. Although buttressing the legitimacy of philosophical exegesis—one should note—*Fasl* is careful to circumscribe and delimit the philosopher's role in several ways. First of all, as mentioned before, the philosopher is also part of a practical community and not merely an external spectator. This stipulation is further solidified by a number of corollaries and caveats. For Ibn Rushd, not everyone can indiscriminately be counted as a philosopher, but only someone with proper training and proven competence in that field. (Writing of commentaries on classical texts would presumably establish competence.) What Ibn Rushd seems to guard against here is the role of half-educated charlatans and their frequently disorienting effect on social life. Closely associated with this caveat is the proviso that philosophers should not randomly disclose their findings but rather be circumspect in their speech and actions. Without endorsing esotericism or hermeticism, Ibn Rushd here simply seems to wish to counteract the temptation of philosophers to degenerate into demagogues or public agitators bent on manipulating public opinion (which is unprepared, or not sufficiently educated, to resist or critically screen ideological appeals).[13]

Within these specified limits and provisos, depth interpretation—the excavation of hidden from apparent meanings—was to be chiefly the task of philosophers, a task that they necessarily had to shoulder in the case of opaque or confusing textual passages. In the performance of this task, philosophers for Ibn Rushd should not be subject to the reprimands and often severe penalties demanded by clerics and their theological allies. In his *Tahafut al-falasifa* and other writings, Ghazali had attacked a great number of unorthodox or "non-scriptural" opinions of philosophers (especially of Ibn Sina); three such opinions, however, he had earmarked for particularly harsh indictment by condemning them not merely as heretical but as signs of disbelief (*kufr*). These three opinions or alleged doctrines had to do with the "eternity" of the world, the character of divine knowledge, and the issue of bodily resurrection. While responding to "Abu Hamid" (i.e., Ghazali) in his *Tahafut al-tahafut* in a comprehensive manner covering multiple issues, Ibn Rushd in *Fasl* limits himself to rebutting the three central or most incriminating charges. As one should note, the strategy of *Fasl* is again not to vindicate Eastern or Neoplatonic philosophy as such, but rather to defend Aristotle's teachings. This strategy is immediately evident in the issue of divine knowledge to which Ibn Rushd turns first of all. Here a version of Neoplatonic philosophy—bent on elevating the divine over the mundane, the absolute over the contingent—had asserted that divine knowledge was of a universal kind in which all finite particulars vanished or disappeared. Abu Hamid had stylized this view into the claim that God "does not know particulars at all" and had attacked it as evidence of the denial of God's omniscience and omnipotence. While granting the lopsidedness of the view, *Fasl* proceeds to "deconstruct" the latter charge by showing it to be inapplicable to classical Aristotelian teachings.[14]

To Ibn Rushd, as a good Aristotelian, it was clear that knowledge or reasoning of any kind involves a correlation of universals and particulars. Hence, he could not readily subscribe to a speculative metaphysics (as described and critiqued by Ghazali). Differently phrased: divine knowledge and human knowledge could not be radically separated—but they could also not be simply collapsed or identified (leading to a charge of immanentism). Congruent with his typology of levels or modes of understanding, Ibn Rushd here resorts again to a non-antithetical differentiation of genres. With regard to knowledge of particulars, he writes, classical "Peripatetic" philosophers hold "that God the Exalted knows them in a way which is not of the same kind as our way of knowing them." For, while human knowledge of particulars is tied to and dependent on concrete objects, God's knowledge is starkly different by being the source and origin of all objects and existing things. Moreover, the stress of Peripatetics on differentiated forms of knowing extends not only to particulars but also to universals; "for the universals known to us are the effects of the nature of existing things, while in God's knowledge the reverse is the case." For Ibn Rushd, to collapse the different kinds of knowing means to collapse and identify the character of distinct, and even opposite things—which is "the extreme of ignorance." Given the differential relations of humans and the divine, he insists, there exists in principle no uniform definition "embracing both kinds of knowing at once, as the theologians in our time imagine." If this is so, then philosophers are clear of the charge that God does not or cannot know particulars (in a certain way). Hence, with regard to this issue, there was no point in arguing about the orthodoxy or heterodoxy of philosophers, and especially of debating "whether to call them unbelievers (*kafirs*) or not."[15]

The second charge involved the (alleged) belief in the "eternity" of the world—a belief that Ghazali and a host of clerics denounced as undermining God's sovereign omnipotence as creator "*ex nihilo.*" This point was clearly a Pandora's box and a hornet's nest for philosophers as it involves the status of temporality or time. If creation "out of nothing" includes the creation of time, and if this creation is said to happen temporally "before time," then there seems to be an incoherence in creation as it seems to presuppose what it calls into being. In his response, Ibn Rushd does not simply assert such incoherence—which would have further fueled clerical animosity. Instead, he limits himself in *Fasl* to showing, first of all, that the opinions of philosophers *and* Muslim theologians differ greatly on the problem of creation and eternity and, second, that even sacred scripture does not unequivocally assert creation "*ex nihilo.*" Regarding the opinions of philosophers and theologians, both agree on the status of polar extremes: namely, that some things (objects) are entirely created in time, while something else is uncreated and eternal—this being God, "the sustainer of the universe." However, there is a third class of being whose character is unclear: the status of "the world as a whole." Here, some writers approximate this status to createdness, while others ascribe it to God's eternal being; some view temporality as moving infinitely into the future, while others see it as stretching also infinitely into the past. For Ibn Rushd, disputes in this domain are not really substantial and "almost resolvable into a disagreement about naming" (involving the meaning of creation and eternity). In any event, the different views about the world "are not so far apart that some of them should be called irreligious (*kufr*) and others not." This conclusion is further buttressed for Ibn Rushd by the testimony of sacred scripture, which affirms nowhere that God "existed with absolutely nothing else" and hence created radically "*ex nihilo.*" Thus, for instance the verse that states that "God created the heavens and the earth in six days, and His throne was on the water" (*Qur'an*, 11: 7) clearly implies (in its manifest meaning) that there was something before creation, namely the throne and the water. Treating passages like this, even theologians were forced to adopt a metaphorical reading— which they attacked in the case of philosophers.[16]

The situation with regard to the third issue—bodily resurrection— is similar, and Ibn Rushd's response follows in many respects his previous arguments. To begin with, he points again to the (limited) range within which scholarly disagreement in scriptural matters is legitimate: there are passages of scripture where consensus (*ijma*) stipulates a literal reading, while some other passages are consensually open to metaphorical or allegorical reading. Between them there is a field where interpretative method is not settled; in Ibn Rushd's view, the issue of bodily resurrection belongs to this field and hence allows for different readings or construals. Although scripture definitively and unequivocally establishes the prospect of a future life (hence barring disagreement on this point), it leaves open the character of this future life and the precise meaning of resurrection. In *Fasl*, Ibn Rushd does not fully explore this question, limiting himself to brief suggestions. However, in a sequel to *Fasl*, the basic issues are neatly profiled (together with indications of his own view). As he observes there, there are basically three positions regarding the future life and resurrection. According to orthodox literalists, resurrection in the world to come involves the revival of the same body that exists in the present world. According to some theologians and Neoplatonic philosophers, life in the world to come means the cessation of the physical body and only the survival of the soul or spirit. According to Ibn Rushd, however, a third position is possible: one that maintains the notion of "bodily" resurrection while differentiating between the meaning of "body" in the present and the future world. As he writes, the latter position holds that resurrection is "corporeal," but that "corporeality existing in the life beyond differs from the corporeality of this life in that the latter is perishable while the former is immortal." Although leaning perhaps toward this third option, Ibn Rushd in that context does not urge its adoption but merely states that, in this question, it is "every man's duty to believe whatever his study leads him to conclude"—provided that the basic tenet of a future life is not denied. Similarly, in *Fasl*, he simply notes that "a scholar who commits an error in this matter is excused, while one who is correct receives thanks or a reward."[17]

The concluding section of *Fasl* returns to the basic and more general issue of the relation between religion and philosophy, scriptural faith and reasoning. Proceeding from the defense of philosophical inquiry to an offensive against its inveterate detractors, Ibn Rushd sharply rebukes the latter for their ill-designed machinations. The target here are again the clerics and would-be theologians who, by moving randomly between faith and reason, have been the cause both of intellectual confusion and of social conflict and dissensus. These people, he writes, follow neither the common-sense beliefs of ordinary people nor the rules of rational inquiry: they diverge from ordinary people because their methods are "more obscure than the methods common to the majority" and they diverge from philosophy because, on inspection, their methods are "found deficient in the conditions required for rational demonstration." The result of their hybrid machinations was dismal, because "they threw people into hatred, mutual detestation and wars, tore the scriptures to shreds, and completely divided people." As an antidote to these ills, Ibn Rushd counsels the sober differentiation of approaches, especially the distinction between scriptural faith and philosophy, which yet recognizes their common horizon of truth: namely, their shared devotion to human flourishing on a deep level. On the last page of *Fasl*, the philosopher pours out his anguish over the prevailing state of affairs in a moving and memorable passage:

> For our soul is in the utmost sorrow and pain on account of the evil fancies and perverted beliefs which have infiltrated this religion, and particularly such afflictions as have happened to it at the hand of would-be philosophers. For injuries from a friend are more severe than injuries from an enemy. I point to the fact here that philosophy is the friend and milk-sister of religion. Thus injuries from would-be philosophers are the severest injuries [to religion]—apart from the enmity, hatred and quarrels which such injuries stir up between the two, which are companions by nature and lovers by essence and instinct.

Thus, *Fasl* ends with a paean to differential friendship, to a loving relationship that respects difference without fusion or mutual separation.[18]

Platonic-Aristotelian Politics

Ibn Rushd's work, and its contemporary significance, are not restricted to his celebration of the friendship of reason and faith. The range of his arguments also extends into the social and political domain, providing important impulses for political thought and philosophy. To a considerable extent, *Fasl* can itself be read as a political treatise. By carefully distinguishing between different methods or approaches and safeguarding their integrity, the book clearly seeks to establish an open arena of discourse, making room for diverse kinds of discursive genres; in pleading for greater freedom of philosophical interpretation, the book aims to expand tolerance for intellectual disagreements (at least in the absence of a binding consensus).[19] Most important, in arguing against the tactics of clerics, Ibn Rushd basically took aim at their extremist affirmation of God's unlimited omnipotence and sovereignty, a sovereignty completely removed from any kind of reason or rational intelligibility. By extending this model of arbitrary divine power to the mundane-political domain, these theologians in effect were allies and pacemakers of political despotism and tyranny—a despotism sharply at odds with the Prophet's own benevolent and fair-minded rule. Oliver Leaman seems quite correct when he points to divine will, or the relation between will and reason, as a central issue between Averroes and the theologians (including Ghazali). The strategy of the latter, he writes, was to accuse philosophy of holding a pale view of divine omnipotence, with the result that "the philosophical model of the world could do without a deity quite easily." In response, Averroes charged Ghazali and fellow theologians with "only being prepared to accept a concept of God which is remarkably similar to that of a very powerful human being, God with a status rather similar to that of Superman."[20]

Ibn Rushd's political leanings can be discerned not only indirectly or by way of inference from his arguments on other topics; they are also more directly disclosed in his writings on classical texts, especially on the political or ethical-political texts of Plato and Aristotle. In the case of Aristotle, he left behind a ("middle") commentary on *Nicomachean Ethics* and also shorter comments on *Topics, Rhetoric* and *Poetics*. His most detailed treatment of politics, however, can be found in his commentary on Plato's *Republic* (which can be counted among his longer or great commentaries). In many respects, it is unfortunate that he did not have access to Aristotle's *Politics*—a text that, as he regretfully notes, "has not yet fallen into our hands." Judging from his other writings, one can surmise that the teachings of *Politics* might have been even more congenial to him than the *Republic*—mainly because of Aristotle's sympathy for a middle-of-the-road "polity" and his greater attention to social and cultural contexts. By comparison, Plato's *Republic* is marked by a certain stress on hierarchy, that is, by the subordination of the sensible to the intelligible domain accompanied by the subordination of ordinary people to "guardians" and the "philosopher-king." While faithfully and often sympathetically commenting on Plato's text, one should note that Ibn Rushd's treatment of hierarchy is distinctive in at least three respects. First of all—in opposition again to the theologians of his time—he insists on the just, rationally motivated and hence non-despotic character of philosophical "rule" (where the latter could ever be established). Second, as follows from *Fasl* and other works, the philosopher's rule or role is necessarily subdued and hedged in both by sacred scripture and the bounds of social consensus in practical matters. Finally and perhaps most importantly, structural hierarchy is problematized and contested by the Islamic belief in the basic equality of all Muslims—a belief Ibn Rushd seemed to share. On repeated occasions, he is fond of citing a statement of the Prophet Muhammad (recorded in *Hadith*) that he has been "sent to the White and the Black"—which means: to all people alike.[21]

Ibn Rushd's commentary on the *Republic* starts out in a somewhat un-Platonic and decidedly Aristotelian vein. First of all, he describes politics as part of "practical science" or practical philosophy, as opposed to strictly "theoretical" philosophy (a distinction not quite germane to Plato's thought). Next, he explicitly adopts Aristotle's definition of "man" as a "political animal," a creature "political by nature"—which means that "man" becomes properly human only in association with other humans. He illustrates this point by reference to the cultivation of human "virtue"—a discussion that again seems heavily indebted to Aristotle's *Nicomachean Ethics* (and in part to al-Farabi's *Virtuous City*). As he writes, it seems impossible or at least highly improbable for one person to attain all the virtues single-handedly, whereas it is quite possible to find all the virtues spread out or dispersed among a multitude of individuals. Likewise, it appears "that no man's substance can be realized in any of these virtues unless other humans help him, and that hence to acquire his own virtue a person has need of other people." As he adds, this insight concurs with the teachings of the *Republic* insofar as Plato there declares it "inappropriate that any of the citizens engage in more than one art" (corresponding to a distinct virtue), finding that "the employment of a person in more than one art is either altogether impossible or, if possible, not best." With regard to the structure of the *polis,* this argument entails that different people have different aptitudes and that hence "not every person is fit to be a warrior or an orator or a poet, let alone a philosopher." While clearly indebted to Platonic teachings, the preceding statements also can (and perhaps should) be read with an Aristotelian twist: pointing to the conclusion that no single human virtue or aptitude can be cultivated in isolation—including that of the philosopher. In his straightforward manner, Ibn Rushd adds: "All this being as we have characterized it, there ought to exist an association of humans—an association perfect in every species of human perfection."[22]

Over long stretches, Ibn Rushd's text offers a running commentary on the structure of Plato's "republic," especially on the perfection of "justice" in the *polis* through the hierarchical ordering of human virtues corresponding to an ordering of classes of citizens. Since these Platonic teachings are quite well known, little purpose would be served here to replicate the pertinent passages. What one should note (and is not always sufficiently noted), however, is a certain tension or tensional relation prevailing between Plato, or Ibn Rushd the Platonist, on the one hand, and Ibn Rushd the Muslim and Aristotelian, on the other. Sometimes, the Muslim and Aristotelian struggles against or raises a critical voice against the Platonist; sometimes, Platonic teachings are invoked as critical antidotes to abuses in Islamic communities of his time (all of which shows the Cordoban as a critically engaged thinker, not a mere commentator). The first time Ibn Rushd challenges Plato is with regard to the latter's distinction between Greeks and barbarians and his assumption that only the former have philosophical aptitudes. This opinion, he writes, "would only be correct if there were but one type of humans disposed to human perfection, and especially to the philosophical [theoretical] type." Yet, even if one were to grant a certain advantage in this matter to the Greeks, one cannot disregard the fact that philosophically minded individuals are "frequently to be found." Thus, he adds, one can find them "in the land of the Greeks and surrounding areas, such as in this land of ours, namely Andalusia, also in Syria, Iraq and Egypt—although this may have been more widespread in Greece." Another critical rejoinder to Plato occurs in relation to the desirable size of a *polis*—which Plato had specified in a definite way. Proceeding cautiously, Ibn Rushd first muses that perhaps Plato did not mean his specification to be "unalterable like the other general things he mentions" in the *Republic,* but rather stated it "in accord with his time and also with his people, the Greeks." For Ibn Rushd, showing his Aristotelian colors, it made more sense to say that the proper size of cities will "vary according to the localities" and social contexts; any determination of size should be in "conformity with the natural climates" and actual condition of peoples. This fact, he asserts, is "alluded to in the saying of the Lawgiver [Prophet]: 'I have been sent to the White and the Black'"—adding: "If this be the correct view, Plato does not favor it; but it is Aristotle's opinion, and it is the indubitable truth."[23]

While critical rejoinders to Plato are relatively rare, there are many passages in the text where Plato (sometimes in conjunction with Aristotle) is invoked as a critical yardstick by which to judge conditions in Islamic societies at the time. A prominent instance has to do with the character of virtuous rulership in a city—which, on Platonic premises, means the rule of a just, rational, and unselfish sage. This tenet—as previously mentioned—collided head-on with the absolutist leanings of Muslim clergy and theologians (both then and now). Some of the most eloquent and stirring passages of the text are devoted to this controversy. As Ibn Rushd notes, perfect rulership is often identified with rule in accordance with God's will—with the added proviso that the only way of knowing God's will is through prophecy, not through any inquiry or rational insight. This posture was aggravated in the case of clerics and theologians (the so-called *mutakallimun*) by their insistence that "what God wills has no definite nature and merely turns on what the will—namely, the will of God (may He be exalted)—lays down for it." According to this voluntarist (and Hobbesian) view, there is in this world "nothing beautiful or base other than by fiat"; likewise, there is "no end [*telos*] of man other than by fiat." Thus, in their zeal to elevate and absolutize divine rule, these theologians concluded that God "is capable of doing whatever He wills" and that hence "all things are possible" without rhyme or reason. Proceeding in this manner, the *mutakallimun* leaped headlong into a whirlpool of random assertions and opinions "close to sophistry"—in any event, into a stance "very far from the nature of man, and also far from the content of the *shari'ah*." The entire confusion, however, could be avoided by some attention to classical philosophers, especially their teachings regarding the relation between reason and will, between theoretical and practical virtues, and especially regarding the requirements of just rulership (whether the ruler be a philosopher-king or a Prophet or an Imam). As these teachings clearly indicate, just rulership requires practical wisdom and judgment (*phronesis*), theoretical insight into how states of affairs are "brought about in nations and cities," and above all "great moral virtue through which alone governance of cities in justice is possible."[24]

Another instance in which Plato serves as a critical yardstick involves the role of women in cities. Taking his bearings from Plato's famous discussion of female guardians and the "community of wives" (in Book 5 of the *Republic*), Ibn Rushd declares it a "fit topic of investigation" to inquire "whether there exist among women natures resembling the natures of each and every class of citizens, and in particular the guardians, or whether women's natures are radically different from men's natures." If the former is the case—as Plato held—then women would have the same standing as men in all social roles "so that there would be among them warriors, philosophers, rulers, and the rest." On the other hand, on the assumption of radical difference, women would only be fit for activities for which men are less or unfit "such as upbringing, procreation, and the like." Taking resolutely Plato's side, Ibn Rushd states: "We say that women, insofar as they are of one kind with men, necessarily share the same ends as men," differing only perhaps in "less or more." Thus, one can see women—though perhaps physically weaker—practicing the same arts as men, and sometimes practicing them more diligently. Most important, since women (like men) are formed "with eminence and a praiseworthy disposition," it is by no means excluded that there be "philosophers and rulers" among them. Turning to the situation in Islamic societies at his time, Ibn Rushd finds a dismal contrast. "In these (Muslim) cities," he writes, the aptitude or competence of women is "unknown" since they are considered only fit for procreation and "placed at the service of their husbands for purposes of procreation, upbringing, and nursing"—which "nullifies their other aptitudes." For Ibn Rushd, the disregard and exclusion of women from most roles has dire social and political consequences. As they are unprepared for any of the higher virtues, he complains, "women in these cities frequently resemble plants." Uneducated and unproductive, they become a burden upon men and the entire society, which is "one of the causes of the poverty of these cities."[25]

Another critical invocation of Platonic teachings concerns the topic of warfare, and especially of "holy war" (*jihad*)—where an extremist or fanatical use of the latter term had prompted Muslim societies not only to launch war against outsiders or infidels, but to engage in internecine warfare among Muslims, leading to deep internal cleavages and a destruction of the *umma*. Ibn Rushd's reference point here is Plato's discussion of warfare and factional strife (in Book 5 of the *Republic*). Plato there argues that strife between Greeks or Hellenes— that is, between peoples bound together by shared ethnicity and culture—should stop short of the enslavement of enemies, of the burning down of their cities and the devastation of their forests and fields. In the words of the commentary, it is hence "not fitting that Greeks, for example, should enslave Greeks, burn down their houses, and cut down their trees." Factional strife should be called "discord and sedition" rather than war properly, for such strife resembles the dispute that sometimes "breaks out between members of a single household or between lovers." Turning to factional strife between

Muslim sects or Muslim societies, Ibn Rushd in a Platonic vein counsels restraint: opponents in such cases, he states, should be called "ones who have gone astray, not unbelievers." In another context—his commentary on Aristotle's *Nicomachean Ethics*—he is even more outspoken in his critique of random warfare by and among Muslims, now extending this critique to certain readings of the *shari'ah*. The formulations of the Muslim law regarding warfare, he writes there, are "very general," to such a point that many Muslims have proceeded to "destroy, root and branch, whoever differs from them." Since many members of the Muslim community interpret the concept of war (*jihad*) as a blanket prescription to be used indiscriminately, "great damage has been inflicted on account of their ignorance of the intent of the Lawgiver [Prophet]." For Ibn Rushd, it is important and proper to say "that peace is preferable at times to war."²⁶

The most explicit critique of political conditions in Muslim countries, especially countries in "Western" Islam, occurs in the final section of the commentary, where Ibn Rushd takes up the decline or deterioration of cities (as discussed in Book 8 of the *Republic*), that is, the descent from the perfect or virtuous *polis* through timocracy, oligarchy, and democracy to the abyss of tyranny. Regarding the latter, Ibn Rushd is again emphatic in distinguishing it from virtuous rulership, saying that the tyrant only seeks power moved by brute self-interest whereas virtuous rulers aim at the well-being of all citizens (thus acting more like "guides" or educators). Concerning timocracy—rulership based on "honor"—Ibn Rushd finds it "most preferable" among the "non-virtuous" cities, because people there still strive after virtue, though based on "unexamined opinion." Actually, the main concern of the commentary is not with timocracy as such, but with its status as a transitional gateway to even less desirable political regimes, especially oligarchy and "democracy"—the former being characterized by the rule of wealth and the latter by random pleasure-seeking among all citizens. In oligarchy or the "governance of the vile," we read, all life is geared toward "wealth, riches, and their acquisition in excess of need." The rulers in such cities, the oligarchs, are bound to be the wealthiest and hence most powerful of people—which results in a division of society into two parts. For, since wealth is scarce and the aptitude to acquire uneven, it necessarily follows that the rich "will be few and the majority in this city be poor." As far as democracy is concerned, it is described (in a Platonic vein) as a community in which "everyone is unrestrained." Every individual here does "what his heart desires" and seeks to grasp "whatever pleasure his soul yearns for." Since this kind of regime is entirely grounded in private self-interest and self-seeking, it is evident that the "household" functions as the primary unit and that the city exists "only for its sake." What this means is that the core of democracy is entirely private or "domestic," contrary to what happens in the virtuous city: in the former, "every person, if he so wills, may have all goods in private."[27]

Applying these observations to Islamic societies, Ibn Rushd finds them amply supported by historical evidence. As he notes, the slippery slope or downhill slide through timocracy to political decay can be illustrated in at least three phases of Islamic history. One phase is the founding period of Islam and its aftermath. In Ibn Rushd's view, the rule of the Prophet Muhammad and the early "righteous" caliphs imitated or resembled the virtuous city. However, with the rise of the Umayyad dynasty (in 661), conditions changed, giving rise to timocracy and possible further deteriorations. In the context of Western Islam, the Platonic theory of decline is exemplified both in the reign of the Almoravides (1062–1145) and the reign of the Almohads (1147–1248). In the case of the former dynasty, the initial ruler (Yussuf Ibn Tashfin) earnestly strove to imitate the governance of the virtuous city; but under his son and grandson, the regime deteriorated first into timocracy and then into democratic hedonism and pleasure-seeking. The following Almohad dynasty—which ruled during Ibn Rushd's adult life—also began by imitating virtuous governance; but conditions soon entered a downhill slide. Ibn Rushd is stern and uncompromising in castigating the combination of oligarchy and democratic pleasure-seeking prevailing in most Islamic societies, including those in Western Islam. "Most of these cities existing today," he writes, "are democratic," or rather mixed plutocratic-democratic, and the individuals lording over them are those capable "of so governing that every man attains his desire and preserves it." For many people, this kind of regime appears admirable for "every man there asserts on the basis of unexamined opinion that he deserves to be free" and to act as he chooses. Given the reliance on untrammeled self-interest, the regimes of "many Muslim kings today" are entirely "domestic" in character, in the sense that all property is domestic or private (with no concern for public needs). Since property or wealth, however, is unevenly distributed—revealing the oligarchic strand—Muslim society resembles no longer the virtuous city, but rather older "Oriental" societies with their invidious class structure:

> Men are of two classes: a class of the multitude and a class of the mighty—as was formerly the case with the people in Persia and as is now the case in many of these cities of ours. Among the latter, the multitude

are plundered by the mighty, and the mighty go so far in seizing their property that this occasionally leads them to tyranny—just as it happens in this time of ours and in this city of ours [Cordoba] . . . [When these things happen,] the ship of state is prepared for destruction. And so is the case with this city when it is not a single city, but rather two cities—the city of the poor and the city of the rich.[28]

Ibn Rushd's Historical Legacy

By hindsight or from a contemporary perspective, Ibn Rushd's critical comments acquire a broader significance: showing their relevance not only to Muslim societies of his time but to many modern societies, including societies in the modern West. Needless to say, his comments were not appreciated by his Muslim contemporaries, just as they are unlikely to be appreciated by many modern Western "democrats" (regrettably so, since critics of corruption are usually the best friends of a society, as shown by the example of Socrates). As many students have noted, Ibn Rushd's fate in Muslim civilization after his death has been puzzling and disappointing; partly because of his political criticisms and partly because of his "liberal" religious views, his work has failed to gain the resonance in the Muslim world it would seem to deserve by virtue of its quality and sheer quantity. In the centuries after his death, the influence of his work among Muslims declined and—perhaps not unexpectedly—was steadily eclipsed by the ascendancy of clerics and would-be theologians (whose excessive claims he had challenged). As Leaman writes, with a touch of melancholy irony: in his dispute with Abu Hamid, Ibn Rushd had "the last word," but in many ways "Ghazali had the last laugh," since "the form of philosophy represented and defended by Averroes went into a sudden decline in the Islamic community after his death" while the status of Ghazali "has remained formidable up to today."[29]

This, of course, is not the entire story. While insufficiently appreciated in the Muslim world, Ibn Rushd's work found considerable resonance elsewhere: first of all among Jewish philosophers and then, in part through their mediation, among Christian thinkers in Western Europe. It is well known that his work was highly valued by the slightly younger Moses ben Maimon (Maimonides, 1135–1204), the great rabbi and fellow-Cordoban, as well as by the latter's disciple Joseph ben Judah. Partly due to their influence, many of Ibn Rushd's writings were translated into Hebrew, with intellectuals like Moses ben Tibbon, Simeon Anatoli, and Zerachia ben Isaac serving as some of the main translators and transmitters.[30] A second wave of reception occurred in the thirteenth and fourteenth centuries in Western Europe, facilitated by the translation into Latin of numerous texts from Arabic and Hebrew. This reception led to the rise of what has come to be known as "Latin Averroism," a movement represented by such figures as Siger of Brabant and John of Jandun—but whose precise meaning is unsettled or controverted. Largely under the impact of much later "modernist" tendencies, Latin Averroists have sometimes been interpreted as radical free-thinkers hostile to the medieval church—with the corollary result (as Majid Fakhry notes) that Ibn Rushd himself came to be viewed as an iconoclast and "a kind of Muslim Siger of Brabant." More recent scholarship, however, has shown the lopsidedness of this reading. What Latin Averroists seemed to advocate was a sharper distinction (than was common at the time) between philosophy and religion, thus juxtaposing a radical fideism and a self-confident rationalism—though without endorsing a sharp break or antithesis. As Leaman writes, Ibn Rushd would have been happy to concede "that there are different ways of establishing propositions in different universes of discourse"; but he would not have been happy being credited with the idea "that these universes of discourse exist in splendid isolation." For, although he *did* emphasize "the differences between religious and philosophical language," he also argued that "both types of language describe the same reality" (or honor the same horizon of truth).[31]

Some of the motifs of Latin Averroism were carried forward by various Renaissance thinkers, like Pietro Pomponazzi—though now with a classical humanist agenda (which often preferred original texts to later commentaries). In the following two centuries interest in medieval philosophy generally subsided, being eclipsed by the rise of Baconian and Cartesian modes of reasoning. It was only in the nineteenth century, in the context of spreading positivist and secular-agnostic ideas, that attention was paid again to Ibn Rushd—who now was seen as an unabashed fighter for rational science against the encroachments of religious dogma. It was chiefly Ernest Renan's *Averroes et l'Averroisme* (of 1852) which in this respect exerted a pervasive (and largely distorting) influence, pushing the distinction between reason and faith in the direction of a dubious "double-truth" theory (whereby faith appeared as a disposable camouflage of reason). Renan's initiative was paralleled by a partial revival of interest in the Muslim world, promoted chiefly by the so-called *Nahda* ("Islamic renaissance") movement, which sought to retrieve rationalist elements in the Islamic past and combine them with the scientism of the modern West. As Leaman reports, one of the leaders of this movement, Farah Antun, translated Renan's book on "Averroes" in a typically Renanian spirit, presenting Ibn Rushd as a victim of religious persecution as a result of his iconoclastic, anti-religious opinions. Although widely supported by "liberal" intellectuals both in the West and the Islamic world, this "rationalist" reading conflicts head-on with his carefully nuanced balancing of reason and faith—and also with reported life-experiences of the philosopher. A particularly telling experience concerns an event that happened late in Ibn Rushd's life (around 1194) when he and his son Abdallah entered a mosque in Cordoba at the time of the evening prayer. Probably at the incitement of clerics, some people in the mosque made a "commotion" and ejected them from it—an event that Ibn Rushd describes as "the worst thing that happened to me in my afflictions."[32]

In the contemporary setting, the effects of nineteenth-century positivism and materialism still linger—although there are signs of more perceptive and innovative approaches. To a considerable extent, discussions in this area are still dominated by the Renanian antithesis of science versus faith, with Ibn Rushd serving as a kind of litmus test separating intellectuals. For many interpreters both in the West and the Islamic world, Ibn Rushd represents indeed the iconoclastic rationalist and agnostic favored by Renan's Enlightenment agenda, an agnostic capable of renovating Islamic societies through an infusion of modern science and technology. Reacting to this view but sharing its basic premises, other intellectuals denounce Ibn Rushd as an infidel and an enemy of the orthodox doctrines of Islam—which they seek to vindicate in the same manner as the clerics and *mutakallimun* of earlier times.[33] Curiously, the latter position is also supported or buttressed by some Western intellectual circles that, reacting against modernist scientism, sometimes denounce rational-philosophical inquiry as such, preferring to leap either into a radical fideism or else a mystical intuitionism or illuminationism (akin to the teachings of traditional "Eastern" Islam). In the midst of this agonistic babel of tongues, Oliver Leaman provides again some helpful pointers when he insists on the need to distinguish the Cordoban's thought both from a one-sided fideism and an iconoclastic rationalism—the latter often being identified with "Averroism." What should be remembered, he writes, is Ibn Rushd's argument that "faith and reason are two very different approaches" whose diversity should be respected "in any attempt at grasping their relationship" or communality. Hence, there is a need to distinguish "between the doctrine that religion and philosophy are different routes to the same truth, and the doctrine that only one of them [reason] is capable of reaching that truth." Given that these issues are still confused and unresolved in our time, he adds, "Ibn

Rushd sets us an intellectual and practical problem which modern culture is still struggling to address."[34]

Fortunately, as indicated, there are signs of new departures in this ongoing struggle. In contemporary Western philosophy, the older paradigms of positivism and scientism no longer enjoy undisputed hegemony, having been challenged for some time now by such newer initiatives as phenomenology, existentialism, and post-structuralism. At least in some instances, these initiatives seem able to throw a promising new light on the complicated faith-reason nexus. Thus, relying precisely on Aristotelian teachings, Martin Heidegger in some of his writings and lecture courses has insisted on the need to differentiate between philosophy and theology—without on this count disparaging genuine faith as such nor the possibility of a subterranean liaison between reason and faith. In a similar vein—though invoking a heavier dose of extra-rational "transcendentalism"—Jacques Derrida has begun to explore the relation between religion and philosophy, with an accent on the relation between human understanding and Messianic intervention.[35] More important for the future fate of Ibn Rushd are signs of a renewed preoccupation with his work among contemporary Muslim intellectuals and philosophers, including philosophers located in the context of "Western" Islam. Anke von Kügelen, in her far-ranging study titled *Averroes und die arabische Moderne* (Averroes and Arab Modernity, 1994), detects a significant difference in Muslim discussions of Ibn Rushd during the first and second half of the 20th century. In the second half, she writes, one can find "both a quantitative and substantive change" in these discussions, manifest in more intensive and widespread concerns with political issues or implications and in more resolute efforts to tackle the troubling question of the relation between philosophical reasoning and faith, and more specifically between traditional Islam and Western modernity. Among present-day Muslim intellectuals, von Kügelen singles out prominently the Egyptians Muhammad 'Ammara and Hassan Hanafi and the Moroccan Mohammed al-Jabri for their contributions in this field.[36]

A prolific writer and publisher—among his books is a new edition of *Fasl*—Muhammad 'Ammara presents himself deliberately as follower of a middle path mediating between reason and faith, a path initially cleared by Ibn Rushd (and in part by Mu'tazilite thinkers). Pursuit of this path, in his view, necessarily has a double critical edge, being opposed both to reactionary fundamentalism and a slavish imitation of Western rationality. In contrast to the latter perspective, "genuine Islam" for him is itself "rationalist" in a distinctive sense: namely, by treating reason and faith as two branches of a tree, developing separately without antithesis. Among the factors contributing to the decline of genuine Islam, 'Ammara mentions the penchant for Neoplatonic mysticism, the anti-intellectualism of Ottoman rulers, and (of course) the impact of colonialism and imperialism. As antidote to these factors and as gateway to a regeneration, he recommends the renewed study of Ibn Rushd—seen not only as a philosopher but as a political thinker. Attention to the Cordoban's work could contribute to a productive resolution of the religion/politics conundrum, and also (still more important) to the fostering of a social (or socialist) democracy not along materialist-Marxist but along Qur'anic lines. In a similar vein, philosophical and political motives are also operative in the work of Hassan Hanafi. Educated both in Cairo and in Paris—where he was a student of Paul Ricoeur—Hanafi is one of the more controversial figures in contemporary Islam, a status due to his vehement opposition both to religious fundamentalism and to Western-style "modernization." Together with 'Ammara (and Ibn Rushd), he assigns partial responsibility for the decline of Islamic reasoning to clerical literalists as well as to (overly ambitious) Neoplatonic mystics. Although favoring social change, he charges Western-style modernizers with neglecting basic hermeneutical insights (as well as democratic principles): namely, the need to transform society from within by relying initially on popular beliefs and indigenous traditions (here the tradition of Islam). Both philosophically and politically, Ibn Rushd can still serve as a guidepost: philosophically by reconciling "God and world" (faith and reason), and politically by encouraging a genuine renewal of the Islamic *umma*.[37]

The third Muslim intellectual highlighted by von Kügelen is Mohammed al-Jabri, professor of philosophy in Rabat and recipient of a UNESCO prize for Arabic culture (1988). As a native of the region of Western Islam, al-Jabri shows a particular affinity to the legacy of Ibn Rushd. Like the philosopher of Cordoba, he voices strong criticism of clerical literalists and would-be theologians (*mutakallimun*), and also of the excessive flights of fancy of adepts of esoteric mysticism or gnosticism. In fact, one of the central points of his writings is the need to accentuate Western Islamic thinkers (in the Maghrib) over proponents of Eastern illuminationism (in the Mashriq). Among these proponents, al-Jabri castigates especially Ibn Sina for his esoteric, "Orientalist" leanings, and al-Ghazali for his anti-rational fideism. One of the glaring defects of illuminationism, in his view, is the indiscriminate fusion of reason and faith—a fusion detrimental to both (as Ibn Rushd had shown). For al-Jabri, the legacy of the Cordoban is helpful for renovative purposes on several levels. On the philosophical level, he stresses the distinction between discursive genres, especially between metaphorical speech (*bayan*) and argumentative reasoning (*burhan*), and the vindication of the latter's legitimacy. In terms of social or political transformation, his argument echoes or resembles that of Hanafi, by distinguishing between several strategies: those of clerical fundamentalists, Western liberals, and Marxists. While rejecting the reactionary nostalgia of clerics, he charges Western liberals and Marxists with ignoring the concrete historical experiences of Muslim societies. Like Hanafi, al-Jabri finds it impossible to renovate or transform society without a "creative appropriation" of the past—which, for Muslims, should include renewed study of Ibn Rushd.[38]

As is evident from contemporary discussions, the import of Ibn Rushd's legacy is assessed not only under "theoretical," but also under practical-political auspices. The Cordoban's critique of clericalism, fideism, and esoteric mysticism was advanced with the purpose not only of defending philosophical reasoning, but also of extending the scope of public space to accommodate a broader range of opinions and genres of discourse. This connotation is by no means lost on contemporary defenders of his work. Almost with one voice they castigate religious fundamentalism not only for its irrationalism, but also for jeopardizing the political balance between reason and faith in a manner that often culminates in a clerically sanctioned "theocracy" (or autocracy). Similar complaints are lodged against radical fideism and esoteric mysticism. Thus, Hanafi deplores in illuminationism the tendency to replace public discourse by a divinely inspired monologue— or a discourse intelligible only to self-selected sages. In a like manner he criticizes Neoplatonism for its addiction to vertical hierarchical schemes that radically subordinate human affairs and questions of social justice to abstract-spiritual concerns; in terms of political organization, these schemes give preference to a "pyramidal state" governed from the top in disregard of due process and popular participation. As arguments like these indicate, interest in Ibn Rushd is by no means antiquarian but part and parcel of ongoing moral-political struggles—as befits the both philosophical and practical legacy of the Cordoban. Basically, the Cordoban's name can be taken as a stand-in for the yearning for a tolerantly open, yet morally responsible society, a society in which reason and faith, respect for humans and for the divine are balanced (not collapsed) in a carefully calibrated way. To conclude, it may be appropriate to cite some hopeful comments found toward the end of Ibn Rushd's "treatise of difference" or *Fasl*:

> But God directs all men aright and helps everyone to love Him. He unites their hearts in the fear of Him, and removes from them hatred and loathing by His grace and His mercy.[39]

CHAPTER 8

WEST-EASTERN DIVAN

Goethe and Hafiz in Dialogue

To God belongs the Orient,
to God belongs the Occident,
Northerly and Southern lands
Peacefully rest in His hands.

Even in this awkward translation, readers of these lines can still detect the hand of one of the great literary geniuses of the Western world: Johann Wolfgang Goethe. What many readers will not readily perceive, however, is the fact that the lines are a variation of Qur'anic verses, more specifically of these verses of the second Sura: "To God belongs the rising and the setting of the suns, and wherever you may turn, you find God's face."[1] Slightly varying the Qur'anic words, Goethe extends the scope of God's "face" from East and West to North and South—a rephrasing that is likely to resonate strongly with contemporary readers living in (what is often called) the "age of globalization." Still, what may startle or disorient the same contemporary readers is the deep religiosity reflected in Goethe's lines, a religiosity bordering on religious "surrender" (which is the literal meaning of Islam). Clearly, such religiosity concurs ill with the popular image of Goethe as a self-possessed Olympian patterning his life on pagan-Greek models; it also agrees poorly with his image as a fellow-traveler of modern enlightenment or enlightened modernity—especially in view of the fact that the latter is often identified summarily with such ailments as logocentrism, egocentrism, and Eurocentrism.

Goethe's lines are found in his *West-Eastern Divan* (*West-Östlicher Divan*), a collection of poems composed between 1814 and 1819 in the midst or in the aftermath of the Napoleonic wars, the national wars of "liberation," and the settlement reached at the Congress of Vienna. Written at a time when Goethe was in his late sixties and early seventies, the collection exudes an aura of seasoned wisdom, cheerful serenity, and unregimented piety (not at odds with a kind of sublimated worldliness). In part, the collection owed its origin to Goethe's encounter with the Persian poet Hafiz (1320–1389), who himself was a witness and survivor of extremely turbulent upheavals ravaging Islamic societies at the time—upheavals associated with the Mongol invasion and especially with the exploits of the mighty Timur or Tamerlane. To be sure, historical parallels should not be overstated here. In writing his *Divan,* Goethe's intent was never to identify himself with Hafiz, but only to encounter and converse with the Persian poet in the mode of traveler or sojourner attentively visiting that poet's world. At the beginning of his own "Annotations" to the *Divan,* Goethe invited his readers to become travelers or sojourners with him:

> If poetry you wish to understand,
> you must go to poetry's land;
> and if you seek the poet's mind,
> the poet's world you need to find.[2]

As these lines make clear, the objective is neither psychic fusion nor an empirical-geographical excursion, but rather a poetic or imaginative journey (in poetry's land). The following pages are meant for imaginative travelers across borders—and not specifically for Goethe experts or Islamicists (safely ensconced in their respective expertise). The first part seeks to retrace the story of Goethe's evolving relationship with Islam, and more particularly with Persian poetry. The second or middle part offers glimpses of the *West-Eastern Divan,* with a special focus on the dialogue between Goethe and Hafiz. The third or concluding part seeks to highlight possible lessons of the *Divan* for contemporary readers and for the pursuit of cross-civilizational dialogue in our time.

If "Islam" God-Surrender Means . . .

Goethe's encounter with Hafiz was not a sudden chance meeting; it was preceded by a nearly life-long interest on Goethe's part in Islamic (or "Oriental") culture and literature. A major factor triggering this interest in the young poet was the influence of Johann Gottfried Herder, who—along with a lively spiritedness—bequeathed to him a taste for cultural pluralism and inter-religious tolerance and appreciation. Ever since his student days in Strasbourg (1769–71), Goethe followed with keen attention and sympathy the writings of his older friend; thus he was no doubt familiar with the latter's unconventional views (unconventional for a Protestant minister) regarding Islamic religion, views that remained a steady part of his evolving opus. These views surfaced with particular eloquence in Herder's *Ideas for a Philosophy of Human History* (*Ideen zur Philosophie einer Geschichte der Menschheit*). In that work, Herder praised the Prophet Muhammad for his "fervent devotion to the idea of one God" and for showing the proper way of "serving God through purity, prayer, and good deeds." According to the text, the triumphant expansion of Islam during the early period was due jointly to certain corruptions besetting Judaism and Christianity at the time, to the exquisite Arabic idiom of the *Qur'an*, and (last but not least) to the remarkable personal talents of the Prophet. Venturing an unflattering comparison, Herder added: "If the Germanic conquerors of Europe had possessed a book in their tongue on a par with the *Qur'an*, Latin would never have become the dominant language, nor would many Germanic tribes have strayed so hopelessly into errancy."[3]

Accepting or absorbing Herder's impulses, Goethe proceeded to deepen and enrich them with his own characteristic élan. Basically, what mattered to him was not so much expanded knowledge about Islam (and other religions); rather, the issue was "existential": having to do with his search for genuine religiosity, particularly a religiosity fitting to him as a poet. In her remarkable books *Goethe and Islam* and *Goethe and the Arab World*, Katharina Mommsen persuasively stresses this point. As she notes, Goethe's interest went far beyond the Enlightenment motto of tolerance, "which is often only a cover-up for religious indifference." Without relinquishing tolerance, Goethe entered into a "much more personal relation" with Muhammad and his religion—which explains the fact that, "in their provocative boldness," many of his statements go "far beyond anything heard or said in Germany before." What fostered this close relation, in Mommsen's account, was an affinity of Goethe's own beliefs and thoughts with certain key teachings of Islam, an affinity that nurtured a "deeply grounded sympathy." The strength of this sympathy surfaced soon in his writings, and initially in a letter written to Herder in July 1772. In that letter, Goethe expressed his passionate quest for a path leading to poetic "mastery," as that mastery had been exemplified by Pindar in ancient times. The letter culminated in the sentence: "I would like to pray like Moses in the *Qur'an*: Lord, make room in my narrow chest." The sentence is taken almost verbatim from the twentieth Sura, where we read: "Moses said: O my Lord, make room in my breast. Make my mission easy, and remove the impediment of my tongue."[4]

Goethe's quotation or borrowing from the *Qur'an* was by no means fortuitous. As research in his sprawling opus has shown, Goethe during this time was busy copying numerous verses from the *Qur'an* for his own purposes. He also wrote a review of a new German translation of the *Qur'an* produced by a somewhat bigoted Frankfurt professor—who in his preface did not hesitate to denounce Muhammad as a "false prophet and anti-Christ" and the *Qur'an* as a "tissue of lies" (*Lügenbuch*). Although appreciating the labor invested by the professor, Goethe's review expressed the hope that another translation might soon be produced—written "under Oriental sky" and with greater sensitivity for Islamic poetry and religion. Partly in response to continued bigotry, Goethe in late 1772 conceived the plan of a great tragedy titled *Mahomet* (Muhammad)—a project that, unfortunately, has remained a torso. The extant pieces, however, convey a glimpse of the drama's spirit. Two passages in particular deserve attention. The first passage is the drama's opening hymn in which "Mahomet" recounts his search for true faith—a search that leads him from the starry skies to moon and sun and finally to worship of the one God who is both revealed and sheltered in natural phenomena. Patterned on the sixth Sura of the *Qur'an*, the hymn is indicative also of Goethe's own religiosity: his delicate blending of immanence and transcendence, of worldly piety (*Weltfrömmigkeit*) and God-seeking—which goes far beyond any simple pantheism. The other passage deals with the task or mission of the Prophet as divine messenger and religious law-giver. Titled "Mahomet's Song," the passage portrays the Prophet's mission under the image of a stream or river, a stream that—starting from small beginnings—progressively gathers into itself a multitude of diverse side-rivers or tributaries until it finally delivers itself into the mighty ocean. For Goethe, the stream was a metaphor for Islam's hope to gather people from all walks of life, and without regard for race or ethnic background, into a pious community bonded by fraternal equality. Here are some lines:

> And the rivers from the plains
> and the brooklets from the mountains
> salute it [the stream] calling: brother!
> Brother take your brothers with you,
> take them to your old father,
> to the timeless mighty ocean
> who with widely outstretched arms
> us awaits. . . . [5]

With the torso of 1772/73, Goethe's preoccupation with the life and mission of "Mahomet" did not come to an end. Toward the end of that century, in 1799, he had to deal with another Mahomet tragedy—this time not his own, but the work of the great protagonist of French *lumières*: Voltaire. The occasion was a specific request, addressed to Goethe by his prince and employer, to translate and put on stage in Weimar the French drama (whose composition dated back to 1742). The request or commission was anything but enticing or congenial to Goethe. In his drama, titled *Le fanatisme ou Mahomet le Prophète*, Voltaire had depicted the prophet as a vile bigot and deceiver, and above all as a man consumed by lust for tyrannical power and for excessive sexual-sensual indulgence. The source of these abominations was traced in the drama not to accidental character blemishes but to the Prophet's fanatical religiosity—a ploy that enabled the French philosopher to attack in the person of Mahomet religion as such, including Christianity and above all Roman Catholicism. Although obeying the wishes of his prince, Goethe clearly chafed under the imposed obligation that in so many ways contravened his own convictions and his own different appreciation of Islam and its Prophet. As he wrote in a letter to a friend: "It was the request of my prince alone which pushed me into this enterprise—perhaps strange or peculiar to many—of translating Voltaire's *Mahomet*." In his own autobiographical account *Dichtung und Wahrheit* (Poetry and Truth), begun about a decade later, Goethe preferred to return to his own "Mahomet" fragment (which was lost for a while but recovered posthumously). The account leaves no doubt about his own persisting sympathies for the Prophet and for core tenets of Islamic faith. Referring to the opening "Mahomet's Song," the poet recalls: "The piece begins with a hymn intoned by Mahomet standing alone under the starry sky." After pursuing his quest through the epiphanies of the firmament, Mahomet finally "raises his soul to the one, eternal and unlimited God to whom all finite beings owe their existence. This hymn," Goethe concludes, "I composed with much love."[6]

Goethe's affection for Islam and Islamic faith was reinforced in many (sometimes surprising) ways during the time of the Napoleonic wars and wars of national liberation. While up to this time his acquaintance had been mostly literary or based on book-learning, the far-flung movements of armies and peoples during this period brought Goethe into more direct contact with Muslims and Muslim beliefs. In late 1813 and early 1814, as part of the allied campaign against Napoleon, groups of Russian officers and soldiers were stationed in Weimar, and among them were numerous Muslims. As we know from his letters and diary, several of these Muslims befriended Goethe, visited his home, and exchanged gifts with him. The high point of this interaction came in early 1814 when, together with other townspeople, he attended a Muslim religious service. As he wrote excitedly to a friend:

> Talking about prophesies I have to tell you that things are happening in our time which no prophet would have dared to utter. Who would have foretold even a few years ago that, in the auditorium of our Protestant *Gymnasium* [high school], a Muslim service would be held and that we would hear Suras of the Qur'an recited there. And yet it did happen.

The lively impression left by this service was further deepened by a few additional events that drew Goethe's attention to Islamic religion and culture. Shortly before the Muslim service, some soldiers returning from Spain had brought to him a hand-written Arabic text that, on inspection, turned out to be the last and culminating Sura of the *Qur'an*. Not long afterwards, a Leipzig merchant offered to the Weimar library (administered by Goethe) a valuable collection of Arabic, Persian, and Turkish manuscripts—a collection the library promptly acquired. Still a few months later, Goethe's publisher (Cotta) sent to him as a gift a new German translation of a collection of Persian poems: Hafiz's *Divan*.[7]

To this battery of impressions and events Goethe responded in his own way: as a poet. In the summer of 1814, during one of his customary excursions to the Rhineland, he began his own collection of "West-Eastern" poems for which he borrowed Hafiz's title *Divan*—a term that may be rendered as collection, gathering, assembly, even public assembly or council. There can be no doubt that, in composing his poems, Goethe also meant to pay tribute to the religious and cultural world of Islam (or at least to certain core teachings of Islamic faith). In announcing the impending publication of his new work, he did not hesitate to insert a phrase to the effect that the author "does not reject the suspicion that he may himself be a Muslim" (a phrase, of course, that may contain poetic license). As previously indicated, some key passages of the *Divan* are direct quotations from or variations on Qur'anic verses; other passages invoke more freely Islamic traditions and beliefs. The entire collection opens with a poem titled "Hegire," which is a German rendering of the Arabic *hijra*—a term, as is well known, referring to the Prophet's exodus from Mecca to Medina (the pivotal event in the Muslim calendar). In Goethe's case, the exodus or *hijra* leads from a world of external turbulence ("thrones collapse, kingdoms tremble") into a realm of cheerful piety, a realm devoted to "purity and rightness" but also welcoming "love, song, and wine" (as part of poetry's land). In keeping with this serene friendly piety, the collection's "Book of Proverbs" contains these lines:

> Foolish, how everyone esteems
> his special convictions aloud!
> If "Islam" God-surrender means,
> in Islam we all live and die no doubt.

As we know, on later occasions—especially in the face of misfortune and suffering—Goethe repeatedly returned to these verses of the *Divan* and to the notion of a "natural" or unavoidable Islam in which we all live and die. The same sentiment surfaces in a startling way in a comment of the old Goethe, where he confesses an intent or inclination: namely, the desire "reverently to celebrate that holy night in which the Qur'an was fully revealed to the Prophet."[8]

Guiding Motifs in the Divan

Goethe's *West-Eastern Divan* is a gathering of a large number of poems loosely assembled or strung together in twelve books (after a Persian fashion). As befits a poetic collection, the text deals with a great variety of themes—not all of which can possibly be mentioned here. Following the suggestion of one Goethe specialist, one might feasibly cluster the topics in four closely interrelated thematic rubrics: first, the encounter with Hafiz, whose poetry elicits a poetic response; second, the theme of love culminating in the "duodrama" of Hatem (=Goethe) and Suleika; third, the interlacing of sensual and intelligible, of earthly and spiritual motifs (throughout the collection and especially in the "Cupbearers Book" or "Schenkenbuch"); and finally, an assortment of proverbs and sage teachings.[9] In this listing, the encounter with Hafiz occupies first place—quite sensibly because the Persian poet's work clearly was a crucial catalyst for Goethe's own poetic endeavors at that time. In his "Annotations" to the *Divan,* Goethe speaks in some detail of the attraction exerted by Hafiz, whom he describes as "a dervish, Sufi, and sheikh" who lived and worked in his native city of Shiraz "well liked and appreciated." He also points to the meaning of "Hafiz," which is actually an honorary title given to persons solidly grounded in the *Qur'an*—an observation that leads Goethe to draw a parallel to his own generation and its grounding in biblical texts (at least in Protestant circles). Regarding

Hafiz's poetry, he praises its "ever-new, but temperate liveliness," its cheerful wisdom, its willingness to enjoy "part of the bounty of the earth" and simultaneously to probe "divine mysteries from afar," while firmly rejecting both arid ritualism and blatant sensuality. All in all, this poetry was able to maintain a delicate balance of diverse trends through a kind of "skeptical flexibility."[10]

In heeding Hafiz's appeal, Goethe aimed not so much to merge as rather to converse with his Persian counterpart in a friendly manner—across the boundaries of time and space. The "Book Hafiz," placed near the opening of the collection, begins precisely with a dialogue in which the two poets recognize and pay tribute to each other. To Goethe's request to explain the meaning of his name, Hafiz responds that the name was given to him because "in happy remembrance" he has steadily guarded "the Qur'an's sacred legacy" in such a way as to attain piety far removed from "mundane vileness." The Western poet happily perceives here an affinity, noting that he too had integrated "the sublime message of our sacred scriptures" into his own life, in such a way as to subdue vileness and negativity through "the serene gift of faith." Goethe does not leave unmentioned certain troubles Hafiz experienced with the religious orthodoxy of his time, troubles deriving from an occasional liberal divergence of his poetry from the rigid letter of the law (*shar'iah*). Here again, the Western poet detects a fortunate linkage or affinity. In a poem entitled "The German Thanks You," he exclaims that "such saints are indeed welcome to the poet," for precisely those slight divergences from the law are the poet's patrimony where he can "move cheerfully even in sorrow." This observation supports the poem's conclusion that now "the old [German] poet" also can hope for redemption when the "Huris" (angels) in paradise shall "receive him as transfigured youth." A following poem, titled "Infinite," intones an exuberant paean to the Persian poet who is praised as "the true source of all poetic joys," a source generating an untold number of cheerful songs. The poem concludes:

> And if the world should end tomorrow,
> Hafiz, with you, with you alone
> I shall compete! Joy and sorrow
> we share as twins in common.[11]

Several other poems or verses in the *Divan* deal with or pay tribute to Hafiz, either directly or indirectly. A frequent theme in these verses is Hafiz's immanent-transcendent piety, that is, his ability to bridge or reconcile sensible and super-sensible dimensions. Thus, one of the opening poems pays homage to Hafiz's worldly religiosity, praising it as something worthy of emulation. Addressing the Persian poet, Goethe expresses the hope that "your gentle song and holy example" may lead us too "at the sound of wine glasses to the temple of our creator." As Goethe notes, Hafiz's combination of immanence/transcendence has sometimes been described as "mystical"; but he cautions against use of this term, which carries different meanings and is liable to create misunderstanding. In the poem "Manifest Secret" we learn that "they have called you a mystical tongue, o holy Hafiz." The "they" here refers to orthodox clerics and literalists who fail to "grasp the sense of the word." They called Hafiz mystical because they associate mysticism with something weird and phantastical, and because they like to "pour their own spoiled wine in your name." For Goethe (and Hafiz), however, genuine mysticism means something different: not an extravagant or "gnostic" leap beyond the world, but rather a loving contemplation of the mystery of God's world and its "manifest secret." Thus, the poem concludes by saying: "But you, Hafiz, are mystically pure — something they cannot understand." What they are unwilling or unable to admit is that "without being bigoted you are blessed (*selig*)." In his "Annotations" to the *Divan,* Goethe is more explicit in his critique of a false or arrogant kind of mysticism that rashly exits from the world and pontificates in the name of a presumed higher wisdom: "What else does such a mystic do but to bypass genuine problems or else to postpone them as far as this is possible?"[12]

Hafiz's "mystical" blending of immanence and transcendence is particularly evident in his love poetry — which Goethe in his own way seeks to emulate. Blending here means a precarious navigation between human and divine, earthly and heavenly love, a navigation accomplished by means of image, analogy, and metaphor. In this sense, Goethe's entire *Divan* is metaphorical; its effort, in terms of the poem "Hegire," is to migrate into a realm where one might still perceive "divine message in earthly tongues" ("Himmelslehr' in Erdensprachen"). The name given to the beloved in the *Divan* is Suleika — who expresses her own complex status in these lines:

The mirror tells me I am fair!
But aging too I must allow.
In God all things must perservere,
in me love Him, at least for now.

Seen in this light, Suleika throughout the *Divan* is both near and far, both intimate and distantly receding; despite the playfulness of joyful embraces, there remains a gap—allowing for "blessed longing" and infinite allure. In this context, it is useful to remember that, in the Islamic tradition (and especially in the twelfth Sura of the *Qur'an*), Suleika is the wife of Potiphar, who is grasped by a deep, consuming desire for Joseph (Jussuf)—but a desire that never reaches fulfillment and thus remains an exemplar of chaste and non-possessive love. In the words of Katharina Mommsen: "This famous love story of the Islamic tradition, which celebrates the love between Suleika and Jussuf as passionate but chaste, prompted Goethe to address the beloved in the *West-Eastern Divan* under the name of Suleika." As an aside, it may not be inappropriate to recall that, at the time of writing his *Divan*, Goethe himself was moved by deep love for Marianne Willemer—who, as the wife of a trusted friend, remained eventually out of reach (but did contribute some verses in her own right). Whatever the relation between life and poetry (or between *Wahrheit* and *Dichtung*) may be, it is clear that Goethe was deeply touched by the Islamic story. In the concluding "Book of Paradise," Suleika figures first among those "elect women" rightly admitted into paradise:

> First Suleika, beauty's warden,
> for Jussuf filled with desire,
> now in paradise's garden
> renunciation we admire.[13]

As a further aside, to gain interpretive perspective, it may be helpful to undertake a brief excursion into Hafiz's own poetry. As readers of the Persian poet will surely agree, his work is unmatched in its spirited liveliness, its boldness of images and metaphors, and its richness of subtle allusions and intimations. To illustrate particularly his worldly piety (at the cusp of immanence and transcendence), here are a few of his *ghazals*. One poem, called in translation "When I Want to Kiss God," reads:

> When no one is looking
> I swallow deserts and clouds
> And chew on mountains knowing
> They are sweet bones.
> When no one is looking
> and I want to kiss God,
> I just lift up my hand
> to my mouth.

Another *ghazal* says equally boldly and perhaps brazenly:

When your hands, feet, and tongue
Can move in that free unison
That conjoins this longing earth
With rare knowledge—
When your soul has been groomed
In His city of love;
And when you can make others laugh
With jokes that belittle no one
And your words always unite:
Then Hafiz votes for you.
Hafiz votes for you to be
The minister of every country in the world.
He will vote for you, my dear:
Vote for you to be God.[14]

In yet another poem, Hafiz refers specifically to the Islamic story mentioned above, but does so in a playful-ambivalent manner:

For that ever-increasing beauty of Jussuf,
I ventured that love was going to tease
Suleika even out of chastity's veil?[15]

These few examples should suffice to convey the point at issue here: the similarity and difference between the two poets, and hence their incipient dialogue. As indicated before, despite his deep sympathies, Goethe was keenly aware of the distance separating him from his Persian counterpart (and from "Oriental" poetry in general). In the initial announcement of the *Divan,* the book still carried the cumbersome title "Collection of German Poems with Constant Reference to Hafiz's Divan"—a formulation clearly signalizing the complex character of the relation. In Goethe's own view (as recorded in his "Annotations"), "Oriental" poetry was distinguished by its genial lightness of spirit (*Geist*), its infinity variety, and its free use of metaphors—traits that, however, could on occasion decay into formlessness and a playful repetition of clichés. In his *Divan,* he compares such poetry sometimes with a liquid or watery element that can freely move in any direction and on any terrain. Thus, a poem in the opening sequence expresses the poet's delight of being able "gleefully to descend into the Euphrates' waters and to move freely around in its fluid waves." The reference to the Euphrates recurs in a poem spoken or sung by Suleika, which reports a dream and a riddle:

When on Euphrates I was sailing,
ah, the golden ring, your gift,

slipped and sank beyond the railing
into river's depth so swift.

Asked about the meaning of the dream, Hatem (=Goethe) interprets it
as a glad omen foretelling a possible wedding between himself and the
river containing Suleika's ring (and the treasure of "Oriental" poetry).
As one should note, however, the wedding does not signify a complete
merger or fusion. This point is indicated in the first poem referring to
the "Euphrates' waters," where the poet's gleeful descent is followed by
these verses:

> Once the soul is thus restored [through the watery descent],
> song becomes alive;
> if the poet's hand is pure,
> water [itself] takes shape.[16]

The "taking shape" of the water in the poet's "pure hand" suggests
that, traveling eastward, the German poet cannot simply aim to drown
himself in the Euphrates (or the Orient) in a gesture of total self-nega-
tion or self-abandonment. Even when fully immersed in the fluid element of the East, his own creativity and imagination must remain
vibrant to permit a genuine poetic "response." In his "Annotations,"
Goethe states specifically that, in order to catch a glimpse of Eastern
poetry, culture, and religion, a distinct effort is required. "If we want to
participate in the productions of these marvelous intellects, we have
to 'orientalize' ourselves; the Orient is not simply going to come over
to us." This means that cultural empathy and receptivity—no matter
how desirable—cannot simply be equated with passivity. Like every art
or important competence, the Orient has to be patiently acquired—
which means that its texts have to be studied, its languages and music
savored, its unfamiliar life-forms experienced. In Heideggerian language, one might say that the Orient has to be "undergone" (*erfahren*)
in such a manner that we are both ourselves transformed and enabled
to respond adequately to its challenge. Goethe's aversion to sheer passivity, to a mindless tourism in foreign lands, and his emphasis on genuine responsiveness are reflected in a poem in the "Book of
Reflections" that deserves to be quoted in full:

> Markets tease you with their wares,
> yet insipid are your stares.
> Only who quietly attends
> learns how love restores and mends.

If you spend your days and nights
accumulating vain sounds and sights,
then pause in different surroundings
to perceive more truthful soundings.
If you seek right things in life,
rightly you yourself must strive:
Who in genuine love can burn,
will be loved by God in turn.[17]

What needs to be added immediately, however, is that poetic creativity and initiative cannot cancel the required receptivity, the needed
willingness patiently to "undergo" the difference of other cultures and
ultimately of the divine. In emphasizing poetic engagement, Goethe
does not wish to encourage cultural self-aggrandizement, the strategy
of assimilating or appropriating the other in an imperial or possessive
gesture—a gesture that has rightly been termed "Orientalism" (in the
pejorative sense). In the German context of Goethe's time, this strategy was particularly manifest in the tendency to measure Oriental poetry by classical Western (Greek or Roman) standards. In his
"Annotations," Goethe deplores the "narrow prejudice which does not
wish to acknowledge anything that cannot be traced to Rome or
Athens"—a prejudice he considers "obnoxious." Although Oriental
poets may occasionally remind one of Homer or Horace, the latter
should not serve as measuring rods; rather, Goethe states, these poets
should be "compared among each other and honored on their own
terms—quite independently of Greeks and Romans." The "Annotations" also provide helpful clues regarding the proper relation between
self and other, native and foreign cultures. Under the heading "Über-
setzungen," the text distinguishes between three types of translations:
one (called "prosaic") that merely transliterates foreign thoughts in an
empirical-descriptive way without personal engagement; a second one
(called "parodistic") that seeks to internalize and assimilate the foreign
in a self-assertive or possessive manner; and finally a translation that en-
gages the other without any intent to copy or subdue—that is, one that
honors the distinctness of the other by allowing the echoes of the
other's language to resonate in the native tongue. For Goethe, this third
type is clearly the most admirable and appropriate; for in it, he says, we
find "completed the entire circle in which the encounter between the
foreign and the native, between the familiar and the unfamiliar moves."
As one might add, this type is also the proper locus of dialogue—a dialogue that occupies the midpoint between self and other, the "in-between" (*metaxy*) between address and creative response.[18]

Goethe's *Divan* Today

Considerable time has passed since the first appearance of Goethe's *West-Eastern Divan;* turbulent events of the intervening period have opened a distance, perhaps a gulf between his "classical" age and ours. What lessons can contemporary readers draw from his poetry, and especially his *Divan?* No doubt, many readers today are estranged from Goethe's work, feeling alienated by the Olympian aura surrounding his legacy and also by his status as courtier or court official (*Geheimer Rat*). Above all, the agonies of the twentieth century have produced a certain sea-change in European culture rebounding strongly on its classical period. Several leading European intellectuals have noted this sea-change and its effects on Goethe. Thus, reacting against the evalation of the Weimar poet to a cultural icon, Ortega y Gasset after the Second World War issued a call "begging for a Goethe from within." Similarly, on the occasion of the bicentennial of Goethe's birth (1949), Romano Guardini in his book *The End of Modernity* (*Das Ende der Neuzeit*) reflected on the distance from classical Weimar. Referring to Goethe's opus as a whole he observed:

> This work obviously cannot mean for the future—and even for the present—what it has meant for the period before the first World War. The Goethe image of that earlier time was closely linked with distinct features of the modern world-view and hence, to the extent of that linkage, belongs now to the past. However, that Goethe who will be relevant to future generations is today not yet clearly visible or perceptible.[19]

A main point of the present pages is precisely the claim that at least glimpses of his present and future relevance can be gleaned from a close reading of his late work, especially his *West-Eastern Divan.* The following discussion will seek to highlight some features that seem particularly relevant and instructive in our time. One of these features is the lesson Goethe's late work, including the *Divan,* holds for Germans. As will be recalled, the *Divan* was written in a time of upheaval, in the midst of the wars of liberation (against Napoleon and the French). In Germany, the period witnessed a massive upsurge of "patriotic" literature and poetry glorifying warfare and German nationalism. A good deal of (so-called) Romantic poetry at the time was replete with references to bloody swords, sacrifice (*Opfer*), and heroes' death (*Heldentod*). Thus, a poem by Ernst Moritz Arndt proclaimed: "Today we shall, every one of us/drench our weapons in blood/French blood. . . ." Seen against this background, Goethe's *Divan* stands as a radical antipode to this popular "patriotic" literature—a fact that explains in part its lukewarm reception among his contemporaries. As mentioned, the opening poem "Hegire" invited his readers not to the battlefield but into a realm of "purity and rightness." This does not mean that Goethe was blithely indifferent to the current ideas of liberty and national independence, nor that he was coldly detached from the lot of his compatriotes. What he opposed, however, was the political instrumentalization of poetry, that is, its abuse for militarisitic purposes. Above all, he feared that "patriotic" songs might open the floodgates to chauvinism and xenophobia with their devastating effects. (In light of the experiences of the twentieth century, his fears assume a prophetic quality.) For Goethe, the task of literature and culture was not to unleash the worst in people, but to cultivate their better aptitudes and talents. In this sense one can understand his well-known lines in *Zahme Xenien:* "To become a nation, Germans, you try it in vain; rather, as you are able, aim to humanize yourselves more freely."[20]

Goethe's opposition to chauvinism is manifest not only in *Xenien* and numerous conversations but also in the *Divan* itself, especially in the "Book of Annoyance" ("Buch des Unmuts"). There, with oblique reference to patriotic-Romantic poets, we read:

> But if you wish to know them better,
> keep your standards right and sane;
> for what they call golden letter
> is quite probably inane.
> For to earn in rightness praises,
> rightly living one must be;
> and to soar in grandiose phrases
> seems like tawdry alchemy.

Critique of chauvinism in that book, one should note, extends beyond German confines to all European nationalities who have traditionally been engaged in enmity and mutual disdain. As one poem in the book remarks, with a good deal of annoyance: whatever the nationality, "whether French, British, Italian or German," each party only practices "what egotism dictates." Directly aiming at the tumultuous warmongering of the period, another poem complains:

> Have I ever offered counsel
> how to wage your wars and feuds?
> Have I ever scolded anyone,
> when to peace you turned your moods?

The concluding poem of the *Divan,* titled "Good Night," commends the peaceful collection or gathering ("Divan") to Goethe's compatriots, and readers in general, saying: "Now, dear songs, bed yourselves at the bosom of my people" and in a cloud may angel Gabriel "guard your weary limbs" so that "fresh and healthy, cheerful and sociable" you may savor fully "how beauty and newness constantly grow on all sides."[21]

Apart from holding lessons for Germans (and nationalities in general), Goethe's *Divan* also offers valuable pointers to contemporary philosophy (especially its Continental or European variant). In some quarters of recent philosophy—often labeled "postmodern"—it has become customary to denounce the entire spectrum of Western thought and culture as being gravely disfigured by logocentrism, egocentrism, and anthropocentrism; according to this line of argument, Western reasoning—dating back as far as Socrates—has always been self-centered, predatory, and basically monological. While perhaps containing a kernel of truth (especially regarding Cartesian and post-Cartesian thought), the accusation seems vastly overstated, approximating the status of a doctrinaire shibboleth. Both in premodern and modern times, one can find a host of counter-examples undermining the broad indictment. One of these counter-examples is precisely Goethe's *Divan,* which, as has been shown, celebrates the blessings of unconditional love—a love that does not aim to dominate or possess but finds its joy in generously resigned cherishing and "letting-be." In this non-possessive attitude Goethe could rightly find a soul-mate in the Persian poet Hafiz, who was the epitome of self-giving and prodigality. History records that, on one of his military ventures, the mighty Timur arrived in Shiraz and there ordered Hafiz to appear before him. The conqueror was upset over a poem by Hafiz that said that he would gladly "give away Samarkand and Bokhara" for a little dark mole on the cheek of his beloved (Samarkand and Bokhara being the seat and backbone of Timur's empire). Called to account for his verses, Hafiz is reported to have bowed to the ground and replied: "Alas! O prince, it is this prodigality which is the cause of the misery in which you see me." On hearing this Timur relented and, according to a historian, treated the poet henceforth "with kindness and generosity."[22]

The philosophical import of the *Divan* goes beyond logocentrism, touching on the central question of self/other relations. In this respect, much of contemporary philosophy shows a deeply conflicted, even schizoid, character. According to some influential intellectuals, the accent today must be placed squarely on otherness or alterity (seen as an antidote to traditional Western self-centeredness). In some formulations, the entire goodness, integrity, or self-worth of an individual is derived from a nondescript "Other" — a claim that radically devalues the endeavor of self-care and the attentive self-cultivation of virtues. In regard to foreign texts or cultures, the claim tends to cancel the labor of interpretation in favor of a passively pliant receptivity. In contrast to this argument (and sometimes in tandem with it), a very different, even opposite approach is favored by some intellectuals: an approach that, in quasi-Nietzschen fashion, celebrates the sovereign will-power of the reader over the text, of self over other. By proclaiming every interpretation to be an arbitrary construction or invention, this approach in effect devalues the integrity of the text (or foreign culture) by stripping it of its right to a fair hearing. To both kinds of strategies, Goethe's *Divan* offers a helpful rejoinder. As previously indicated, his "Annotations" provide important clues for a proper construal of interpretation and translation. Particularly significant is his distinction between three types of interpretation: a prosaic-receptive, a parodistic or imperialistic, and (what one may call) a hermeneutical reading. To recall an earlier point, it is chiefly the third type that is favored by Goethe as capturing the complete circle "in which the encounter between the foreign and the native, between the familiar and the unfamiliar moves." The point is also reflected (playfully) in these verses, addressed to Suleika:

> As she lavishes my day,
> I retain my precious ego;
> but whenever she turns away,
> instantly I shrink to zero.[23]

In our rapidly contracting world, Goethe's comments on self/other relations acquire global significance, pointing in the direction of a dialogue of cultures and civilizations. As is well known, Goethe throughout his life was deeply committed to an amicable interaction and conversation between cultures and religions. In his later years, he eagerly sponsored the notion of global literary and intellectual exchange. As he commented to Eckermann (in 1827): "National literature today does not mean much, for the epoch of world literature is dawning"—where "world literature" does not mean the establishment of a uniform global canon, but the fostering of an ongoing dialogue between writers and thinkers across boundaries.[24] A similar spirit animated his views on relations between religious faiths. A concrete event, which occurred during the wars of liberation, illustrates his attitude poignantly. After the great battle of Leipzig (October 1813), in which the allied troops—including many Muslim soldiers—defeated Napoleon, Goethe was dismayed to learn that the Protestants in Weimar were planning to celebrate the annual Reformation Day as usual. As he wrote in an essay of the time, such a celebration was bound to separate and split apart peoples and denominations that, just a while before, had been united in a common cause; religious separation, in turn, was liable to remind thoughtful observers of the "discord and belligerence" that had been the "enormous blight" of previous centuries. In lieu of the celebration, Goethe suggested an interfaith service—what he called a "festival of the purest humanity"—in which different denominations and religions, without entirely abandoning their own traditions, would come together to venerate jointly the divine source of all being. In poetic language, a similar thought is expressed in the *Divan,* in the "Book of Reflections," where we read:

> Do not ask through which portal
> you have entered God's holy city,
> just remain, a sober mortal,
> at the place that now seems fitting.[25]

As is evident from the tenor of the entire *Divan,* Goethe favored not the "clash" but the peace of civilizations; or else: he sought to counteract, wherever possible, the ever-renewed clashes between cultures and societies through the cultivation of dialogue and mutual affection. This endeavor is highlighted with forceful clarity in the shortest book of the *Divan:* the "Book of Timur." Although short in size, containing only two poems, the book may be considered the pivot around which the *Divan* turns. The two poems are titled respectively "Winter and Timur" and "For Suleika." In the first poem, the icy, bone-chilling figure of winter addresses Timur, comparing itself to Saturn and Timur to Mars—both "evil-spirited stars." In this contest of planets, winter promises to vanquish Timur, called the "tyrant of injustice," saying: "Note, my storms are icier even than your heart." In the end, winter conjures up the icy grip of death as Timur's final judge and executioner: "Yes, old man, from death's coldness nothing shall protect you, neither embers of the hearth nor December fires." In sharp contrast to this desolate scene, the second poem celebrates affection and the playful joys of love. Although recognizing that to fetch perfume for his beloved may require "a thousand roses," the poet here enlists nature's bounty not in the service of death and destruction but for the enhancement of joy and the fullness of life. In the words of the poem: "In order to have a flask containing the heavenly scent [of roses], tender like your finger tips, a whole big world is needed." The "world" invoked in these verses is the poet's world or land—the same

land into which Goethe in his epigram invited his readers to migrate.
It is in this poet's world that all beings are nurtured, cherished, and ul-
timately salvaged from destruction. In one of his posthumous poems,
Goethe returned to Hafiz in a moving "éloge de la poésie":

> Yes, I hear how in your songs,
> Hafiz, you sing poets' praises;
> look, I gladly go along,
> thanking you whom laurel graces.[26]

Chapter 9

Islam and Democracy

Reflections on Abdolkarim Soroush

Islam demands loyalty to God, not to thrones.

—*Mohammad Iqbal*

In his *Political and Social Essays,* Paul Ricoeur addresses forthrightly the situation of the religious believer in the modern world, especially in modern secular society. Quoting from scripture (Matthew 5, 13), he insists that believers are meant to be "the salt of the earth"—a phrase militating against both world domination and world denial, that is, against the dual temptation of either controlling or rejecting worldly society. As he writes poignantly, "the salt is made for salting, the light for illuminating," and religion exists "for the sake of those outside itself," that is, for the world that faith inhabits. In Ricoeur's view, religion—including (especially) Christianity—has been for too long enamored or in collusion with political power and domination, a collusion that some recent theologians have aptly labeled "Christendom" and that has exerted a "demoralizing effect" on believers and non-believers alike, driving them to "cynicism, amoralism, and despair." However, the situation is perhaps not entirely bleak. When it emerges from this collusion, he adds, religion "will be able to give light once more to all men—no longer as a power, but as a prophetic message," that is, as a light that illuminates but does not blind. In a similar vein, Emmanuel Levinas has defined the role of Judaism or Judaic faith "in the time of the nations," namely, as a non-domineering voice of conscience that remembers and faithfully reiterates the call to justice.[1]

Among all the great world religions today, Islam is still most sorely tempted by the lure of worldly power and public dominion; this at least is the impression given by a large number of its adherents, especially by many so-called Islamic governments and Islamist movements (often labeled "fundamentalist" in Western media). As in the case of Christianity, this lure or collusion is baffling and disconcerting—given the strong opposition of Islam to any kind of idolatry, that is, to the substitution of any worldly images or power structures for the rule of the one transcendent God. How can Muslim believers be expected to submit or surrender themselves to any worldly potentates, no matter how pious or clerically sanctioned, if their faith is defined as surrender ("*islam*") to nothing else but the eternal "light" of truth? How can they be asked to abandon their religious freedom (in the face of the divine) for the sake of contingent political loyalties to rulers who often lack even a semblance of public or collective legitimation? As in the case of traditional Christendom, Islam's collusion with public power has exerted (in Ricoeur's words) a "demoralizing effect" on believers and non-believers alike, driving many of them to "cynicism, amoralism, and despair." In this situation, it is high time for Muslims and all friends of Islam to take stock of the prevailing predicament. Concisely put: it is time, not to relinquish Islam in favor of some doctrinaire secularism or laïcism, but to reinvigorate the "salt" of Islamic faith so that it can become a beacon of light both for Muslims and the world around them. Differently phrased: it is time to recuperate the meaning of Islam as a summons to freedom, justice, and service to the God who, throughout the *Qur'an,* is called "all-merciful and compassionate" (*rachman-i-racheem*).

As it happens, such soul-searching recuperation is actually going on in the Islamic world today—often accompanied by intense conflict, recrimination, and even persecution. To this extent, contemporary Islam is in a state of agony, with the fortunes of recovery hanging in the balance. The point here is not to impugn the motives of political Islam or political Islamicists—motives that in many ways are historically understandable, given the backdrop of colonialism, Western hegemony, and perceived military insecurity. What is at issue is rather the wisdom and sensibility of politicized religion, seeing that the yoking together or collusion of power and religion inevitably exacts a heavy toll both on the sobriety of political judgment and on the integrity of religious faith. Among contemporary Muslim philosophers and public intellectuals no one has been more eloquent in exposing the pitfalls and costs of this collusion than the Iranian Abdolkarim Soroush. In a long series of writings, Soroush has vindicated the compatibility of Islam and modern democracy, by showing that it is precisely in the context of political democracy that Muslims can reclaim and exercise their religious freedom, being released from religious absolutism or oppressive clerical tutelage. Recently, some of these writings have become available to English-speaking readers in a volume titled *Reason, Freedom, and Democracy in Islam*.[2] In the following I shall explore Soroush's argument by proceeding in three steps. In a first section, I seek to profile his position against the backdrop of political Islam, especially the backdrop of the Islamist rejection or sidelining of democracy in favor of traditionalist versions of quasi-theocracy. The second section offers an exposition and interpretation of Soroush's reconciliation of Islam and democracy under the rubric of a religiously sensitive civil society. By way of conclusion, this reconciliation is inserted into the context of contemporary politics, especially the emergence of an inter-religious and inter-civilizational global society.

Democracy as Ignorance (Jahiliyya)

In common parlance, religion and politics are neither synonyms nor necessarily antonyms. On a theoretical level, one can distinguish a limited number of ideal-typical constellations involving the two terms. On the one hand, there is the paradigm of complete separation or isolation (an extreme version of the Augustinian formula of "two cities"). In this paradigm, religious faith withdraws onto a "holy mountain" while politics maintains a radical indifference or agnosticism vis-à-vis scriptural teachings or spiritual meanings. As can readily be seen, both sides pay a price for this mutual segregation: faith by forfeiting any relevance or influence in worldly affairs, and politics by tendentially shriveling into an empty power game. In the historical development of religion and politics, this segregationist paradigm has been relatively rare (leaving aside the phenomenon of monastic retreat). Much more common has been another paradigm or constellation: that of fusion or amalgamation—which may be accomplished in two ways or along two roads: either religion strives to colonize and subjugate worldly politics, thereby erecting itself into a public power, or else politics colonizes religious faith by expanding itself into a totalizing, quasi-religious panacea or ideology. History shows that the former strategy has been the preferred option of most religions in the past.

The same strategy also characterized traditional Islam. With minor variations, public power in Islamic society during the early centuries was wielded either by semi-divine leaders (the "righteous caliphs") or else by a combination of dynastic imperial rulers (presumably descendants of the Prophet) and a battery of clerical jurists or jurisconsults (*fuqaha*). In his account of political authority in early Islam, Ira

Lapidus distinguishes between two models or (what he calls) two "golden ages": namely, an "integral" or holistic model and a more "differentiated" or symbiotic structure. In the first model, he writes, Islamic society "was integrated in all dimensions, political, social, and moral, under the aegis of Islam." The prototype of this model was the unification of Arabia under the guidance of the Prophet and his immediate successors. In the second, more differentiated model, imperial Islamic government—from the Umayyads and Abbasids to the Ottomans—was erected on the diversified structures of traditional Middle Eastern societies, thus yielding a complex, symbiotic amalgam. In this case, the original caliphate was transformed "from the charismatic succession to the religious authority of the Prophet" into a far-flung imperial regime governed both by religious norms (*shari'ah*) and more adaptive political laws, or rather by a mixture of imperial-political authority and clerical jurisprudence (resembling the medieval theory of "two swords"). This mixture gave rise to a more complex socio-political theory. To quote Lapidus again: "Muslim political theorists, such as al-Baqillani, al-Mawardi, and Ibn Taimiyya, devised a theory of the caliphate that symbolized the ideal existence of the unified *umma*, while at the same time allowing for historical actualities."[3]

According to Lapidus, contemporary Islamic traditionalists or "revivalists" harken back—though often unsuccessfully—to the two models of Islam's "golden ages." To this extent, Islamic revivalism necessarily is at odds with the basic features of modern life—given that, in its core, "modernity" (at least in its Western form) aims at the disaggregation and radical diffusion of the unified, holistic worldviews and political structures of an earlier age. Being an integral part of modernity and its way of life, modern democracy inevitably falls under the same verdict of traditionalists: namely, as testifying to the modern abandonment of faith in favor of an "un-godly" secularism or nihilism. At this point, it is important to observe the strategy of the revivalist argument—a strategy that presents the transition from tradition to modernity (and postmodernity) under the simplistic image of reversal or antithesis. Thus, traditionalists are wont to erect a series of binaries to capture the historical change—claiming, for instance, that modernity (or modernization) means a lapse from faith into non-faith, from religious devotion into agnostic rationalism, and from the holistic unity of "truth" into a radical relativism (denying "truth"). In a similar vein, the argument is sometimes advanced that, while earlier ages were founded on "virtue," modernity is founded on freedom and non-virtue (as if a virtue without freedom were somehow plausible or even desirable). In the most provocative formulation, traditionalists assert that modernity has replaced the reign of God with the reign of "man" or humanity—a replacement equalling a lapse into paganism and the state of pre-Islamic "ignorance" (*jahiliyya*).

In the present context, the latter formulation is particularly significant. Under political auspices, the charge implies a reversal of public supremacy—namely, the replacement of God's sovereignty with the sovereignty of the people (the latter equated with democracy). In larger measure, this charge is at the heart of the anti-democratic sentiments espoused by many revivalists and/or "fundamentalists." In discussing the "political discourse" of contemporary Islamicist movements, Youssef Choueiri highlights this point as central to that discourse. Referring to the writings of Sayyid Qutb, al-Maududi, and Ayatollah Khomeini, Choueiri underscores the holistic religious quality of "God's sovereignty," writing that the phrase affirms God's authority "in the daily life of His creatures and servants," revealing that "the universe is judged to be one single organic unity, both in its formation and movement: The unity of the universe mirrors the absolute oneness of God." Judged by the standard of this holistic unity, modern humanity—including modern democracy—exists in a state of disarray and incoherence, that is, in "a second *jahiliyya,* more sinister in its implications than the *jahiliyya* of pre-Islamic days." Pushing this point still further, radical Islamicists tend to view the entire course of Western history as "a connected series of *jahiliyyas:* Hellenism, the Roman Empire, the Middle Ages, the Renaissance, the Enlightenment, and the French Revolution" (and its democratic offshoots). As an antidote to modernity and modern democracy, Islamicist thinkers typically propose a return to "God's sovereignty," that is, to a semi- or quasi-theocracy (which usually means some form of clerical despotism or elitism). Thus, Qutb supported the idea of a "Muslim vanguard" (patterned on various revolutionary vanguards of the twentieth century). In turn, al-Maududi called for an "international revolutionary party" ready to wage Islamic *jihad,* while Khomeini placed his trust in the guardianship of a supreme jurist (*velayat-e faqih*).[4]

It becomes urgent here to look at the presumed transfer of sovereignty and its underlying premises. Is such a transfer plausible or persuasive (even on strictly religious grounds)? The idea of sovereignty implies the rule of absolute will or will power untrammeled by any rational constraints or intelligible standards of justice. To ascribe such sovereignty to God means to construe God as a willful and arbitrary autocrat—which is hardly a pious recommendation. Several of the great Islamic philosophers (of the classical period) had already objected to this construal, complaining that it transforms God into a tyrant or despot similar to such tyrants as Genghis Khan or Tamerlane.[5] As it happens, contemporary Islamicists seeking to revive "golden ages" of the past tend to be attracted precisely to this aura of despotism (undeterred by the horrible examples of the twentieth century). Whatever the status of God's sovereignty may be, however, modern democracy represents by no means a simple reversal in the sense of installing the people as sovereign despots. On the contrary, whatever else modern democracy means, it certainly means a dispersal of power and a constant circulation of power holders. Several leading democratic theorists, including Hannah Arendt, have gone so far as to urge the removal of "sovereignty" from political discourse, in order to make broader room for grassroots participation. This initiative has been continued and further fleshed out by "postmodern" political thinkers, and especially by defenders of radical democracy, for whom democracy is defined by the removal of the "markers of certainty" and thus by the disintegration of traditional holistic shibboleths (like sovereignty, the nation, or "the people"). What emerges here is a conception of democracy not as a static entity but as an open-ended and experimental process—though one needs to guard again against a simple reversal that would replace earlier holistic structures with utter fragmentation and incoherence.[6]

Transplanted into the Islamic context, this conception of democracy entails not a simple transfer of sovereignty (from God to people), but a radically different understanding of political rule, and also a radically new view of the relation between religion and worldly politics, or between the sacred and the secular. In fairness, the sea-change involved here has not gone unnoticed by leading Muslim intellectuals in our time, including Mohammed al-Jabri, Muhammed Arkoun, Hassan Hanafi, and others. Thus, al-Jabri has proposed a "critique of Arab reason" that would open up holistic structures of the past to new and diversified inquiries, while Arkoun has urged examination of the "unthought" dimensions in traditional Muslim thought in order to tap recessed resources of both secular and religious insight.[7] In the specific idiom of political theory, Lahouari Addi has contrasted Islamicist "utopian" revivalism with the demands of modern democracy. Rejecting as debilitating the tendency of Islamicists to denounce every innovation (domestic or foreign) as *jahiliyya*, he complains that, for too long, the Islamic world has "held itself apart from the social debates" of the West, preferring instead to encapsulate itself in a nostalgic and "apologetic historiography." Drawing on the lessons of modernity, Addi formulates a crucial precondition for democracy in the Islamic world: "It is necessary to show how political modernity is incompatible with the public character of religion and how modernity is built on the depoliticization of religion"—where depoliticization, however, has the "precise content" not of abolishing religion but of assigning it a new domicile in civil society. Regarding the prospect of such a change to take root, Addi is moderately hopeful, stating: "Such a creation of modernism by way of Arab-Islamic culture is theoretically possible, for there is no reason—everything else kept the same—why democracy should be inherently Western and absolutism inherently Muslim."[8]

Soroush and Religious Democracy

As one can see, the path toward a reconciliation of Islam and democracy has been prepared in several quarters. What Abdolkarim Soroush adds to this endeavor is an unusual breadth of erudition and an unfailing grasp of key issues. These qualities are clearly evident in his *Reason, Freedom, and Democracy in Islam* (as well as in his other writings, interviews, and recorded statements). His book forthrightly takes aim at the association of Islam with absolutism or an absolutist and despotic sovereignty. Surveying the history of Muslim societies, he bemoans the forced submissiveness of Muslims, a submission due to "a political culture deeply influenced by centuries of tyranny." In large measure, this political culture can be traced to traditional theological and jurisprudential teachings. As Soroush writes: "The theoreticians of the past used to say: 'Sovereigns are mirrors of the sovereignty of God'." In traditional theology (*kalam*), God was portrayed as "an absolute bearer of rights and free of all duties toward human beings"; accordingly, kings and imperial rulers were viewed in the same light, as mirrors or replicas of divine authority. Predictably, vested in human hands, this absolute power produced dismal effects on social and moral life. "Is it not true," the text asks, "that tyrannies attract a considerable retinue of corrupt panegyrists and sycophants? What is this but moral and social corruption?" Such venality may explain why those "who miss few occasions to deliver a litany against the evils of freedom refuse to put two words together about the evil of absolute power." In modern times, however, and recently also in Muslim societies, a rebellion has been mounted against tyranny and its corrupting effects. This rebellion, one should note, is directed not so much against God or religion, but against human rulers arrogantly usurping divine authority. The modern world, Soroush writes, has long challenged and undermined a notion that has always been "a source of evil and corruption": namely, "the right to act as a God-like potentate with unlimited powers." Modern society rejects such God-like pretensions "because it does not consider government to be an extension of divine power within human society. Management skills require merely human, not God-like powers."[9]

As crucial antidote to tyrannical oppression, Soroush's text celebrates the value of human freedom (a defense that surely reflects also his personal experiences and those of many of his contemporaries). In Soroush's account, human freedom is not merely equivalent to will power or arbitrary choice, but harbors ontological and even religious connotations. As he notes, freedom is not treasured by, or only receives lip service from, the powerful and arrogantly mighty. "Only those," he writes, "who consider themselves to be directly inspired by God, who profess to possess the absolute truth" tend to refuse "the gifts of freedom." But these gifts are vital to the oppressed and downtrodden: "Freedom is the slogan of the humble and the needy; it is the catchword of those who are aware of the penury of their own reason." In line with a longer tradition of philosophical thought, Soroush distinguishes not so much between positive and negative freedom as rather between internal and external freedom. The former type is achieved "by liberating oneself from the rein of passion and anger," that is, from inner (though often socially induced) compulsions. The second, external type consists in "emancipating oneself from the yoke of potentates, despots, charlatans, and exploiters"; its requisite is "participation in the contest of freedom, which is a public process based on rules and regulations." In their joint operation, internal and external freedom are the gateway to deliverance and the pursuit of justice—for freedom is clearly "one of the components of justice," and the seeker of freedom is "in pursuit of justice" in the same way as the seeker of justice "cannot help but pursue freedom as well." Soroush at this point reminds his Muslim readers of such Qur'anic verses as "No compulsion in matters of faith" and "Shall we compel you to accept it when ye are averse to it?," adding emphatically that religion is "by definition, incompatible with coercion," while freedom has the virtue of endowing life and life choices with meaning. In the same context, we find this moving paean to the benefits of freedom:

No blessing is more precious for mankind than the free choice of the way of the prophets. Nothing is better for humanity than submission based on free will. Blessed are those who are guided in this manner, who freely choose the way of the prophets and are awash in a cascade of divine grace. . . . But in the absence of this state of grace, nothing is better for humankind than the possession of freedom. All free societies, whether they are religious or nonreligious, are humane. But totalitarian societies abide neither divinity nor humanity.[10]

For Soroush, freedom is closely associated with reason or rational understanding, in the sense that such understanding provides a supplement and corrective to (arbitrary) will. Concisely put: freedom, to be non-capricious or non-despotic, requires reason, just as reason requires the help of freedom, specifically the freedom of thought (or *libre examen*). The latter freedom has always been anathema to proponents of dogmatism (theological or otherwise), who consider "truth" as a property and settled doctrine. "The vision of reason as a treasure trove of truths," he states, "is not conducive to thinking about the origin and the manner of arriving at truths." This view of reason as a storehouse or warehouse of doctrines entails the notion of an "enforced" or "administered" truth that leaves "no room for questioning and doubt." By contrast, anti-dogmatists construe reason as a path of reasoning, that is, as "a truth-seeking, sifting, and appraising agent" where the method of pursuing truth deserves as much respect as the goal itself. In this latter construal, freedom is a crucial requisite. What those who shun freedom as the "enemy of truth" do not realize, Soroush emphasizes, is that "freedom is itself a truth (*haq*)," namely, as the necessary gateway to truth of any kind. At this point, in an effort to underscore the importance of freedom of thought or reasoning, the text draws a parallel that is scarcely flattering to radical Islamic fideists utterly disdainful of reason. "It is hardly surprising," we read, "that hatred of reason rises under tyranny and dictatorship. Fascists found a friend in the passions of youth and a foe in the rationality of the mature." Like all dogmatic ideologists, "Nazis despised democracy and public deliberation because they carried the aroma of reason"; hence, "worshipping Hitler was encouraged because it was based on blind and brutish obedience."[11]

Defense of reason, or rather of the process of reasoning, is linked with the vindication (albeit qualified) of modernity and modernization. For Soroush, premodern social life was marked by a certain static quality, averse to innovative inquiry and deliberate change. Modern humankind, he writes, is no longer satisfied with a passive acceptance of things, but is asserting its transformative potential; it has assumed the role of "an active agent in the world," whereas traditional humankind perceived itself as "a guest in a ready-made house in which the occupant had no opportunity or right to object or to change anything." In the language of Kant (invoked by Soroush in several contexts), modern humankind has in a way "grown up" or achieved a state of adult maturity—a condition that has opened up a host of opportunities, but also entailed heavy new responsibilities. Following the European example, reaching maturity signals a kind of "enlightenment," that is, the growth of a critical reflectiveness evident in the critique of traditional metaphysics and traditional holistic worldviews. Against this backdrop, the history of humankind equals in many ways the history of the unfolding of human knowledge—where "knowledge" does not mean a finished set of propositions but rather a mode of knowledge-seeking or critical inquisitiveness (for which the development of modern science is, at least to some extent, an impressive testimonial): "Modern scientific knowledge has transformed not only humanity's view of the world, but also its view of its own abilities and place in it." As a corollary of enlightened inquisitiveness, modernity has carried in its wake a certain metaphysical "disenchantment," which is usually described as the process of "secularization." As Soroush observes (echoing in part Weberian insights): "From an epistemological point of view, the presecular [or premodern] age is marked by the hegemony of metaphysical thought in political, economic, and social realms." By contrast, modernization unsettles earlier holistic premises, bringing about a regime in which "no values and rules are beyond human appraisal and verification" and where "everything is open to critique"—which is "the meaning of secularism."[12]

Modernization, however, denotes not only a change of cognitive perspectives, but also a change of concrete social or socioeconomic practices—which explains the nexus of modernity and "development." This linkage is usually ignored or sidelined by radical traditionalists enamored with the past as an era of piety and morality. Soroush is adamant in challenging this kind of nostalgia. As he admits, development sometimes brings in its wake "leisure and occasionally pride, obliviousness, and disdain for traditional values." However, what is frequently neglected is the circumstance that it also provides the opportunity "for cultivating the higher and more spiritual needs"—and, in fact, for cultivating any values whatever, for "the distress of acquiring one's daily bread, shelter, and clothing" hardly leaves room for engagement in arts and the pursuit of "mystical gnosis." Only once humans are liberated from the "worrisome tasks" of daily survival can they be expected to take wing and "fly in the sphere of higher concerns." It be may be correct to say that socioeconomic development only fulfills the primary needs and not the "higher values," such as justice, freedom, wisdom, and the like. However, while in the clutches of physical want, the laboring masses of humankind have little or no chance to reach these higher goals. For Soroush, in any case, the God of those struggling for subsistence is "the God of the oppressed, not that of the mystics"; he is a God "that vanquishes the oppressors, facilitates survival, pays off debts, and grants wishes" (in other words, he is "*rachman-i-*

racheem"). Viewed against this background, socioeconomic development should be seen not as an aberration, but as "an important stage in the evolution of humanity and, as such, even ethically [and religiously] sanctioned."[13]

Construed in this sense, development is beneficial not only for the pursuit of spiritual goals, but also for the fostering of an uncoerced public life and political praxis—that is, for the flourishing of modern democracy. Without postulating a narrow economic determinism (even in the "last instance"), Soroush perceives a close affinity between the struggle against economic misery and exploitation and the struggle against despotism. "Democracy," he writes pointedly, "is desirable for all, but in practice it is not available to all"—a restriction that is usually due to unfavorable socioeconomic circumstances. The greatest dictatorship, he adds (with a sideglance at conditions in many Middle Eastern countries), is that of "poverty and ignorance"; and it is in their shadows "that tyrannical [political] rule rises and prospers, extinguishing the torch of liberty and justice in human hearts." Democracy, one should note, is aligned in this account with liberty and justice, or rather with the liberty or freedom to strive for justice and truth—values that are "extinguished" by despotism. Far from being equivalent to popular sovereignty or arbitrary popular will, democracy emerges here as a searching or "zetetic" enterprise, as a transformative and constantly self-transforming regime in the direction of justice. In Soroush's words, democracy in a developed society is for ever "brimming with new values and facts"; its very existence hinges on "a matrix of freedom of research and adversarial dialogue of ideas"—practices that are incompatible with tyranny or political repression. A crucial instrument for furthering free inquiry and dialogue is an open public sphere, a sphere well informed but not domesticated or manipulated by the media: "Democratization of the spread of knowledge and the establishment of popular control over the flow of information (in addition to that of wealth and power) is among the most significant promoters and properties of democracy in developed societies."[14]

In articulating his view of democracy, Soroush adopts an unusual stance that does not fit well into the established rubrics of democratic theory. On the one hand, he describes democracy as a "method"—which seems to place him in the camp of "proceduralism" or a purely procedural construal of democracy (devoid of intrinsic moral qualities). But on the other hand, he insists that the operation or maintenance of democratic procedures is impossible without a general commitment to "substantive" goods, such as justice and truth. This ambivalence or complexity is clearly reflected in his statement that democracy is "a method of harnessing the power of rulers, rationalizing their policies, protecting the rights of the subjects, and attaining the public good." What this statement reveals (or so one might argue) is an effort to break out of established metaphysical and political binaries—an effort that one can (cautiously) label "postmodern" (provided the term is not identified with a simple relativism or nihilism).[15] This effort is intrinsic to the notion of a "zetetic" or transformative democracy. For clearly, an open-ended search for "truth" (implied in "zetetic") militates *both* against a conception of truth as property or storehouse and against its dismissal as illusory (rendering search futile). In a similar way, search for the public good is at odds *both* with the dogmatic imposition of a collective formula and with a stance of radical indifference or neutrality toward goodness as such. Soroush's difficult or nuanced position is also evident in his attitude toward another binary shibboleth of our time: the doublet of "foundationalism/antifoundationalism" or determinacy/indeterminacy. In his view, democracy requires a blending of the two, namely, a commitment to just means and a certain open latitude of ends. Here is a crucial passage:

> The proposition that "democracy denotes the use of specific means to attain unspecific ends" is a fundamentally correct assertion—but lends itself to misunderstanding. Far from denying the a priori principles of democracy [commitment to public good], it is meant as a response to those who believe ends justify means and thus misguidedly characterize a totalitarian system that purportedly dispenses justice and human rights as a democracy. They are reminded: "method" is of essence in democracy. It is not evident, from the outset, who is right and who deserves certain privileges and powers.... Reality, here, follows the method of discovering the reality.... It is in this sense that democracy may be said to have a determined method toward undetermined ends. The indeterminacy, however, refers to instances and specific cases, not the basic principles and criteria of democracy which, like the fundamental precepts of jurisprudence, are determined, honored, and inviolable.[16]

Soroush's unorthodox stance surfaces in several other respects, especially in his discussion of modernity and Western liberal democracy. Although generally supportive of the former, he is not unaware of the pitfalls of a certain doctrinaire "modernism" (an awareness displaying, perhaps, a postmodern flavor). Thus, while clearly championing reason and modern science, his text also acknowledges "profound scientific, humanist, and philosophical critiques" of modernization that have arisen in the West as byproducts of development. From the vantage of these critiques, technology and development may have "run their course," allowing societies to advance beyond technological gadgets, toward new and possibly more elevated horizons (more attentive, for example, to ecological needs). With regard to Western liberal democracy, Soroush critiques both the exclusive glorification of one type of liberty and the retreat into a spurious and deceptive kind of moral neutrality. Returning to the distinction between internal and external freedom, he finds that Western society is one-sidedly preoccupied with the second type, constantly engaged in battling external enemies—from king, church, and nobility to unfair taxation and a host of imaginary foes. What has been forgotten or forsaken is the internal battle, the struggle against desires and inner compulsions. The truth, however, is that "if internal and external freedom are not combined, both will suffer." This one-sidedness is sometimes associated in Western liberal society with a complete indifference or neutrality toward moral and religious concerns. Some liberal philosophers, Soroush observes, consider arguments in this domain "unverifiable and unfalsifiable"; hence, they deem controversy over such issues utterly futile and prone to lead into a "quagmire of delusions." As it happens, however, this kind of liberalism is by no means identical with democracy, or at least far from exhausting its meaning. "Equating liberalism and democracy," we read, "signifies, at once, great ignorance of the former and grave injustice toward the latter." Hence, "decoupling" this kind of liberalism from democracy is "analogous to the attempts of social democrats to separate democracy from capitalism."[17]

The uncoupling of democracy from a morally neutral liberalism leads Soroush to his most important contribution: the idea of a "religious democracy" or a democratic religious society. Here it is important, first of all, to distinguish clearly between government and civil society, a distinction that is needed to prevent the usurpation of public power by a religious group or movement in violation of democratic rules of open competition and contestation. Equally important are two other requisites or corollaries: namely, the need not to conflate religion with dogmatism or dogmatic certainty and, further, the refusal to equate democracy with amoral indifference (a refusal implicit in the critique of liberal neutrality, mentioned before). Regarding the last point, religion can bolster moral sensibilities in a democratic society, just as general moral standards (like justice and human rights) can bolster religious sensibilities. In Soroush's view, democracy cannot possibly prosper without commitment to moral precepts, such as "respect for the will of the majority and the rights of others, justice, sympathy, and mutual trust." Slackening of these bonds will endanger democratic life in any society. This is why "sympathetic voices" are beginning to call for "a return to virtues" in Western countries today; and this is where "the great debt of democracy to religion" is revealed, for the latter can serve as "the best guarantor of democracy." This service, of course, can only be fruitful if the other conflation is avoided: that of religion and dogmatic absolutism. Returning to the story of modernization, Soroush reminds his readers that the difference between premodern and modern ages is the "difference between certainty and uncertainty," between a closed worldview (claiming possession of truth) and an open-ended search for truth and genuine insight. Just as modern science depends on a continuous testing and correction of assumptions, so also religious doctrines must be open to continuous scrutiny, that is, to the cauldron of interpretation and re-interpretation (*ijtihad*), which engenders doctrinal modesty and tolerance: "Tolerance in the domain of beliefs is the correlative of a fallibility in the domain of cognition that has encroached upon traditional dogmas."[18]

As a moral disposition, tolerance has a somewhat ambivalent character: it requires a moral or religious commitment to tolerance—which hence cannot be unbounded, so as to include tolerance of intolerance. For Soroush, religious democracy does not require the endorsement of a radical relativism, and certainly not the abandonment of moral or religious convictions. To this extent, democratic tolerance is not contingent on indifference or lack of beliefs, but only on the readiness to expose one's cherished beliefs and those of others to questioning and possible correction. In this sense, Soroush writes, the chief requisite for tolerance is the willingness to jettison "infantile and immature attachments" to one's own omniscience or infallibility. Like all moral dispositions, tolerance is a difficult virtue requiring steady practice and cultivation in a public context. Practice in a public context, however, is liable to infuse religious belief with a measure of open-mindedness or reasonableness—thereby promoting in the long run a "concordance" of reason (*aql*) and divine revelation (*shar'*). In a passage that is liable to upset radical fideists, Soroush maintains that a precondition for democratizing religious society is "historicizing and energizing the religious understanding by underscoring the role of reason in it"—where "reason" does not mean an isolated individual capacity but "a collective reason" or public "common sense" arising from "the kind of public participation and human experience that are available only through democratic methods." Democratic religious societies, he adds, thus do not need to "wash their hands of religiosity" nor turn their backs on revelation; however, they do need to absorb "an adjudicative understanding of religion," in such a way that an "informed religiosity can thrive in conjunction with a democracy sheltered by common sense."[19]

Removed from the lure of public power, religious democracy—or a religiously nurtured democratic society—cannot insist on religious uniformity or homogeneity, but must allow and even foster religious freedom and the diversity of religious beliefs. In Soroush's view, such a democracy necessarily has to be heterogeneous and pluralistic; in fact, its diversity is liable to exceed the vaunted pluralism of secular-liberal society—where some voices (particularly religious voices) tend to be silenced or ignored. As he writes: "The faithful community is more like a wild grove than a manicured garden. It owes the fragance of its faith to this wild independent spirit"—which cannot be harnessed without being strangled. In this respect, his text offers some truly captivating passages exuding the spirit of (a democratized) Sufism:

> Those who have endured ebbs and flows of the heart, avalanches of doubt, clashes of belief, surges of faith, the violence of spiritual storms, and the plundering swell of visions that restlessly and ruthlessly assail the delicate sanctuary of the heart understand that the heterogeneity of souls and the wandering of hearts is a hundred times greater than that of thoughts, tasks, limbs, and tendencies. Belief is a hundred times more diverse and colorful than disbelief. If the pluralism of secularism makes it suitable for democracy, the faithful community is a thousand times more suitable for it.

Addressing the defenders of religious orthodoxy and conformism, he adds: "You respect uniformity, emulation, and obedience to religious jurists"; but "I implore you to appreciate the complexity and colorfulness of belief, liberty, subtlety, and the agility of faiths and volitions." For indeed, "the plurality of religious sects is but a coarse and shallow indicator of the subtle, elusive, and invisible plurality of souls."[20]

Islam and Global Conversation

Soroush's arguments are important and challenging in the context of Islamic societies, a context that traditionally has favored conformism over independent judgment (*libre examen*). Not fortuitously—but perhaps with some hyperbole—some Western journalists have labeled him the "Martin Luther of Islam" (albeit a very modern and perhaps postmodern Luther).[21] However, the significance of his arguments is not narrowly restricted to the Islamic context, but appeals today to a broader, potentially global audience. From the angle of political theory or philosophy, one of the crucial features of his work is the shift of attention from the "state" or central governmental structures to the domain of "civil society" seen as an arena of free human initiatives. This shift of focus is a prominent ingredient in recent Western political thought which, in this respect, has derived significant lessons from Eastern European experiences (particularly the atrophy of society under totalitarian state bureaucracies).[22] Even more crucial is Soroush's attempt to foster a symbiosis or reconciliation of religion and democracy, an attempt that seeks to bypass both rigid separation and totalizing (or totalitarian) fusion.[23] In his account, such a symbiosis would be able *both* to re-energize democracy by elevating its moral fiber (its commitment to the public good) and to enliven and purify religion by rescuing it from conformism and the embroilment in public power. By renouncing domination or "religious despotism," religion is capable of regaining its basic spiritual quality and thereby to serve (in Ricoeur's words) as the "salt of the earth" or the salt of democracy.[24]

In order to perform its role, religious discourse has to broaden its range and accommodate a more general humanistic vocabulary: especially the vocabulary of human rights, individual freedoms, and social justice. In our time, engagement or confrontation with these issues is a requisite for the relevance and viability of religion (Islamic or otherwise). Discussion of human rights, Soroush observes, belongs to "the domain of philosophical theology (*kalam*) and philosophy in general" and in a way constitutes an "extrareligious area of discourse." Although not directly nurtured by religious motives (at least in the modern era), human rights discourse is today religiously unavoidable, and a religious faith oblivious to human rights—as well as to human freedom and justice—is no longer "tenable in the modern world." For Soroush it is axiomatic that humanity cannot be placed in stark antithesis to divine revelation—which entails that respecting human rights and freedoms is important not only for promoting democracy but also for safeguarding its religious dimension or character. Even the tendency of many religious people to accentuate duties or obligations over rights should not be construed in a binary sense, but rather as a supplement or corrective to narrowly secular "rights talk." In a positive vein, religious discourse enriched by human rights vocabulary counteracts the pretense of "inalienable a priori rights," sometimes termed "divine rights," of public or clerical elites. In a religious democracy—no less so than in a secular regime—rulers (including religious judges) cannot be self-appointed but need to be selected through democratic methods accepted by all. In fact, it is "not only the right but the duty" of religious people to elect their rulers in this manner. Underscoring the democratic feature of religious democracy, Soroush asserts forcefully: "The ultimate right of the people to govern, that is, to manage rationally the society in such a way as to reduce errors of deliberation and policy making, shall not be abrogated under any circumstances. . . . The government of the people is a government fit for people, not for Gods."[25]

By inserting religious faith into an open-ended democratic discourse, Soroush's text makes a contribution to a major conundrum that has beleaguered Islam as well as other religions throughout the course of their historical development: the dilemma of the relation between reason and faith. Religious democracy cannot resolve this dilemma through fiat: either through fusion or radical separation. Rather, what such a regime brings into view is a difficult and tensional relationship, an ongoing mutual enrichment and contestation where both sides resist self-enclosure. In Soroush's words, "religious scholars cannot afford to be oblivious to extrareligious knowledge," especially to such key categories of public discourse as social justice, public interest, and human rights. Self-encapsulation in a religious or theological idiom can only lead here to circularity and doctrinaire rigidity—which is detrimental to both reason and faith. On the other hand, religious or spiritual vocabulary can serve as an antidote to sluggish or conformist tendencies in modern public life—an antidote highlighted by the role of prophets whose mission has always been that of "accelerating human spiritual evolution" by "bringing the path of humanity closer to God, augmenting justice, and eradicating tyranny." Once reason and faith are correlated in this manner, an enviable symbiosis is achieved; in Soroush's words: "Heaven and earth are reconciled and the severity of the paradox of religiosity and rationality is reduced." He also describes this nexus as "an auspicious reconciliation" where "religious morality would be the guarantor of democracy" and where "the rights of the faithful to adopt a divine religion would not vitiate the democratic, earthly, and rational nature of the religious government."[26]

In our globalizing age, the correlation of faith and reason carries over into the relationship between historical faith traditions and the broader conversation of humankind, a conversation that includes as participants a variety of religious and non-religious voices. In this broader context, every particular faith tradition is compelled to look at itself both from the inside and the outside, that is, to shoulder the dual task of self-affirmation and self-assessment or self-critique. For a weak or shallow faith, this task is likely to be further debilitating and perhaps destructive. A living faith, however, will welcome the challenge of re-interpretation as the gateway to continuous self-renewal and reformation. In his *In the Time of the Nations,* Levinas—reiterating Talmudic teachings—speaks of the insertion of Israel into "the seventy nations," that is, into humanity at large, presenting this insertion not as a damaging confinement, but rather as an opportunity or invitation for faith to reveal its leavening potential. In a similar vein, harkening back to medieval Islamic formulations, Soroush speaks of "the battle of seventy-two denominations" seen not as an arena of conquest or conversion, but as the "wild grove" of faith nurturing the soil of religious freedom. Each of these denominations or traditions, he writes (affirming the importance of interfaith dialogue),

> is deemed praiseworthy and honorable in his or her own place. . . . "Excusing the battle of the seventy-two nations" is the wise counsel of our righteous sages and is not a result of their "liberal-mindedness," faithlessness, or skepticism. It is the result of their profound philosophical anthropology and their intimate knowledge of the intricacies of the human soul.[27]

CHAPTER 10

RETHINKING SECULARISM —
WITH RAIMON PANIKKAR

For a long time, Western society has been defined as secular and modernization has tended to be equated with secularization. Today, however, these notions are suddenly contested. More than a century after Nietzsche's proclamation of the "death of God," Gilles Kepel speaks alarmingly of "the revenge of God," while Mark Juergensmeyer points to the prospect of a "new cold war" inspired by religious motives—a prospect that is often far from "cold" or speculative.[1] Having emerged not long ago from European domination, Algeria has been plunged into a bloody nightmare pitting against each other religious "fundamentalists" and a "secular" military and business elite. On a lesser scale, similar feuds are brewing throughout North Africa and the Middle East—incipiently even extending to Turkey, which Kemal Pascha had supposedly made "safe" for secularism. Taking note of the brewing turmoil, many Western observers are wont to adopt a superior, condescending stance (not far from colonial conceit), blaming the conflicts on cultural and economic backwardness. Though comforting, this stance ignores, however, the emergence of similar troubles in the West, especially the rise of a militant religious "Right" bent on salvaging traditional faith from the inroads of secular democracy. Observers with a somewhat longer memory will recall the deep fissures afflicting many Western societies during the nineteenth century, especially the agonies of the so-called culture struggle (*Kulturkampf*) dividing these societies along religious versus secular lines. Viewed against this background, contemporary conflicts lose some of their novelty; in a sense, one might say that *Kulturkampf* today has been globalized.

At this juncture, it seems appropriate and timely to reexamine the meaning of secularism and secularization and their relation to religious faith. As one should note at the outset, this examination cannot simply amount to an arid conceptual analysis. Terms like "secularism" and "secularization" are emblems of intense historical conflicts and transformations, struggles aiming in large measure at the liberation of social life from clerical tutelage and the forced imposition of dogmas. These are matters of historical record; the cultural identities of many Western—and also non-Western—societies are deeply, perhaps indelibly marked by these conflicts. The question that remains open is whether these struggles were basically anti-religious in their effects, or whether they harbored perhaps an emancipatory potential for religion itself, namely, by enabling the latter to perform more properly its task: that of cultivating faith without embroilment in public power. In the following an effort will be made to explore dimensions of this question against the backdrop of the pervasive secular or secularizing propensities of modernity—propensities that are steadily globalized in our time. The first section seeks to stake out the general parameters of the topic by reviewing arguments advanced by a number of prominent social scientists, social theorists, and philosophers. In a second step, the presentation turns to the interpretive work of one of the most innovative and widely influential comparative philosophers and philosophers of religion in the contemporary world: Raimon (or Raimundo) Panikkar. Given the impressively sprawling character of his opus, the discussion here has to be selective and will focus chiefly on Panikkar's views on the secular or "worldly" character of religion, with additional side glances on inter-religious encounters in our globalizing scenario. By way of conclusion, some inferences will be drawn from the preceding considerations regarding such vexing questions as the "religion of the future" or the "future of religion" as well as the future of global politics.

Social Science and Secularization

Secularism and secularization are not merely marginal or incidental features of modern social life; in many ways, they are central or constitutive categories defining the character of modern society as such. This fact has always been emphasized (at least until recently) by the leading practitioners of social analysis: the social scientists. All the great founding pioneers of the discipline of sociology, from Comte to Weber, insisted with varying accents on one crucial feature of social dynamics: the steady historical evolution from a religion-centered life-form to one centered on secular, especially scientific, knowledge and human self-regulation. This historical scheme was epitomized (though perhaps not inaugurated) by Auguste Comte's well-known evolutionary sequence leading from religious myth via metaphysical speculation to "positive" science—a formula curiously (and tellingly) twisted by his elevation of science to a new religion. The scheme was continued, in modified form, by subsequent social analysts like Marx and Spencer and reached a point of crisp succinctness in Durkheim's famous distinction between "mechanical" and "organic" solidarity (the first term referring to a ritually or mythically imposed, the second to a self-generated social structure). In many ways, Max Weber added further historical depth to these accounts by linking secularization with the Protestant Reformation and the rise of capitalism, developments ultimately leading to "disenchantment" in the "iron cage" of modernity. In their combination, these intellectual precedents lend ample support to Gerhard Lenski's observation, as stated in *The Religious Factor,* that "from its inception sociology was committed to the view that religion in the modern world is merely a survival from man's primitive past, and doomed to disappear in an era of science and general enlightenment. From the positivist standpoint, religion is, basically, institutionalized ignorance and superstition."[2]

Building on the premises of the founding pioneers, social scientists in recent times have—on the whole—sought to solidify or systematize their predecessors' views. In the hands of "mainstream" practitioners, the arguments of the founders—often couched with tentativeness and surrounded by many provisos—have tended to congeal into a solid doctrine or creed: the so-called secularization thesis. As articulated especially by "functionalist" social scientists (stressing functional utility), the thesis involves the evolutionary progress of society from a holistic traditional life-form permeated by religion toward a steadily increased differentiation of social functions leading to the marginalization and even obsolescence of religion. By all accounts, the most prominent "functionalist" theorist was Talcott Parsons, whose influence radiated far beyond his home discipline (sociology) and whose basic tenets were summarized by C. Wright Mills in these terms:

Once the world was filled with the sacred—in thought, practice, and institutional form. After the Reformation and the Renaissance, the forces of modernization swept across the globe and secularization, a corollary historical process, loosened the dominance of the sacred. In due course, the sacred shall disappear altogether except, perhaps, in the private realm.[3]

To illustrate the influence of this formula, it may suffice to point to the work of two prominent political scientists whose stature nearly equaled that of Parsons: Gabriel Almond and Bingham Powell. In their trend-setting study *Comparative Politics: A Developmental Approach,* the authors anchored social evolution or development in two key processes: structural differentiation and cultural secularization (or rationalization of worldviews). On a more sophisticated level, Jürgen Habermas also paid tribute to the formula when he linked modernization with expanding structural complexity and a growing rational reflexivity of lifeworlds.[4]

Lately, however, the intellectual landscape has changed or become more diversified. Partly in respond to the upsurge of new religious, especially fundamentalist, movements around the world—Kepel's "revenge of God"—many social scientists and social theorists have begun to challenge the traditional "secularization thesis" or at least to surround it with many caveats and question marks. On a theoretical plane, a number of books have sought to reassess or redefine the social place of religion under contemporary, post-Enlightenment auspices; among these texts, one may prominently mention Robert Bellah's *Beyond Belief,* Phillip Hammond's *The Sacred in a Secular Age,* and Harvey Cox's *Religion in the Secular City.* At the same time, a host of sociological practitioners have endeavored to replace the traditional formula with a new and more flexible interpretive framework, termed "transformation thesis," according to which religion in modern times has not so much vanished as rather evolved and adapted itself in novel ways to the requirements of post-industrial society.[5] As a result of these and related initiatives, secularization no longer enjoys the status of a firm or unassailable doctrine—although the import of the various counter-moves remains ambivalent and beset with numerous quandaries. For one thing, in the portrayal of some authors, secularization is simply erased in favor of a restoration of religion to its earlier supremacy and triumphal authority—an assessment that ignores the liberating effects of secular modernity and its contributions to human and social maturation. On the other hand, while duly paying heed to modernity, sociological adepts of "transformation" often reinscribe religion into a set of functional coordinates governed by post-industrial "systemic" needs—thereby acknowledging the continued prevalence of functionalist (Parsonian) premises.

At this point, without proceeding any further, it may be helpful to attend to some terminological clarifications—which in turn may yield some theoretical purchase. Obviously, a key term here is "secular" or secularity, which—as many authors have noted—derives from the

Latin "*saeculum*" meaning century or world-age (*aion*) or, still more broadly, temporality. Seen from this angle, attention to the "secular" implies a concern with the temporal dimension of human and social life, with the character of human experience in a given age, including experience of the sacred or divine. Some insightful comments on this score have been provided by the Turkish philosopher Ioanna Kuçuradi. In an essay on "Secularization and Human Rights," Kuçuradi mentions the derivation of "secular" from the Latin terms "*saeculum*" and "*saecularis*" designating a century or world-age. If this is so, she observes, then the term "secularization" would seem to express not necessarily a denial of religion but rather a kind of temporal change, an adjustment of religious faith to the experiences and "exigencies of an age"; what happens in secularization would then be a sort of temporalization—which in the modern age goes by the name of "modernization." Kuçuradi is at pains to differentiate secular and secularity from the French terms "*laïc*" and "*laïcité*," which received their historical edge or contours in the French Revolution. As she writes, *laïcité* (laïcism) is in essence "only a negative concept"; it expresses "what *should not* determine the structure and functioning of an institution," especially the institution of the modern state. By contrast, secularization has a more positive connotation and denotes what should legitimately permeate or influence the functioning of modern government: "these are the ideas shaped by the philosophical thought of 'the age'," that is, by the reflective seasoning of successive generations.[6]

Another clarification may be in order at this point. Not every secularization is equally open to the full range of the experiences and agonies of an age. Some types of secularization may be flexible and tolerantly open to a broad spectrum of religious beliefs, while others may be more rigid and doctrinaire, thus shading over into "laïcism." Hence, some form of differentiation seems desirable that remains attentive to the great diversity of historical and cultural examples. In an essay on "Secularization and Cultural Diversity," the Canadian philosopher John Mayer has offered a suggestive distinction. In Mayer's view, it seems plausible to distinguish between "secularism" and "secularization," by giving the first term a more pejorative, doctrinaire connotation and the latter a more tolerant meaning. As he writes, secularization implies a "turning toward this world" or toward this age, a turning that serves as an antidote to an extreme other-worldliness where the "supernatural" was given "too much priority." For Mayer, such a turning is legitimate or warranted whenever the stress on other-worldliness has led to "world-negation and world-indifference" to such an extent that ordinary "secular" life has been "undervalued and trivialized." By contrast, "secularism" pursues a more militant agenda by "denying the reality of any transcendence whatever." It may indeed be the case, he adds, "that if secularization succeeds too well, secularism will result"; but this need not be the case. Rather, "valuing the here-and-now need not negate the need to recognize and also value that 'otherness' which can be called the transcendent or supernatural."[7] For present purposes, it may suffice to accept Mayer's plea for differentiation, but without adopting his terminological usage—which seems needlessly forced. While there is ample reason to distinguish between militant and tolerant agendas, it seems preferable to honor the customary usage of secularism/secularization and to place the distinction inside the semantic scope of both terms.

Panikkar's "Cosmotheandric" Perspective

Deliberately non-exhaustive and non-systematic, the preceding discussion was merely intended to provide some broad benchmarks or guideposts for orientation. Needless to say, secularism and secularization have been the concern not only of social scientists and social theorists but also—and importantly—of philosophers of religion and practitioners of religious studies. Among the latter, one of the most prominent figures in our time is Raimon Panikkar, for many years professor of religious studies at Santa Barbara. In many respects, Panikkar is the epitome of a multidimensional thinker, befitting the needs of a multicultural age. Of mixed (Spanish-Indian) ancestry, he has studied at various universities in Spain, Germany, Italy, and India, and acquired doctorates both in chemistry and in philosophy and theology. Perhaps his most notable intellectual contributions have been in the field of inter-religious and cross-cultural studies, where he has persistently criticized both a bland universalism neglectful of differences and a narrow (ethnic or religious) particularism hostile to reciprocal learning. A recurrent theme in Panikkar's writings has been the exploration of "discordant concord," that is, the reconciliation of starkly opposed tendencies or perspectives—an exploration aiming not at a homogenized unity but at a correlation of diverse elements (acknowledged in their diversity).[8] An example of this endeavor is his treatment of secularism and secularization, a topic to which he has repeatedly been attentive over the years. As he writes boldly and provocatively in one of his early books, *Worship and Secular Man:* "To put forward my thesis straightaway: only worship can prevent secularization from becoming inhuman, and only secularization can save worship from being meaningless."[9]

With this thesis, Panikkar puts himself sharply at odds both with a purely other-worldly religiosity and with a secular "worldliness" destructive of religious faith. In the encounter of worship and the world, he notes, a mutual "total risk" emerges: namely, that worship may wish to "eliminate or anathematize secularization, as being the main evil confronting man," while secularism may try to "get rid of worship as being a remnant of an age dead and gone." To make headway in this confrontation, Panikkar first of all elucidates some of the key terms employed. As he states, worship in this context means a "human action symbolizing a belief" or, more precisely, a "symbolical act arising from a particular belief" (where "symbolic" carries transcendental or ontological significance). On the other hand, secularism can be traced to the Latin *saeculum* denoting a particular world-age (in the sense of *aion* or *kairos*). To this extent, the term "secular"—as previously noted—designates the "temporal world" or the "temporal aspect of reality," and its status or worth varies with the evaluative assessment of temporality. If time and temporality are viewed negatively, then *saeculum* will mean the "merely" secular and transient world as distinct from the sacred and eternal world; in that case, secularization will be seen as the process of "invading the realm of the sacred, the mystical, the religious." By contrast, if temporality is positively valued, then *saeculum* will stand as a symbol for "regaining or conquering the realm of the real, monopolized previously by the sacred and the religious;" accordingly, secularization will denote the "liberation of mankind from the grip of obscurantism," with "secular man" emerging as the "full human being" shouldering genuine responsibility in and for the world. Phrased differently, secularization will mean the "penetration of [ultimate] reality into the world, the process of making the world real" or else sacred or divine. As Panikkar writes, with characteristic verve:

> Now, what is emerging in our days, and what may be a "hapax phenomenon," a unique occurrence in the history of mankind, is—paradoxically—not secularism, but the sacred quality of secularism. In other words, what seems to be unique in the human constellation of the present *kairos* is the disruption of the equation sacred-nontemporal with the positive value so far attached to it. The temporal is seen today as positive and, in a way, sacred.[10]

The revaluation of temporality, in Panikkar's view, is linked with a reinterpretation of human existence: a shift from the traditional conception of the "animal with reason" (*animal rationale*) to that of a symbolic or symbolizing being (*homo symbolicus*) designating a distinctive mode of being-in-the-world open to, or standing out into, the meaning of reality (or Being). In a phrase deliberately patterned on Heidegger's key notion of ontological difference, Panikkar speaks of a "symbolic difference" indicating the differential entwinement between symbol and (ontological) reality—an entwinement that allows him to say that reality "discloses itself only as a symbol" with the result that "what reality *is*, is its symbol." With regard to human experience, symbolic difference entails that human "secular" worldliness is genuine only in an "ek-static" mode that reaches out to "the other pole, the other shore." This aspect inevitably puts pressure on secularization, revealing it as a "constitutively ambivalent" process, a process implying a change—for good or ill—in fundamental human and religious symbols: on the one hand, it can erode or destroy traditional forms of worship while, on the other, it can purify and renew them. The fruitful or promising dimension of secularization emerges only against the background of an "integral anthropology," which sees human personhood as ultimately symbolical or liturgical. The basic aim of his book, Panikkar observes, is to affirm

> the liturgical nature of man, thus considering worship to be an essential human dimension, while, at the same time, recognizing secularization to be a major phenomenon of our age, a phenomenon which, from now on, is assuredly destined to assist the growth of man's consciousness. Today, anyone who is not exposed to secularization cannot hope to realize his humanity to the full, at least not in terms of the twentieth century. On the other hand, man without worship cannot even subsist.[11]

In addition to refocusing personhood or existential anthropology, *Worship and Secular Man* also offers broader reflections on secularization silhouetted against the backdrop of the history of Western metaphysics. According to Panikkar, this history can be conveniently grouped and heuristically expounded under the three headings of "heteronomy, autonomy, and ontonomy"—where "heteronomy" designates a worldview relying on a hierarchical structure of reality regulating behavior from above, whereas "autonomy" insists on radical human self-reliance and self-determination; "ontonomy" finally refers to a perspective shunning both internal and external constitution and accentuating instead a web of (ontological) relationships. Ontonomy, he writes, means "the realization of the *nomos* of being" at that profound level "where unity does not impinge upon diversity"; it rests on the "*specular* character of reality" where each part "mirrors the whole" in a refracted way. Sharply deviating from recent celebrations of heteronomous "exteriority," Panikkar criticizes an approach that denudes or de-sacralizes the world in favor of religious, often clerical authority and authoritarianism (sometimes culminating in theocracy or caesaropapism). In Western history, the Renaissance and Reformation ushered in the age of "profane autonomy," which privileges the "state" over the church, science over philosophy, and the profane over the sacred. As Panikkar astutely perceives, autonomy is in the last analysis always "a reaction against heteronomy," that is, a rebellion "against the abuses of the heteronomic structure"; in this context, there is still a limited place for God, but "for a God who respects the rules of the game, for a God, as it were, whose nature and whose attributes I discover and in a sense I postulate." Above all, the divine here is radically privatized and reduced to a target of subjective choice or preference.[12]

What is coming into view in our age—partly as a result of secularization—is the perspective of a "theandric" or else "cosmotheandric" ontonomy that stresses the integral connection between the divine, the human, and nature (or the cosmos). What this outlook opposes above all are traditional metaphysical dualisms or dichotomies: "The field of the sacred is no longer defined in opposition to that of the secular, nor is a development of worship made at the cost of work, politics or any other human activity." Human beings in this view are considered neither as sovereign agents nor as passive victims of authority but rather as participants in the ongoing disclosure or epiphany of "being," in the effort of a "*consecratio mundi*" pervading the deepest strands of reality. Whereas heteronomy typically views secularization as a "blasphemous" undertaking soiling the garment of hierarchical authority, and whereas autonomy greets secularization as the "grand achievement" of modernity and the "greatest victory for the liberation of man," ontonomy construes the same process in a different light: namely, as the tapping of the hidden potential or promise of the world. In doing so, Panikkar comments, ontonomy seeks to "enlighten our vision" so as to make us realize "that the worship that matters is the worship *of* the secular world"—interpreting this genitive all the while as a subjective genitive: "it is the worship *of* (possessed by, coming from, corresponding and fitting to) this secular world."[13]

About a decade after *Worship and Secular Man* Panikkar returned to the topic of secularization and the meaning of "secularity," focusing now more specifically on the relation between religion and politics. In the new text—titled "Religion or Politics: The Western Dilemma"— the earlier notion of "symbolic difference" was modified or amplified by a further difference or differential entwinement equally opposed to both fusion and separation. According to Panikkar, the history of

Western civilization has been dominated by two contrasting models: either religion and politics have been fused or identified, leading to forms of theocracy or caesaropapism, or else they have been separated and pitted against each other "as if religion and politics were mutually incompatible and antagonistic forces." The first model gives rise to such dangers as religious opportunism, fundamentalism, and even variants of totalitarianism; in the second model, favored by agnostics and "all types of liberalisms," separation readily leads to degeneracy in politics by reducing it to a "mere application of techniques." Adopting again a secularization perspective (focusing on our *saeculum*), Panikkar sees our age as capable of moving beyond the "Western dilemma" of monism/dualism. As he notes, various developments in our time warrant the conclusion that "we are approaching the close of the modern Western dichotomy between religion and politics, and we are coming nearer to a nondualistic relation between the two." This rapprochement is liable to be beneficial to both sides by rescuing each from an endemic mode of pointlessness or aporia: "Religion without politics becomes uninteresting, just as politics without religion turns irrelevant."[14]

As in his earlier text, Panikkar attends again to a clarification of terms. In his view—distantly echoing Aristotle—"politics" denotes the "sum total of principles, symbols, means, and actions" whereby humans endeavor to attain "the *common good* of the *polis*"; the term "religion," on the other hand, refers to the "sum total of principles, symbols, means, and actions" whereby humans expect to reach "the *summum bonum* of life." Differently phrased, politics is concerned with the "realization of a human order," while religion aims at "the realization of the ultimate order"—with the two concerns highlighting the tensional polarity (though not segregation) between politics and religion. In the history of Western culture, the latter polarity has often been captured in institutional terms, for example, by opposing to each other papacy and empire, church and state; on a different level, the opposition has been between professional clergy and laity, or between private faith and public neutrality (vis-à-vis all faiths). Panikkar's aim is to challenge these and related dichotomies. Employing vocabulary introduced earlier, he opposes to intrinsic fusion and extrinsic cleavage the perspective of "ontonomy." As he states: "The relationship can also be *ontonomous;* that is to say, it can be one of constitutive interdependence regulated by the very nature of both religion and politics as being two elements of one and the same human reality." This outlook rescues both terms from a mutual isolation that undermines their meaning. All too often, he notes, it is taken for granted that religion is "only concerned with the divine, the supernatural, the eternal, the sacred," while politics is consigned to "the earthly, the natural, the profane." The task today is to move beyond these dualisms without lapsing into monistic coincidence:

> God and the world are not two realities, nor are they one and the same. Moreover, to return to our subject, politics and religion are not two independent activities, nor are they one indiscriminate thing. There is no politics separate from religion. There is no religious factor that is not at the same time a political factor. . . . The divine tabernacle is to be found among men; the earthly city is a divine happening.[15]

To illustrate the history of religion-politics relations in the West, Panikkar offers the image of a somewhat tumultuous marriage. While at the outset the partners promised each other "eternal fidelity," soon mutual disenchantment set in, with accusations and recriminations being levied on both sides. Eventually, accusations gave way to a legal divorce, followed finally by attempts to "declare the marriage null and void": in the view of both fundamentalists and agnostics, politics and religion should never have been married and there must have been a "misunderstanding" on both sides. In Panikkar's account, this story has played itself out over the past centuries. However, the situation we face in our time, in our *saeculum,* is rather a question of "legitimizing or recognizing the son [or daughter] born of this union": an offspring in which the respective natures of the parents are correlated in such a way as "to offer us today a new intuition about both politics and religion." This offspring, he adds, is not yet baptized and thus has no name; but, heeding the "signs of our times," we can already describe his/her physiognomy. For today, people speak of a "politics of engagement" and a "religion of incarnation"; in doing so, people are discovering "the sacred character of secular engagement and the political aspect of religious life." In the confines of "Christian" societies, one witnesses the growth of a faith that is "less and less ecclesiastical" and of civil and political activities that are "less and less subject to party disciplines" or ideologies. Using Augustinian vocabulary, one might say that the heavenly or celestial city is not "a second city for the elect" but rather represents, so to speak, "the channels of communication and the joy of earthly paradise constantly lost and refound." By the same token, "love of God" cannot subsist without "love of neighbor" and vice versa. With regard to the goal of salvation (or *moksha*) this means that "one does not enter heaven alone" but that somehow "the earth enters [or must enter] with us"; for, "those who are deaf to the cries of men are blind to the presence of God."[16]

By referring to a concrete "politics of engagement" and its religious significance, Panikkar ultimately undercuts the institutional division of church and state, shifting attention instead to the ordinary life-world where religious and "wordly" motifs are inevitably linked. For the proverbial "man in the street," he notes, the institutional division is remote and opaque. Seen from this vantage, humans do not have "two natures, two countries, two vocations"; rather, religion is impregnated with politics and politics with religion. Using language distinctly resonating with contemporary "political theology" or "theology of liberation," Panikkar asserts that a "religion for our times" must be political in the sense that it cannot keep itself aloof of "problems of injustice, hunger, war, exploitation, the power of money, armaments, ecological questions, demographic problems." By the same token, a politics that is really concerned with the well-being of the *polis* and desires to be more than "a technocracy at the service of an ideology" cannot ignore the deeper religious and (perhaps) metaphysical roots of the problems beleaguering our age. For Panikkar, none of the preceding means that politics and religion can simply be fused or identified, for there always remains an excess or left-over. For believers in the "transcendent" life's aspirations can never be reduced to private whim or political manipulation; and even for non-believers life is likely to retain an "imponderable factor" or even a "mystery." Hence, politics is always "more- or other-than just 'politics'," just as religion is always "less- or other-than 'religion'." Ultimately, for Panikkar, the relation between the two domains is "non-dualistic" or "*advaitic*" (in the sense of Indian *Advaita Vedanta*): "It is an intrinsic and thus nonmanipulable relationship that distinguishes but does not separate, allows for diversity but not for rupture, does not confuse roles, but equally does not raise roles to ontological status."[17]

Waiting for God(ot)?

Readers of Panikkar's texts—at least readers not mired in conformism—are likely to experience a sense of invigorating zest. Lucidly and engagingly composed, his writings have the ability of unclogging intellectual arteries blocked by dogmatisms of all kinds, and thus of opening up fresh new vistas. One zestful insight is the conception of an "integral anthropology" that, by stressing the self-transcending or ek-static character of human existence, is capable of counteracting fashionable behavioral or socio-biological forms of reductionism. Closely connected with this insight is the emphasis on the "theandric" or "cosmotheandric" character of experience—an emphasis that is meant to restore a certain balance between the human and the divine by inserting both in a broader cosmological and (genuinely) ecological fabric. The same search for balance also animates Panikkar's plea for "ontonomy" or a "middle voice" between and beyond heteronomy and autonomy—a plea that mounts a critical challenge both to religious traditionalists or fundamentalists (enamored with heteronomy) and to advocates of liberal modernity bent on erecting modernity into a creed. Perhaps the most innovative contribution of Panikkar's work, however, resides in his reinterpretation of secularity, where secular temporality emerges as the gateway to a possible deepening and enrichment of faith (a faith adequate to our *saeculum*). In one of his as yet unpublished texts, Panikkar speaks pointedly of the prospect of "sacred secularity," a prospect that would mark our time as the privileged site of a sacred happening or disclosure.[18]

It is precisely on the latter score that some qualms or reservations may surface. After all, our age has not been particularly hospitable to faith or the realm of the sacred; in fact, more than others, our *saeculum* has been overshadowed by unspeakable horrors (like genocide and ethnic cleansing) and a host of lesser afflictions (like rampant technocracy and consumerist self-indulgence). At this point, it may be beneficial to compare Panikkar's arguments briefly with those of a philosopher whose teachings he frequently invokes: Martin Heidegger. As is well known, Heidegger in *Being and Time* presented human existence as a mode of "being-in-the-world"—where "world" does not at all designate an external container but the open site for an ek-static encounter with transcendence (or the ongoing disclosure of "being"). Moreover, the latter encounter was emphatically inscribed in that text in the framework of "time" or "temporality"—a conception that, far removed from a bland historicism, was meant to highlight the experiential locus of the human quest and of interpretations of all kinds. A closer look at *Being and Time,* however, reveals some features that have a distinctive bearing on secularization. For one thing, human existence for Heidegger was marked not only by ek-static openness but also by "fallenness," that is, by the constant danger or proclivity to forget itself and its own deeper calling. In the context of social relations, this proclivity was prone to foster self-abandonment or a mindless surrender to the anonymous forces of ruling opinion (*das Man*). In some of his later writings, Heidegger elevated this feature into a characteristic trademark of our time or *saeculum,* which he saw increasingly as an age marked by ontological oblivion and abandonment (*Seinsvergessenheit, Seinsverlassenheit*). In large measure, this oblivion was supported and buttressed by the triumphant sway of an all-embracive technology (*das Gestell*) bent on reducing the entire world, including human beings, to productive resources and targets of technocratic manipulation, thus jeopardizing the very premises of a proper human life-form or dwelling.[19]

As can readily be seen, these lines of argument put an enormous pressure on the notion of "sacred secularity," revealing that phrase as inhabited by a deep rift or cleavage. Yet—to remain for the moment within the Heideggerian ambit—this rift or cleavage is not necessarily, or not at all, synonymous with antimony or contradiction. As Heidegger repeatedly insisted, ontological abandonment does not by itself cancel ek-static human existence; by the same token, technological "enframing"—far from being an inexorable fate—may harbor an unexpected mode of liberating disclosure. Differently phrased: disclosure and concealment are mutually contaminated and subtly entwined. Precisely by withdrawing or retreating in our age or *saeculum*, the call of "being" may reach us in a new or different register; more specifically: Nietzsche's vaunted announcement of the "death of God" may be a device protecting or sheltering the unexpected arrival of the divine—in our time or *saeculum*. What emerges at this point is a tensional kind of secularity: one where the sacred is not simply manifest but rather sheltered, withdrawn or lying in wait—in a mode of resistance and quiet contestation. This kind of secularity has recently been underscored by a number of philosophers attentive to the "religious" dimension of Heidegger's work. Thus, concentrating on the latter's lecture courses in Marburg and Freiburg, Jean Greisch reaches the paradoxical conclusion that philosophy "can properly turn toward God only by initially seeming to turn away." Likewise, exploring some Nietzschean affinities, Manfred Riedel stresses Heidegger's *attentismo,* his relentless "waiting for God" (*Erharren vor Gott*), which is irreducible to autonomous whim. This emphasis concurs with Heidegger's own statement that contemporary philosophy's "turning away" is a "difficult kind of remaining 'with'" the divine.[20]

Shifting attention to our contemporary social and political world, tensional secularity holds important lessons precisely for our *saeculum*. Clearly, not every kind of secularism or secularization is equally conducive to the "arrival" of the divine or sacred; by the same token, not every form of religion or religiosity is equally attuned to the experiences of our age, especially to the spreading contagion of democracy averse to heteronomous domination. As John Mayer has noted (in accord with many others), secularism can assume an aggressively intolerant shape in which the *saeculum* is seen no longer as a shelter of expectancy but rather as a prison-house tightly controlled by ideological or technocratic guards, sometimes invoking religious symbolisms.

In turn, religiosity may wish to retreat from the "world" in a radical gesture of *fuga mundi,* or else adopt a more militant, "fundamentalist" stance by enlisting political power in the pursuit of a renewed clerico-religious triumphalism. In the face of these perilous possibilities—not infrequently translated into *Realpolitik*—it seems urgent to maintain a sober vigilance by preserving the tensional character of "sacred secularity"—that is, the cleavage or cleft operating in that phrase despite the close entwinement of its terms. In this respect, Raimon Panikkar seems to be on the mark when he speaks of a differential relation between politics and religion, insisting that politics properly understood is always more and other than *Realpolitik,* and religion more and other than established doctrine. The same aspect of differential connectedness, or "symbolic difference," is also reflected in his comments that religion and politics are not "two independent and separate activities," but that they are "certainly not identical either." For both believers and non-believers, there remains an imponderable factor, always "something more."[21]

This "something more" is inevitably elusive—without on this count being irrational or whimsical. In Heidegger's terms, it has the character of a calling or beckoning, leading to a stance of waiting or expectancy. Not long ago, Panikkar has reflected on this beckoning, in a series of essays dealing with "The Future of Religion." In these texts, Panikkar points to a religious crisis inhabiting our *saeculum,* namely, a growing distance between official religion and the actual religiosity of peoples. Within the orbit of Christianity, for example—he writes—it takes considerable imagination to perceive in the practices and beliefs of most denominations "an authentic expression of the spirit of the founder as stated in the Sermon on the Mount." But the crisis is more widespread; almost everywhere the "chasm between 'religiousness' and 'religion'" is deepening in the mind and heart of many people. To some extent, religiousness has migrated into the "world," that is, moved "from the temple to the street, from sacred rite to secular practice, from institutional obedience to the initiative of conscience." Thus, many people today perceive the pressing religious problems to be "hunger, injustice, the exploitation of man and the earth, intolerance, totalitarian movements, war, the denial of human rights, colonialism and neo-colonialism." In these respects, most official religions lag far behind popular religiosity. For Panikkar, however, there is another important dimension of this lag: a dimension having to do with the emergence of the global village and the need for inter-religious cross-fertilization. As he writes, in our present situation we need "a mutual fecundation among the different human traditions of the world—including the secular and modern traditions," without lapsing into a bland syncretism. At this point, the "essentially liberating character" of the religion of the future comes into view. For, just as the global future of humankind tends toward conciliation (not uniformity), so contemporary religiosity can and should contribute to the "conciliation between persons and peoples":

> It is not a matter of speaking the same language nor of practicing the same religion, but of remaining with an awake consciousness, aware that we are intoning different notes in the same symphony, and that we are walking on different paths toward the same peak. This then is faith (*religio*): the experience of the symphony, of catching a glimpse of the summit, while being attentive to the path we follow, and trying not to stumble on the way.[22]

Chapter 11

Freedom East and West

A Tribute to D. P. Chattopadhyaya

Ever since the Enlightenment, Western culture has presented itself emphatically as a culture of freedom. Constitutional documents and charters celebrate the importance of human freedom and individual liberty, sometimes to the point of erecting the entire constitutional structure on this foundational premise. Needless to say, self-presentation of this kind feeds on an opposition or contrasting foil. Thus, when America presents itself quite specifically as the "land of the free," there is at least the implication that other countries or societies are marked by a lesser degree of freedom and perhaps by unfreedom. This contrast, to be sure, is not entirely of a modern vintage. As we know, ancient Greek and Roman cultures defined themselves largely in terms of the dichotomy between civilized and "barbarian" peoples—with barbarian peoples being basically characterized by their unfreedom or servile submission to despotic rule. Over the centuries, this legacy congealed into the doctrine of Oriental or Asian despotism, a doctrine that functioned for a long time as a staple in Western political thought. More recently, with the demise of colonialism, the doctrine has come to be muted, though not entirely abandoned. Recast in an evolutionary mold, the ancient legacy resurfaces as the contrast between developed and developing societies—where the latter, though steeped in servility, are seen as at least moving in the direction of Western freedom.

Based on dubious assumptions, the described legacy is bound to be troubling or offensive to reflective intellectuals everywhere, and particularly in non-Western societies. Among the many aspects neglected by the doctrine is the multiplicity of possible conceptions of freedom when viewed from both a historical and a cross-cultural perspective.

There is, hence, an evident need today to take a broad-gauged and fair-minded (though not disinterested) look at these conceptions, with the aim of assessing their distinctive merits and shortcomings. One of the most probing and insightful assessments in this domain has been offered by the Indian philosopher D. P. Chattopadhyaya, longtime chairman of the Indian Council of Philosophical Research and now director of the Center for the Study of Civilizations in Delhi. Trained in both classical Indian philosophy and in modern Western philosophy—in both its analytical and Continental varieties—Chattopadhyaya seems well-equipped and even predestined to overcome narrowly confining modes of philosophical (and political) ethnocentrism. One of the crucial premises of his work is that the conception of freedom is not an exclusively Western monopoly, just as philosophical reflection on freedom (like philosophy as such) is not a Western prerogative. As he writes in one of his major texts, *Knowledge, Freedom and Language:* "I think that the concept of freedom is central to the proper understanding of the individual's place in the world"—although different cultural contexts may color the meaning(s) of the term.[1] In the following I shall review Chattopadhyaya's discussion of freedom as presented chiefly in that text, paying special attention to both the similarities and differences between Western and Indian conceptions. By way of conclusion I shall briefly indicate the contemporary relevance of the discussion.

Freedom as Self-Liberation

In modern Western culture, freedom stands in the crucible of science, free will, and social responsibility or connectedness. The title of Chattopadhyaya's book, *Knowledge, Freedom and Language,* clearly is indebted to this crucible—which, in a very broad sense, can be related to Kant's famous three Critiques. As Chattopadhyaya notes, freedom in the modern West emerged basically as a rebellion against, or emancipation from, unexamined religious and metaphysical dogmas—dogmas enshrined at the time in autocratic forms of political domination. The engine of liberation or emancipation was initially or in the first instance "reason" or rationality, and only secondarily human willing or spontaneity. The meaning of reason, however, remained for a long time ambivalent. In Chattopadhyaya's account, modern reason can be traced distantly to classical, especially Platonic, rationalism—although the latter was distinctly more metaphysical. In his words:

> The essence of the European model, as I see it, is rooted in the Platonic view that reason in its pure form can truly and infallibly grasp the whole

of reality, all its nooks and corners, without a remainder. This robust optimism, faith in the power of reason, one might say, turns out to be more speculative and less empirical at the stage of its self-formulation.

What happened during the Renaissance and the early Enlightenment period was that reason was stripped of its cosmic-transcendental ambitions and tailored to the dimension of a human-centered or "anthropological" capacity, that is, the dimension of a cognitive-rational subjectivity standing over against the world (of which the Cartesian *cogito* is the prototype).[2]

Despite this reductive or tailoring effort, however, reason's broader ambitions were not quickly or completely curbed. Throughout much of the seventeenth and eighteenth centuries, concentration on human reason was conceived not so much as the negation of a higher divine purpose, but rather precisely as the gateway to a more accurate and reliable perception of a hidden master plan or *telos*. Given that both human reason and nature were assumed to be divinely structured or ordained, rational-scientific inquiry, properly pursued, could still hope to find the secret passageway to the deeper layers of cosmic order. This hope persisted even when nature began to be seen as a mechanical clockwork and reason to be approximated to mathematics or algebra (a *mathesis universalis*). As Chattopadhyaya comments, the "book of nature" remained "the first and most important book to be read for attaining the highest possible knowledge." Despite his radical skepsis, Descartes basically reached the same conclusion, namely, "that the book of nature can be clearly and distinctly, that is, scientifically, read only by the grace of a veracious or non-deceiving God." Thus, what prevailed at the time was a rationalism (*cum* empiricism) whose boundaries toward metaphysics were hazy and ill-defined: "All these moving spirits of the European Renaissance—Copernicus, Bacon, Galileo and Descartes—willingly or unwillingly (at least in some cases unwillingly) were called upon to read and decipher simultaneously two seemingly unrelatable, if not incompatible, books—nature and holy writ." The result, Chattopadhyaya adds, was a curious amalgam: "the emergence of naturalism, on the one hand, and deism, on the other."[3]

In a highly perceptive and erudite manner, *Knowledge, Freedom and Language* traces the historical permutations of this amalgam through the writings of Newton, Spinoza, Leibniz, and Locke. What increasingly came to the fore in these permutations was an intrinsic dilemma or fissure afflicting the European Enlightenment: the realization that the relentlessly pursued scientific discovery of the laws of nature was liable to jeopardize the goal of human freedom and self-determination, which had been the initial impulse fueling the dawn of European modernity. Precisely to the degree that the metaphorical "book of nature" was replaced by a comprehensive natural-scientific determinism, pressure was placed not only on inscrutable divine providence but also on the conception of a self-propelled or undetermined human freedom. As Chattopadhyaya writes, in a passage evocative of Horkheimer's and Adorno's *Dialectic of Enlightenment:*

> The leading spirits of the European Enlightenment were working under some basic perceptions which did not prove easily reconcilable. First, they all sincerely believed that scientific knowledge, based on experimental reasoning and expressible in mathematical language, had to be taken very seriously. Secondly, deeply impressed by the law-governed characters of the universe, they were earnestly, almost desperately, searching for similar, at least comparable, sets of laws in the realm of human society. Their second concern invited some basic difficulties for them. They could not see how exactly the paradigm of scientific lawfulness could be transferred to social life without seriously impairing the ideal of individual freedom—the ideal which many of them . . . seriously defended as the most powerful argument against despotism.

What happened was that the unbounded expansion of scientific knowledge was purchased at a price comparable to the bargain of the sorcerer's apprentice: the progressive "disenchantment" of nature boomeranged by casting a disenchanting shadow on human life and initiative. The dilemma was sensed with particular acuteness by Locke, Montesquieu, and Rousseau. These thinkers, Chattopadhyaya states, were "engaged simultaneously in defending the *mechanical* concept of nature and in vindicating the *freedom* of the individual and the state on the basis of some principles allegedly derived from nature itself"—a daunting and probably impossible task.[4]

Faced with this formidable task, European thinkers were driven to choose one of two options: either to accept the natural determinism of human will—a course followed by nineteenth-century positivism and its offshoots—or else to transcendentalize human freedom by placing it beyond the bounds of nature. The latter path was pursued most prominently and most nobly by Kant, who proceeded to anchor the moral law in the "noumenal" freedom of human consciousness. As can readily be seen, this move did not so much overcome as rather radicalize the Cartesian subject-object (or mind-matter) division: namely, by further "spiritualizing" or internalizing freedom and thus by driving freedom more deeply into the inner recesses of subjectivity (and thus into a kind of "worldlessness," to use Hannah Arendt's term). To be sure, Kant still wrestled with both sides of the equation—but by tilting the balance in one direction. In Kant's philosophy, Chattopadhyaya observes, "the rationality of human will is independent of the rationality or intelligibility of nature." Viewed from another angle, however, nature's intelligibility owes its "main characters" to human reason, while the latter does not owe its own rationality to nature or the natural universe. For Chattopadhyaya, Kant's work constitutes the "high water mark of the age of Enlightenment." The main spokesman of that age, in his view, tried to achieve three things: to vindicate science, to ground moral freedom, and to search for a viable social order. In his imposing opus, Kant sought to accomplish all three, by projecting rationality onto the "starry skies" as well as on morality and society. Yet, in his rationalist eagerness he may have overreached himself and "invented light of reason where it was not." In a phrase again reminiscent of Horkheimer and Adorno, Chattopadhyaya concludes: "The age of Enlightenment does not mean all light and no darkness. Most of its chapters, to extend the metaphor, are grey."[5]

Freedom as Liberation from Self?

The discussion of modern Western freedom—more specifically, the freedom embroiled in the crucible of the Western Enlightenment—is followed in Chattopadhyaya's text by a close review of the conception of freedom as found in classical Indian and Buddhist thought. Crudely speaking, one might say that freedom in the modern West was anchored in a metaphysical subject-object scheme: a scheme in which humans were first projected as autonomous purveyors and masters of the natural universe and finally driven back into the inner core of private subjectivity in a disenchanted world. On the whole, classical Eastern thought pursued a different path: one that, undercutting the metaphysical (Cartesian) scheme, sought to liberate humans from both external and internal bondage, that is, both from material determinism and subjective self-enclosure or solipsism. Given its different character and orientation, this path could not—as in the Western model—rely centrally on "reason" or rational-scientific inquiry, and certainly not on human rationality seen as an instrument of self-aggrandizement and world-appropriation. Without bypassing or negating reason (broadly understood), classical Indian and Buddhist thought tended to invoke more the resources of reflective-poetic thinking, of symbolic expression—and sometimes of the disclosive potential of silence (as the antipode of propositional claims). As Chattopadhyaya writes, the spirit of the Western Enlightenment was freedom, which was said "to be attainable by [rational] knowledge. But one must not think that there are no other paths as well leading to that ideal." As experience teaches, a person can be "wise and virtuous" without formal scientific training and gain insight without Western-style rationality. Thus, the ancient Rig-Vedic "poet-philosophers" of India read in their own way the "book of nature" and, in doing so, were able to "liberate" themselves from illusions and from the bondage induced by ignorance and ill-will.[6]

Basically, the divine pantheon celebrated by the Vedic seers was not so much the target of cognitive-propositional knowledge, but rather the emblem of a poetic world-disclosure, revealing a reality where transcendence and immanence were intimately meshed. In Chattopadhyaya's words, the array of Vedic gods and divinities represented primarily "the powers of light, energy, and fertility"; simultaneously they were "the symbols of needs, protection, and elevation or inspiration." Over time, the Vedic deities evolved into a "synonym for the life-breath" itself, into metaphorical stand-ins for the "infinite and inexhaustible source of light and life, things and thoughts" that could assume such different names as Agni, Indra, and Varuna for "different beings according to their cravings, responding to their prayers." Contemplation of, and participation in, the higher reality animated by the divine pantheon were assumed to yield genuine freedom in the sense of a liberation from selfish desires and cognitive delusions. The Vedic tradition was modified, but not radically changed or transformed by later Upanishadic teachings. Basically, Upanishadic texts integrated the Vedic deities into a more recessed spiritual matrix, the supreme *brahman,* which again was understood as encompassing, or at least interlacing, immanence and transcendence as well as selfhood and otherness. In Chattopadhyaya's words: "The Upanishadic view of moral life is not to be understood as logical-conceptual in a narrow sense. It rather requires one to open oneself up to the higher forces of light and the delight of the universe." This means that the individual self (*jiva*) must realize that it cannot find true fulfillment and liberation "without the help of other fellow beings" and without the help and caring attention of *brahman* signaling the complex interrelation of all things.[7]

In opposition to the modern Western fascination with sharp conceptualization and the subjection of nature to propositional claims, ancient Indian thought was more elusive and reticent—and in any case averse to any kind of domineering rationality. While not disdainful of language, classical thought often placed itself at the boundary of language or at the interstices of the "said" and the "unsaid"; differently put: it gestured toward a depth dimension of language where the latter harbors or makes room for silence. "To say," Chattopadhyaya writes, "that the highest stage of realization is a stage of endless ecstasy (*purnananda*) or of perfect freedom (*vimukti*) does not make the matter, intellectually [conceptually] speaking, very clear." This is why, at the border of the effable and the ineffable, classical thought often took recourse to metaphors and symbols, employing such images as "evaporation of camphor in air," "dissolution of a lump of salt into water," or "convergence of the jar-bound sky (*ghatakasha*) and the unbounded sky (*patakasha*)." The classical ambivalence between saying and unsaying persisted in the long line of Vedantic and post-Vedantic thinkers, which prominently included Shankara, Mishra, and Ramanuja. Unable to assert cognitively or conceptually either the complete coincidence of the individual human (*jiva*) and the divine, nor their absolute distance or separation, these thinkers were constrained to navigate a precarious path between self-maintenance and self-surrender, that is, between the active-purposive pursuit of the divine and the attainment of liberation through contemplative releasement from such pursuit. Thus, while insisting on the primacy of contemplation (*jñana*) over self-propelled seeking, Shankara also acknowledged the need for moral action and practical devotion (*bhakti*). Conversely, although privileging self-conscious and "independent" human striving, Ramanuja simultaneously recognized the divine as the inner wellspring (not merely the goal) of this search. As Chattopadhyaya observes: "Shankara's view of knowledge maximally exploits the notion of identity—identity of the knower and the known, and scrupulously avoids their discursive association. But he, like Ramanuja, recognizes the necessity of worship, prayer and also *bhakti* for salvation from worldly bondage." Hence, in both cases, *jñana* is neither antithetical nor alien to *bhakti:* "both can take the soul to the same goal of supreme realization" or liberation.[8]

Transposed into a somewhat different key, with perhaps greater emphasis on un-saying than saying, elements of classical Indian thought were continued and elaborated by Buddhism. As is well known, the central motive of the Buddha's teaching is liberation from suffering, a suffering induced by ignorance and self-centered or clinging desire. In his famous eight-fold path, the Buddha delineated the road leading from the initial understanding of the cause of suffering to the final stage of blissful freedom or *nirvana*. However, in pointing or rather gesturing toward *nirvana*, the Buddha remained (and had to remain) ambivalent regarding the character and role of the human self: whether *nirvana* was the achievement of a goal-seeking self (*atman*) or whether it signaled in effect the cessation of, and liberation from, self (*anatman*). For the Buddha, Chattopadhyaya notes, the liberated self is "like an extinct lamp," an image expressed in such phrases as "blowing out" or "cooling down" and in the synonymous use of such terms as "sheenlessness," "disappearance," or "liberation." However, when the lamp is literally extinct, who or what can still be claimed to be liberated or blissful? Hence, Chattopadhyaya adds, the Buddha's teaching here was "figurative"; for the Buddha was keenly aware that figurative expression is "the only possible approximation available to the normal human mind for the understanding of the unspeakable nature of *nirvana*." A similar difficulty affects the prominent Buddhist notion of *sunya* or *sunyata*, meaning emptiness and sometimes likened to "speckless space or windless air." Here again, understanding has to proceed circumspectly. For, when radically separated from ordinary or "full" reality and the normal flux of things, emptiness is liable to be converted into something distinct in itself (or to be objectified). Hence, its meaning can only be approximated through a series of negations or else through figurative speech. In Chattopadhyaya's words:

> Perhaps, because of its intrinsic indefinability, the Buddha did not think it fit even to try to define this enigmatic negation of every phenomenon. To affirm that *nirvana* is eternal or to state that it is a temporal process . . . is equally untenable. The real truth of the matter is not itself a position, still less a third position, trying to reconcile the said two positions. Both affirmation and denial of any position are two equally distorted ways of theoretization: Buddha's is not a theory, not a position" (without being a negative theory or nihilism).[9]

The intrinsic and insuperable ambivalence of Buddhist teachings was highlighted with unmatched force and clarity by the great Madhyamika philosopher Nagarjuna. Faithful to the "middle path" adumbrated by the Buddha himself, the Madhyamika school steered a kind of "dialectical" course between affirmation and negation, between being and non-being. Without endorsing a reductive relativism, this approach emphasized the "relationality" or relational connection of all beings, while denying the absoluteness of any essential self-nature (or any distinct entity as such). A particularly telling or revealing term employed by the school was that of "empty self-nature" (*svabhavasunya*), a term that, as Chattopadhyaya notes, was meant to indicate that the emptiness of every being is due precisely to "its essential relational character." It was in the writings of Nagarjuna that this dialectical, or better aporetic, view of things found its most powerful articulation.

Reflecting on the ultimate nature of reality, Nagarjuna took recourse to a "tetralemma," that is, to a series of four, mutually deconstructive sentences: *nirvana* is not a positive entity (*bhava*); *nirvana* is not a negative entity (*abhava*); *nirvana* is not both positive and negative; *nirvana* is neither something positive nor something negative. For Chattopadhyaya, it would be "rash" to conclude from these statements that Nagarjuna simply dismissed logic or cognitive rationality; what he did, instead, was to pursue rationality to its limit, forcing it to disclose its own aporia: "The proper use of logic, the Madhyamika points out, lies in *showing* the limits of logic." Only through a firm reliance on reason can the truth-seeker finally "see for himself the flaws and faults of the logical formulation of the so-called 'knowledge' of the highest truths, of *nirvana* for example." By accepting aporia as a virtue, Madhyamika Buddhism left room for open-ended inquiry, thereby rejoining insights of early Western philosophical thought. In Chattopadhyya's words: "The Madhyamikas like Nagarjuna are bound to remind one of the Socratic method followed by Plato in his dialogues. The seemingly discursive 'fault-finding' is in reality rooted in, and oriented toward, truth-seeking" and genuine liberation.[10]

Freedom as Praxis

Having reviewed the conceptions of freedom in Western modernity and classical India, what lessons can one plausibly derive from these varying accounts, especially for our contemporary situation? Clearly, the two accounts rely on different premises and follow divergent, perhaps even opposite, trajectories. Yet, despite these divergences, one can also detect a subterranean linkage: in their different ways, both the dilemmas of Western Enlightenment and the aporias of classical India point to the elusive and even enigmatic character of human freedom. In classical Indian Vedanta, freedom was wedged between transcendent knowledge and individual desire or striving, while Madhyamika Buddhism located it in the interstices of self-being and non-self-being, presence and absence. In the case of Western modernity, freedom signified first of all a self-propelled appropriation and cognitive mastery of nature—an outreach that in the end jeopardized human agency by radically internalizing or privatizing its role. Chattopadhyaya is lucidly eloquent in portraying the latter process. "The most important component of the European Enlightenment," he writes, was "reason and reason-based knowledge," a reason that was "praised for its discursive functions, associated with the marvels of experimental sciences, and put to classificatory, measurable, and system-making uses." Buoyed by the advances of natural science, "the European felt—for the first time and perhaps with some justification—that he could now successfully penetrate into the secrets of the universe and . . . conquer the world physically as well." The underlying engine of these advances was the "*cogito*" or cognitive "I think," which succeeded in "largely freeing itself from the dogmatic and dying institutional moorings of theology" and in "humbling religion." In the pursuit of world conquest or appropriation, however, something unexpected happened: the initial impulse of liberation "started yielding the pride of place to the concept of a rational order" governed by scientific determinism. In the end, under the increasing pressures of science and social conventions, "the self got somewhat smothered" (or was driven into world-alienation).[11]

One lesson driven home by this story—and actually by the accounts of both Western and Asian freedom—has to do with the limitation of discursive-propositional language and, more specifically, with the limited competence of cognitive rationality in deciphering the "book of nature" as well as the complex textuality of human lives. It is in the context of a critique of propositional language that Chattopadhyaya draws attention to the teachings of Heidegger and Gadamer. As he notes, with particular reference to *Being and Time,* communication for Heidegger is never a mere "information-conveying process," but rather involves "an experience of co-sharing." In the conversation of *Dasein* with co-*Dasein,* communication comprises both what is "talked about" and the "talking itself," and in fact "the two are hardly distinguishable." Moreover, besides oral and non-oral communication, there is for Heidegger the important dimension of silence—which is not outside, but a part of language: "It may look like a dark and rugged island encircled by a boundless and bottomless see, but in fact it is always supported by submarine firm territory of unheard and unspoken language." A similar insight may be gleaned from *Truth and Method,* where Gadamer speaks of an "inner dimension" of language and a hidden "dialectic of words." For Gadamer, Chattopadhyaya comments, language has "a life of its own," which first of all becomes "manifest and articulated in speech." Looked at from the reverse side, however, speech derives its meaning from language itself, which comprises silence as a "built-in" component: "If language is a plenum, uninterrupted continuum, it is so under the aspect of meaningfulness and not definable in terms of words, however large their number might be and however complex their syntax. The whole to which a word belongs contains in it meaningful slices of silence which interweave words but themselves are not words."[12]

Another, still more important lesson in the present context concerns the status and meaning of human freedom itself. As it appears from the above accounts, freedom cannot be grasped in cognitive-propositional terms—under the rubric of the familiar subject-object scheme—without either being surrendered to external determinism or being reduced to private solipsism. Differently phrased, freedom's aporetic status does not yield to a cognitive-theoretical solution offered in a spectatorial stance; if at all, its enigma can only be resolved in a participatory stance or the mode of public action—though an action which is not willfully self-centered but rather self-transcending. In the Indian classical tradition, this kind of action was prominently thematized in the *Bhagavad Gita,* which celebrated self-transcending or non-attached praxis (*karma yoga*) as an eminent passageway to liberation. In the modern Indian context, no one has more ably and persuasively embodied this praxis in public life than the Mahatma Gandhi. It is thus perhaps not surprising that, in some of his recent writings, D. P. Chattopadhyaya has turned his attention increasingly to the Gandhian legacy. As he writes in a recent essay, titled "Gandhi on Freedom and Its Different Facets": Gandhi's conception of freedom rested on a "philosophical-cum-religious assumption," in the sense that individuals for him "existed in God" and hence were wayfarers on the path to self-realization that simultaneously transgressed the self. Humans, in this view, were indeed "makers of their own destiny," but not in a self-centered or solipsistic way, which would violate the sacred "relationality" of all beings. For all his manifold insights, and especially for alerting readers again to the legacy of the Mahatma, students and colleagues in India and throughout the world owe D. P. Chattopadhyaya a profound debt of gratitude.

CHAPTER 12

WHAT IS SELF-RULE?

Lessons from Gandhi

Behind the screen of flux and turbulence, our age seems to be pervaded worldwide by a dominant idea: the idea of "democracy" or at least the aspiration of "democratization." Despite the immense diversity of social and cultural traditions, humankind today seems agreed on the superiority of democracy over any competing alternative. People of diverse political convictions—from conservative to radical—all share at least the proposition that, to be legitimate, governments need popular approval and guidance. Seen in this light, humankind seems indeed united by a common purpose or *telos*—whose meaning, however, appears puzzling on closer inspection. For, what is the meaning of democracy when translated as popular self-government or self-rule? How can the people govern themselves—more precisely: how can the people be both rulers and the ruled, and perform their roles legitimately without domination or oppression? In the well-known phrase of Lincoln—"government of the people, by the people, for the people"—How can the people exercise government (by the people) over themselves (of the people) and do so in way as to promote the common good (for the people)? Differently and more simply put: How can the self rule itself? How is popular self-rule—or to use the Indian term, *swaraj*—possible and even conceivable?

Questions of this kind are liable to appear strange or alien to many contemporary democrats wedded to the belief that popular rule means satisfaction of the people's wants and needs. But what if human wants are intrinsically infinite (or at least can be infinitely generated) and if available resources (especially ecological resources) are limited? And what if efforts to secure these resources willy-nilly involve people (some people) in mastery and domination? The above questions were not as alien to the older tradition of political philosophy in the West. Despite differences in detail, Plato and Aristotle both insisted on a qualitative differentiation between modes of rule or rulership. In their view, rulership exercised for purely selfish interests or the sole benefit of the rulers was illegitimate or unjust, while rulership performed unselfishly or virtuously for the common benefit was deemed just and legitimate. With regard to popular rule, this criterion meant that people had to rule themselves unselfishly and wisely—which presupposed a widespread practice of self-restraint and the cultivation of ethical dispositions. The classical distinction persisted throughout the Roman period and well into the Christian Middle Ages. According to Augustine, there was a need to sharply distinguish between two opposing "cities" or regimes: the one (called "earthly city") was governed by self-love manifest in lust for power and self-aggrandizement, while the other (termed "heavenly city") was marked by self-giving, self-surrender, and service. In our time, all these teachings have become nearly apocryphal and persist only at the margins of modern consciousness. In large measure, this eclipse is due to the modern tendency to replace the "tale of two cities" with a stark public-private dichotomy: a formula whereby self-transcendence is consigned to a purely private sphere of inner spirituality, while the public square is increasingly equated with power struggles and the pursuit of self-interest. This equation, needless to say, exacts a price, especially for democratic politics. Stripped of qualitative connotations, self-rule shades over into self-indulgence and into the restless search for (what Augustine aptly calls) "sottish pleasures."[1]

The present pages are an exercise of retrieval. Basically the attempt is to retrieve some public voices who, in the midst of our modern and contemporary era, have resisted the lure of consumerism and selfish complacency while holding fast to the principle of popular self-rule. Among these voices easily the most prominent is that of Mahatma Gandhi, who led India in her prolonged struggle for independence and self-rule from England—but who never lost sight of the difficulties and paradoxes of self-rule. Although vigorously opposed both to British colonialism and native fundamentalism, Gandhi's writings and speeches made it amply clear that, with the demise of empire, the struggle for self-rule would not come to an end but really only begin. The presentation here proceeds in three steps. The first section reviews some of Gandhi's numerous comments on self-rule or *swaraj,* from his early plea for "Indian home rule" to statements made on the eve of independence. The second part advances an interpretation of the Gandhian view of *swaraj,* partly by relying on the insights of prominent Gandhi scholars and their writings. To round out the presentation, the concluding section seeks to underscore the continuing relevance of Gandhian *swaraj* by comparing that notion with, or profiling it against, significant recent initiatives in Western ethical and political thought.

Gandhi and Swaraj

Long before he emerged as leader of the independence movement and was hailed as the Mahatma, Gandhi had warmly embraced and eloquently articulated the idea of self-rule or home-rule for India or the Indian subcontinent. His legal studies in England and his subsequent prolonged stay in South Africa never alienated Gandhi from the cause of India's freedom, to which he remained committed throughout his life. One of the most clear-sighted and pithy formulations of the idea was penned by Gandhi during the later phase of his South African period. Titled *Hind Swaraj*—translated as *Indian Home Rule*—the booklet was written on board an ocean liner that carried him back from London to South Africa in November of 1909. To be sure, the goal of Indian self-rule or home-rule was not an invention or discovery of Gandhi. At the time when his booklet was published, there was already an ongoing home-rule movement on the subcontinent, sponsored in part by the Indian National Congress (founded in 1885). Several political leaders, including Dadabhai Naoroji and Gangadar Tilak, had specifically employed the term *swaraj* to designate the goal of their political aspirations. However, as used by these leaders, the term had a narrowly ideological or strategic cast, suggesting basically nothing more than the expulsion of the British from India. It was the momentous merit of Gandhi's booklet to raise the issue of *swaraj* from purely strategic concerns to the level of political ethics and a vision of the "good life": the vision of democratic self-government transcending self-centeredness or selfish interests. In doing so, Gandhi articulated a standard of democratic life applicable to Indians and non-Indians alike—in any event, a standard that urgently needs to be remembered fifty years after India's independence.

Gandhi's text ranges over a number of topical issues, all discussed in dialogue form; for present purposes, it must suffice to highlight briefly passages directly relating to *swaraj*. Following a discussion of the present condition of India—the state of ferment and unrest pervading the subcontinent due to British colonial policies—the text turns immediately to the central issue of self-rule, finding that issue mired in perplexity and confusion. Addressing himself to his interlocutor, Gandhi observes that "you and I and all Indians are impatient to obtain *swaraj,* but we are certainly not decided as to what it is." In the opinion of many people, self-rule consists simply in driving the English out of India; but "it does not seem that many have properly considered why it should be so." For Gandhi, the goal of *swaraj* could not be obtained by simply replacing British rulership with Indian rulership; the problem was much deeper and more complex, involving a change in the very meaning and character of rulership. Those people wedded to the simple policy of expulsion, he notes, seem to want "English rule without the Englishman" or "the tiger's nature but not the tiger." Successful pursuit of this policy would "make India English, and when it becomes English," Gandhi adds, "it will be called not Hindustan but Englistan. This is not the *swaraj* that I want."[2]

Seen against this background, the issue turns on the character of British rulership, which Gandhi exhorts his countrymen not to imitate or adopt as their own. Examining first the political condition in England, he describes it as "pitiable" and unworthy of emulation—as is evident in the profligacy of Parliament, its subservience to vested interests and the fluctuating whims of opinion. For Gandhi, this political condition is not accidental, but must and can be traced to a deeper underlying source: the state of modern British civilization and of modern (Western) civilization in general. Focusing on modern civilization, the text portrays it in stark terms as "a civilization only in name," a mode of life under which "the nations of Europe are becoming degraded and ruined day by day." What is the nature of this degradation or ruination? Apart from pointing to British politics, *Hind Swaraj* details a number of developments in ordinary living practices that testify not to steady progress but to a spreading malaise or decay. What links or unifies these diverse phenomena, however, is one central feature: the upsurge of self-centeredness and self-indulgence, at the cost of binding (or bonding) commitments. Gandhi is not unaware that modernity has also brought greater freedom for many people, including political freedom in democracies. This freedom, however, is tarnished by its misuse. In his words, the true test of modern civilization lies in the fact that "people living in it make bodily welfare the object of life." What is basically lacking in modern civilization is any sense of self-transcendence and responsiveness. In the stark and uncompromising language of *Hind Swaraj:*

> This civilization takes note neither of morality [*niti*] nor of religion [*dharma*]. Its votaries calmly state that their business is not to teach religion. Some even consider it to be a superstitious growth. . . . Civilization

seeks to increase bodily comforts, and it fails miserably even in doing so. This civilization is irreligion [*adharma*], and it has taken such a hold on the people in Europe that those who are in it appear to be half mad. They lack real physical strength or courage. They keep up their energy by intoxication. They can hardly be happy in solitude.[3]

If such is the state of modern (Western) civilization, Indians are well advised to keep their distance from it; as it happens, however, many Indians have been influenced and thus been colonized not only externally but internally in their minds. In fact, Gandhi attributes the persistence of colonialism not to the might of British arms but to the selfish weakness of Indians. In his provocative formulation: "The English have not taken India; we have given it to them. They are not in India because of their strength, but because we keep them." Evidence for this fact, in Gandhi's view, can be found in the behavior of Indians, especially Indian elites, from the days of Britain's entry into India to the present time: "Who assisted the Company's officers? Who was tempted at the sight of their silver? Who bought their goods? History testifies that we did all this." In order to become "rich all at once," Indians "welcomed the Company's officers with open arms. We assisted them." This situation continues unabated and has even become more widespread and pronounced. It follows, Gandhi summarizes, that "we keep the English in India for our base self-interest. We like their commerce, they please us by their subtle methods, and get what they want from us. . . . We further strengthen their hold by quarrelling amongst ourselves."[4]

The remedy proposed in the text for this spreading malaise is self-rule or *swaraj*—a notion whose clarification now becomes Gandhi's central aim. As he points out, self-centeredness or self-seeking is contrary not only to moral and spiritual rightness (one sense of *dharma*) but to the teachings of practically all the great religions of the world—including, next to Hinduism, Islam, Christianity, and Zoroastrianism. What all these religions try to teach us is "that we should remain passive about worldly pursuits and active about godly pursuits, that we should set a limit to our worldly ambition, and that our religious ambition should be illimitable." Between the two courses of action our endeavors "should be directed into the latter channel." Despite differences of accent or detail, all religions and spiritual paths can thus be seen as "different roads converging to the same point." People following these paths or teachings are liable to achieve not "civilization only in name" but genuine or true civilization fitting for free human beings. Here is Gandhi's terse formulation: "Civilization is that mode of conduct which points out to man the path of duty. Performance of duty and observance of morality [*niti*] are convertible terms. To observe morality is to attain mastery over our mind and our passions. So doing, we know ourselves." Observance of morality requires self-restraint and moderation, for "the more we indulge our passions, the more unbridled they become." The chief implication of this view of civilization is a new and transformative understanding of *swaraj*. In a section titled "How can India become free?" Gandhi proceeds to offer a definition of the term as he sees it: "It is *swaraj* when we learn to rule ourselves." And he adds: "The *swaraj* that I wish to picture before you and me is such that, after we have once realized it, we will endeavor to the end of our lifetime to persuade others to do likewise. But such *swaraj* has to be experienced by each one for himself."[5]

Although composed relatively early in his life (and during an arduous sea voyage), the basic tenets of *Hind Swaraj* remained firm guideposts illuminating Gandhi's mature years. Although willing to revise minor details, he never disavowed his early text; in fact, he reconfirmed its central argument on repeated occasions in subsequent years. Little purpose would be served here in recapitulating Gandhi's numerous statements on the topic; a few selected examples should be sufficient. In his "constructive program" submitted to the Indian National Congress in 1941, Gandhi strongly reaffirmed his commitment to *swaraj,* paraphrasing the meaning of the term as "complete independence through truth and non-violence" and "without distinction of race, color or creed." A letter written to Jawaharlal Nehru a few years later made explicit reference to the text of 1909, stating: "I have said that I still stand by the system of government envisaged in *Hind Swaraj.* These are not mere words." In retrospect, what appeared to Gandhi then as the central lesson of his book was the emphasis on moral self-rule and self-restraint: "The essence of what I have said is that man should rest content with what are his real needs and become self-sufficient. If he does not have this control he cannot save himself." The most dramatic and direct application of the idea of *swaraj* came in Gandhi's "Quit India" speech delivered in Bombay in 1942. In that speech, Gandhi—now leader of a nationwide *satyagraha*—contrasted his vision of Indian self-rule with the kind of freedom and political rulership found in Britain and the Western world. Here are some of his statements (still providing food for thought):

> I do not regard England, or for that matter America, as free countries. They are free after their own fashion, free to hold in bondage the colored races of the earth. Are England and America fighting for the liberty

of those races today? . . . The English and American teachers, their history and their magnificent poetry have not said you shall not broaden the interpretation of that freedom. And according to my own interpretation of that freedom, I am constrained to say: they are strangers to that freedom which their poets and teachers have described. If they will know real freedom, they should come to India.[6]

Self Ruling Self?

Gandhi's statements on *swaraj* are forthright and certainly not couched in coded or esoteric language. Nevertheless, their very forthrightness screens from view a number of theoretical problems or quandaries—which call for sustained interpretive labor on the part of readers. Among these problems, the following deserve primary attention. If *swaraj* is identified with moral self-rule or self-restraint, why should such self-restraint be hampered or obstructed by British colonialism (or any other political regime)? If restraint is equated with internal discipline or mind-control, why should internal freedom not be compatible even with external slavery (as shown in the case of Epictetus)?[7] Moreover, does mind-control not also involve a kind of mastery or domination, with possibly repressive consequences—for how would "duty" conceived as pure discipline otherwise mold human inclinations? On the other hand, if self-restraint is extended to the social and political domain, are the common people perhaps consigned to indigence, need deprivation, or "backwardness"? To put things differently: Does the accent on self-restraint encourage the rise of a moral and intellectual elite, perhaps an elite of ascetic virtuosi, with an attendant division of society into more restrained and less restrained segments, into ruling "guardians" and ruled "artisans"? But in this case, what would be the relevance of *swaraj* for democracy and popular self-government? Yet, if moral restraint is deemphasized in favor of popular politics, does self-rule not shade over into a simple strategy of national independence, and *swaraj* into a synonym for the pursuit of nationalist goals (perhaps to the detriment of the global community)?

These are surely difficult issues—which all in diverse ways point up the paradox of self-rule. To disentangle some of these issues, it may be well to remember a few points from *Hind Swaraj,* especially Gandhi's critique of modern Western civilization and politics. Despite his fondness for Western writers like Ruskin, Thoreau, and Tolstoy, Gandhi was not a radical individualist (in the modern "liberal" sense) ready to separate a vast arena of private freedom and inwardness from a narrowly (perhaps procedurally) circumscribed public domain. Faithful to older philosophical traditions (both in India and the West), he preferred to stress a qualitative differentiation between modes of human and political conduct—a differentiation that cannot readily be collapsed into modern private/public or internal/external polarities. Without blandly fusing individual and society or subordinating one to the other, his thought was able to hold the two elements in fruitful, perhaps tensional balance—thus demonstrating the possibility of reconciling difference and mutual correlation. This aspect is clearly shown in another letter Gandhi wrote to Nehru in 1945. Picking up Nehru's suggestion regarding the importance of human and social "development," he fully agreed that it was crucial to "bring about man's highest intellectual, economic, political and moral development." The basic issue was how to accomplish this goal. For Gandhi this was impossible without thorough attention to rightness (*dharma*) and without social engagement or responsibility. Echoing Aristotle, he wrote: "Man is not born to live in isolation but is essentially a social animal independent *and* interdependent. No one can or should ride on another's back." A similar view was expressed in an interview of summer 1946 where Gandhi stated that, though "ultimately, it is the individual who is the unit," this "does not exclude dependence and willing help from neighbors or from the world. It will be a free and voluntary play of mutual forces."[8]

Another issue concerns the role of self-restraint, and especially of moral asceticism, in its relation to practical life and to the range of human inclinations, including yearnings for pleasure (*kama*) and worldly success (*artha*). As is well known, Gandhi during his early years was strongly under the influence of the Jain mystic Rajchandra Mehta, whose teachings stressed liberation from passions, ascetic self-purification, and withdrawal from the world; partly under the impact of these teachings, Gandhi decided to practice sexual celibacy (*brahmacharya*) during his mature years. Yet, Gandhi did not accept all the tenets of the Jain mystic, especially not the idea of world-withdrawal. As Anthony Parel correctly observes in his introduction to *Hind Swaraj,* Gandhi soon "went beyond the intellectual horizons that Rajchandra had opened up for him: already by the first decade of the century his spiritual life was focusing more on the *Gita* and the Tulsidas *Ramayana.*" One of the central lessons of the *Gita,* however, is the possibility of active world-engagement (*karma yoga*) carried out in an unselfish or unattached and hence purified manner; in addition, the *Gita* also suggests the path of self-transcendence not through repression but through transformation of human wants. Closely connected with the role of restraint is the charge of moral or intellectual elitism sometimes hurled at Gandhi by his critics. This charge stands in complete contrast with Gandhi's fervent popular or democratic leanings—as expressed, for example, in the interview of 1946: "The rulers should depend on the will of those who are under their heels. Thus, they have to be servants of the people, ready to do their will. Independence begins at the bottom." Notwithstanding his ascetic practices, Gandhi never sought to impose his own austerity on the entire country. Again, Parel's comments seem to be judiciously on target when be writes:

> Gandhi wants Indians to be well fed, well housed, well clothed, well governed, well read, and cognizant of the place and function of aesthetics and art in life. It is therefore absolutely essential to separate the asceticism peculiar to Gandhi as an individual from the humanism that he promotes as a social and political philosopher. If there was one thing that pained him more than anything else, it was the poverty of the Indian masses. His asceticism is a penitential expression of that pain: he wanted to suffer voluntarily in his person what the multitude suffered involuntarily in their person—so that their pain may be brought to a quicker end.[9]

What surfaces in the preceding discussion, in diverse guises, is the basic paradox of self-rule: the notion that self rules self. To repeat an earlier query: How is this possible without domination or empty circularity? Here it is important to remember a qualitative distinction regarding selfhood found in traditional Indian philosophy: the distinction between a "higher" or spiritual self called "*atman*" and an ordinary, mundane self termed "*dehin*" or "*jiva,*" where the former may be thought of as an imperishable divine spark and the latter as a mode of finite existence. As one should note, the distinction should not be confused or identified with the familiar metaphysical binaries of mind and matter, spirit and body, or otherworldliness and worldliness. On inspection, none of these binaries are properly able to clarify the notion of self ruling over self. However, matters are not much simpler regarding the *atman/dehin* distinction. On this issue, the Indian Vedantic tradition offers a rich profusion of alternative solutions—ranging from radical monism and non-dualism (*advaita*) over qualified non-dualism to radical dualism (*dvaita*). Fully cognizant of this profusion, Gandhi can reasonably be assumed to have adopted a flexible or experimental course—as one of his "experiments with truth"—and thus to have steered a path somewhere between monism and dualism.[10] Such a course seems indeed required for the very intelligibility of self-rule or *swaraj*. On the assumption of a radical dualism or separation, self would not be ruling over self, but over something alien or external (or else be ruled by something alien). On the assumption of a radical monism or coincidence, by contrast, the aspect of rule or ruler-ship vanishes from view. The issue thus hinges on the character of the rule exercised by self over self—where "rule" denotes a kind of bridge or link mediating between *atman* and *dehin/jiva*.

Here it seems advisable to return to the *Gita*—always a source of profound inspiration for Gandhi. As is commonly recognized, the *Gita* also steers a course somewhere between rigid separation—the dualism of spirit (*purusha*) and matter (*prakriti*) as advocated by the Samkhya school—and an intimate fusionism blending human and divine being. The central teaching of the *Gita*, however, is the delineation of various paths—called *yogas* or *margas*—through which finite humans might become reconciled with the divine, or *dehin* with *atman*. Using the vocabulary of the *Gita*, Gandhi defined himself expressly as a follower of *karma yoga*, the path of action or active service. Nevertheless, in opting for service, Gandhi certainly did not mean to brush aside the other soteriological paths (those of insight and devotion). Although incredibly busy in worldly affairs, one should recall that Gandhi was also a sincere Vaishnava *bhakta*, a Krishna devotee traveling along the royal highway of loving devotion (*bhakti*). In his pursuit of *karma yoga*, Gandhi did not act in a domineering or a condescending or paternalistic fashion; non-attachment to the fruits of action in his case did not mean careless indifference toward the people he served. Seen from this perspective, it is probably not quite correct to say that moral self-rule for Gandhi meant the rule of mind over matter or of spirit over body; instructively, the key faculty of transformation singled out in his work was not mind or rationality but rather the "heart" or the "soul"—which (as we know) rules not by coercion but by caring solicitation. Evidence for this emphasis can be found in many of Gandhi's writings—including the concluding section of *Hind Swaraj*, where we read: "Real home-rule is self-rule or self-control. The way to it is passive resistance [*satyagraha*]: that is soul-force or love-force." And in his autobiography we find these lines (reflecting the genuine spirit of Vaishnava devotion).

> To see the universal and all-prevading spirit of truth face-to-face one must be able to love the meanest of creation as oneself. And a man who aspires after that cannot afford to keep out of any field of life. That is why my devotion to truth has drawn me into the field of politics; and I can say without the slightest hesitation, and yet in all humility, that those who say that religion has nothing to do with politics do not know what religion means.[11]

Given the inner linkage of *atman* and *dehin*—the wellspring of loving solicitation—self-rule involves a process of transformation that is neither self-destructive (or alienating) nor preordained. For Gandhi, pursuit of soteriological paths, especially the path of *karma yoga*, requires sustained work or labor—though not in the sense of modern industrial productivity. Freedom as the goal of self-transformation cannot be willfully engineered, but constitutes an experiential task that needs to be patiently and courageously shouldered and undergone. In Gandhi's words, freedom is not an instant boon, but is "attained only by constant heart-churn" or self-suffering. In his book *Self and Society: A Study in Gandhian Thought,* Ramashray Roy thoughtfully connects *karma yoga* with self-giving, sacrifice, and sanctification, stating: Gandhi "equates action with *yajna* (sacrifice), that is, the performance of action as a sacred duty. This sacred duty lies, for Gandhi, in exerting oneself to the benefit of others, that is, service."[12] This statement, of course, resonates again with the teachings of the *Gita,* where we read (4, 32): "In many ways men sacrifice, and in many ways they go to *brahman.* Know that all sacrifice is holy work, and knowing this thou shalt be free." Viewed from this angle, achievement of self-rule or *swaraj* involves self-transcendence and a diligent training in the ways of freedom—but a training which is aided or facilitated by the solicitation of truth (*satya*) and *brahman* (being). In a manner akin to Aristotelian ethics, pursuit of soteriological paths demands steady practice and habituation; again in an Aristotelian vein, such practice revolves around the nurturing of a set of virtues—which Gandhi reformulated under the rubric of "vows" (adapted from the traditional Indian doctrine of *yamas* and *niyamas,* meaning cardinal and casual vows). Steadied or braced by the practice of vows, cultivation of freedom emerges as a kind of venture or journey—not an aimless or nomadic errancy, but a movement of self toward self, a seasoning of *dehin* by *atman.* In religious language, the journey resembles a pilgrimage or a "pilgrim's progress" (in St. Bonaventure's language: *itinerarium mentis in Deum*).

Transferred to the social and political arena, *swaraj* translates into the self-rule of a larger community, that is, into a synonym for national democratic self-government or "home rule." When operating on this level, popular *swaraj* is closely linked with the idea of *swadeshi,* a broad term designating national self-reliance, preference for home-grown products, and cultivation of indigenous (material and spiritual) resources of development. This linkage was often made by Gandhi, for example, in the concluding pages of *Hind Swaraj.* There the phrase equating *satyagraha* with "soul-force or love-force" is immediately followed by the statement: "In order to exert this force, *swadeshi* in every sense is necessary." Although intuitively plausible, the connection between home rule and national self-reliance needs to be carefully pondered and weighed. Occasionally, interpreters have tended to place the major accent on *swadeshi* in the sense of national self-determination, with the result that the aspect of moral self-rule or self-transcendence is sidestepped or at least partially displaced. In his instructive study, *Gandhi's Political Philosophy*, Bhikhu Parekh comes close to this displacement when he writes: "For Gandhi the *swadeshi* spirit extended to all the elements composing the *desh* [community] and implied a love of not only the traditional way of life but also the natural environment and especially the people sharing it"—amplifying these comments further by stating: "Gandhi used the term *swaraj* to describe a society run in the *swadeshi* spirit. It meant self-rule or autonomy and implied not only formal independence but also cultural and moral autonomy." Pursued to its logical extreme—something Parekh carefully avoids—the subordination of self-rule to *swadeshi* would reduce *swaraj* ultimately to a form of political nationalism or a strategy of independence in the name of national self-interest. Such a reading would surely not accord with Gandhi's understanding, who was firmly opposed to the maxims of "national interest" and "reason of state" (slogans he attacks in *Hind Swaraj*).[13]

The issue is to strike a sensible balance that does not rupture the link between ethics and politics, between moral self-rule and democratic self-government. Here again Parel's approach seems on target when he notes that "Gandhi draws a subtle distinction between *swaraj* as [moral] self-rule and *swaraj* as self-government or home rule," but immediately adds that "the good state or good self-government is possible only if Indians acquire the capacity for self-rule" and that political *swaraj* requires people "who rule themselves." National self-reliance thus needs to be buttressed and animated by sustained moral practice, to prevent its deterioration into a myopic nationalism. On the other hand, self-reliance or *swadeshi* has a good and legitimate sense if *swaraj* is to operate in the context of democracy or popular rule. Here one needs to take seriously Gandhi's comments (previously cited) that *swaraj* has to be "experienced by each one for himself" and that "independence must begin at the bottom." For Gandhi, self-government cannot be imposed on people from above—neither by a foreign power nor by the modern nation-state (an institution he always regarded with suspicion). Rather, self-government must first be nurtured, through education and example, on the local or village level and then be encouraged to spread out into larger communities and the world through a series of (what Gandhi called) "oceanic circles." Seen in this light, democracy means indeed people ruling themselves—ruling not as arbitrary tyrants nor as indulgent nurse-maids pampering every whim, but as caring benefactors seeking to enhance the goodness of people or the "good life" (in accordance with *dharma* and *brahman*).[14]

Toward an Ethical-Political Freedom

Having reviewed Gandhi's idea of *swaraj,* and attempted an interpretation, it seems appropriate to inquire finally into its contemporary relevance, and especially its compatibility or incompatibility with trends in Western ethical and political thought. What springs into view right away is the distance of *swaraj* from the dominant modern versions of freedom: those of "negative" and "positive" liberty (as articulated by Isaiah Berlin). In this binary conception, negative liberty basically designates the freedom to be left alone, that is, liberalism's favorite strategy of withdrawal into private inwardness and the satisfaction of individual wants. Positive liberty, by contrast, denotes the unhampered pursuit of communal or collective goals, a pursuit sometimes shading over into social engineering on behalf of ideological blueprints. As can readily be seen, neither of these options shows kinship with Gandhian *swaraj:* even when highly spiritualized, negative liberty still bears traces of self-centeredness, while the positive type— though actively involved—seems ignorant of self-restraint and non-attachment (to the fruits of action). This distance is clearly perceived and pinpointed by Ramashray Roy. As he notes in *Self and Society,* negative liberty insists on "the absence of constraints on whatever one wishes to do," with happiness being sought in the "satisfaction of desires," the "realization of creative urges," or the like. Lacking a criterion for discriminating between desires, wants, and urges, the negative brand is unable to negotiate the *dehin/atman* relationship and ultimately leads to the "chaos of conflicting claims" (eventually tamed by the will of the strongest). On the other hand, while emphasizing social and political commitments, positive liberty sidesteps self-transcendence in favor of some collectively chosen goals. It was "Gandhi's genius" to have "squarely faced" this dilemma and have shown an exit from this binary opposition. The central point of Gandhian *swaraj* was the emphasis on self-rule as self-transcendence; liberty in his sense means "the freedom of self-actualization in a transcendental sense"— which, however, must be "realized in this world."[15]

What surfaces behind the negative/positive binary is another, still deeper bifurcation characterizing modern Western metaphysics: that between inner subjectivity and external world, between consciousness and unconscious nature, or, in Kantian terms, between "noumenal" freedom and "phenomenal" causality. Basically, this metaphysics bears the imprint of the Cartesian turn to mental inwardness—perhaps to the point of solipsism—in opposition to the "extended matter" of the world. In the Kantian reformulation of this scheme, inner consciousness or reason becomes the categorical law-giver, the legislator of universally binding norms and duties—but norms that relate elusively, if at all, to the realm of human inclinations and social political aspirations. Abandoning the Aristotelian model of self-transformation—the seasoning of inclinations through the practice of virtues—categorical morality erects a wall between duty and human motivation, between higher (noumenal) self and empirical self, in a manner vaguely reminiscent in the Indian context of rigid dualism (*dvaita*) and some aspects of the Samkhya doctrine. While displaying an appropriate respect for Kantian moralism, Ramashray Roy again voices some telling reservations inspired by the Gandhian example. In the Kantian and neo-Kantian scheme of morals, he writes, reason must

> take the place of desire. The Kantian emphasis on self-determination by the moral *and* rational will, points to the impossibility of concentrating on desire as the grounds either for freedom or for morality because of its contingent nature. But reason as the imperial governor and as the ground for freedom and morality brings about a diremption with nature and suppresses what is truly human. Freedom [however] must take note of the totality of the human being and must mean self-determination as an instrument for the expressive fullness of life.[16]

As one should note in fairness, not all contemporary theorizing is held hostage to modernist metaphysics. In the context of political theory, one of the bolder moves to escape its confines has been made by Hannah Arendt in a string of writings, especially in *The Human Condition*. Rupturing the inner/outer metaphysical paradigm, Arendt resolutely placed human freedom not in a sphere of self-centered inwardness but rather in the open arena of human interaction in practical political life—what she called the *vita activa*. During the classical period, she affirmed, Greeks on the whole took for granted that "freedom is exclusively located in the political realm"—whereas physical need-fulfillment and technical production are "prepolitical" phenomena. Only by interacting and communicating in an open space were humans thought to be capable of showing free initiative and displaying their unique talents. For Arendt, political freedom decayed in subsequent centuries and reached a nadir in later modern times when the *vita activa* was steadily submerged in the pursuit of need-fulfillment and economic productivity (in the "social" domain). A corollary of these developments has been the atrophy of active political life and the truncation of freedom through its confinement in a private solipsim.[17] Challenging this modern trajectory, Arendt sought to revitalize the worldly character of freedom (as distinguished from freedom of thought or will). "We first become aware of freedom and its opposite," she asserted, "in our intercourse with others, not in the intercourse with ourselves." Before being transmuted into "an attribute of thought or a quality of the will," freedom was understood to be "the free man's status." To salvage this legacy, everything depended hence on a recuperation of public space as a platform for human agency: "Without a politically guaranteed public realm, freedom lacks the worldly space to make its appearance."[18]

Although admirable in its élan, Arendt's defense of public freedom is not without quandaries or drawbacks. Her stress on overt activity made little allowance for the promptings or motives of the heart; moreover, geared toward public "virtuosity" and self-display, *vita activa* falls short of the Gandhian notions of self-rule and self-transcendence. Some remedies for these defects can be found in the writings of other contemporary thinkers, particularly the work of Charles Taylor. Together with Arendt, Taylor has sought to recapture political freedom from the snares of a purely subjective privacy; like Arendt, he has thereby transgressed the negative/positive binary (outlined by Berlin). As he wrote, in an attack on this binary, negative liberty is untenable since freedom cannot just denote "the absence of external obstacles, for there may also be internal ones." Once this is recognized, freedom must mean not only the removal of external obstacles, but also the ability to deal with "emotional fetters" and to channel human inclinations.[19] In appealing to motivational guidance and self-rule, Taylor placed the accent not just on action but on its ethical quality and significance—thus preserving the classical (and Hegelian) linkage between ethics and politics, between moral self-rule and self-government. This linkage, and hence the notion of freedom as self-rule, have been eloquently articulated in some of Taylor's ethical writings—in a manner reminiscent of Gandhian *swaraj*. Using "authenticity" as a code word for the ambivalence of modern freedom, Taylor acknowledges that, under the impact of modern subjectivism, freedom easily deteriorates into self-centeredness and self-indulgence. Conceived as a selfishly domineering agency, he writes, freedom pushed to its limit "does not recognize any boundaries, anything that I *have* to respect in my exercise of self-determining choice"; hence, it can "easily tip over into the most extreme forms of anthropocentrism." To this deviant type, Taylor opposes a vision of freedom understood as responsiveness and self-transformation. Properly construed, authenticity points us towards a more self-responsible form of life . . . [it] opens up an age of responsibilization, if I can use this term. . . . The nature of a free society is that it will always be the locus of a struggle between higher and lower forms of freedom. . . . Through social action, political change, and winning hearts and minds, the better forms can gain ground, at least for a while.[20]

The distinction between types of freedom has also been endorsed by Tu Weiming in his reflections on Confucian thought. As Tu Weiming shows, Confucianism opposes the negative/positive binary, that is, the construal of freedom in terms of either private self-withdrawal or domineering self-enhancement. "It rejects," he writes, "both an introspective affirmation of the self as an isolable and complacent ego and an unrestrained attachment to the external world for the sake of a limitless expansion of one's manipulative power." In lieu of these alternatives, the Confucian *tao* (or way) involves an "unceasing process of self-transformation as a communal act," and thus a linkage of ethics and social engagement whose seasoning effect "can ultimately free us from the constrictions of the privatized ego." In addition to social engagement, Confucianism also fosters the "mutuality between man and Heaven," and ultimately human reconciliation with "Heaven, Earth, and the myriad things"—with clearly spiritual (or religious) implications. Tu Weiming also points to the Confucian stress on exemplification, on the need not merely to hold fine theories but to exemplify them in daily conduct. Despite his deep modesty, Confucius himself can be seen as an "exemplar" or "exemplary person" (*chün-tzu*) who taught the way not through doctrines but through the testimony of engaged living—thereby appealing to the "heart-and-mind" (*hsin*).[21] Gandhi, in all his modesty, can also be seen as such an exemplary person or practical *guru*. Averse to abstract formulas and ideologies, Gandhi in his own life-conduct demonstrated and exemplified the meaning of *swaraj*. As he repeatedly insisted, *swaraj* cannot be left on the level of abstract principles and empty theorizing, but must be instantiated in daily practice—something he did throughout his life. To conclude with these lines (in part cited before) of *Hind Swaraj*:

> Do not consider this *swaraj* to be like a dream. Here there is no idea of sitting still. The *swaraj* that I wish to picture before you and me is such that, after we have once realized it, we will endeavor to the end of our lifetime to persuade others to do likewise. But such *swaraj* has to be experienced by each one for himself.[22]

NOTES

Introduction

1. See United Nations General Assembly, Resolution 53/22 of November 4, 1998; also "World Day of Peace Message," January 1, 2001, as reported in *Catholic Worker* 21 (Jan.-Feb. 2001): 1, 5–6. For the text of the UN Resolution and also for the text of a parallel Declaration adopted by the Organization of Islamic Conference (OIC) in Tehran, May 3–5, 1999, see Victor Segesvary, *Dialogue of Civilizations: An Introduction to Civilizational Analysis* (Lanham, MD: University Press of America, 2000), pp. v-vii, 99–105.

2. Martin Buber, *I and Thou* (New York: Scribner, 1970), and *Between Man and Man* (New York: Macmillan, 1965). As Maurice Friedman aptly notes in his "Introduction" to *Between Man and Man:* "To say that 'all real living is meeting' is not to say that one leaves one's ground in order to meet the other or that one lets oneself get swallowed up in the crowd or trades in one's individuality for a social role" (p. xv). Another prominent defender of the dialogical principle in recent history is the linguist Mikhail Bakhtin; see especially his *The Dialogic Imagination: Four Essays,* ed. Michael Holquist (Austin: University of Texas Press, 1981); also Tzvetan Todorov, *Mikhail Bakhtin: The Dialogical Principle,* trans. Wlad Godzich (Minneapolis: University of Minnesota Press, 1984). Regarding Gadamer see also Richard Shapcott, "Conversation and Coexistence: Gadamer and the Interpretation of International Society," *Millennium* 23 (1994): 57–84.

3. Buber, *Between Man and Man,* pp. xvii, 7. As Buber adds: "Only then will genuine common life appear, not that of an identical content of faith which is alleged to be found in all religions, but that of the situation, of anguish and of expectation" (pp. 7–8).

4. Charles Taylor, *Sources of the Self: The Making of Modern Identity* (Cambridge, MA: Harvard University Press, 1989), p. 520. On the issue of modern boundaries or demarcations see also Alan Schnaiberg and Kenneth A. Gould, *Environment and Society: The Enduring Conflict* (New York: St. Martin's Press, 1994); Erazim V. Kohák, *The Embers and the Stars: A Philosophical Inquiry into the Moral Sense of Nature* (Chicago: University of Chicago Press, 1984). Compare also Martin Heidegger, *Identity and Difference,* trans. Joan Stambaugh (New York: Harper & Row, 1969).

5. The notion of dialogue as a "mid-point" between self and other has also been eloquently articulated by Paul Ricoeur; see especially his *Oneself as Another,* trans. Kathleen Blamey (Chicago: University of Chicago Press, 1992), pp. 180–194; also my "Oneself as Another: Paul Ricoeur's 'Little Ethics,'" in *Achieving Our World: Toward a Global and Plural Democracy* (Lanham: Rowman & Littlefield, 2001), pp. 171–188.

6. Charles Taylor, "Two Theories of Modernity," *Public Culture* 11 (1999): 162–163. Compare also my "Modernity in the Crossfire: Comments on the Postmodern Turn," in John Paul Jones III, Wolfgang Natter, and Theodore R. Schatzki, eds., *Postmodern Contentions: Epochs, Politics, Space* (New York: Guilford Press, 1993), pp. 17–38.

7. In Dussel's words, a philosophy of dialogue is necessary "as part of a philosophy of liberation of the oppressed, the excommunicated, the excluded, the Other." See Enrique Dussel, *The Invention of the Americas: Eclipse of the "Other" and the Myth of Modernity,* trans. Michael D. Barber (New York: Continuum, 1995), p. 12.

8. Compare in this context especially Elmer Bender, *The Rise and Fall of Paradise: When Arabs and Jews Built a Kingdom in Spain* (New York: Dorset Press, 1983). For a more general discussion compare Osman Bakar, *Islam and Civilizational Dialogue: The Quest for a Truly Universal Civilization* (Kuala Lumpur: University of Malaya Press, 1997).

9. The accusation is raised in Edward W. Said, *Orientalism* (New York: Vintage Books, 1979), especially pp. 154, 167–168. On this point, I find persuasive the judicious statement by the late Wilhelm Halbfass who writes: "What he [Goethe] did had nothing to do with 'Orientalizing the Orient' or 'Occidentalizing the Occident.' On the contrary, it was meant to neutralize and supersede any potential reification and essentialization of Orient and Occident." See Eli Franco and Karin Preisendanz, eds., *Beyond Orientalism: The Work of Wilhelm Halbfass and Its Impact on Indian and Cross-Cultural Studies* (Amsterdam: Rodopi, 1997), p. 12.

10. These lectures have not yet been published; however, Ruth Abbey offers some glimpses in her *Charles Taylor* (Princeton: Princeton University Press, 2000), pp. 195–212. At an earlier point, Taylor observed tellingly: "It is impossible in our days to be a Christian, atheist, or anything else, without a degree of doubt. Our situation is characterized by its instability, much more than by the idea that secularism has swept away religion." See his "From Philosophical Anthropology to the Politics of Recognition," *Thesis Eleven* 52 (February 1998): 111; also his "Modes of Secularism," in Rajeev Bhargava, ed., *Secularism and Its Critics* (Delhi: Oxford University Press, 1998), pp. 31–53.

11. See "*Sunyata* East and West: Emptiness and Global Democracy," in my *Beyond Orientalism: Essays on Cross-Cultural Encounter* (Albany: State University of New York Press, 1966), pp. 175–199; "Humanity and Humanization: Comments on Confucianism," in my *Alternative Vi-*

sions: Paths in the Global Village (Lanham: Rowman & Littlefield, 1998), pp. 123–144; also "Liberation Perspectives East and West" and "'Return to the Source': African Identity (After Cabral)," in the same text, pp. 17–103, 169–190. Compare also my "Nothingness and *Sunyata:* A Comparison of Heidegger and Nishitani," *Philosophy East and West* 42 (1992): 37–48; and "Tradition, Modernity, and Confucianism," *Human Studies* 16 (1993): 203–211. For additional literature see, e.g., Eliot Deutsch, *Introduction to World Philosophies* (Upper Saddle River, NJ: Prentice Hall, 1997), Ninian Smart and B. Srinivasa Murthy, eds., *East-West Encounters in Philosophy and Religion* (Long Beach, CA: Long Beach Publications, 1996); J. J. Clark, *The Tao of the West: Western Transformations of Taoist Thought* (London: Routledge, 2000); Chenyang Li, *The Tao Encounters the West: Explorations in Comparative Philosophy* (Albany: State University of New York Press, 1999); and Daniel A. Bell, *East Meets West* (Princeton: Princeton University Press, 2000).

12. For Hölderin's poems and Heidegger's comments, see Martin Heidegger, *Erläuterungen zu Hölderlins Dichtung,* ed. Friedrich-Wilhelm von Herrmann (*Gesamtausgabe,* vol. 4; Frankfurt-Main: Klostermann, 1981), pp. 38–40, 123–124. Compare also, e.g., Michael A. Sells, *Mystical Languages of Unsaying* (Chicago: University of Chicago Press, 1994); David Abram, *The Spell of the Sensuous: Perception and Language in a More-Than-Human World* (New York: Vintage Books, 1996).

Chapter 1

1. United Nations General Assembly, Resolution 53/22 of November 4, 1998.

2. Hans-Georg Gadamer, *Truth and Method,* 2nd rev. ed., trans. Joel Weinsheimer and Donald G. Marshall (New York: Crossroad, 1989), p. 312. See also Oswald Spengler, *The Decline of the West,* 2 vols. (New York: Knopf, 1926–28); Arnold Toynbee, *Civilization on Trial* (New York: Oxford University Press, 1948); Samuel Huntington, "The Clash of Civilizations?" *Foreign Affairs* 72 (Summer 1993): 22–49; also Huntington, *The Clash of Civilizations and the Remaking of World Order* (New York: Simon & Schuster, 1996).

3. *Encyclopaedia Britannica* (Chicago: Benton Publ., 1964), vol. 5, p. 824.

4. See, for example, R. Grant Steen, *DNA and Destiny: Nature and Nurture in Human Behavior* (New York: Plenum Press, 1996), and Theodore D. Wacha, *The Nature of Nurture* (Newbury Park, CA: Sage Publ., 1992). The above presentation bypasses the distinction between "culture" and "civilization" (which sometimes carries invidious overtones, devaluing the second term). Occasionally, "culture" (from Latin *colere*) is associated with an agricultural society, while "civilization" is said to denote an urban, perhaps industrial society. Use of the

term "culture" is further complicated by its frequent association with education or educational accomplishment (*Bildung*).

5. Norbert Elias, *The Civilizing Process* (New York: Urizen Books, 1978); also *Power and Civility* (New York: Pantheon books, 1982). In the wake of the Hobbesian initiative, John Locke sought to mitigate the gulf between the natural and civil states—but only by partially civilizing the "natives" (in the state of nature). On the assumption that people are naturally civilized, subsequent laissez-faire liberalism reduced the role of the civil state (giving free rein to private economic ambitions).

6. St. Augustine, *The City of God*, ed. Vernon J. Bourke (Garden City, NY: Image Books/Doubleday, 1962), pp. 321–322.

7. Gadamer, "Philosophy and Literature," trans. Anthony J. Steinbook, *Man and World*, vol. 18 (1985), pp. 243–244.

8. In the words of Eric Voegelin: "The understanding of the medieval empire as the continuation of Rome was more than a vague historical hangover; it was part of a conception of history in which the end of Rome meant the end of the world in the eschatological sense. . . . Western Christian society thus was articulated into the spiritual and temporal orders, with pope and emperor as the supreme representatives in both the existential and the transcendental sense." See *The New Science of Politics: An Introduction* (Chicago: University of Chicago Press, 1952), p. 110.

9. This goal is clearly manifest in Nicolo Machiavelli's *Discourses on the First Ten Books of Titus Livius*. See Machiavelli, *The Prince and the Discourses*, introd. Max Lerner (New York: Modern Library, 1950).

10. The most perceptive and instructive account of the emergence of modern individualism is Charles Taylor, *Sources of the Self: The Making of Modern Identity* (Cambridge, MA: Harvard University Press, 1989).

11. Gadamer, "Citizens of Two Worlds," in Dieter Misgeld and Graeme Nicholson, eds., *Hans-Georg Gadamer on Education, Poetry, and History: Applied Hermeneutics* (Albany, NY: State University of New York Press, 1992), pp. 212–213.

12. Compare in this context, e.g., Jürgen Habermas, *The Philosophical Discourse of Modernity*, trans. Frederick G. Lawrence (Cambridge, MA: MIT Press, 1987); Maurizio Passerin d'Entrèves and Seyla Benhabib, eds., *Habermas and the Unfinished Project of Modernity* (Cambridge, UK: Polity Press, 1996); Agnes Heller, *Can Modernity Survive?* (Cambridge, UK: Blackwell, 1990); Albrecht Wellmer, *In Defense of Modernity* (Cambridge, MA: MIT Press, 1990); Anthony Giddens, *The Consequences of Modernity* (Stanford, CA: Stanford University Press, 1989); Lawrence E. Cahoone, *The Dilemma of Modernity* (Albany, NY: State University of New York Press, 1988); Gianni Vattimo, *The End of Modernity*, trans. Jon R. Snyder (Baltimore, MD: Johns Hopkins University Press, 1988).

13. Gadamer, *Truth and Method*, pp. 278, 281. The statement occurs in his discussion of European Romanticism construed as a counter-move to the Enlightenment. As he writes, Romanticism treated tradition (especially medieval tradition) as the "antithesis to the freedom of reason," regarding it as "something historically given, like nature." In Gadamer's view, however, the celebration of nature and tradition "before which all reason must be silent" is just as "prejudiced" (in the pejorative sense) as the "anti-tradition" of radical Enlightenment; even the deliberate preservation of nature and the past reflects "an act of reason, though an inconspicuous one." Regarding the ambivalent status of modernity and the Enlightenment see especially Max Horkheimer and Theodor W. Adorno, *Dialectic of Enlightenment*, trans. John Cumming (New York: Seabury, 1972); also Sigmund Freud, *Civilization and Its Discontents*, trans. and ed. James Strachey (New York: Norton & Co., 1962).

14. See, e.g., Abdolkarim Soroush, "The Three Cultures," in *Reason, Freedom, and Democracy in Islam*, trans. and ed. Mahmud Sadri and Ahmad Sadri (Oxford: Oxford University Press, 2000), pp. 156–170. In addition to the main historical layers it is also desirable, within the Islamic tradition, to differentiate between scriptural theology, Graeco-Hellenistic philosophy, and Sufi mysticism and poetry.

15. *Truth and Method*, pp. 363, 367. As Gadamer adds: "What characterizes dialogue . . . is precisely this: that here language in questioning and answering—in giving and taking, in miscommunicating and mutual understanding—performs that communication of meaning whose artful elaboration (especially with regard to written texts) is the task of hermeneutics. Hence it is more than a metaphor but an original insight if the task of hermeneutics is described as dialoguing with a text" (p. 368; translation slightly altered).

16. *Truth and Method*, pp. 295, 353–354, 383. Compare also John Llewelyn, *The Middle Voice of Ecological Conscience* (London: Macmillan, 1991).

17. See Edward W. Said, *Orientalism* (New York: Vintage Books, 1979); also my *Beyond Orientalism: Essays on Cross-Cultural Encounter* (Albany, NY: State University of New York Press, 1996), especially the chapter on "Gadamer, Derrida, and the Hermeneutics of Difference," pp. 39–62.

18. See Martin Heidegger, "A Dialogue on Language," in *On the Way to Language*, trans. Peter D. Hertz (San Francisco: Harper & Row, 1982).

19. In Gadamer's words: "Essential to the meaning of situation (or situatedness) is the concept of '*horizon*'. The horizon is the range of vision that includes everything that can be seen from a particular vantage point. . . . The concept of 'horizon' suggests itself because it expresses the superior breadth of vision that the person who is trying to understand must have. To acquire a horizon means that one learns to look

beyond what is close at hand—not in order to look away from it but to see it better, within a larger whole and in truer proposition." See *Truth and Method,* pp. 302, 305. Although the text also speaks of a "fusion of horizons" (p. 306), the phrase probably should not be taken in the sense of a bland consensualism.

20. *Truth and Method,* p. 469; see also Heidegger, "Language," in *Poetry, Language, Thought,* trans. Albert Hofstadter (New York: Harper & Row, 1971), pp. 207–208. As Gadamer adds (p. 469), the speculative account of language is "epitomized in the poetic word." Elsewhere, he elaborates on this point: "The poetic incarnation of meaning in language consists in the fact that it need not insert itself in the one-dimensionality of an argumentative context and logical lines of deduction but gives, so to speak, its third dimension to the poem through what Paul Celan has once called the multifariousness of each word." See "Philosophy and Literature," p. 248.

21. As Gadamer writes: "Creation once took place through the word of God. In this way the early [church] fathers used the miracle of language to explain the un-Greek idea of the creation. More importantly still: the actual redemptive act, the sending of the Son, the mystery of incarnation, is portrayed in John's prologue in terms of the word." See *Truth and Method,* p. 419. In more theological language he continues: "Christology prepares the way for a new philosophy of man, which mediates in a new way between the mind of man in its finitude and the divine infinity. Here what we have called the 'hermeneutical experience' finds its own, special ground" (p. 428). With regard to the divine, Heidegger's position is in many ways the reverse of contemporary fundamentalism. In his *Beiträge zur Philosophie,* he speaks of the possibility of the quiet passing-by of the "last God"; elsewhere he has commented on, and affirmed, Hölderlin's notion of the "want of holy names" in our time. See *Beiträge zur Philosophie (Vom Ereignis),* ed. Friedrich-Wilhem von Herrmann (*Gesamtausgabe,* vol. 65; Frankfurt-Main: Klostermann, 1989), pp. 409–417; "The Want of Holy Names," trans. Bernhard Radloff, *Man and World,* vol. 18 (1985), pp. 261–267.

22. St. Augustine, *The City of God,* pp. 459–460.

23. Bhikhu Parekh, "A Varied Moral World," in Joshua Cohen, Matthew Howard, and Martha C. Nussbaum, eds., *Is Multiculturalism Bad for Women?* (Princeton, NJ: Princeton University Press, 1999), p. 74. See also Parekh, *Rethinking Multiculturalism: Cultural Diversity and Political Theory* (London: Macmillan, 2000).

Chapter 2

1. Michael Oakeshott, "The Voice of Poetry in the Conversation of Mankind," in *Rationalism in Politics, and Other Essays* (New York: Basic Books, 1962), pp. 197–199.

2. "The Voice of Poetry," p. 198. See also Immanuel Kant, "Idea for a Universal History with a Cosmopolitan Purpose [Intent]," in Hans Reiss, ed., *Kant's Political Writings* (Cambridge, UK: Cambridge University Press, 1970), pp. 41–53.

3. In the words of Charles Taylor: "Explanations of modernity in terms of *reason* seem to be the most popular. Even social explanations tend to invoke reason: Social transformations, like mobility and industrialization, are thought to bring about intellectual and spiritual changes because they shake people loose from old habits and beliefs—religion or traditional morality—which then become unsustainable because they lack the kind of independent rational grounding that the beliefs of modernity—such as individualism or instrumental reason—are assumed to have." See Taylor, "Two Theories of Modernity," *Public Culture* 11 (1999): 155.

4. See Edward W. Said, *Orientalism* (New York: Random House, 1978); also my *Beyond Orientalism: Essays on Cross-Cultural Encounter* (Albany, NY: State University of New York Press, 1996).

5. See in this respect Karl August Wittfogel, *Oriental Despotism: A Comparative Study of Total Power* (New Haven, CT: Yale University Press, 1957); also Patricia Springborg, *Western Republicanism and the Oriental Prince* (Austin: University of Texas Press, 1992).

6. Compare, e.g., Gabriel A. Almond and G. Bingham Powell, Jr., *Comparative Politics: A Developmental Approach* (Boston: Little, Brown & Co., 1956); Lucian W. Pye, *Aspects of Political Development* (Boston: Little, Brown & Co., 1966); also my "Introduction" to *Border Crossings: Toward a Comparative Political Theory* (Lanham, MD: Rowman & Littlefield, 1999), pp. 1–2.

7. See Ian Shapiro, "Enough of Deliberation: Politics Is About Interests and Power," in Stephen Macedo, ed., *Deliberative Politics: Essays on Democracy and Disagreement* (New York: Oxford University Press, 1999), pp. 28–38. The above discussion of "power" is predicated on the customary Weberian view, widely accepted by professional political scientists, and not on Hannah Arendt's notion of shared "empowerment."

8. See Carl Schmitt, *The Crisis of Parliamentary Democracy*, trans. Ellen Kennedy (Cambridge, MA: MIT Press, 1985); *The Concept of the Political*, trans. George Schwab (New Brunswick, NJ: Rutgers University Press, 1976); *The Leviathan in the State Theory of Thomas Hobbes*, trans. George Schwab and Erna Hilfstein (Westport, CT: Greenwood Press, 1996); also Chantal Mouffe, ed., *The Challenge of Carl Schmitt* (London: Verso, 1999), and Thomas Hobbes, *Leviathan* (New York: Dutton, 1953), chapters 18 and 28, pp. 91, 169.

9. Samuel P. Huntington, "The Clash of Civilizations?" *Foreign Affairs* 72 (Summer 1993): 22, 39, 41. Huntington's arguments are examined more extensively in chapter 4 below.

10. See Jürgen Habermas, *The Theory of Communicative Action,* trans. Thomas McCarthy, 2 vols. (Boston: Beacon Press, 1984); *The Philosophical Discourse of Modernity: Twelve Lectures,* trans. Frederick Lawrence (Cambridge, MA: MIT Press, 1987); also *Communication and the Evolution of Society,* trans. Thomas McCarthy (Boston: Beacon Press, 1979); *Legitimation Crisis,* trans. Thomas McCarthy (Boston: Beacon Press, 1975); and *Toward a Rational Society,* trans. Jeremy J. Shapiro (Boston: Beacon Press, 1970).

11. Habermas, "The Unity of Reason in the Diversity of Its Voices," in *Postmetaphysical Thinking: Philosophical Essays,* trans. William M. Hogengarten (Cambridge, MA: MIT Press, 1992), pp. 115–148. For the German original see *Nachmetaphysisches Denken: Philosophische Aufsätze* (Frankfurt-Main: Suhrkamp, 1988), pp. 153–186. Compare also Habermas, "Kant's Idea of Perpetual Peace: At Two Hundred Years' Historical Remove," in *The Inclusion of the Other: Studies in Political Theory,* ed. Ciaran Cronin and Pablo De Greiff (Cambridge, MA: MIT Press, 1998), pp. 165–201. For a similar argument, largely along Habermasian lines, see Seyla Benhabib, "Cultural Complexity, Moral Interdependence, and the Global Dialogical Community," in Martha C. Nussbaum and Jonathan Glover, eds., *Women, Culture and Development: A Study of Human Capabilities* (Oxford: Clarendon Press, 1995), pp. 235–255.

12. Habermas, "The Unity of Reason," pp. 115–117 (translation slightly altered).

13. "The Unity of Reason," pp. 118–122 (translation slightly altered).

14. "The Unity of Reason," pp. 124–127 (translation slightly altered).

15. "The Unity of Reason," pp. 128–131 (translation slightly altered).

16. "The Unity of Reason," pp. 134, 136–137 (translation slightly altered). Compare in this context Richard Rorty, *Consequences of Pragmatism* (Minneapolis, MN: University of Minnesota Press, 1982), and "Solidarity or Objectivity?" in John Rajchman and Cornel West, eds., *Post-Analytic Philosophy* (New York: Columbia University Press, 1985), pp. 3–19; Hilary Putnam, "Why Reason Can't Be Naturalized," in Kenneth Baines, James Bohman, and Thomas McCarthy, ed., *After Philosophy—End or Transformation?* (Cambridge, MA: MIT Press, 1987), pp. 222–244.

17. Habermas, "The Unity of Reason," pp. 137–139 (translation slightly altered).

18. "The Unity of Reason," pp. 139–142, 144–146 (translation slightly altered).

19. See Claude Lefort, *Democracy and Political Theory,* trans., David Macey (Minneapolis, MN: University of Minnesota Press, 1988), p. 19.

20. For the distinction of discourses and counter-discourses or anti-discourses see especially *The Philosophical Discourse of Modernity,* pp. 83–86, 96–97; and for a critical review my "The Discourse of Modernity: Hegel, Nietzsche, Heidegger and Habermas," in Maurizio Passerin d'Entrèves and Seyla Benhabib, eds., *Habermas and the Un-*

finished Project of Modernity (Cambridge, UK: Polity Press, 1996), pp. 59–96.

21. See Iris Marion Young, "The Ideal of Community and the Politics of Difference," in Linda J. Nicholson, ed., *Feminism/Postmodernism* (New York: Routledge, 1990), pp. 300–323; "Impartiality and the Civic Public," in Seyla Benhabib and Drucilla Cornell, eds., *Feminism as Critique* (Minneapolis, MN: University of Minnesota Press, 1987), pp. 56–76; and *Inclusion and Democracy* (Oxford: Oxford University Press, 2000), especially pp. 52–80.

22. Diana Coole, "Habermas and the Question of Alterity," in d'Entrèves and Benhabib, *Habermas and the Unfinished Project of Modernity*, pp. 221, 225, 231.

23. Habermas, *The Philosophical Discourse of Modernity*, pp. 326, 363; "Modernity: An Unfinished Project," in d'Entrèves and Benhabib, *Habermas and the Unfinished Project of Modernity*, p. 45; Coole, "Habermas and the Question of Alterity," p. 242.

24. Charles Taylor, *Sources of the Self: The Making of Modern Identity* (Cambridge, MA: Harvard University Press, 1989), p. 510; *A Catholic Modernity?*, ed. James L. Heft (New York: Oxford University Press, 1999), pp. 111–113. For an effort to steer a course, or "split the difference," between Taylor and Habermas, see Thomas McCarthy, "On Reconciling Cosmopolitan Unity and National Diversity," *Public Culture* 11 (1999): 175–208.

25. *Sources of the Self*, pp. 22, 113. The text repeatedly speaks of "exclusive humanism" as a mode of anthropocentrism (pp. 120–124). The notion of "thick conversation" is indebted distantly to Clifford Geertz's discussion of "thick description" in his *The Interpretation of Cultures* (New York: Basic Books, 1973), pp. 3–30; and also to Michael Walzer's distinction between "thick" and "thin" moral cultures in *Thick and Thin: Moral Argument at Home and Abroad* (Notre Dame: University of Notre Dame Press, 1994).

26. Due to this emphasis not on one's own, but on the "other's" (the interlocutor's) deepest strivings, the critique and correction of prevailing social practices or conditions needs to rely preferably on "internal" critique, that is, on liberating resources made available in a given cultural and/or religious tradition—although these resources need occasionally be supplemented by "external" arguments offered in a communicative spirit. Regarding this combination of resources see especially Abdullahi Ahmed An-Naim, "Introduction," in An-Naim, ed., *Human Rights in Cross-Cultural Perspective: A Quest for Consensus* (Philadelphia: University of Pennsylvania Press, 1992), pp. 2–4; also his "The Cultural Mediation of Rights," in Joanne R. Bauer and Daniel A. Bell, eds., *The East Asian Challenge for Human Rights* (Cambridge, UK: Cambridge University Press, 1999), pp. 147–168.

27. Oakeshott, "The Voice of Poetry," in *Rationalism in Politics*, pp. 234, 240, 244. See also Aristotle, *Nicomachean Ethics*, trans. Terence Irwin

(Indianapolis: Hacket Publishing Co., 1985), Book 8, pp. 212–213 (1156b).

28. Jalal ad-Din Rumi, "Open Door." Poem translated from the Turkish by Deniz Ugur.

Chapter 3

1. My doctoral dissertation, submitted to the University of Munich in 1955, dealt with the beginnings of European "supranational" integration at that time; the more theoretical argument was published under the title "Initiation à l'idée du 'supranational'" in *Chronique de politique étrangère* 8 (Brussels, 1955): 1–9. Shortly afterwards I wrote an essay for a post-graduate journal issued by the Istituto di Studi Europei in Turin, Italy, titled "Um ein Europa von innen bittend"—a title that was adapted from Ortega y Gasset's famous plea for a Goethe "from within" (that is, removed from his olympian pedestal).

2. Samir Amin, *Eurocentrism,* trans. Russell Moore (New York: Monthly Review Press, 1989), p. vii.

3. Enrique Dussel, *The Invention of the Americas: Eclipse of 'the Other' and the Myth of Modernity,* trans. Michael D. Barber (New York: Continuum, 1995), pp. 20, 72. As he adds in a footnote (p. 172, note 39): "These prophetic pages warn about the brutal violence that modernity will scatter throughout the peripheral, colonial world, only recently called the Third World. Las Casas would not be surprised to see the desolation of Iraq's poor, suffering people." The citation is taken from Las Casas, *De único modo de atraer a todos los pueblos a la verdadera religión* (1536; Mexico City: FCE, 1975), pp. 343–344. In another text, Dussel cites these comments of Las Casas: "Then it was that they [the indigenous peoples] knew them [the Europeans] as wolves and tigers and the cruelest of lions who had been hungry for many days. And the latter have done nothing else these forty years in this part of the world until this very day than [inflict] havoc, slaughters, distresses, afflictions, tortures and destructions by strange, new, and varied forms of cruelty that have never been seen, or read about, or heard of before." See Dussel, *Para una ética de la liberación latinoamericana,* vol. 4 (Bogotá: Universidad Santo Tomas, 1979), p. 41; cited in Michael D. Barber, *Ethical Hermeneutics: Rationalism in Enrique Dussel's Philosophy of Liberation* (New York: Fordham University Press, 1998), p. 65.

4. Dussel, "Beyond Eurocentrism: The World-System and the Limits of Modernity," in Fredric Jameson and Masao Miyoshi, eds., *The Cultures of Globalization* (Durham, NC: Duke University Press, 1999), pp. 3–5.

5. Jacques Derrida, *The Other Heading: Reflections on Today's Europe,* trans. Pascale-Anne Brault and Michael B. Naas (Bloomington: Indiana University Press, 1992), pp. 6, 20–21, 24. As he adds: "Europe takes itself to be a promontory, an advance—the avant-garde of geography

and history. It advances and promotes itself as an advance, and it will never have ceased to make advances on the other: to induce, seduce, produce, and conduce, to spread out, to cultivate, to love or to violate, to love to violate, to colonize, and to colonize itself " (p. 49). The reference is to Paul Valéry, "The European," in *History and Politics,* trans. Denise Folliot and Jackson Mathews (New York: Bollingen, 1962), pp. 311–312.

6. Derrida, *The Other Heading,* pp. 14–15, 17, 26, 28–29.

7. *The Other Heading,* pp. 9–10, 39, 69. Intensifying the paradoxical status of Europe, another passage states: "It would seem that European cultural identity, like identity or identification in general, if it must be equal to itself and the other, to the measure of its own immeasurable difference 'with itself,' belongs or must belong to this *experience and experiment of the impossible*" (p. 45).

8. *The Other Heading,* pp. 47–48, 50–52, 54–55. As Derrida adds: "Claiming to speak in the name of intelligibility, good sense, common sense, or the democratic ethic, this discourse tends . . . to discredit anything that complicates this model. It tends to suspect or repress anything that bends, overdetermines, or even questions, in theory or in practice, this idea of language. With this concern, among others, in mind, it would be necessary to study certain rhetorical norms that dominate analytical philosophy or what is called in Frankfurt 'transcendental pragmatics'" (p. 55). See in this context Jürgen Habermas, "What is Universal Pragmatics?" in *Communication and the Evolution of Society,* trans. Thomas McCarthy (Boston: Beacon Press, 1979), pp. 1–68; *The Postnational Constellation: Political Essays,* trans. Max Pensky (Cambridge, MA: MIT Press, 2001).

9. Habermas, "Modernity: An Unfinished Project," in Maurizio Passerin d'Entrèves and Seyla Benhabib, eds., *Habermas and the Unfinished Project of Modernity* (Cambridge, UK: Polity Press, 1996), p. 45–46, 51 (translation slightly altered).

10. "Modernity: An Unfinished Project," pp. 46, 53–54. In Habermas's terminology, Young Conservatives (including Nietzsche, Derrida, and Foucault) are basically "antimodern," while Old Conservatives (including Leo Strauss and Hans Jonas) are "premodern," and New Conservatives "postmodern."

11. Bassam Tibi, *Europa ohne Identität? Die Krise der multikulturellen Gesellschaft* (Munich: Bertelsmann, 1998), pp. 45–47.

12. *Europa ohne Identität?,* pp. 24–26, 28, 59, 67–68.

13. *Europa ohne Identität?,* pp. 56, 181, 183.

14. There is by now a broad literature on this topic. See, e.g., Will Kymlicka, *Multicultural Citizenship: A Liberal Theory of Minority Rights* (Oxford: Oxford University Press, 1995); Joseph H. Carens, *Culture, Citizenship and Community* (Oxford: Oxford University Press, 2000); Bhikhu Parekh, *Rethinking Multiculturalism: Cultural Diversity and Political Theory* (London: Macmillan, 2000).

15. On the importance of cultural dialogue, including conflictual dialogue, see Tibi, *Europa ohne Identität?*, pp. 179–180, 258–263; on multiculturalism, pp. 49–50, 81–82, 92–97.

16. *Europa ohne Identität?*, pp. 28, 149–151. For many interpreters (including myself), "multiculturalism" tends to coincide more or less with Tibi's notion of "cultural pluralism."

17. Charles Taylor, "The Politics of Recognition," in Amy Gutmann, ed., *Multiculturalism and "The Politics of Recognition"* (Princeton, NJ: Princeton University Press, 1992), pp. 31–32. The importance of Herder has recently also been emphasized by the distinguished international policy expert David P. Calleo in his book *Rethinking Europe's Future* (Princeton, NJ: Princeton University Press, 2001), pp. 53–56, 373–374.

18. Taylor, "The Politics of Recognition," pp. 37–39, 43. Compare in this context also my "'Rights' versus 'Rites': Justice and Global Democracy," in *Alternative Visions: Paths in the Global Village* (Lanham, MD: Rowman & Littlefield, 1998), pp. 253–276.

19. Amy Gutmann, "Introduction," in *Multiculturalism and "The Politics of Recognition,"* pp. 16, 18, 20–21. Gutmann adds an important caveat regarding the difference between respect and toleration: "Not every aspect of cultural diversity is worthy of respect. Some differences— racism and anti-Semitism are obvious examples—ought not to be *respected,* even if expressions of racist and anti-Semitic views must be *tolerated*" (p. 21).

20. Derrida, *The Other Heading,* pp. 12–13, 18–19, 29, 76–77. As he adds (p. 44): "One must therefore try to invent gestures, discourses, politico-institutional practices that inscribe the alliance of these two imperatives, of these two promises or contracts: the capital and the a-capital, the other of the capital."

21. Dussel, *The Invention of the Americas,* pp. 132, 136–137.

22. Tibi, *Europa ohne Identität?*, pp. 108, 185–186.

23. Taylor, *Sources of the Self: The Making of the Modern Identity* (Cambridge, MA: Harvard University Press, 1989). See also Michel Foucault, "What is Enlightenment?" in Paul Rabinow, ed., *The Foucault Reader* (New York: Pantheon Books, 1984), pp. 32–50.

24. Hans-Georg Gadamer, *Das Erbe Europas* (Frankfurt-Main: Suhrkamp, 1989), pp. 30, 33–34. For an English translation (not followed here) see Dieter Misgeld and Graeme Nicholson, eds., *Hans-Georg Gadamer on Education, Poetry, and History: Applied Hermeneutics* (Albany: State University of New York Press, 1992), pp. 234–236. In a similar vein, linking identity and self-transcendence, Martin Heidegger states: "Thinking has needed more than two thousand years really to understand such a simple relation as that of the mediation within identity. Do *we* then have a right to the opinion that the thoughtful entry into the basic source of identity could be achieved overnight? . . . Whatever and however we may try to think, we think

within the ambiance of tradition—which holds sway by freeing us from nostalgia into a fore-thought which is no longer planning." See his *Identity and Difference,* trans. Joan Stambaugh (New York: Harper & Row, 1969), p. 41 (translation slightly altered).

Chapter 4

1. See, e.g., Jean-François Lyotard, *The Differend: Phrases in Dispute,* trans. Georges Van den Abbeele (Minneapolis: University of Minnesota Press, 1988). Perhaps it would be better to treat conceptions like asymmetry and radical alterity as expressions of reverence or reverential praise rather than as philosophical principles.

2. Another possible drawback of the tradition is that equality often tends to be extended only to co-religionists—as if the divine could be appropriated and monopolized by a particular faith or religious creed.

3. Regarding the "rule of law" compare, e.g., Franz Neumann, *The Rule of Law* (Dover, NH: Berg, 1986) and Randy E. Barnett, *The Structure of Liberty: Justice and the Rule of Law* (Oxford: Clarendon Press, 1998); and regarding modern citizenship Ronald Beiner, ed., *Theorizing Citizenship* (Albany: State University of New York Press, 1995) and Will Kymlicka and Wayne Norman, eds., *Citizenship in Diverse Societies* (Oxford: Oxford University Press, 2000).

4. See Helen Marie Casey, "Chandra Muzaffer Reflects on a Just World," *Boston Research Center for the 21st Century, Newsletter* No. 16 (Winter 2001), p. 18.

5. Samuel P. Huntington, "The Clash of Civilizations?" *Foreign Affairs* 72 (Summer 1993): 39.

6. "The Clash of Civilizations?," p. 40.

7. Huntington, *The Clash of Civilizations and the Remaking of World Order* (New York: Simon & Schuster, 1996), pp. 29, 83–84, 318.

8. *The Clash of Civilizations,* pp. 31–36, 91.

9. Huntington, "Culture, Power, and Democracy," in Marc F. Plattner and Aleksander Smolar, eds., *Globalization, Power, and Democracy* (Baltimore, MD: Johns Hopkins University Press, 2000), pp. 3, 5–6. The volume arose out of a conference on "International Relations and Democracy" held in Warsaw, Poland, on June 25–28, 1998.

10. "Culture, Power, and Democracy," pp. 3, 5, 11.

11. See United Nations Development Program (UNDP), *Human Development Report 1999* (Oxford: Oxford University Press, 1999).

12. Developments in different parts of the world have been diverse. Thus, in East Asia the number of people living on less than $1 a day fell from around 420 million to about 280 million between 1987 and 1998. However, in Latin America, South Asia, Central Asia, and Sub-Saharan Africa the numbers of poor people (less than $1 a day) have been increasing, in Central Asia more than twentyfold. See World Bank,

World Development Report 2000 (Oxford: Oxford University Press, 2000); cited from *World Faiths Development Dialogue,* Occasional Paper No. 4 (Oxford, 2000), p. 3.

13. See, e.g., Andrew Hurrell and Ngaire Woods, "Globalization and Inequality," *Millennium* 24 (1995): 447–470; Saskia Sassen, *Globalization and Its Discontents: Essays on the New Mobility of People and Money* (New York: New Press, 1998); Richard Falk, *Predatory Globalization: A Critique* (Cambridge, UK: Polity Press, 1999). For revealing economic data see also David Held, Anthony McGrew, David Goldblatt, and Jonathan Perraton, *Global Transformations: Politics, Economics, Culture* (Stanford, CA: Stanford University Press, 1999), esp. pp. 168–188.

14. See Charles Derber, "Change the World!" in *Boston Research Center for the 21st Century, Newsletter* No. 16 (Winter 2001), pp. 1, 16. Amplifying the figures of the United Nations and the World Bank, Derber notes that 450 billionaires today own more wealth than half of all humanity and that the three richest shareholders of Microsoft own more wealth than all the people living in Africa. He adds, in terms of wealth, "Wal-Mart is bigger than 163 countries. General Electric (GE) is bigger than Israel or Finland." Compare also Derber, *Corporation Nation: How Corporations are Taking Over Our Lives and What We Can Do About It* (New York: St. Martin's Press, 1998).

15. Amartya Sen, *Inequality Reexamined* (Cambridge, MA: Harvard University Press, 1992), pp. 21, 24. In this context, Sen opposes the abstract opposition between freedom and equality (often advanced by neo-classical economists) as a "category mistake" (pp. 22–23): "It is neither accurate nor helpful to think of the difference . . . in terms of 'liberty *versus* equality'. . . . They are not alternatives. Liberty is among the possible *fields of application* of equality, and equality is among the possible *patterns* of distribution of liberty."

16. *Inequality Reexamined,* pp. 110–111, 150. Regarding differential incentives one should note his comment: "To the extent that gender or age is responsible for inequality of capabilities, the policy response may take the form of providing special help to members of the more deprived gender or age categories. Since it is impossible to change one's age rapidly, and particularly hard to change one's sex, the special treatments may not generate incentive problems of the standard kind" (p. 142). It seems clear that considerations of this kind can be extended to other deprived or marginalized categories.

17. Sen, *Development as Freedom* (New York: Random House/Anchor Books, 2000), pp. 18, 25–26, 111.

18. *Development as Freedom,* pp. 20–21, 119, 126–129.

19. See David Crocker, "Functioning and Capability: The Foundations of Sen's and Nussbaum's Development Ethic," in Martha Nussbaum and Jonathan Glover, eds., *Women, Culture, and Development: A Study in Human Capability* (New York: Oxford University Press, 1995), pp.

153–198; Iris Marion Young, *Inclusion and Democracy* (Oxford: Oxford University Press, 2000), pp. 31–32, 34, 50.

20. See in this respect, e.g., European Knowledge Acquisition Workshop, *Knowledge Engineering and Knowledge Management* (New York: Springer, 2000): Michael E. Porter, *Measuring the "Ideas" Production Function: Evidence from International Patent Output* (Cambridge, MA: National Bureau of Economic Research, 2000).

21. See Wayne Gabardi, "Contemporary Models of Democracy," *Polity* 33 (Summer 2001): 559–560, 562; also Danilo Zolo, *Democracy and Complexity: A Realist Approach* (University Park: Pennsylvania State University Press, 1992), p. ix, 1–3; Scott Lash and John Urry, *Economies of Signs and Space* (Thousand Oaks, CA: SAGE Publications, 1994); Edward S. Herman and Robert W. McChesney, *The Global Media: The New Missionaries of Global Capitalism* (London: Cassell, 1997).

22. Hans-Georg Gadamer, *Reason in the Age of Science,* trans. Frederick G. Lawrence (Cambridge, MA: MIT Press, 1981), pp. 2–3 (translation slightly altered). Some of these comments are clearly reminiscent of Max Horkheimer's and Theodor W. Adorno's *Dialectic of Enlightenment,* trans. John Cumming (New York: Seabury, 1972). See also Alexis de Tocqueville, *Democracy in America,* ed. Phillips Bradley (New York: Random House/Vintage Books, 1945), esp. vol. 2, pp. 9–12, 239–241.

23. Gadamer, *Reason in the Age of Science,* pp. 70–73 (translation slightly altered). As he adds: "The society of experts is simultaneously a society of functionaries as well, for it is constitutive of the notion of the functionary that he be completely concentrated upon the execution of his function" (p. 74). For a similar concern about the role of experts see also Jürgen Habermas, *Toward a Rational Society,* trans. Jeremy J. Shapiro (Boston: Beacon Press, 1970), esp. pp. 62–80.

24. Gadamer, *Reason in the Age of Science,* pp. 76–77, 84–86 (translation slightly altered).

25. Martin Heidegger, "A Dialogue on Language," in *On the Way to Language,* trans. Peter D. Hertz (San Francisco: Harper & Row, 1971), pp. 15–16; "Zur Seinsfrage," in *Wegmarken* (Frankfurt-Main: Klostermann, 1967), p. 252.

26. Robert Kagan, "The Centrality of the United States," in Plattner and Smolar, eds., *Globalization, Power, and Democracy,* p. 110. As he adds: "And is there anyone who believes that democracy will continue to flourish without the continued exercise of American power on its behalf?" (p. 111). The comments appear in a subsection titled "American Democracy at Home and Abroad." See also Zbigniew Brzezinski, "Epilogue: Democracy's Uncertain Triumph," in the same volume, p. 149; Huntington, "Culture, Power, and Democracy," pp. 9, 11–12.

27. For the above citations see Sheldon Wolin, "Fugitive Democracy," in Seyla Benhabib, ed., *Democracy and Difference: Contesting the Boundaries of the Political* (Princeton, NJ: Princeton University Press,

1996), pp. 31, 43–44. Compare also my "Beyond Fugitive Democracy: Some Modern and Postmodern Reflections," in Aryeh Botwinick and William E. Connolly, eds., *Democracy and Vision: Sheldon Wolin and the Vicissitudes of the Political* (Princeton: Princeton University Press, 2001), pp. 58–78.

28. Iris Marion Young, *Inclusion and Democracy* (Oxford: Oxford University Press, 2000), pp. 17, 31–33.

29. *Inclusion and Democracy*, pp. 236, 250, 265. See also my "Global Governance and Cultural Diversity," in *Achieving Our World: Toward a Global and Plural Democracy* (Lanham, MD: Rowman & Littlefield, 2001), pp. 35–50; Thomas W. Pogge, ed., *Global Justice* (Cambridge: Blackwell, 2001); Darrel Moellendorf, *Cosmopolitan Justice* (Boulder, CO: Westview Press 2001); and Charles Jones, *Global Justice: Defending Cosmopolitanism* (Oxford: Oxford University Press, 1999).

30. Young, *Inclusion and Democracy*, pp. 48, 50.

Chapter 5

1. The Sung dynasty in China (960–1279 A.D.) is sometimes described by historians as "early modern." Regarding the same period in Islamic civilization, see, e.g., Ira M. Lapidus, "The Golden Age: The Political Concepts of Islam," *The Annals of the American Academy of Political and Social Science* 524 (1992): 13–25.

2. Compare in this context the comments of the American political scientist Lucian W. Pye, who defined modernization as the process "by which tradition-bound villages or tribal-based societies are compelled to react to the pressures and demands of the modern, industrialized and urban-centered world. This process might also be called Westernization, or simply advancement and progress; it might, however, be more accurately termed the diffusion of a world culture—a world culture based on advanced technology and the spirit of science, on a rational view of life, a secular approach to social relations." See his *Aspects of Political Development* (Boston: Little Brown, 1966), pp. 44–45.

3. Richard Falk, "Religion and Politics: Verging on the Postmodern," *Alternatives* 8 (1988): 379. See also Henry Sumner Maine, *Ancient Law* (New York: Dutton & Co., 1931); Emile Durkheim, *The Division of Labor in Society,* trans. George Simpson (New York: Free Press, 1933); Reinhard Bendix, "Tradition and Modernity Reconsidered," *Comparative Studies in Society and History* 9 (1967): 326; Bruce B. Lawrence, *Defenders of God* (San Francisco: Harper & Row, 1989), p. 27. Compare also the discussion of Roxanne L. Euben in *Enemy in the Mirror: Islamic Fundamentalism and the Limits of Modern Rationalism* (Princeton, NJ: Princeton University Press, 1999), pp. 21–24.

4. See Jürgen Habermas, *Toward a Rational Society,* trans. Jeremy J. Shapiro (Boston: Beacon Press, 1970); *Legitimation Crisis,* trans. Thomas

McCarthy (Boston: Beacon Press, 1975); *Communication and the Evolution of Society,* trans. Thomas McCarthy (Boston: Beacon Press, 1979); *The Theory of Communicative Action,* vol. 1: *Reason and the Rationalization of Society,* and vol. 2: *Lifeworld and System: A Critique of Functionalist Reason,* trans. Thomas McCarthy (Boston: Beacon Press, 1984); *The Philosophical Discourse of Modernity: Twelve Lectures,* trans. Frederick Lawrence (Cambridge, MA: MIT Press, 1987).

5. *The Theory of Communicative Action* (hereafter cited as *TCA*), vol. 1, pp. 146–147, 149.

6. *TCA,* vol. 1, pp. 149, 153–155.

7. *TCA,* vol. 1, pp. 158–165. See also Max Weber, *Economy and Society,* 2 vols., ed. Guenther Roth and Claus Wittich (New York: Bedminster Press, 1968); and *The Protestant Ethic and the Spirit of Capitalism,* trans. Talcott Parsons (New York: Scribner, 1958).

8. Habermas, *TCA,* vol. 1, pp. 167–172.

9. *TCA,* vol. 1, pp. 175–176, 180. As Habermas adds: "Regarding those aspects of validity under whose guidance both the independently arisen value spheres of modernity and the corresponding social subsystems have been formally rationalized: we should not confuse or mix up these aspects with contingent *value contents,* with historically changing patterns of value. Rather, however fraught with internal tensions, these validity claims form a system that indeed emerged first in the form of Occidental rationalism, but that—beyond the peculiarity of that specific culture—lays claim to a universal validity binding on *all* 'civilized human beings' (*Kulturmenschen*)" (pp. 183–184).

10. *TCA,* vol. 1, pp. 45–47, 50.

11. *TCA,* vol. 1, pp. 48–49, 51. Regarding the distinction between three worlds compare the statement: "The objective world is presupposed in common as the totality of facts, where 'fact' signifies that a statement about a certain state of affairs . . . can count as true. A social world is presupposed in common as the totality of all interpersonal relations that are recognized by members as legitimate. Over against this, the subjective world counts as the totality of experiences to which, in each instance, only one individual has privileged access" (p. 52).

12. *TCA,* vol. 1, pp. 15, 42, 70. For a detailed discussion of Talcott Parsons's "theory of modernity," see *TCA,* vol. 2: *Lifeworld and System,* pp. 283–299.

13. See Habermas, "Modernity—An Incomplete Project," trans. Seyla Benhabib, in Hal Foster, ed., *The Anti-Aesthetic* (Port Townsend, WA: Bay Press, 1983), pp. 3–15. See also Albrecht Wellner, *In Defense of Modernity* (Cambridge, MA: MIT Press, 1990), and Maurizio Passerin d'Entrèves and Seyla Benhabib, eds., *Habermas and the Unfinished Project of Modernity* (Oxford: Polity Press, 1996).

14. See Oswald Spengler, *The Decline of the West* (New York: Knopf, 1939); René Guénon, *The Crisis of the Modern World,* trans. M. Pallis and R. Nicholson (London: Luzac, 1962); Romano Guardini, *The*

End of the Modern World (New York: Sheed & Ward, 1956); and Alasdair MacIntyre, *After Virtue* (Notre Dame, IN: University of Notre Dame Press, 1984). Compare also Johan Huizinga, *La Crisi della civiltá* (Torino: Einaudi, 1939); Hilaire Belloc, *The Crisis of Civilization* (New York: Fordham University Press, 1937); Eric Voegelin, *Modernity Without Restraint* (Columbia: University of Missouri Press, 2000); and Leo Strauss, "The Crisis of Our Time," in *The Predicament of Modern Politics,* ed. Harold J. Spaeth (Detroit, MI: University of Detroit Press, 1964), pp. 41–54.

15. Enrique Dussel closely links Western modernity with colonial expansion, namely, the conquest of the Americas—but without indicting modernity as such. As he writes: "My hypothesis is that Latin America, since 1492, is a constitutive element of modernity. . . . The European ego or subjectivity . . . continues to develop. Finally, it surfaces in the person of Hernán Cortés presiding over the conquest of Mexico, the first place where this ego effects its prototypical development by setting itself up as lord-of-the-world and will-to-power. This interpretation will permit a new definition, a new world vision of modernity, which will uncover not only its emancipatory concept, but also the victimizing and destructive myth of a Europeanism based on Eurocentrism and the developmentalist fallacy." As he adds, however: unlike some radical detractors, "I will not criticize reason as such; but I do accept their critique of reason as domineering, vicitimizing, and violent. I will not deny universalist reason its rational nucleus, but I do oppose the irrational element of its sacrificial myth." Still later, he explains: "I propose two contradictory paradigms: mere Eurocentric modernity and a modernity subsumed in a world horizon. While the first paradigm functions ambiguously as emancipative and mythically violent, the second, transmodern paradigm embraces both modernity and its alterity." See Dussel, *The Invention of the Americas: Eclipse of "the Other" and the Myth of Modernity,* trans. Michael D. Barber (New York: Continuum, 1995), pp. 26, 139.

16. The status of both capitalism and modern state bureaucracy remains ambivalent in Habermas's conception, as they seem to be exempt from the range of communicative rationality.

17. The terms mentioned above are taken respectively from Martin Heidegger, *Identity and Difference,* trans. Joan Stambaugh (New York: Harper & Row, 1969); Jacques Derrida, *Margins of Philosophy,* trans. Alan Bass (Chicago: University of Chicago Press, 1982); and Maurice Merleau-Ponty, *The Visible and the Invisible,* ed. Claude Lefort, trans. Alphonso Lingis (Evanston, IL: Northwestern University Press, 1968). The above considerations also affect the relation between Habermasian "value spheres," in the sense that factual assertions cannot be as readily separated from normative and poetic-hermeneutical concerns as he claims.

18. Compare in this context, e.g., Eric Katz, *Nature as Subject: Human Obligation and Natural Community* (Lanham, MD: Rowman & Lit-

tlefield, 1997); Al Gore, *Earth in the Balance: Ecology and the Human Spirit* (Boston: Houghton Mifflin, 1992); Paul W. Taylor, *Respect for Nature: A Theory of Environmental Ethics* (Princeton, NJ: Princeton University Press, 1986); J. E. Lovelook, *Gaia: A New Look at Life on Earth* (Oxford: Oxford University Press, 1979).

19. For reconsiderations of transcendence, see, e.g., Philippe Capelle, *Philosophie et théologie dans la pensée de Martin Heidegger* (Paris: Editions du Cerf, 1998); R. Kearny and J. O'Leary, eds., *Heidegger et la question de Dieu* (Paris: Grasset, 1980); also Jacques Derrida and Gianni Vattimo, eds., *Religion: Cultural Memory in the Present* (Stanford, CA: Stanford University Press, 1996). One a more practical level, the ferment of religious longings on the grassroots (or lifeworld) level is demonstrated by the mushrooming of "liberation theologies" in many civilizational contexts. See in this respect my "Liberation Perspectives East and West," in *Alternative Visions: Paths in the Global Village* (Lanham, MD: Rowman & Littlefield, 1998), pp. 71–103.

20. Charles Taylor, *The Ethics of Authenticity* (Cambridge, MA: Harvard University Press, 1992), pp. 11, 22–23. As used by Taylor, the term "authenticity" is in many ways close to the notions of human autonomy and integrity.

21. Taylor, *Sources of the Self: The Making of the Modern Identity* (Cambridge, MA: Harvard University Press, 1989), pp. 509–510, 512–513.

22. Taylor, *A Catholic Modernity?*, ed. James L. Heft, S. M. (New York: Oxford University Press, 1999), pp. 16–19. Regarding the possibility of "alternative modernities" see also Taylor, "Two Theories of Modernity," *Public Culture* 11 (1999): 153–173.

23. *A Catholic Modernity?*, pp. 14–15, 19, 21. As he realizes, recognition of transcendence can mean different things. In his words, "the acknowledgers of transcendence are divided. Some think that the whole move to secular humanism was just a mistake, which needs to be undone. We need to return to an earlier view of things. Others, among whom I place myself, think that the practical primacy of life [in modernity] has been a great gain for humankind and that there is some truth in the 'revolutionary' story: this gain was, in fact, unlikely to come about without some breach with established religion" (p. 29).

24. Regarding the prospect of different global modernities, see Mike Featherstone, Scott Lash, and Roland Robertson, eds., *Global Modernities* (London: SAGE, 1995); also Scott Lash, *Another Modernity, a Different Rationality* (Oxford: Blackwell, 1999), and Dilip P. Gaonkar, ed., *Alternative Modernities* (Durham, NC: Duke University Press, 2001). Regarding Islam and modernization see, e.g., Aziz al-Azmeh, *Islams and Modernities* (London: Verso, 1993); Ali Mirsepassi, *Intellectual Discourse and the Politics of Modernization: Negotiating Modernity in Iran* (Cambridge: Cambridge University Press, 2000), and Farhang Rajaee, "Islam and Modernity: The Reconstruction of an Alternative Shi'ite Islamic Worldview in Iran," in Martin E. Marty and

R. Scott Appleby, eds., *Fundamentalisms and Society,* vol. 2: *Reclaiming the Sciences, the Family, and Education* (Chicago: University of Chicago Press, 1993), pp. 103–125.

25. The notion of *"gharbzadegi"* was prominently articulated by Jalal Al-e Ahmad (1923–1969) in his book *Gharbzadegi* (Tehran: Ravaq, 1962); it was later fleshed out in his *Occidentosis: A Plague from the West,* trans. R. Campbell (Berkeley, CA: Mizan, 1984). His work is discussed by Mehrzad Boroujerdi in his *Iranian Intellectuals and the West: The Tormented Triumph of Nativism* (Syracuse, NY: Syracuse University Press, 1996), pp. 65–76.

26. Qutb's statements are taken from his *Signposts along the Road,* as translated and quoted by Roxanne L. Euben in *Enemy in the Mirror,* pp. 55–57. Euben's book offers a splendid summary of Qutb's basic teachings (pp. 49–92).

27. Seyyed Hoseyn Nasr, *Islam and the Plight of Modern Man* (New York: Longman, 1975), p. 12. See also his *Man and Nature: The Spiritual Crisis of Modern Man* (London: Unwin, 1976); and for a discussion of his work Boroujerdi, *Iranian Intellectuals and the West,* pp. 120–130.

28. See Boroujerdi, *Iranian Intellectuals and the West,* pp. 159–160. There are indications that Davari more recently has softened his stance in favor of a position more sympathetic to cross-cultural encounters with the West.

29. See Boroujedi, *Iranian Intellectuals and the West,* pp. 142–143, 161–162. Compare also Hamid Enayat, *Modern Islamic Political Thought* (Austin: University of Texas Press, 1982).

30. See Farish A. Noor, "Interview with Abdolkarim Soroush," in *Commentary: International Movement for a Just World,* No. 37, New Series (June 2000), pp. 10–11. For Soroush, the task of Muslim intellectuals today is to have "their feet planted" (p. 12) both in religious or local traditions and in modernity. Compare also Soroush, *Reason, Freedom, and Democracy in Islam,* trans. and ed. Mahmoud Sadri and Ahmad Sadri (New York: Oxford University Press, 2000), and the discussion below in chapter 9.

31. Mohammed 'Abed al-Jabri, *Arab-Islamic Philosophy: A Contemporary Critique,* trans. Aziz Abbassi (Austin, TX: University of Texas, Center for Middle Eastern Studies, 1999), pp. 2–3, 6–7, 129. (I have substituted "superstition" for "gnosticism" as the latter term may be unfamiliar to many readers. For al-Jabri, gnosticism means the claim of a privileged, esoteric access to divine wisdom.)

Chapter 6

1. Milan Kundera, *The Book of Laughter and Forgetting* (New York: Harper-Perennial, 1996).

2. Herbert Marcuse, *Eros and Civilization: A Philosophical Inquiry into Freud* (New York: Vintage Books, 1962), pp. 17–18, 212. Regarding

memory-work, with a focus on Walter Benjamin, Theodor Adorno, Herbert Marcuse, and Martin Heidegger, see my "Liberating Remembrance: Thoughts on Ethics, Politics and Recollection," in *Alternative Visions: Paths in the Global Village* (Lanham, MD: Rowman & Littlefield, 1998), pp. 145–165; compare also Myrian Sepulveda Santos, "Memory and Narrative in Social Theory: The Contributions of Jacques Derrida and Walter Benjamin," *Time and Society* 10 (2001): 163–189.

3. Compare Tzvetan Todorov, *The Conquest of America: The Question of the Other*, trans. Richard Howard (New York: Harper & Row, 1984), pp. 133–137.

4. Comissão pelo Desaparecidos Politicos Brasileiros, *Onde Estão? Desaparecidos Politicos Brasileiros* (n.d.), pp. 36–44.

5. Marguerite Feitlowitz, *A Lexicon of Terror: Argentina and the Legacies of Torture* (New York: Oxford University Press, 1998), p. ix. One should add that the crimes of the junta went basically unpunished. Despite some trials and convictions in 1985, all ex-commanders were finally pardoned in 1990 "in time for Christmas" (p. x).

6. Jo Fischer, *Mothers of the Disappeared* (Boston: Sound End Press, 1989), pp. 12, 18, 25–26. As Fischer notes: "The families never got the condemnation they were expecting from the Catholic Church. The ecclesiastical hierarchy had never hidden its identification with the social and political vision of the Argentina military and its close relationship with the state remained untroubled by the events following the coup of 1976. . . . It remained silent even as its own members became victims of the *proceso*. During the later 1960's and early 1970's the traditional conservatism of the Argentine church had been challenged by the growth of progressive sectors within its ranks, such as the group of Third World priests who expressed concern about social justice and the worker priests who lived and worked amongst the poor. At least 30 of these priests and nuns, together with those individuals who dared to speak out against the kidnappings, disappeared in the months following the coup" (p. 23).

7. Marguerite Guzman Bouvard, *Revolutionary Motherhood: The Mothers of the Plaza de Mayo* (Wilmington, DE: Scholarly Resources, 1994), p. 1.

8. Bouvard, *Revolutionary Motherhood*, p. 214.

9. Human Rights Watch/Americas, *Colombia's Killer Networks: The Military-Paramilitary Partnership and the United States* (New York: Human Rights Watch, 1996). In its report, Human Rights Watch documented the "disturbing role" played by the United States in the Colombian military-paramilitary partnership (p. 3). To give a few examples: A U.S. Defense Department and Central Intelligence Agency (CIA) team worked with Colombian military officers on the 1991 intelligence reorganization that "resulted in the creation of killer networks that identified and killed civilians suspected of supporting

guerrillas" (pp. 3–4). More concretely still: "Massacres committed by just one of the units that received U.S. military aid, the Palacé Battalion, took the lives of at least 120 people since 1990, killings that remain largely unpunished."

10. ACAFADE, *Desaparecidos en Centroamérica 1988* (San Jose, Costa Rica: ACAFADE, 1988).

11. Ramsey Clark, "Foreword," in Bill Hutchinson, *When the Dogs Ate Candles: A Time in El Salvador* (Niwot: University Press of Colorado, 1998), p. xiv. See also William Dean Stanley, *The Protection Racket* (Philadelphia: Temple University Press, 1996).

12. Clark, "Foreword," p. xv. As he adds: "By October 1982, U.S. ambassador Dean Hinton estimated that '30,000 Salvadorans had been murdered—not killed in battle, murdered'" (p. xvi).

13. Marilyn Anderson and Jonathan Garlock, *Granddaughters of Corn: Portraits of Guatemalan Women* (Willimantic, CT: Curbstone Press, 1988). The figures of the study were based mainly on facts supplied by Amnesty International, Americas Watch Committee, and the Human Rights Commission of the Organization of American States (OAS). Compare also Greg Grandin, *The Blood of Guatemala: A History of Race and Nation* (Durham, NC: Duke University Press, 2000).

14. Anderson and Garlock, *Granddaughters of Corn*, p. 67. The book is replete with similarly gruesome stories. One further detail: "What does it mean, 'signs of torture?' Cadavers are found without eyes, testicles, or with hands out off. Bodies are found without fingernails, teeth, or nipples. Women's bodies appear with chests burned, brands from hot iron on their skin, and with their scalp pulled off. Amputated parts are placed on top of bodies. Now you know what 'signs of torture' implies" (p. 62). See also Susanne Jonas, *The Battle for Guatemala* (Boulder: Westview, 1991).

15. Compare, e.g., Richard Kearney, *Poetics of Imagining: Modern and Postmodern* (New York: Fordham University Press, 1998); Drucilla Cornell, *The Imaginary Domain* (New York: Routledge, 1995); Cornelius Castoriadis, *The Imaginary Institution of Society,* trans. Kathleen Blamey (Boston: MIT Press, 1987); John Sallis, *Force of Imagination: The Sense of the Elemental* (Bloomington: Indiana University Press, 2000).

16. Paul Ricoeur, "Imagination in Discourse and in Action," in Gillian Robinson and John Rundell, eds., *Rethinking Imagination: Culture and Creativity* (London & New York: Routledge, 1994), pp. 121–122. Compare also Ricoeur, *The Rule of Metaphor: Multi-Disciplinary Studies of the Creation of Meaning in Language,* trans. Robert Czerny (Toronto: University of Toronto Press, 1977). For a closer analysis of Kant's theory of imagination see Rudolf Makkreel, *Imagination and Interpretation in Kant* (Chicago: University of Chicago Press, 1990); also John Rundell, "Creativity and Judgment: Kant on Reason and Imagination," in Robinson and Ruddell, *Rethinking Imagination,* pp. 87–117.

17. Ricoeur, "Imagination in Discourse and in Action," pp. 123–124, 126.
18. "Imagination in Discourse and in Action," pp. 129–131. See also Karl Mannheim, *Ideology and Utopia* (New York: Harcourt Brace and Co., 1936).
19. Ricoeur, "Imagination in Discourse and in Action," pp. 130–132.
20. "Imagination in Discourse and in Action," pp. 132–133. As he adds, ideology and utopia thus manifest two directions of social imagination: "The first tends toward integration, repetition, reflection. The second, because it is excentric, tends toward wandering. But neither exists without the other" (p. 133).
21. See Michael D. Barber, *Ethical Hermeneutics: Rationalism in Enrique Dussel's Philosophy of Liberation* (New York: Fordham University Press, 1998), pp. ix-x. As Barber elaborates: "One who lives out the ethos of liberation locates herself in the 'hermeneutic position' of the oppressed and takes on their interests. . . . Beginning with the poor (*desde el pobre*), the hero of liberation thereby discovers a whole new critical perspective, a new criterion of philosophical and historical interpretation, a new fundamental hermeneutics, typical of the Gramsic-type 'organic intellectual'" (p. 69).
22. Enrique Dussel, *Método para una filosofía de la liberación: Superación analéctica de la dialéctica hegeliana,* 3rd ed. (Guadalajara: Editorial Universidad de Guadalajara, 1991), pp. 185–186; for English translation see Barber, *Ethical Hermeneutics,* p. 27.
23. Dussel, *The Invention of the Americas: Eclipse of the "Other" and the Myth of Modernity,* trans. Michael D. Barber (New York: Continuum, 1995), p. 12. Dussel is fully aware of the fact that the Other "covered over" in 1492 were not only the indigenous Americans but also the Muslims in Spain: "I write this preface in Seville as I edit the lectures. This was the land of the Moors, Muslims until that tragic January 6, 1492, when the Catholic kings occupied Granada, handed over by Boabdil, who was the last sultan to tread upon European soil" (p. 13).
24. Dussel, "Théologie de la 'Périphérie' et du 'Centre': Rencontre ou confrontation?" *Concilium,* vol. 191 (1984), p. 158; cited in Barber, *Ethical Hermeneutics,* p. 61. See also Dussel, *The Invention of the Americas,* p. 12; and Augusto Salazor Bondy, *Existe una filosofía de nuestra América?* (Iztapalapa, Mexico: Siglo Veintiuno Editores, 1975).
25. For critical comments on Dussel's work, inspired by such concerns, see, e.g., Ofelia Schutte, *Cultural Identity and Social Liberation in Latin American Thought* (Albany: State University of New York Press, 1993), esp. pp. 186–190; also her "Origins and Tendencies of the Philosophy of Liberation in Latin American Thought: A Critique of Dussel's Ethics," *The Philosophical Forum* 22 (1991): 270–295. Some of these concerns are triggered by an occasional hypostatization of Levinasian "otherness." In Barber's balanced assessment: "Other-oppressive aspects of Dussel's erotics, rightly criticized by Ofelia Schutte, may be traced to residual influences of his earlier natural-law position . . . or even to his

uncritical assimilation of *Totality and Infinity's* patriarchal erotics, which Levinas abandoned by the time he wrote *Otherwise than Being*. . . . Contrary to those critics who claim that he is a naïve populist, Dussel recognizes that 'the people' are not free from inauthenticity, voices misgivings about popular religiosity, observes that the oppressed have often introjected the oppression they have received, and refrains from any uncritical endorsement of populist spontaneity." See *Ethical Hermeneutics,* pp. 67, 73.

26. See Dussel, *The Invention of the Americas,* p. 132; also Barber, *Ethical Hermeneutics,* pp. 64–65.

27. For a fuller account of her life-story see Elizabeth Burgos-Debray, ed., *I, Rigoberta Menchú: An Indian Woman in Guatemala,* trans. Ann Wright (London: Verso, 1984). She has returned to Guatemala several times, but always had to leave due to continuing death threats. For some of the controversy surrounding her life-story, see David Stoll, *Rigoberta Menchú and the Story of All Poor Guatemalans* (Boulder, CO: Westview Press, 1999), and Elzbieta Sklodowska, "Author-(dys)function: Rereading *I, Rigoberta Menchú,*" in Benigno Trigo, ed., *Foucault and Latin America: Appropriations and Deployments of Discursive Analysis* (London: Routledge, 2002), pp. 197–207.

28. Rigoberta Menchú, *Crossing Borders,* trans. Ann Wright (London: Verso, 1998), p. 221. As she adds: "I believe in the [indigenous] community as an alternative way forward, and not simply as a memory of the past. . . . It is something dynamic . . . not just nostalgia for eating *tamales.* . . . Identity passes through the community, it passes along pavements, it passes down veins, and it exists in thoughts. . . . Each day it provides the chance to be reborn, to flower again, to be rejuvenated. Identity is not studied in a dark room. It is like the *nawaal,* the shadow that accompanies you. It is the other, the one beside you" (pp. 223–226).

Chapter 7

1. The reference here is to Stendhal, *The Red and the Black* (New York: Modern Library, 1953).

2. For some of this literature compare, e.g., Paul Helm, ed., *Faith and Reason* (Oxford: Oxford University Press, 1999); Robert Sokolowski, *The God of Faith and Reason* (Notre Dame, IN: University of Notre Dame Press, 1982); Alvin Plantinga and Nicholas Wolterstorff, eds., *Faith and Rationality: Reason and Belief in God* (Notre Dame, IN: University of Notre Dame Press, 1983); and Richard Swinburne, *Faith and Reason* (Oxford: Clarendon Press, 1981). In modern Western philosophy, the most famous text is Hegel's "Glauben und Wissen" (1802); for an English rendition see Walter Cerf and H. S. Harris, eds. and trans., *Faith and Knowledge* (Albany: State University of New York Press, 1977).

3. See Oliver Leaman, *Averroes and His Philosophy* (Oxford: Clarendon Press, 1988), p. 5. Compare also Roger Arnaldez, *Averroes: A Rationalist in Islam,* trans. David Streight (Notre Dame, IN: University of Notre Dame Press, 2000).

4. Nasir-e Khosraw, *Kitab jami' al-hikmatayn;* as translated by A. J. Arberry in *Revelation and Reason in Islam* (London: Allen Unwin, 1957), pp. 72–73 (translation slightly altered). Nasir himself aspired toward a genuine "unification" of reason and religion under the auspices of Neoplatonic mysticism—a solution that Ibn Rushd found unattractive (as will be shown).

5. A large number of commentaries of different lengths—labeled "short," "middle," and "great"—testify to Ibn Rushd's relentless endeavor to recapture the genuine meaning of Greek (especially Aristotelian) texts uncontaminated by later mystical or esoteric constructions.

6. See Simon van den Bergh, ed. and trans., *Averroes' Tahafut al-tahafut (The Incoherence of the Incoherence),* 2 vols. (Oxford: Oxford University Press, 1954).

7. George F. Hourani, ed. and trans., *Averroes on the Harmony of Religion and Philosophy* (London: Luzac & Co., 1961), pp. 1, 49, 51, 82 note 1. As one may note, Ibn Rushd in these statements does not postulate a diversity of "truths," but a differential understanding of and "assent to" truth.

8. Hourani, *Averroes on the Harmony of Philosophy and Religion,* pp. 45–46, 64–65. Compare also Majid Fakhry, *A History of Islamic Philosophy* (2nd ed.; New York: Columbia University Press, 1983), pp. 279–280. Given his Aristotelian leanings, it is surprising that (in this context) Ibn Rushd does not mention the differentiation between "theoretical" and "practical" reasoning in philosophy. As one might add, the relation between philosophy (*burhan*) and mysticism might perhaps also be seen as differential and non-antithetical—provided the latter keeps within its proper bounds. Such an approach could explain Ibn Rushd's occasionally favorable comments on Ghazali and on Sufism in general.

9. Hourani, *Averroes,* pp. 44–47. Hourani translates *at-tadhkiya* as "sacrifice"; but perhaps "operation" captures better the sense of the passage—especially in view of the fact that Ibn Rushd was also an accomplished medical doctor.

10. For arguments propounding the need of "esoteric" reading compare, e.g., Leo Strauss, *Persecution and the Art of Writing* (Glencoe, IL: Free Press, 1952); Ralph Lerner, "Introduction" to *Averroes' Commentary on Plato's Republic* (Ithaca, NY: Cornell University Press, 1974), pp. xiii-xxviii. Leaman strongly rebuts the allegation of deliberate dissimulation (*taqiya*) in Ibn Rushd's work and hence the need for esotericism; see *Averroes and His Philosophy,* pp. 10, 124.

11. Hourani, *Averroes,* pp. 48, 53.

12. Hourani, *Averroes,* pp. 51–53.

13. This is clearly a difficult part of Ibn Rushd's argument. Sometimes, his emphasis on the restrictive role of philosophers is interpreted in an elitist sense that, in a Platonic or Neoplatonic manner, would assign to philosophers a privileged status or caste. Thus, according to Hourani, Ibn Rushd might be criticized "by modern opinion for holding an undemocratic view of higher [philosophical] education and wishing to limit it to a privileged elite." He softens the charge only slightly by pleading "educational necessity" and invoking a "very strong aristocratic tradition in philosophy." See *Averroes*, p. 36. However, the evidence may also be read differently. First of all, by restricting the influence of philosophers Ibn Rushd clearly did not mean to place them in the position of a ruling or privileged elite. Moreover, the restriction seems to have been prompted chiefly by the danger of manipulation, that is, by the ready susceptibility of the uneducated multitude to ideological control and abuse. This seems to have been the situation in his time. In a society where education is more widespread and evenly distributed, the danger would surely be reduced and the relation between philosophers and multitude might be more balanced, approximating the relation between teacher and student— where with the advancing competence of students the teacher becomes increasingly superfluous (as teacher). In his characteristic manner, Ibn Rushd illustrates the danger of spurious or pretended philosophizing through a medical example: Just as a patient who received a wrong nostrum from a charlatan doctor might turn against medicine as a whole, so people instructed by charlatan philosophers are likely to lose confidence in reason and truth as such. This comparison is followed by a remarkable passage that expresses the gist of the Aristotelian and Islamic horizon of truth: "The relation of the doctor to the health of bodies is the same as the relation of the Legislator [Prophet] to the health of souls: the doctor is he who seeks to preserve the health of bodies when it exists and to restore it when it is lost, while the Legislator [Prophet] is he who desires this end for the health of souls. This health is what is called 'fear of God.'" See Hourani, *Averroes*, p. 67.

14. Hourani, *Averroes*, p. 54. Since, in rebutting Ghazali, Ibn Rushd does offer numerous philosophical arguments, Hourani probably overstates his case when he writes that *Fasl* itself "is not a philosophical work; it is a legal treatise *about* philosophy," with Ibn Rushd acting "in his capacity as a legal theorist and practicing judge" (p. 19).

15. Hourani, *Averroes*, pp. 54–55.

16. Hourani, *Averroes*, pp. 55–57. As Hourani intriguingly notes, Ibn Rushd's reduction of disputes in this field to a "disagreement about naming" places him in the company of contemporary language philosophy: analyzing the positions of opposing parties he uses "an 'ordinary language' method, of the type brought into prominence in our day by Wittgenstein, Ryle and their contemporaries in England" (p. 31). For

arguments to a similar effect see Leaman, *Averroes and His Philosophy,* pp. 180–181, 196.

17. Hourani, *Averroes,* pp. 58–61, 76–77. The sequel is a book usually cited by the abbreviated title *Manahij;* excerpts of this book are included in Hourani's *Averroes.* Ibn Rushd's outlook is sometimes identified with the second position (survival of spirit only). Since, in the absence of some material substrate, spirits or souls cannot be differentiated, this position is sometimes labeled "panpsychism" or "unity of intellect." However, this thesis seems to be more germane to Neoplatonists than to Aristotelians—and certainly more germane to the Sufi notion of a "unified world soul" (*wahdat al-wujud*) as advocated by Ibn 'Arabi and others.

18. Hourani, *Averroes,* pp. 68, 70.

19. To be sure, Ibn Rushd's tolerance of opinions was hedged in by such binding consensus—which may seem a severe limitation. However, one should recall that early (British) liberalism likewise stipulated such limits (Locke bluntly excluded the opinion of Catholics and atheists). Subsequently, liberalism steadily broadened the range of tolerance; but even today, liberal regimes are hedged in by a binding constitutional framework (open to reinterpretation). Possibly Ibn Rushd's argument could also be developed in this direction.

20. Leaman, *Averroes and His Philosophy,* p. 14. Following in the footsteps of early theologians, many contemporary Islamic thinkers continue to insist on the untrammeled "sovereignty" of God (as opposed to popular sovereignty)—not suspecting the dubious status of that concept. If (as recent political thinkers like Hannah Arendt have shown) sovereignty is a defective notion in politics, its transfer to religion has no redeeming quality.

21. The actual statement is "to the Red man and the Black man," where "red" refers to the people in Europe and Western Asia (who are now called "white"). In his Introduction to Ibn Rushd's commentary on Plato, Ralph Lerner notes that Plato's position involves "the rejection of the universal society" envisaged in the Prophet's remark, adding: "Averroes can hardly conceal that such universalism does not accord with Plato's opinion; but he is careful to avoid letting this disagreement become an open conflict between philosophy and the *shari'ah.*" However, it is not clear, and Lerner provides no evidence to show, that Ibn Rushd in this matter sided with Plato against Islamic belief; hence his "esoteric" reading seems unwarranted. See *Averroes on Plato's Republic,* trans. with intro. Ralph Lerner (Ithaca, NY: Cornell University Press, 1974), p. xxii.

22. *Averroes on Plato's Republic,* pp. 1–6. The point of the above comments is not to erect a rigid breach between Plato and Aristotle, but only to indicate that philosophers cannot simply exit or extricate themselves from a practical-political community—as has been suggested by some Platonists and Neoplatonists.

23. *Averroes on Plato's Republic*, pp. 13, 45–46.
24. *Averroes on Plato's Republic*, pp. 71–72, 81–82.
25. *Averroes on Plato's Republic*, pp. 57–59.
26. *Averroes on Plato's Republic*, pp. 68–69. See also Ibn Rushd, *Middle Commentary on Aristotle's Nicomachean Ethics* (Cambridge, UK: Cambridge University Library), 1137b24, as cited by Lerner, p. 69 note.
27. *Averroes on Plato's Republic*, pp. 108–111, 114.
28. *Averroes on Plato's Republic*, pp. 111–112, 121–122. In a subsequent context (p. 133), Ibn Rushd explicitly refers to the oscillation between democracy and tyranny in Cordoba during his life-time. The bluntness of his political criticisms surely militates against the claim of an alleged "esotericism."
29. Leaman, *Averroes and His Philosophy*, p. 14. To some extent the decline of Ibn Rushd's influence seems to have been due not only to the resurgence of clerical orthodoxy but also to the upsurge of Eastern-style mysticism and Sufism—represented in the West by the "Great Sheikh" Ibn 'Arabi (1165–1240). According to his own report, Ibn 'Arabi as a young man visited Ibn Rushd in Cordoba, attracted by the latter's reputation. Unfortunately, the report is not very flattering to the young mystic as it discloses a certain arrogance (or know-it-all attitude) unbecoming a young man in this encounter with the aging philosopher. For English translations of this report see, e.g., *Sufis of Andalusia*, trans. with Introd. R. W. J. Austin (Berkeley: University of California Press, 1971), pp. 23–24; H. Corbin, *Creative Imagination in the Sufism of Ibn 'Arabi* (Princeton, NJ: Princeton University Press, 1969), pp. 41–42.
30. See Fakhry, *A History of Islamic Philosophy*, pp. 274–275; Leaman, *Averroes and His Philosophy*, pp. 163–164, 175–176; also *Averroes' Destructio Destructionum*, ed. with Introd. Beatrice H. Zedler (Milwaukee, WI: Marquette University Press, 1961), pp. 23–24.
31. Leaman, *Averroes and His Philosophy*, p. 167. As he adds, with specific reference to Siger and Jandun: "Neither Averroist argued that philosophy and religion produce contradictory conclusions which can nonetheless be true together. What they seem to support is a doctrine of the distinctness of religious and philosophical language, so that religion cannot influence the progress of reason while reason cannot contradict the results acquired by faith in revealed supernatural wisdom" (p. 169).
32. Ernest Renan in his *Averroes et l'Averroisme* (3rd. ed. Paris, 1860), p. 439, mentions the incident, though without drawing inferences. See Leaman, *Averroes and His Philosophy*, p. 177; Hourani, *Averroes*, pp. 38–39. Charles E. Butterworth seems quite correct when he writes: "So intent was he upon discerning the roots of the break with ancient political philosophy that Leo Strauss paid little attention to the way the *falasifa*, and Averroes in particular, seek to defend their teachings from the charge of 'worldly wisdom' . . . not to mention the more damning one of materialism imputed by Renan." He also seems to be on target

when he adds: "What is ever present among the writings of the *falasifa* within the Islamic tradition is constant attentiveness to the political context." See Butterworth, "What is Political Averroism?" in Friedrich Niewöhner and Loris Sturlese, eds., *Averroismus im Mittelalter und der Renaissance* (Zürich: Spur Verlag, 1994), pp. 246–247. Compare also his "New Light on the Political Philosophy of Averroes," in George F. Hourani, ed., *Essays on Islamic Philosophy and Science* (Albany: State University of New York Press, 1975), pp. 118–127.

33. To obtain a flavor of these disputes compare, e.g., Mourad Wahba and Mona Abousenna, eds., *Averroes and the Enligtenment* (Amherst, NY: Prometheus Books, 1996). As A. El Ghannouchi writes there: Ghazali "advocated a strict religious integrality. The dawn of secular thought, revindicating the distinction between religion and philosophy, represented by Ibn Tufayl and Averroes, was the answer to that. But Ibn Taymiyya, the most reactionary theologian, condemned Averroes and all who followed his example as practicing the pagan sciences of the Ancients. Since then the Islamic world has been drowned in obscurantism" (p. 229).

34. Oliver Leaman, "Averroes and the West," in Wahba and Abousenna, *Averroes and the Enlightenment*, pp. 60, 66. Arguing against an Averroist "double truth" theory, he adds that Ibn Rushd "would argue that we do have two routes to the truth, and both are routes to the truth, neither being a misguided or erratic path to error" (p. 64).

35. See Martin Heidegger, *Phänomenologische Interpretationen zu Aristoteles: Einführung in die phänomenologische Forschung*, eds. Walter Bröcker and Käte Bröcker-Oltmans (*Gesamtausgabe*, vol. 61; Frankfurt-Main: Klostermann, 1985) where Heidegger argues that philosophical questioning should not pretend to have knowledge of God and thus stay clear of theology—without being anti-religious: "The trick is to philosophize and be religious in doing so" (p. 197). Compare also Jacques Derrida, "Faith and Knowledge: The Two Sources of 'Religion' at the Limits of Reason Alone," in Derrida and Gianni Vattimo, eds., *Religion: Cultural Memory in the Present* (Stanford, CA: Stanford University Press, 1998), pp. 1–78.

36. Anke von Kügelen, *Averroes und die arabische Moderne: Ansätze zu einer Neubegründung des Rationalismus im Islam* (Leiden: Brill, 199), pp. 17, 161–167.

37. von Kügelen, *Averroes und die arabische Moderne*, pp. 180–237. For the sake of brevity, the above presentation sidelines some of the differences between the two Egyptian thinkers.

38. von Kügelen, *Averroes und die arabische Moderne*, pp. 260–288. Compare in this context also Muhammed Abed al-Jabri, *Arab-Islamic Philosophy: A Contemporary Critique*, trans. Aziz Abassi (Austin: University of Texas, 1999).

39. Hourani, *Averroes*, p. 70; von Kügelen, *Averroes und die arabische Moderne*, p. 224.

Chapter 8

1. *Al-Qur'an;* a Contemporary Translation by Ahmed Ali (Princeton, NJ: Princeton University Press, 1988), p. 25, Sura 2, Verse 115. The opening verses are taken from *Goethes West-Östlicher Divan,* ed. Hans-J. Weitz (Frankfurt-Main: Insel, 1974), p. 12. As there exists no available English translation of the *Divan,* all translations here are my own. As much as possible, I have tried to maintain the simplicity of Goethe's verses.

2. *Goethes West-Östlicher Divan,* p. 127.

3. Johann Gottfried Herder, *Ideen zur Philosophy einer Geschichte der Menschheit,* in *Herders Sämtliche Werke,* ed. Bernhard Suphan, vol. 19 (Berlin: Weidmannsche Buchhandlung, 1880), pp. 425–438. As one should add, Herder was not the only one in the German context to advance a more sympathetic appraisal of Islam (countering its longstanding vilification). His efforts were preceded and complemented by some writings of Leibniz and Gotthold Ephraim Lessing.

4. *Al-Qur'an,* p. 267, Sura 20, Verses 25–27. See also Katharina Mommsen, *Goethe und der Islam* (Stuttgart: Goethe Gesellschaft, 1964), pp. 7–8; *Goethe und die arabische Welt* (Frankfurt-Main: Insel, 1988), pp. 167, 171–172. According to Mommsen (p. 171), the main Islamic teachings attractive to Goethe were these: the idea of the unity of God; the conviction of God's manifestness in nature; the notion that God has spoken to humankind through different messengers; the rejection of miracles; and the need of religiosity to be tested through good deeds.

5. Mommsen, *Goethe und der Islam,* pp. 10–14; *Goethe und die arabische Welt,* pp. 195–200.

6. Mommsen, *Goethe und der Islam,* pp. 6, 13; *Goethe und die arabische Welt,* pp. 220–223. As Mommsen relates (pp. 232–233), Goethe's translation and stage production of Voltaire's drama were a source of consternation for Herder and his wife (and one reason for the growing estrangement between Herder and Goethe).

7. Mommsen, *Goethe und der Islam,* pp. 19–20; *Goethe und die arabische Welt,* pp. 255–262. The cited letter was written to F. W. von Trebra on January 5, 1814; see *Goethe Werke: Briefe* (Weimar: Cotta, 1901), vol. 24, p. 91.

8. Mommsen, *Goethe und der Islam,* pp. 5, 16–17 (citing from several letters of the 1820s and early 1830s); the text also lists several passages that quote from Qur'anic verses (pp. 21–23). See also *Goethe und die arabsiche Welt,* pp. 249–253. For the quoted verses see *Goethes West-Östlicher Divan,* p. 59.

9. Karl Otto Conrady, *Goethe: Leben und Werk,* vol. 2 (Königstein: Athenäum Verlag, 1985), p. 401.

10. *Goethes West-Östlicher Divan,* pp. 160–162. In a letter to Zelter of 1820 Goethe stated: "This Muslim religion, mythology, way of life give

room to a poetry befitting my age." See Conrady, *Goethe: Leben und Werk*, p. 391.

11. *Goethes West-Östlicher Divan*, pp. 22–25. To indicate the non-identity of the two twins, however, Goethe adds: "Now sound, my song, with your own fire! For you are older, you are newer."

12. *Goethes West-Östlicher Divan*, pp. 15, 26, 162. As one might add, pretentious or "gnostic" types of mysticism (and Sufism) can also be politically obnoxious: either by negating politics altogether or else by claiming political supremacy based on "esoteric" knowledge.

13. *Goethes West-Östlicher Divan*, pp. 45, 112. The other "elect women" are Mary, Khadija (first wife of Muhammed), and Fatima (his daughter). See also Mommsen, *Goethe und die arabische Welt*, pp. 383–385.

14. The two *ghazals* are taken, with slight variations, from *The Gift: Poems by Hafiz, the Great Sufi Master*, trans. Daniel Ladinsky (New York: Penguin/Arkana, 1999), pp. 64, 175.

15. See *The Poems of Hafez*, trans. Reza Saberi (Lanham, MD: University Press of America, 1995), p. 3. (Saberi spells Suleika as "Zoleikha.")

16. *Goethes West-Östlicher Divan*, pp. 18, 67, 167–168, 199. For a close reading of the cited poems see Edgar Lohner, "Hatem und Suleika: Kunst und Kommunikation," in Lohner, ed., *Interpretationen zum West-Östlichen Divan Goethes* (Darmstadt: Wissenschaftliche Buchgesellschaft, 1973), pp. 277–304, esp. pp. 285–289.

17. *Goethes West-Östlicher Divan*, pp. 39, 184–185. Compare also George Sebba, "Goethe on Human Creativeness," in Rolf King, ed., *Goethe on Human Creativeness and Other Goethe Essays* (Athens: University of Georgia Press, 1950), pp. 105–178.

18. *Goethes West-Östlicher Divan*, pp. 185–186, 260–263. Edith Ihekweazu speaks in this context of the "synthesis of reception and production" in Goethe's *Divan;* see her *Goethes West-Östlicher Divan: Untersuchungen zur Struktur des lyrischen Zyklus* (Hamburg: Buske, 1971), pp. 94–98. To be sure, the term "synthesis" may conceal the complexity of the self/other relation—a relation that in some ways is also marked by rift and radical transformation. The accent on such radical transformation (beyond a smooth metamorphosis) is particularly highlighted in "Blessed Longing" ("Selige Sehnsucht"), one of the most frequently discussed poems in the *Divan*, which begins with these famous lines: "Tell to no one but the wise / to avoid the people's ire, / living being I will praise / which desires death by fire" and which concludes: "And so long you do not follow / this command of death and birth, / you remain a sorry fellow / on this darkened earth." For conflicting interpretations of this poem see Florens Christian, "Goethes 'Selige Sehnsucht'," Wilhelm Schneider, "Goethe: 'Selige Sehnsucht'," and Ewald Rösch, "Goethes 'Selige Schnsucht'—eine tragische Bewegung," in Lohner, *Interpretationen zum West-Östlichen Divan Goethes*, pp. 1–38, 72–83, 228–249.

19. Romano Guardini, *Das Ende der Neuzeit: Ein Versuch zur Orientierung* (Würzburg: Werkbund, 1950), pp. 60–61. See also José Ortega y Gasset, *Triptico: Mirabeau, o El politico; Kant; Goethe desde dentro* (Madrid: Espasa-Calpe, 1964).

20. *Goethes Werke*, ed. E. Trutz (Hamburg: Wegener, 1956), vol. 1, p. 212; cited by Conrady, *Goethe: Leben und Werk*, vol. 2, p. 118. For the poem by Arndt see Monika Lemmel, *Poetologie in Goethes West-Östlichem Divan* (Heidelberg: Carl Winter-Universitätsverlag, 1987), p. 25—a book that cites many other examples of such "patriotic" literature. As Lemmel writes persuasively: "That Goethe's commitment is to peace, and not to war, is as self-evident in the *Divan* as planing is for the carpenter or casting nets for the fisher. Moreover, it befits the nature of the poet and the nature of poetry. . . . The entire *Divan* is opposed to war, hatred, separation, [heroes'] death, and deals rather of unlimited life and love. . . . To the sacrificial exuberance [of patriotic poetry] stands in contrast the cheerfulness, lightness, and life-affirmation of the *Divan*" (pp. 19, 29–30). This judgment must be qualified somewhat, of course, in light of the poem "Selige Sehnsucht."

21. *Goethes West-Östlicher Divan*, pp. 50–51, 53, 124.

22. See Manfred Eickhölter, *Die Lehre vom Dichter in Goethes Divan* (Hamburg: Buske Verlag, 1984), p. 154. Eickhölter quotes Sir Percey Sykes, *A History of Persia*, vol. 2 (London: Macmillan, 1921), p. 125. According to Sykes, Timur confronted Hafiz complaining: "I have subdued with the sword the greater part of the earth, I have depopulated a vast number of cities and provinces in order to increase the glory and wealth of Samarkand and Bokhara, the ordinary places of my residence and the seat of my empire; yet you, an insignificant individual, has pretended to give away both Samarkand and Bokhara as the price of a little black mole setting off the features of a pretty face." For Hafiz's poem see *The Poems of Hafez*, p. 2.

23. *Goethes West-Östlicher Divan*, pp. 75, 263.

24. See Conrady, *Goethe: Leben und Werk*, vol. 2, p. 498. As Conrady comments: by the notion of "world literature" Goethe did not mean "the simple reading and appropriation of foreign texts nor the construction of a global literary canon of 'great books'. Rather, what he had in mind was a global arena of communication and conversation where writers and literatures would remain in a constant exchange of giving and receiving. Limitation to one's native texts should be overcome without leveling or destroying their distinctness" (in a global uniformity).

25. *Goethes West-Östlicher Divan*, p. 40. See also Mommsen, *Goethe und die arabische Welt*, pp. 255–256. Another poem in the *Divan*, in the "Book of Proverbs," reads: "If God were as bad a neighbor as I am and as you are, we both would have little profit; but God leaves everyone free" (p. 57). Goethe's recognition and appreciation of other cultures and religions does not mean a readiness to suspend all critical judgment. As one poem reminds us: "Tradition, you fool, may well be a

chimera. Now good judgment is needed" (p. 53). His "Annotations," in fact, contain many critical observations regarding dubious aspects of Islamic civilization, particularly its affinity to political despotism and unfreedom (pp. 172–173, 242–244). In her carefully detailed study, Mommen discusses three further critical reservations, as articulated in the *Divan:* the generally unequal treatment of women in Islam; the rigid abolition of wine consumption; and the unfavorable treatment of poetry by the Prophet (a point having ultimately to do with the different roles of Prophet and poet). See *Goethe und die arabische Welt,* pp. 362–475.

26. *Goethes West-Östlicher Divan,* pp. 63–64, 280. In the interpretation of the "Book of Timur" I follow the lead of Manfred Eickhölter, *Die Lehre vom Dichter in Goethes Divan,* pp. 182–188. Some readers have found in the poem "Winter and Timur" an allusion to Napoleon's ill-fated Russian expedition; contemporary readers may also (and perhaps more plausibly) be reminded of Hitler's campaign in Russia. Regarding the praise of poetry, Hafiz was even more pointed: "The great religions are ships, / poets the life boats. / Every sane person I know / has jumped overboard. / That is good for business. / Isn't it, Hafiz?" See *The Gift: Poem by Hafiz,* p. 177.

Chapter 9

1. Paul Ricoeur, *Political and Social Essays,* ed. David Stewart and Joseph Bien (Athens: Ohio University Press, 1974), pp. 105, 123; Emmanuel Levinas, *In the Time of the Nations,* trans. Michael B. Smith (Bloomington: Indiana University Press, 1994). Note especially his statement: "Israel, in its soul and conscience . . . is, from its own point of view, already in alliance with the whole universe of nations" (p. 3).

2. *Reason, Freedom, and Democracy in Islam: Essential Writings of Abdolkarim Soroush,* trans. and ed. Mahmud Sadri and Ahmad Sadri (New York: Oxford University Press, 2000). For biographical background on Soroush see editors' "Introduction" and "Intellectual Autobiography," pp. ix-xix and 3–25; also Robin Wright, "Iran's Greatest Political Challenge: Abdulkarim Soroush," *World Policy Journal* 14 (Summer 1997): 67–74. For a broad overview of his views compare Valla Vakili, *Debating Religion and Politics in Iran: The Political Thought of Abdulkarim Soroush* (New York: Council on Foreign Relations, 1996). See also Forough Jahanbaksh, *Islam, Democracy, and Religious Modernism in Iran, 1953–2000: From Bazargan to Soroush* (Boston: Brill, 2001), and John L. Esposito, *Makers of Contemporary Islam* (Oxford: Oxford University Press, 2001).

3. Ira M. Lapidus, "The Golden Age: The Political Concepts of Islam," *The Annals of the American Academy of Political and Social Science* 524 (November 1992): 14–16. *Umma* means the community of all Muslims. I believe Lapidus is wrong when he finds in the second model a

"separation of state and religion" and the emergence of a "non-religious concept of political authority" (pp. 16–17). On the important role of jurists or legal scholars (*fuqaha*) in traditional Islam compare also Tamara Sonn, "Elements of Government in Classical Islam," *Muslim Democrat* 2 (November 2000): 4–6 (published by the Center for the Study of Islam and Democracy, Washington, DC).

4. Youssef Choueiri, "The Political Discourse of Contemporary Islamist Movements," in Abdel Salam Sidahmed and Anoushiravan Ehteshami, eds., *Islamic Fundamentalism* (Boulder, CO: Westview Press, 1996), pp. 22–23, 28–30. Regarding Qutb, see also the discussion in Roxanne L. Euben, *Enemy in the Mirror: Islamic Fundamentalism and the Limits of Modern Rationalism* (Princeton, NJ: Princeton University Press, 1999), pp. 49–92. Regarding Khomeini, see Majid Tehranian, "Khomeini's Doctrine of Legitimacy," in Anthony J. Parel and Arnold C. Keith, eds., *Comparative Political Philosophy: Studies under the Upas Tree* (New Delhi: SAGE India, 1992), pp. 217–243. Tehranian (p. 235) quotes Khomeini as saying: "Islamic government may therefore be defined as the rule of divine law over men."

5. As Oliver Leaman writes, Averroes (Ibn Rushd) criticized fideist theologians for "only being prepared to accept a concept of God which is remarkably similar to that of a very powerful human being, God with a status rather similar to that of Superman." See Leaman, *Averroes and His Philosophy* (Oxford: Clarendon Press, 1988), p. 14. The mentioning above of Genghis Khan and Tamerlane may be slightly anachronistic (but not by much).

6. For the critique of "sovereignty" see Hannah Arendt, "What is Freedom?" in *Between Past and Future* (New York: Penguin Books, 1980), pp. 164–165; also Jean Bethke Elshtain, *New Wine and Old Bottles: International Politics and Ethical Discourse* (Notre Dame, IN: University of Notre Dame Press, 1998), especially pp. 6–25. The notion of the disappearance of the "markers of certainty" is taken from Claude Lefort, *Democracy and Political Theory*, trans. David Macey (Minneapolis: University of Minnesota Press, 1988), pp. 17–20. For formulations of radical democracy compare Ernesto Laclau, *New Reflections on the Revolution of Our Time* (London: Verso, 1990); Chantal Mouffe, *The Democratic Paradox* (London: Verso, 2000); also my "Democracy and Postmodernism," *Human Studies* 10 (1987): 143–170, and "Postmetaphysics and Democracy," *Political Theory* 21 (1993): 101–127.

7. See Mohammed 'Abed al-Jabri, *Arab-Islamic Philosophy: A Contemporary Critique*, trans. Aziz Abbassi (Austin, TX: Center for Middle Eastern Studies, 1999); Mohammed Arkoun, *The Unthought in Contemporary Islamic Thought* (New York: Palgrave/St. Martin's, 2001) and, *Rethinking Islam: Common Questions, Uncommon Answers*, trans. Robert D. Lee (Boulder, CO: Westview Press, 1994).

8. Lahouari Addi, "Islamicist Utopia and Democracy," *The Annals of the American Academy of Political and Social Science* 524 (November

1992): 122, 124, 126. For arguments along similar lines compare, e.g., Timothy D. Sisk, *Islam and Democracy: Religion, Politics, and Power in the Middle East* (Washington, DC: United States Institute of Peace Press, 1992) and Richard W. Bulliet, ed., *Under Siege: Islam and Democracy* (New York: Columbia University, 1994).

9. Soroush, *Reason, Freedom, and Democracy in Islam,* pp. 63–64, 101. Soroush extends this critique to Khomeini's notions of the "guardianship of the jurisconsult" (*velayat-e-faqih*) and "Islamic government" (*hokoumat-e Islami*).

10. *Reason, Freedom, and Democracy in Islam,* pp. 92, 97, 99, 103. The cited verses are from *Qur'an* 2:256 and 11:28.

11. *Reason, Freedom, and Democracy in Islam,* pp. 90–91, 93. It should be clear that by "reason" Soroush here does not mean simply an instrumental or strategic rationality aiming at the maximization of egocentric benefits. Moreover, reason in his account is always counter-balanced by erotic emotion or love (as celebrated by Sufi poetry)—provided the latter does not seek to demolish reason or reasonableness. As he writes pointedly: "The death or degradation of rational discourse might give rise to ultra-rational states of mind or mystic love-sickness among the rarified elites. It is, however, much more likely that in such a situation utter idiocy and competition over devotees will prevail, precluding the use of the small allotment of practical reason that is available to the people" (p. 93).

12. *Reason, Freedom, and Democracy in Islam,* pp. 54–55, 57, 60.

13. *Reason, Freedom, and Democracy in Islam,* pp. 44–45. As Soroush adds, in poetic terms: "As soon as the veil of these primary needs is removed, the sun of divine beauty will reflect in the mirror of the higher and more refined spiritual yearnings. . . . God will finally shed the garbs of the savior and the benefactor to assume that of the beloved" (or friend) (p. 44).

14. *Reason, Freedom, and Democracy in Islam,* pp. 45–46. At this point, Soroush strikes a blow against certain liberal or libertarian construals of democracy: "It is not true (as some have argued) that the bourgeois mentality and the ethos of haggling alone have primed people's minds for democratic dialogue; a more significant factor in this process is the rational thought and rational management that is the very lifeblood of a democratic social system" (p. 46).

15. *Reason, Freedom, and Democracy in Islam,* p. 148. The notion of "postmodernity" has in the meantime acquired so many connotations as to be virtually unusable. A sensible approach might be to define postmodernity as the rethinking of traditional metaphysics, and especially as the critique of traditional binaries. Soroush's attitude toward the term is ambivalent. On the one hand, he appreciates a certain innovativeness (even vis-à-vis canonical views of enlightenment); on the other hand, he criticizes a potential sliding into relativism and irresponsibility. See pp. 45, 49–50.

16. *Reason, Freedom, and Democracy in Islam*, p. 151. Soroush repeatedly compares democracy in this respect with modern science, which, although constituting an open-ended inquiry, presupposes a commitment to inquiry as such.

17. *Reason, Freedom, and Democracy in Islam*, pp. 45, 103–104, 136–138. Pressing his case against Western liberalism, Soroush adds: "Thus, in the Western world we see injustice, colonialism, and arrogance toward other countries alongside the pursuit of liberty. There is external freedom, but no one is interested in internal freedom" (p. 104). For a well-known attempt to "decouple" liberalism from democracy see C. B. Macpherson, *The Life and Times of Liberal Democracy* (Oxford: Oxford University Press, 1977).

18. Soroush, *Reason, Freedom, and Democracy in Islam*, pp. 125, 152–153. It is in this field of dogmatism and anti-dogmatism that Soroush has formulated some of his theologically most controversial tenets: especially the distinction between religion seen as unchanging, transcendent verity, and religion as inserted into human and social life where it necessarily is exposed to interpretation and hence to the continuous "contraction and expansion of religious knowledge." See in this regard the chapter on "Islamic Revival and Reform: Theological Approaches" in the text, pp. 26–38; also his essay "The Evolution and Devolution of Religious Knowledge," in Charles Kurzman, ed., *Liberal Islam: A Source Book* (New York: Oxford University Press, 1998), pp. 244–251; and his (so far untranslated) books *Contraction and Expansion of Religious Knowledge* and *Our Expectations from Religion;* also John Cooper, "The Limits of the Sacred: The Epistemology of Abdolkarim Soroush," in John Cooper, Ronald L. Nettler, and Mohamed Mahmoud, eds., *Islam and Modernity: Muslim Intellectuals Respond* (New York: Tauris Publ., 2000), pp. 38–56. In *Reason, Freedom, and Democracy in Islam*, Soroush acknowledges the affinity of some of his ideas with the hermeneutics of Hans-Georg Gadamer (p. 7).

19. *Reason, Freedom, and Democracy in Islam*, pp. 127–128, 140. Soroush has written a two-volume treatise on *Tolerance and Governance* that so far has been held back by censors. Compare also Michael Walzer, *On Toleration* (New Haven, CT: Yale University Press, 1997); also Charles Taylor's comment: "It is impossible in our days to be a Christian, atheist, or anything else, without a degree of doubt. Our situation is characterized by this instability, much more than by the idea that secularism has swept away religion." See his "From Philosophical Anthropology to the Politics of Recognition," *Thesis Eleven* 52 (February 1998): 111. As one should note, Soroush's notion of "religious democracy" exceeds the categories provided by John Rawls in *The Law of Peoples:* it fits neither into the category of "liberal peoples" nor into that of "decent hierarchical peoples"; see *The Law of Peoples* (Cambridge, MA: Harvard University Press, 1999), pp. 59–67.

20. Soroush, *Reason, Freedom, and Democracy in Islam*, pp. 143–145.

21. See Robin Wright in *Los Angeles Times* (January 27, 1995); also editors' "Introduction" in *Reason, Freedom, and Democracy in Islam*, p. xv.

22. For some recent Western discussions in this field see Don E. Eberly, ed., *The Essential Civil Society Reader: The Classic Essays* (Lanham, MD: Rowman and Littlefield, 2000); also Jean L. Cohen and Andrew Arato, *Civil Society and Political Theory* (Cambridge, MA: MIT Press, 1992).

23. For recent Western views on the relation between democracy and religion compare Nancy L. Rosenblum, ed., *Obligations of Citizenship and Demands of Faith: Religious Accommodation in Pluralist Democracies* (Princeton, NJ: Princeton University Press, 2000); also Robert Audi and Nicholas Wolterstorff, *Religion in the Public Square: The Place of Religious Convictions in Political Debate* (Lanham, MD: Rowman and Littlefield, 1997).

24. Soroush borrows the term "religious despotism" from Ayatollah Na'ini, stating: "Religious despotism is most intransigent because a religious despot views his rule not only as his right but his duty." *Reason, Freedom, and Democracy in Islam*, p. 155.

25. *Reason, Freedom, and Democracy in Islam*, pp. 128–130, 152.

26. *Reason, Freedom, and Democracy in Islam*, pp. 127, 151–152, 154. Soroush at this point uses the felicitous term of an "examined religiosity" (p. 155). The relation between reason and faith is also at issue in the relation between universities and religious seminaries, as discussed in "What the University Expects from the Hawzeh," pp. 171–183. Soroush's endorsement of public rational discourse also places him at odds with certain forms of esoteric mysticism or Sufism: "I shudder every time I evoke the impassioned poetry of Rumi and Hafez in my lectures, lest their ecstatic odes of love and their contempt for reason be used as a weapon by the enemies of reason and freedom. I am afraid this will lead us to spurn the small measure of reason that we have been granted at the sight of a mirage" (p. 93).

27. Levinas, *In the Time of the Nations*, pp. 1–5 (especially the statement, p. 1, that "seventy nations" is a metaphor that "designates all mankind surrounding Israel," all nations "potentially claimed by Holy History"); Soroush, *Reason, Freedom and Democracy in Islam*, p. 139. In another context (a text of 1994), Soroush distinguished between an insider's and a bifocal view of religion. In the words of John Cooper: "On the one hand, there must be knowledge based on one's love of, and respect for, religion, imbued with the awe of the sacred; on the other hand, one must have an analytic, anatomical knowledge. The difference between a religious devotee ('*alim*) an a religious *roshanfikr* (enlightened thinker) is that the former only permits the first kind of knowledge and understanding of religion. The *roshanfikr* can, or rather has to, have both kinds of knowledge, and this is because the '*alim* only sees religion from the inside, whereas the *roshanfikr* has the perspective of one looking in from the outside as well. All of which imposes on him

the difficult but necessary responsibility of bridging the gap between the sacred and the profane, between heaven and earth." See "The Limits of the Sacred," in *Islam and Modernity*, p. 53.

Chapter 10

1. See Gilles Kepel, *The Revenge of God: The Resurgence of Islam, Christianity and Judaism in the Modern World*, trans. Alan Braley (University Park: Pennsylvania State University Press, 1994); Mark Juergensmeyer, *The New Cold War? Religious Nationalism Confronts the Secular State* (Berkeley: University of California Press, 1993).

2. Gerhard Lenski, *The Religious Factor* (New York: Doubleday, 1961), p. 3. Extending this assessment beyond the confines of sociology, Rodney Stark and William S. Bainbridge reached a similar conclusion: "At least since the Enlightenment, most Western intellectuals have anticipated the death of religion. . . . The most illustrious figures in sociology, anthropology, and psychology have unanimously expressed confidence that their children, or surely their grandchildren, would live to see the dawn of a new era in which, to paraphrase Freud, the infantile illusions of religion would be outgrown." See *The Future of Religion* (Berkeley: University of California Press, 1985), p. 1. Compare also Auguste Comte, *Catechisme positiviste* (Paris: Dalmont, 1852); Emile Durkheim, *The Elementary Forms of Religious Life* (1912; New York: Collier Books, 1961); Max Weber, *The Protestant Ethic and the Spirit of Capitalism* (1905; New York: Sribner's, 1958); and *Economy and Society* (1922; New York: Bedminster Press, 1968).

3. C. Wright Mills, *The Sociological Imagination* (New York: Oxford University Press, 1959), pp. 32–33. Compare also Talcott Parsons, *Sociological Theory, Values and Sociocultural Change*, ed. Edward A. Tiryakian (New York: Free Press, 1963).

4. Gabriel A. Almond and G. Bingham Powell, Jr., *Comparative Politics: A Developmental Approach* (Boston: Little, Brown & Co., 1966); Jürgen Habermas, *Legitimation Crisis*, trans. Thomas McCarthy (Boston: Beacon Press, 1975), pp. 1–8.

5. See Robert N. Bellah, *Beyond Belief: Essays on Religion in a Post-Traditional World* (New York: Harper & Row, 1970); Phillip E. Hammond, ed., *The Sacred in a Secular Age* (Berkeley: University of California Press, 1985); Harvey Cox, *Religion in the Secular City* (New York: Simon & Schuster, 1984); also Richard J. Neuhaus, *The Naked Public Square* (New York: Eerdmans, 1984). Regarding the sociological debate around the "secularization thesis" compare, e.g., David Martin, *A General Theory of Secularization* (New York: Harper & Row, 1978); Karel Dobbelaere, "Secularization Theories and Sociological Paradigms," *Social Compass* 31 (1984): 199–219; Jeffrey K. Hadden, "Toward Desacralizing Secularization Theory," *Social Forces* 65 (1987): 587–611;

Timothy Crippen, "Old and New Gods in the Modern World: Toward a Theory of Religious Transformation," *Social Forces* 67 (1988): 316–336; Frank J. Lechner, "A Case Against Secularization: A Rebuttal," *Social Forces* 69 (1991): 1103–1119; David Yamane, "Secularization on Trial: In Defense of a Neosecularization Paradigm," *Journal of the Scientific Study of Religion* 36 (1997): 109–122.

6. Ioanna Kuçuradi, "Secularization and Human Rights," in Bhuvan Chandel and Kuçuradi, eds., *Cultural Traditions and the Idea of Secularization* (Delhi: Centre for Studies in Civilizations, 1988), pp. 72–73. Turning to the theme announced in her title, Kuçuradi offers a characterization of "the 'secular' state, the state of our age at the turn of the millennium": "secular is the state whose law, in the broadest sense, is deduced from, and which is administered in accordance with, human rights." As an aside, as one might note, the notion of secularization as temporalization does not imply the wholesale submergence of religion in historical flux. Whatever the role of the "eternal" may be, human responses to the calling of faith are inevitably temporal.

7. John Mayer, "Secularization and Cultural Diversity," in Chandel and Kuçuradi, *Cultural Traditions and the Idea of Secularization*, pp. 33, 36.

8. For some of Panikkar's prominent writings see, e.g., *Die vielen Götter und der eine Herr* (Weilheim, Germany: Barth, 1963); *Kerygma und Indien* (Hamburg: Reich, 1967); *L'homme qui devient Dieu* (Paris: Aubier, 1970); *The Intrareligious Dialogue* (New York: Paulist Press, 1978); *Myth, Faith and Hermeneutics* (New York: Paulist Press, 1979); *The Unknown Christ of Hinduism* (Maryknoll, NY: Orbis Books, 1981); *The Silence of God: The Answer of the Buddha* (Maryknoll, NY: Orbis Books, 1989); and *A Dwelling Place for Wisdom* (Louisville, KY: Westminister, 1993). Compare also Joseph Prabhu, ed., *The Intercultural Challenge of Raimon Panikkar* (Maryknoll, NY: Orbis Books, 1996).

9. Panikkar, *Worship and Secular Man* (Maryknoll, NY: Orbis Books, 1973), p. 1. Throughout the text, the reader should sympathetically correct for gender-biased terminology.

10. *Worship and Secular Man*, pp. 2, 7, 10–13.

11. *Worship and Secular Man*, pp. 3–4, 18, 20–22.

12. *Worship and Secular Man*, pp. 28–30, 35–36. Regarding celebrations of heteronomous "exteriority," the work of Emmanuel Levinas has exerted a particularly strong (and occasionally disorienting) influence. Compare, e.g., Levinas, *Totality and Infinity: An Essay on Exteriority,* trans. Alphonso Lingis (Pittsburgh, PA: Duquesne University Press, 1960); also his "God in Philosophy," in *Collected Philosophical Papers,* trans. Alphonso Lingis (Dordrecht: Martinus Nijhoff, 1987), pp. 150–165.

13. Panikkar, *Worship and Secular Man,* pp. 42, 47, 49–52. Offering a personal reflection he adds: "For me secularization represents the regaining of the sacramental structure of reality, the new awareness that real full human life is worship, because it is the very expression of the mystery of existence. Man is priest of the world, of the cosmic sacrament

and we are closer today to accepting this truth also: that he is the prophet of this universe of ours, the celebrant of the sacrament of life and the ambassador of the realm of the spirit" (pp. 92–93). Regarding the "cosmotheandric" perspective see also Panikkar, *The Cosmotheandric Experience,* ed. Scott Eastham (Maryknoll, NY: Orbis Books, 1993). As an aside, one may perhaps prefer to regard the three models of heteronomy, autonomy, and ontonomy more as ideal types than strictly as historical worldviews. Compare in this context also Catherine Pickstock, *After Writing: On the Liturgical Consummation of Philosophy* (Oxford: Blackwell, 1997).

14. Panikkar, "Religion or Politics: The Western Dilemma," in Peter H. Merkl and Ninian Smart, eds., *Religion and Politics in the Modern World* (New York: New York University Press, 1983), pp. 44–46.

15. Panikkar, "Religion or Politics," pp. 45–47, 49–50.

16. "Religion or Politics," pp. 51–53. As he adds: "There is no personhood in isolation. To think that I can go to God or establish friendship with him, to think that I can reach *nirvana, moksha* or heaven by cutting all my ties with the rest of reality has certainly been a constant temptation for the religious soul, but this kind of world-negating attitude leads to the degradation of religion. . . . There is no *moksha* without *dharma*" (p. 54).

17. "Religion or Politics," pp. 55, 57–59.

18. Panikkar, *Sacred Secularity* (forthcoming; a Spanish version is near completion). Regarding the "middle voice" see Suzanne Kemmer, *The Middle Voice* (Philadelphia: John Benjamins, 1993); and John Llewelyn, *The Middle Voice of Ecological Conscience* (London: Macmillan, 1991).

19. For some of these arguments see Heidegger, *Being and Time,* trans. Joan Stambaugh (Albany, NY: State University of New York Press, 1996), pp. 49–58, 107–122, 304–306; "Letter on Humanism" and "The Question Concerning Technology," in David F. Krell, ed., *Martin Heidegger: Basic Writings* (New York: Harper & Row, 1977), pp. 193–242, 287–317.

20. See Manfred Riedel, "Frömmigkeit des Denkens," and Jean Greisch, "Das grosse Spiel des Lebens und das Übermächtige," in Paola-Ludovica Coriando, ed., *"Herkunft aber bleibt stets Zukunft": Martin Heidegger und die Gottesfrage* (Frankfurt-Main: Klostermann, 1998), pp. 39, 55; also Heidegger, "Philosophische Interpretationen zu Aristoteles" (1922), in *Dilthey Jahrbuch,* 6 (1989): 197. Compare Richard Kearney and J. O'Leary, eds., *Heidegger et la question de Dieu* (Paris: Grasset, 1980).

21. Panikkar, "Religion or Politics," pp. 56–58.

22. Panikkar, "The Religion of the Future, Part I," *Interculture* 23 (Spring 1990): 7–8, 11, 18–19. Resuming the theme of "cosmotheandric" experience, he adds: "The religion of the future can no longer be a simple cry toward transcendence nor a merely immanent spirituality. Rather, it

will have to recognize the irreducibility of these three poles of reality, thereby changing forever the unilateral sense of the concept of religion. Religion will still 'religare' certainly, but not exclusively the human person with God but also with the whole universe, and thus discovering it in its cohesion and meaning. . . . Religion is again becoming central in human life, but without dominating anything, for its limited function is to secure linkage (religio) and the cohesion (dharma) between every sphere of reality" (p. 21). Part II of this text appeared in *Interculture* 23 (Summer 1990).

Chapter 11

1. D. P. Chattopadhyaya, *Knowledge, Freedom and Language: An Interwoven Fabric of Man, Time and World* (Delhi: Motilal Banarsidass, 1989), p. 279.

2. *Knowledge, Freedom and Language*, p. 241. Chattopadhyaya himself seems to subscribe to such a reduced or chastized version of reason when the describes himself, in the same text (p. 15), as an "anthropological rationalist" (in opposition to a speculative transcendentalist). However, as is clear from this and other writings, his conception of rationalism is flexible enough to embrace many diverse forms of reasoning or thinking, just as his view of being human is not narrowly anthropocentric but makes room for different ways of being-in-the-world (as attested by his numerous references to Heidegger and Gadamer). Compare in this context also his *Individuals and Worlds: Essays in Anthropological Rationalism* (New Delhi: Oxford University Press, 1976).

3. *Knowledge, Freedom and Language*, p. 242.

4. *Knowledge, Freedom and Language*, pp. 244, 246.

5. *Knowledge, Freedom and Language*, pp. 251, 255–256.

6. *Knowledge, Freedom and Language*, pp. 258–259.

7. *Knowledge, Freedom and Language*, pp. 259–261.

8. *Knowledge Freedom and Language*, pp. 261–263.

9. *Knowledge, Freedom and Language*, pp. 270–271. Regarding the significance and profound sense of the Buddha's silence compare Raimundo Panikkar, *The Silence of God: The Answer of the Buddha* (Maryknoll, NY: Orbis Books, 1989). For a comparison of Western (ego-based) freedom and Buddhist (ego-transcending) freedom see also Charles Taylor, "Conditions of an Uncoerced Consensus on Human Rights," in *The East Asian Challenge for Human Rights*, ed. Joanne R. Bauer and Daniel A. Bell (Cambridge, UK: Cambridge University Press, 1999), pp. 124–144.

10. Chattopadhyaya, *Knowledge, Freedom and Language*, pp. 275–277.

11. *Knowledge, Freedom and Language*, p. 268.

12. *Knowledge, Freedom and Language*, pp. 295–296, 299. The references are to Martin Heidegger, *Being and Time*, trans. John Macquarrie and

Edward Robinson (London: SCM Press, 1962), section 161; and Hans-Georg Gadamer, *Truth and Method*, 2nd rev. ed., trans. Joel Weinsheimer and Donald G. Marshall (New York: Crossroad, 1989), pp. 415–416.

Chapter 12

1. St. Augustine, *The City of God*, trans. Marcus Dods (New York: Modern Library, 1950), p. 35.
2. M. K. Gandhi, *Hind Swaraj and Other Writings*, ed. Anthony J. Parel (Cambridge: Cambridge University Press, 1997), pp. 26–28. Originally composed in Gujarati, the text was translated into English by Gandhi himself. It is one of the great merits of Parel's edition to provide at crucial junctures a comparison of the English version with the Gujarati original.
3. *Hind Swaraj*, pp. 30–33, 35, 37. In the cited passage as well as in subsequent passages, one needs to note the difficulty of rendering *dharma* in English. Gandhi himself translates the term as "religion," but it clearly denotes neither a revealed not an organized religion but more a path of rightness (akin to the Arabic "*zirat al-mustaqim*").
4. *Hind Swaraj*, pp. 39–41.
5. *Hind Swaraj*, pp. 42–43, 67, 73.
6. These and similar statements are collected in the "Supplementary Writings" attached by Parel to his edition of *Hind Swaraj*, pp. 149–150, 171, 185. The sources can be found in *The Colleted Works of Mahatma Gandhi* (New Delhi: Government of India, 1958–1989), vol. 75, pp. 146–147, vol. 76, pp. 399–401, vol. 81, pp. 319–321.
7. A question along these lines was in fact posed to Gandhi by the theosophist W. J. Wyberg in a letter of May 1910; see "Supplementary Writings" to *Hind Swaraj*, pp. 141–142.
8. See "Supplementary Writings" to *Hind Swaraj*, pp. 155, 189. Taken from *The Collected Works of Mahatma Gandhi*, vol. 85, pp. 32–33, and Jawaharlal Nehru, *A Bunch of Old Letters* (London: Asia Publishing House, 1958), p. 512.
9. Introduction to *Hind Swaraj*, pp. xlix, lvii-lviii, and "Supplementary Writings," p. 188.
10. Gandhi's flexibility in these matters is reflected in statements like the following: "I believe in the rock-bottom doctrine of Advaita and my interpretation of Advaita excludes totally any idea of superiority at any state whatsoever. I believe implicitly that all men are born equal." And: "I am an Advaitist and yet I can support Dvaitism (dualism). The world is changing every moment, and is therefore unreal, it has no permanent existence. But though it is constantly changing, it has something about it which persists and it is therefore to that extent real." See *The Collected Works of Mahatma Gandhi*, vol. 64, p. 141; and *The Selected Works of Mahatma Gandhi*, ed. Shriman Narayan (Ahmed-

abad: Navajivan, 1969), vol. 6, p. 107. For an attempt to link Gandhi closely with Advaita Vedanta see the essay by the Mahatma's grandson, Ramchandra Gandhi, "The *Swaraj* of India," *Indian Philosophical Quarterly* 11 (October 1984): 461–471.

11. See M. K. Gandhi, *An Autobiography: The Story of My Experiments With Truth* (London: Phoenix Press, 1949), pp. 370–371; also *Hind Swaraj*, p. 118. Compare also this statement: "I have come to this fundamental conclusion that if you want something really important to be done, you must not merely satisfy the reason, you must move the heart also. The appeal of reason is more to the head, but the penetration of the heart comes from suffering. It opens up the inner understanding of men." See Gandhi, *India's Case for Swaraj* (Bombay: Yeshanand, 1932), p. 369. To this extent I cannot quite agree with Parel when he equates self-rule with mind-control and states: "Thus the mind emerges as the key faculty in Gandhi's political philosophy, *swaraj* being the rule of the mind over itself and the passions. The possession of a disciplined mind — free from *inordinate* desire for property, pleasure and power — is the prerequisite for the proper practice of *satyagraha*." See introduction to *Hind Swaraj*, p. l. This accent is all the more curious as Parel himself reports these comments of Gandhi in 1907 on the topic of restraint and self-reliance: "We should also know what we mean by 'reliance on our own strength.' 'Our strength' means the strength of our body, our mind and our soul. From among these, on which should we depend? The answer is brief. The soul is supreme, and therefore soul-force is the foundation on which man must build. Passive resistance or *satyagraha* is a mode of fighting which depends on such force." See *The Collected Works of Mahatma Gandhi*, vol. 9, p. 118; cited in *Hind Swaraj*, p. 21, note 26. One might add that "soul," for Gandhi, does not seem to be a metaphysical substance but a synonym for soul-force seen as agency of transformation.

12. Ramashray Roy, *Self and Society: A Study in Gandhian Thought* (New Delhi: Sage Publications India, 1984), p. 78.

13. See *Hind Swaraj*, pp. 86–87; also Bhikhu Parekh, *Gandhi's Political Philosophy: A Critical Examination* (Notre Dame, IN: University of Notre Dame Press, 1989), pp. 58–59. To be sure, Parekh does not ignore the issue of moral self-transformation; but he treats it (in this text) as a distinct issue separate from the topic of *swaraj*. More recently, however, he has accepted a closer linkage between these aspects. See his *Gandhi* (Oxford: Oxford University Press, 1997), pp. 75–76: "For Gandhi *swaraj* referred to a state of affairs in which individuals were morally in control of themselves and ran their lives in such a way that they needed no external coercion. . . . For Gandhi *swaraj* thus presupposed self-discipline, self-restraint, a sense of mutual responsibility, the disposition neither to dominate nor be dominated by others, and a sense of *dharma*."

14. *Hind Swaraj*, pp. lii–liii, 73, 188–189 (on "oceanic circle").

15. Roy, *Self and Society,* pp. 63, 189–90. The possibility of a transformative freedom was actually acknowledged by Berlin; but he confined this mode narrowly to mystical or ascetic life-styles—a confinement aptly criticized by Roy (pp. 186–187). See Isaiah Berlin, *Four Essays on Liberty* (London: Oxford University Press, 1977). Compare in this context Michel Foucault, *The Care of the Self,* trans. Robert Hurley (New York: Pantheon Books, 1986).

16. Roy, *Self and Society,* p. 64. Some of these dualistic dilemmas still persist in more recent, quasi-Kantian forms of ethics, for example, in Habermasian "discourse ethics." Although ostensibly departing from Kant through a greater reliance on inter-subjective communication, Habermas fully endorses the Kantian primacy of "right" over the "good," of justice over the good life, of duty over inclination. He frankly admits the "weak motivational force" of discourse ethics coupled with its theoretical abstractness. However, if ethical motivation is weak or non-existent, the theory seems to contribute little to self-rule or self-transformation. See Jürgen Habermas, *Justification and Application: Remarks on Discourse Ethics,* trans. Ciaran P. Cronin (Cambridge, MA: MIT Press, 1995), especially pp. 33, 74–76. For a greater willingness to expand or supplement discourse ethics in the direction of caring self-transcendence see the essay by Habermas's successor, Axel Honneth, "The Other of Justice: Habermas and the Ethical Challenge of Postmodernism," in Stephen K. White, ed., *The Cambridge Companion to Habermas* (Cambridge, U.K.: Cambridge University Press, 1995), pp. 289–323.

17. In her eloquent language: "One of the most persistent trends in modern philosophy since Descartes and perhaps its most original contribution to philosophy has been an exclusive concern with the self, as distinguished from the soul or person or man in general, an attempt to reduce all experiences, with the world as well as with other human beings, to experiences between man and himself. . . . World alienation, and not self-alienation as Marx thought, has been the hallmark of the modern age." See Hannah Arendt, *The Human Condition: A Study of the Central Dilemmas Facing Modern Man* (Chicago: University of Chicago Press, 1958), pp. 230–231.

18. Arendt, "What Is Freedom," in *Between Past and Future: Six Exercises in Political Thought* (Cleveland: World Publishing Co., 1963), pp. 148–149, 153. The essay contains a strong critique of liberal individualism. As she notes (p. 155), liberalism, "its name notwithstanding, has done its share to banish the notion of liberty from the political realm. For politics, according to the same philosophy, must be concerned almost exclusively with the maintenance of life and the safeguarding of its interests. Now, where life is at stake all action is by definition under the sway of necessity, and the proper realm to take care of life's necessities is the gigantic and still increasing sphere of social and economic

life whose administration has overshadowed the political realm ever since the beginning of the modern age."

19. Charles Taylor, "What's Wrong with Negative Liberty?" in Alan Ryan, ed., *The Idea of Freedom: Essays in Honor of Isaiah Berlin* (Oxford: Oxford University Press, 1979), p. 193.

20. Taylor, *The Ethics of Authenticity* (Cambridge, MA: Harvard University Press, 1992), pp. 68, 74, 77–78. The awkwardness surrounding the term "authenticity" had been noted earlier by Theodor W. Adorno in *The Jargon of Authenticity,* trans. Knut Tarnowski and Frederick Will (Evanston, IL: Northwestern University Press, 1973).

21. Tu Weiming, *Confucian Thought: Selfhood as Creative Transformation* (Albany, NY: SUNY Press, 1985), pp. 59, 76–77, 175. Compare also his comments on the Confucian "golden rule": "It is certainly not a categorical imperative in the Kantian sense; nor is it the guiding principle for action to which one is enjoined to conform. Rather, it is a standard of inspiration and an experienced ideal made meaningful to the students through the exemplary teaching of their master" (p. 56). Regarding transformative freedom, he adds, in a passage critical of Western liberalism: "Historically, the emergence of individualism as a motivating force in Western society may have been intertwined with highly particularized political, economic, ethical, and religious traditions. It seems reasonable that one can endorse an insight into the self as a basis for equality and liberty without accepting Locke's idea of private property, Adam Smith's and Hobbes's idea of private interest, John Stuart Mill's idea of privacy, Kierkegaard's idea of loneliness, or the early Sartre's idea of freedom" (p. 78).

22. Gandhi, *Hind Swaraj,* p. 73.

INDEX